Papillon

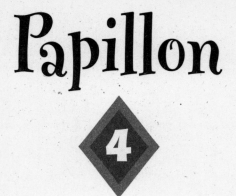

4

Miwa Ueda

Translated and adapted by Elina Ishikawa
Lettered by North Market Street Graphics

Ballantine Books · New York

Papillon volume 4 is a work of fiction. Names, characters, places, and incidents are the products of the author's imagination or are used fictitiously. Any resemblance to actual events, locales, or persons, living or dead, is entirely coincidental.

A Del Rey Manga/Kodansha Trade Paperback Original

Published in the United States by Del Rey, an imprint of The Random House Publishing Group, a division of Random House, Inc., New York.

Publication rights arranged through Kodansha Ltd.

First published in Japan in 2008 by Kodansha Ltd., Tokyo

ISBN 978-0-345-51234-5

Printed in the United States of America

www.delreymanga.com

2 4 6 8 9 7 5 3 1

Translator/Adapter: Elina Ishikawa
Lettering: North Market Street Graphics

CONTENTS

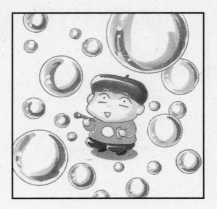

In my 20s, I used to wish I could go back and redo my childhood. I assumed I would have led a different life or become an extraordinary person, but I mysteriously stopped thinking about it as I got older. I think of things that I can accomplish rather than redoing my life. I believe taking things one day at a time will lead to something.

—Miwa Ueda

Honorifics Explained

Throughout the Del Rey Manga books, you will find Japanese honorifics left intact in the translations. For those not familiar with how the Japanese use honorifics and, more important, how they differ from American honorifics, we present this brief overview.

Politeness has always been a critical facet of Japanese culture. Ever since the feudal era, when Japan was a highly stratified society, use of honorifics—which can be defined as polite speech that indicates relationship or status—has played an essential role in the Japanese language. When addressing someone in Japanese, an honorific usually takes the form of a suffix attached to one's name (example: "Asuna-san"), is used as a title at the end of one's name, or appears in place of the name itself (example: "Negi-sensei," or simply "Sensei!").

Honorifics can be expressions of respect or endearment. In the context of manga and anime, honorifics give insight into the nature of the relationship between characters. Many English translations leave out these important honorifics and therefore distort the feel of the original Japanese. Because Japanese honorifics contain nuances that English honorifics lack, it is our policy at Del Rey not to translate them. Here, instead, is a guide to some of the honorifics you may encounter in Del Rey Manga.

-san: This is the most common honorific and is equivalent to Mr., Miss, Ms., or Mrs. It is the all-purpose honorific and can be used in any situation where politeness is required.

-sama: This is one level higher than "-san" and is used to confer great respect.

-dono: This comes from the word "tono," which means "lord." It is an even higher level than "-sama" and confers utmost respect.

-kun: This suffix is used at the end of boys' names to express familiarity or endearment. It is also sometimes used by men among friends, or when addressing someone younger or of a lower station.

-chan: This is used to express endearment, mostly toward girls. It is also used for little boys, pets, and even among lovers. It gives a sense of childish cuteness.

Bozu: This is an informal way to refer to a boy, similar to the English terms "kid" and "squirt."

Sempai/
Senpai: This title suggests that the addressee is one's senior in a group or organization. It is most often used in a school setting, where underclassmen refer to their upperclassmen as "sempai." It can also be used in the workplace, such as when a newer employee addresses an employee who has seniority in the company.

Kohai: This is the opposite of "sempai" and is used toward underclassmen in school or newcomers in the workplace. It connotes that the addressee is of a lower station.

Sensei: Literally meaning "one who has come before," this title is used for teachers, doctors, or masters of any profession or art.

-[blank]:   This is usually forgotten in these lists, but it is perhaps the most significant difference between Japanese and English. The lack of honorific means that the speaker has permission to address the person in a very intimate way. Usually, only family, spouses, or very close friends have this kind of permission. Known as *yobisute,* it can be gratifying when someone who has earned the intimacy starts to call one by one's name without an honorific. But when that intimacy hasn't been earned, it can be very insulting.

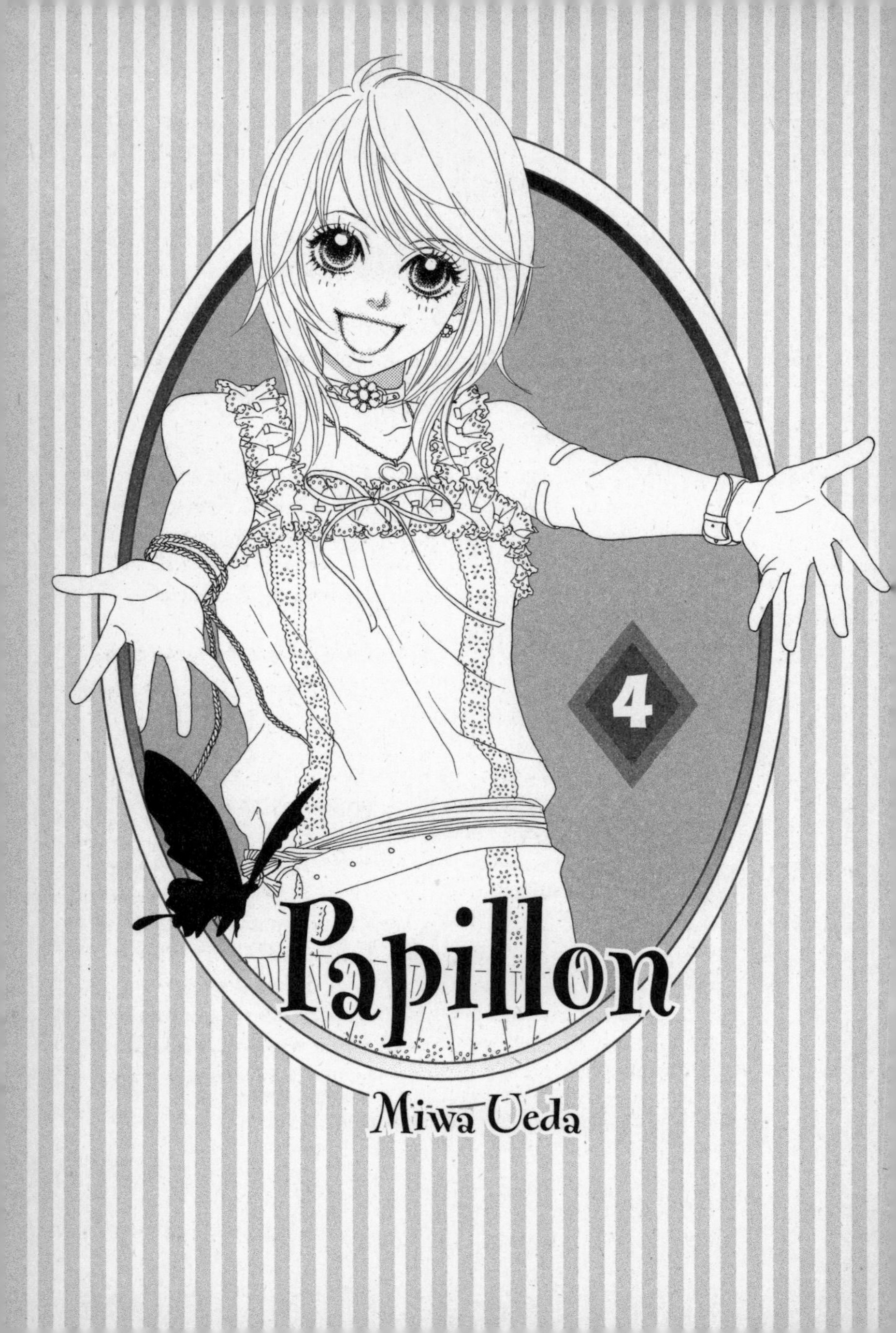
4
Papillon
Miwa Ueda

CONTENTS

The Story So Far

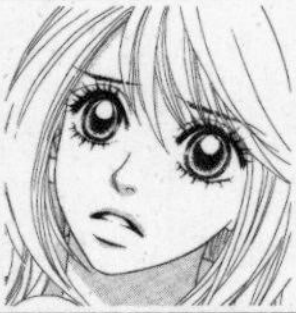

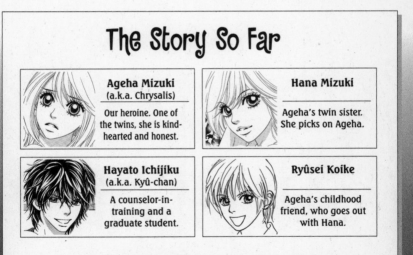

Ageha Mizuki
(a.k.a. Chrysalis)

Our heroine. One of the twins, she is kind-hearted and honest.

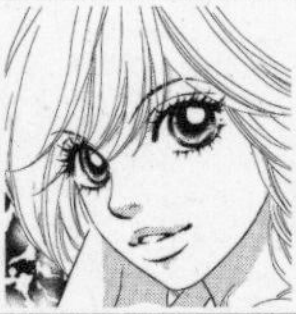

Hana Mizuki

Ageha's twin sister. She picks on Ageha.

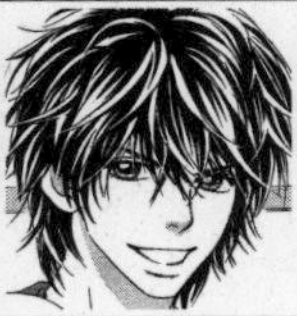

Hayato Ichijiku
(a.k.a. Kyû-chan)

A counselor-in-training and a graduate student.

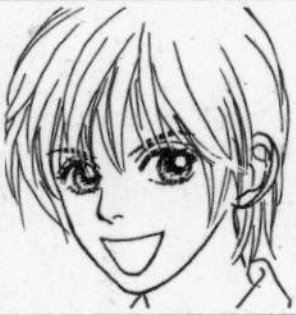

Ryûsei Koike

Ageha's childhood friend, who goes out with Hana.

After she confessed her love to him, Ageha and Kyû-chan, the counselor, began seeing each other. But she caught him kissing another one of his female clients, creating a gap between them. That's when Ageha coerced her former crush, Ryûsei, to kiss her!

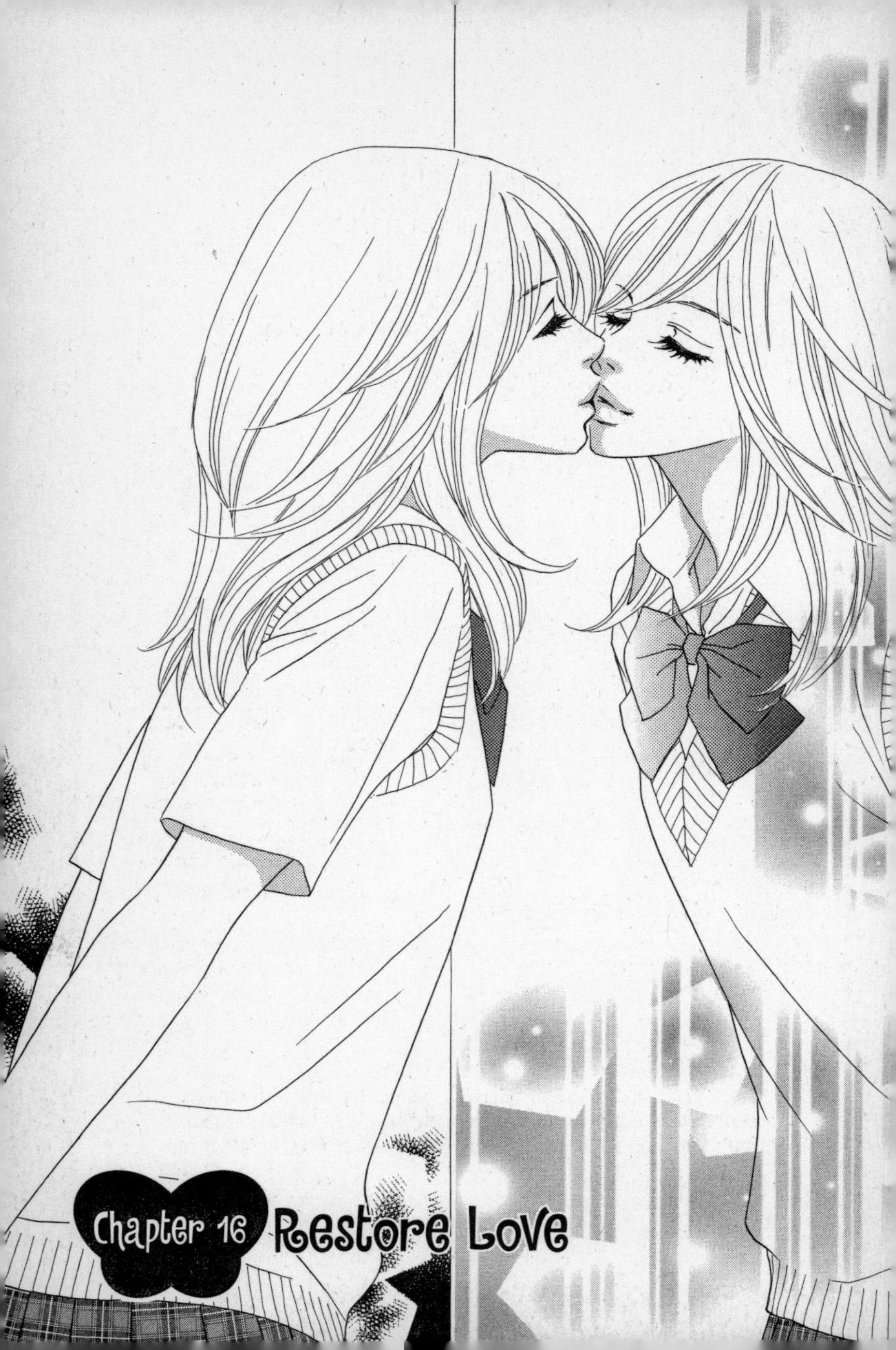
Chapter 16
Restore Love

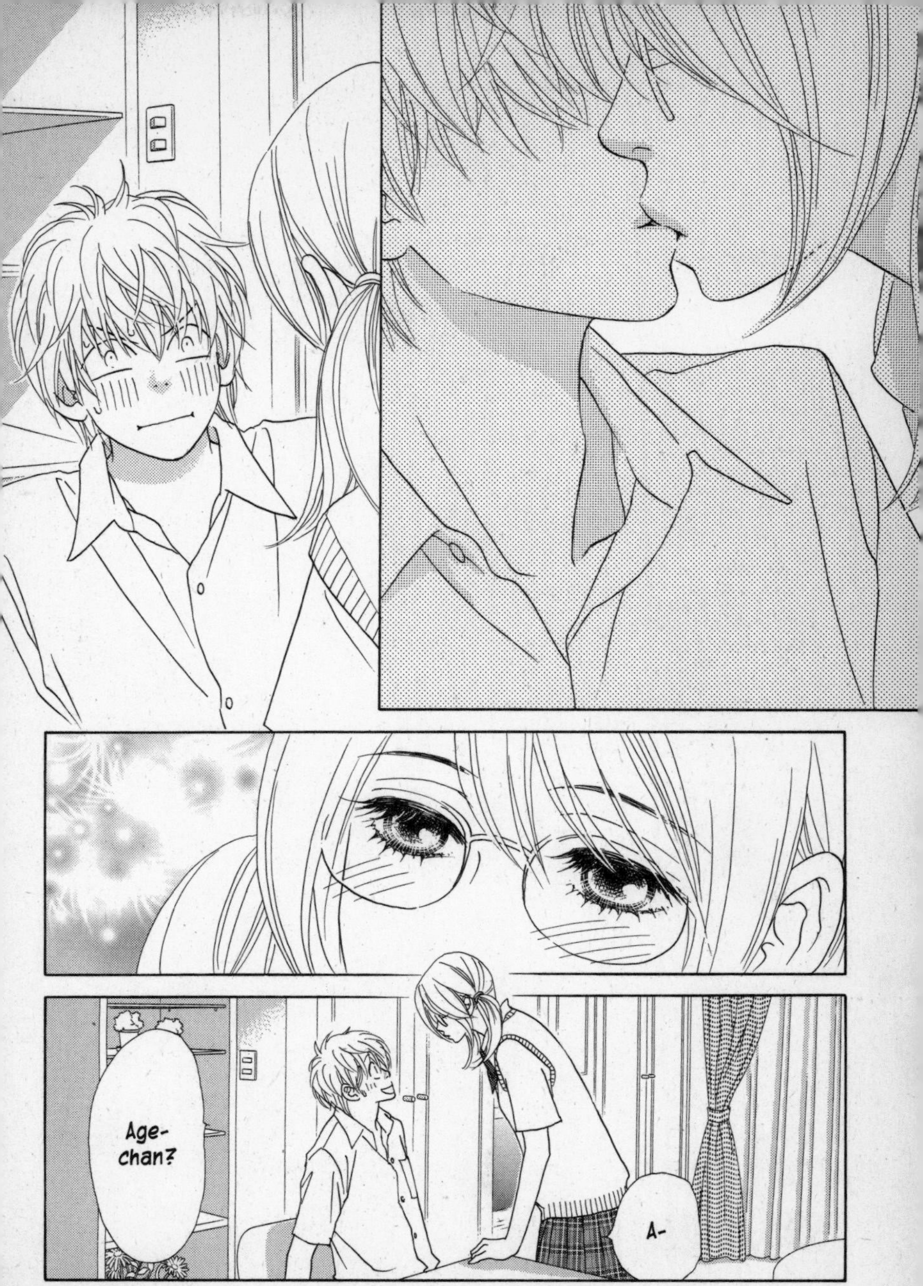
A-
Age-
chan?

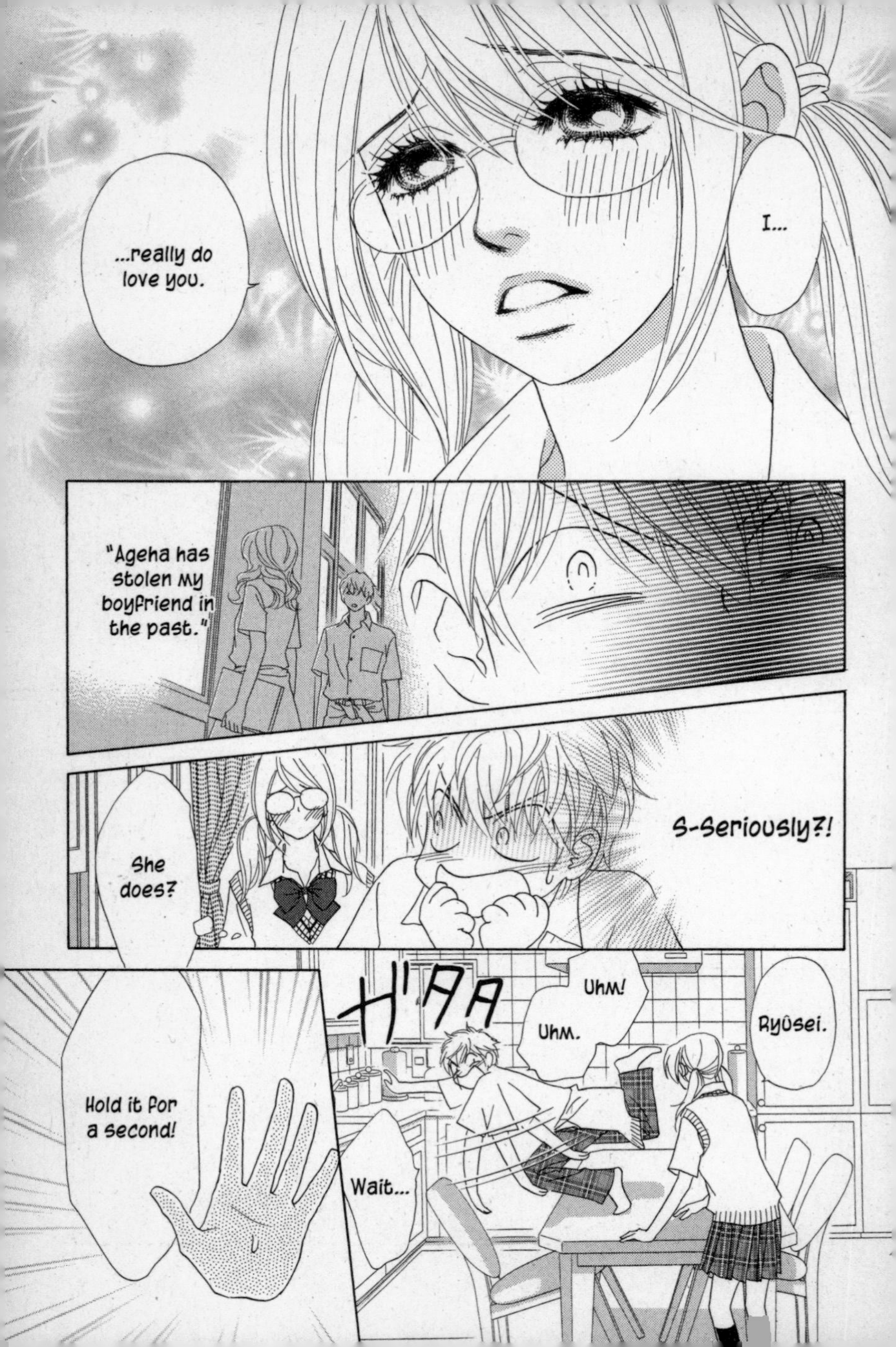
I...
...really do love you.
"Ageha has stolen my boyfriend in the past."
S-Seriously?!
She does?
Ryûsei.
Uhm!
Uhm.
H'AA
Wait...
Hold it for a second!

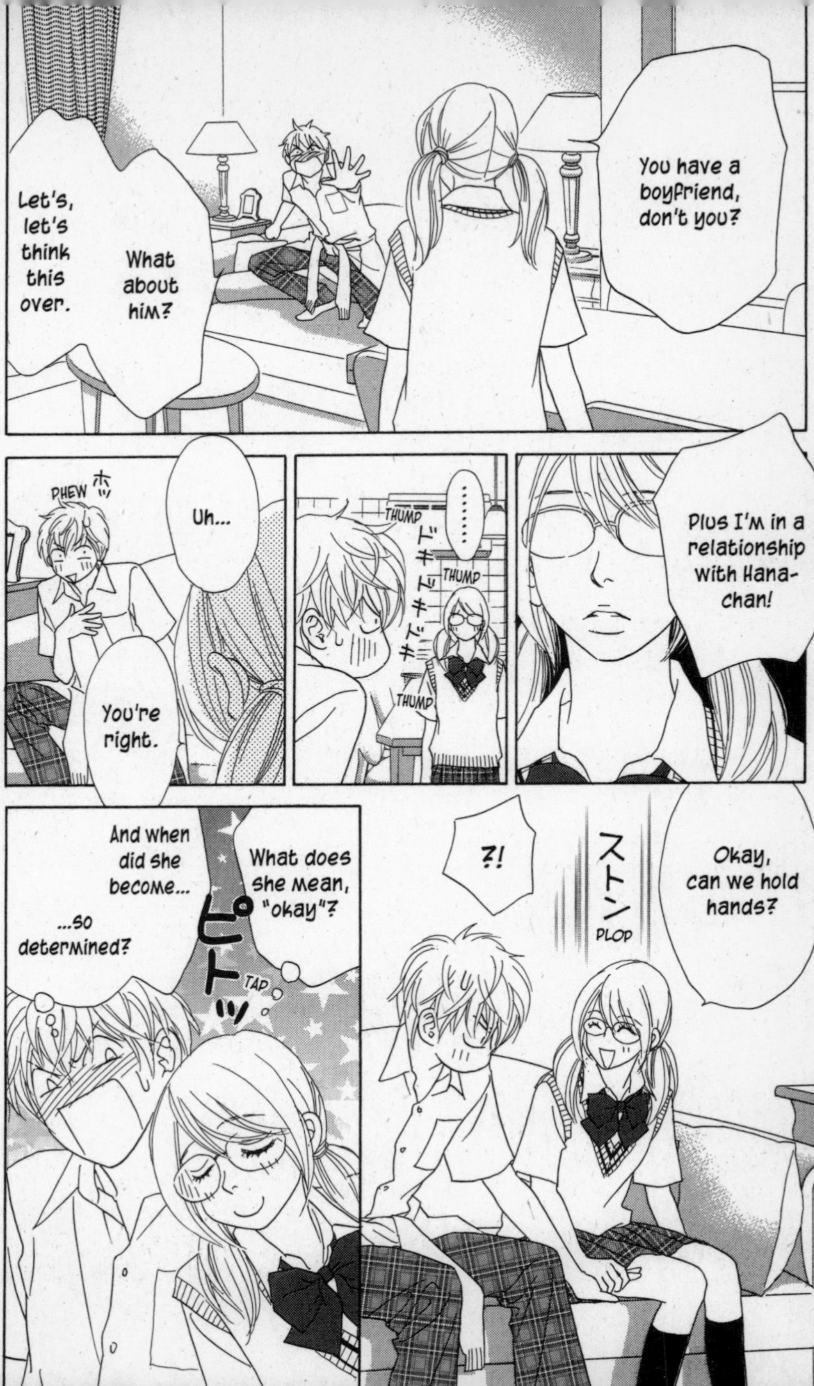
You have a boyfriend, don't you?
What about him?
Let's, let's think this over.
Plus I'm in a relationship with Hana-chan!
....
THUMP
THUMP
THUMP
Uh...
PHEW ホッ
You're right.
Okay, can we hold hands?
ストン PLOP
?!
What does she mean, "okay"?
ピトッ TAP
And when did she become...
...so determined?

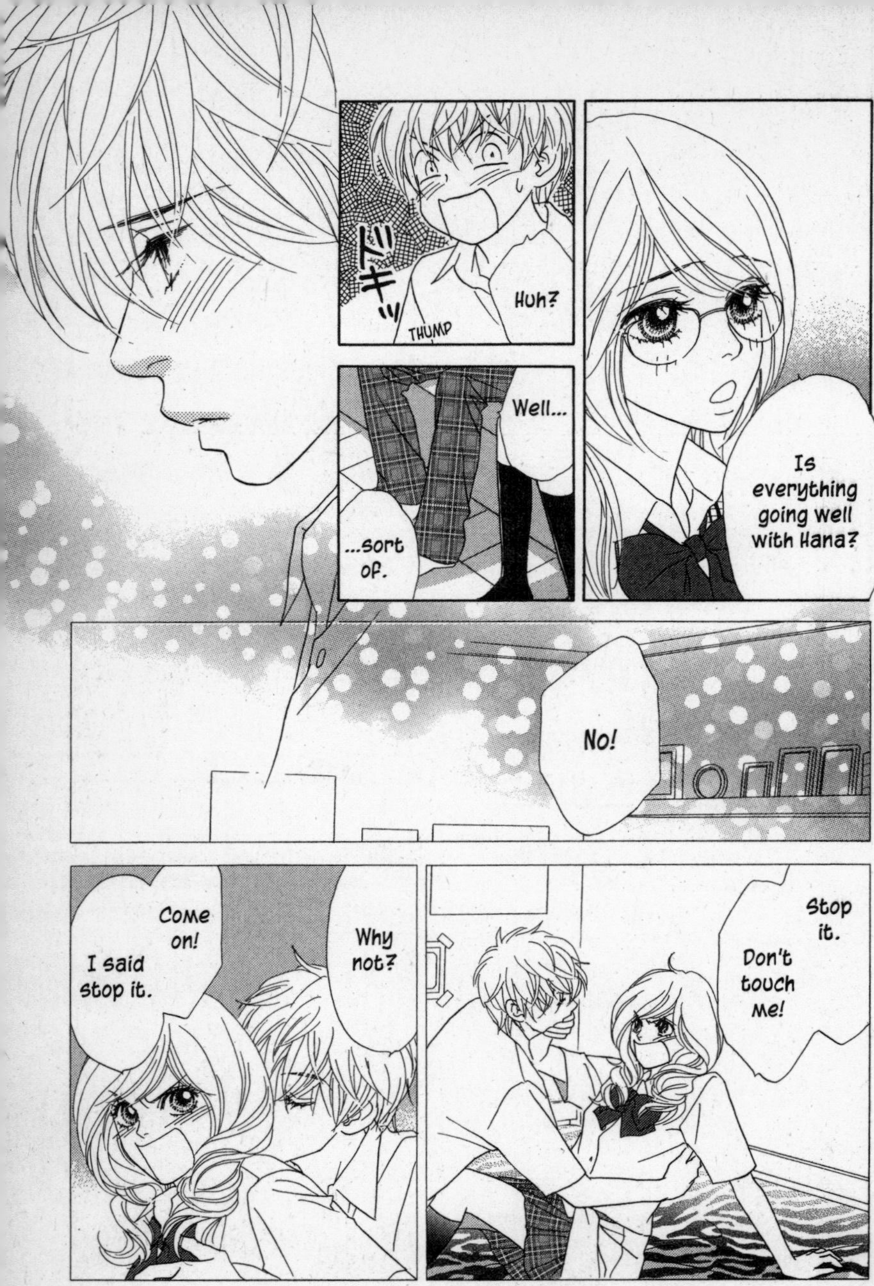
Is everything going well with Hana?
ドキッ
Huh?
THUMP
Well...
...sort of.
No!
Stop it.
Don't touch me!
Why not?
Come on!
I said stop it.

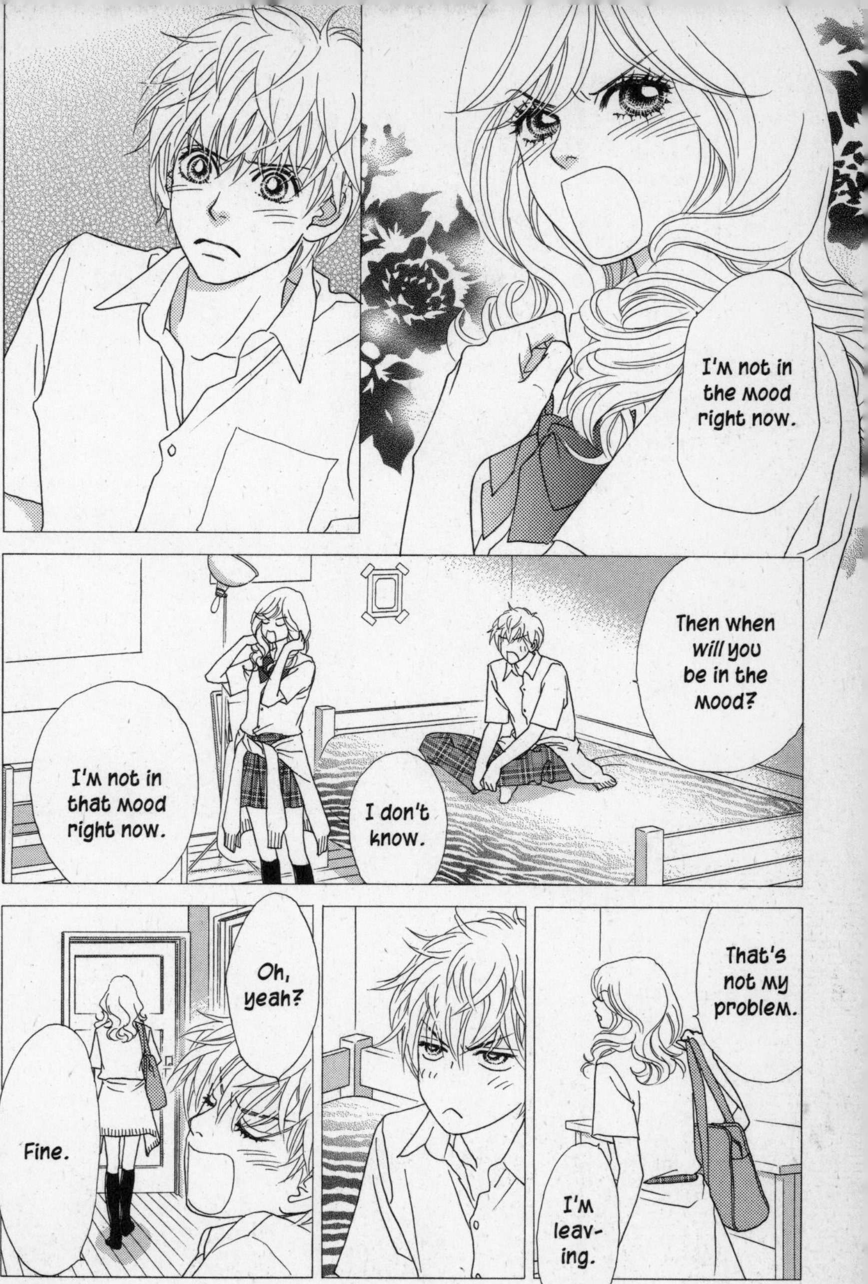

I'm not in the mood right now.
Then when *will* you be in the mood?
I don't know.
I'm not in that mood right now.
That's not my problem.
I'm leaving.
Oh, yeah?
Fine.

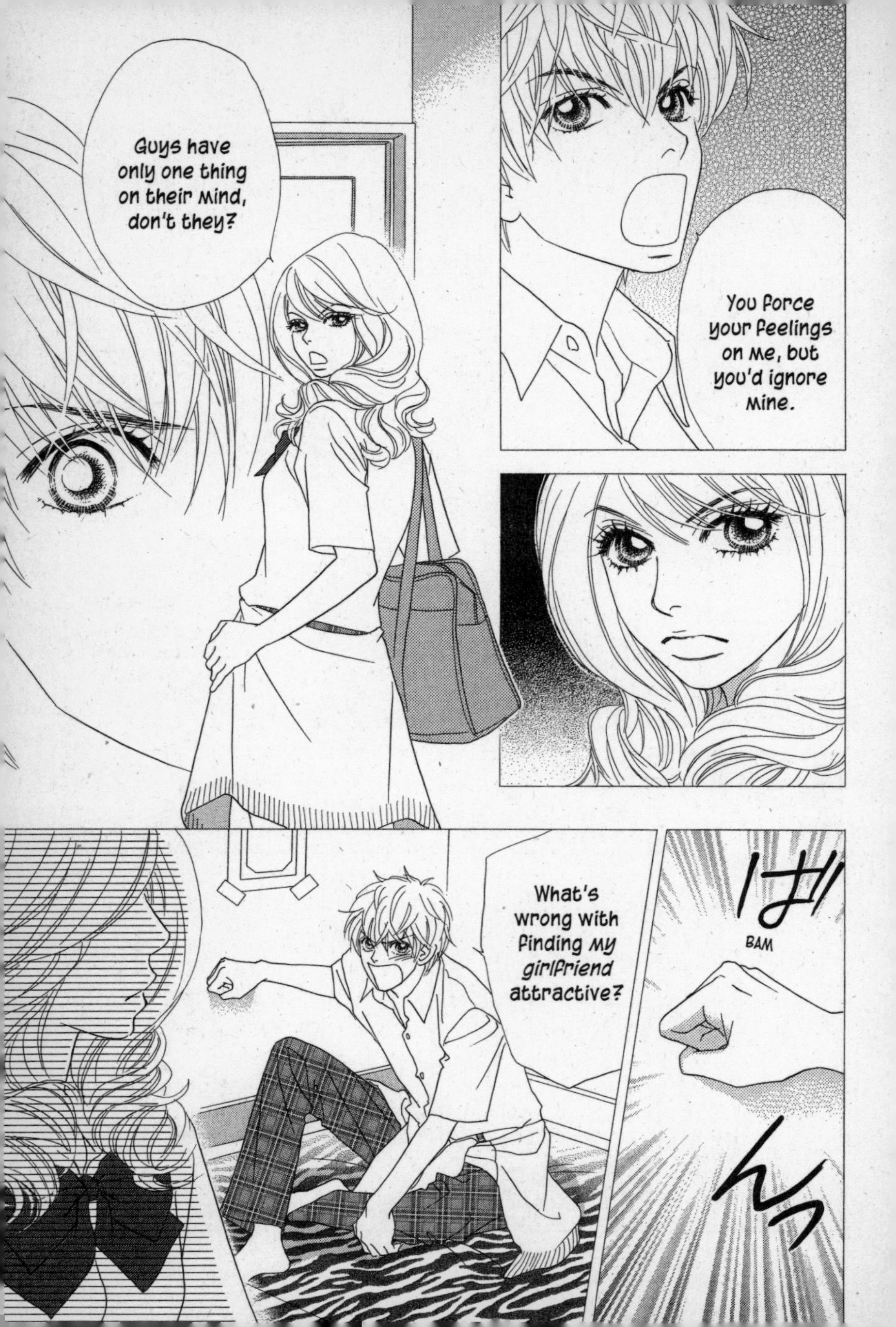
You force your feelings on me, but you'd ignore mine.
Guys have only one thing on their mind, don't they?
ば
BAM
ん
What's wrong with finding my girlfriend attractive?

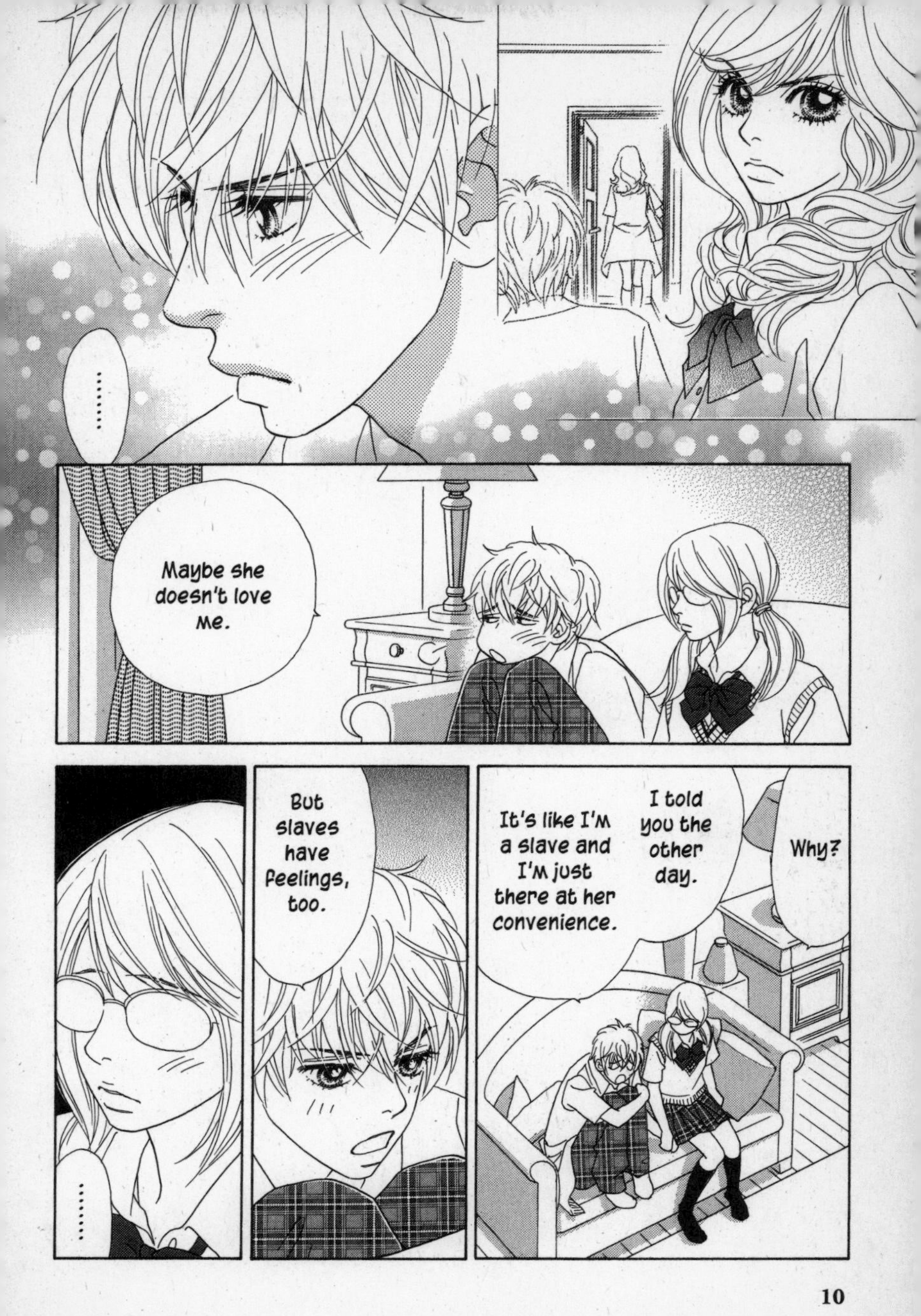
......
Maybe she doesn't love me.
Why?
I told you the other day.
It's like I'm a slave and I'm just there at her convenience.
But slaves have feelings, too.
......

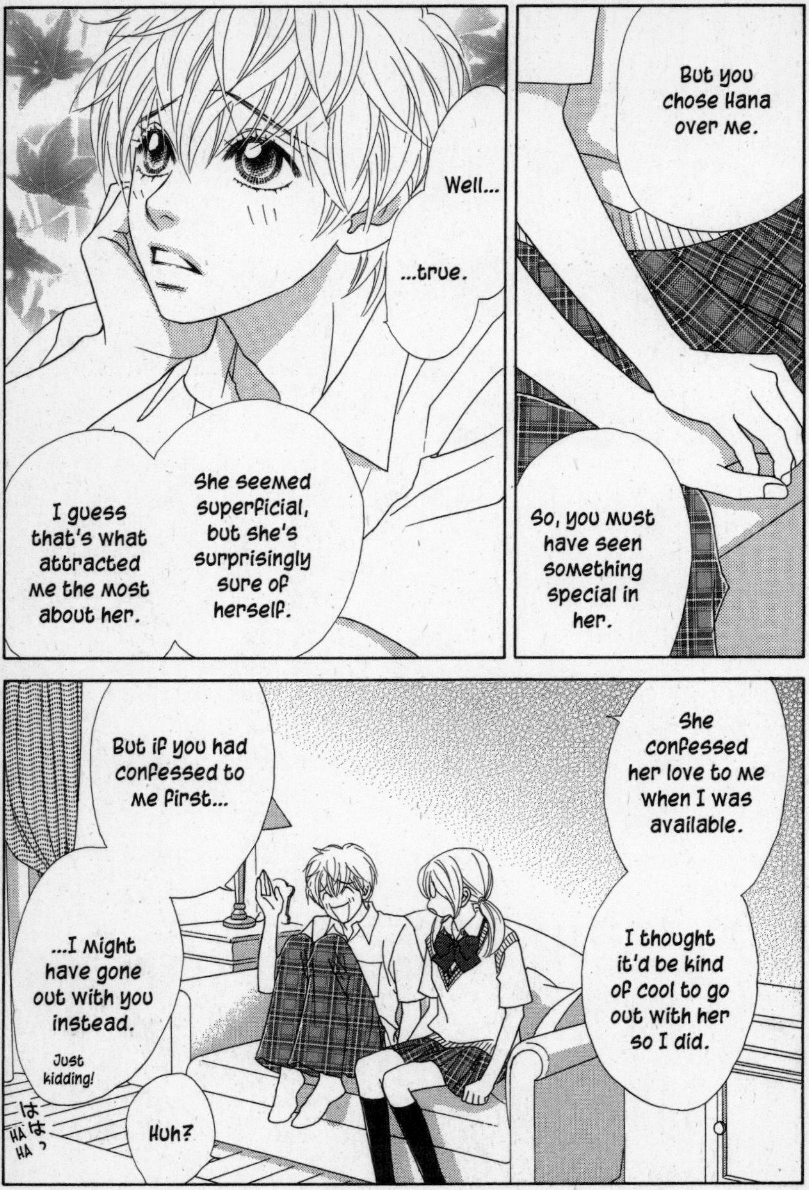
But you chose Hana over me.
So, you must have seen something special in her.
Well...
...true.
She seemed superficial, but she's surprisingly sure of herself.
I guess that's what attracted me the most about her.
She confessed her love to me when I was available.
I thought it'd be kind of cool to go out with her so I did.
But if you had confessed to me first...
...I might have gone out with you instead.
Just kidding!
Huh?
ははっ HA HA

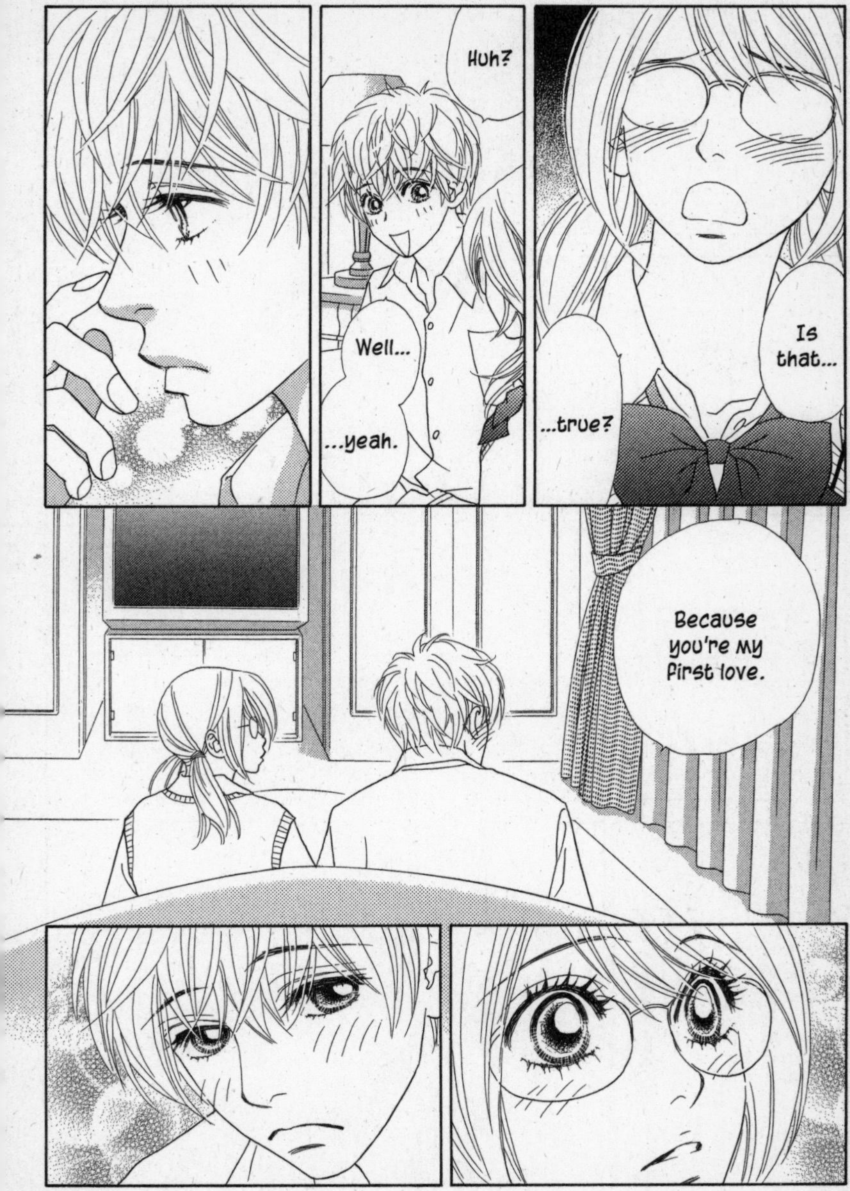
Is that...
...true?
Huh?
Well...
...yeah.
Because you're my first love.

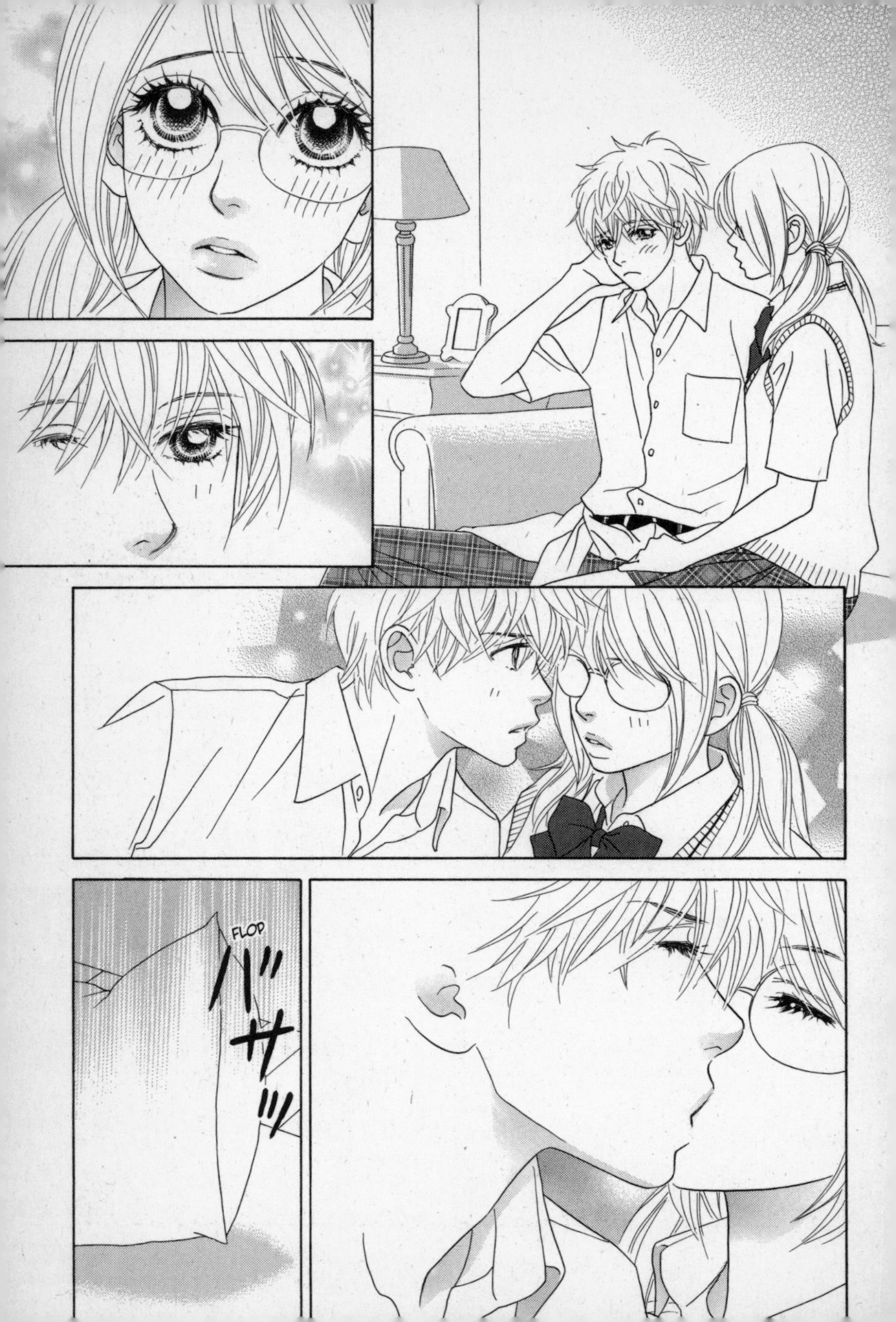
FLOP
バサッ

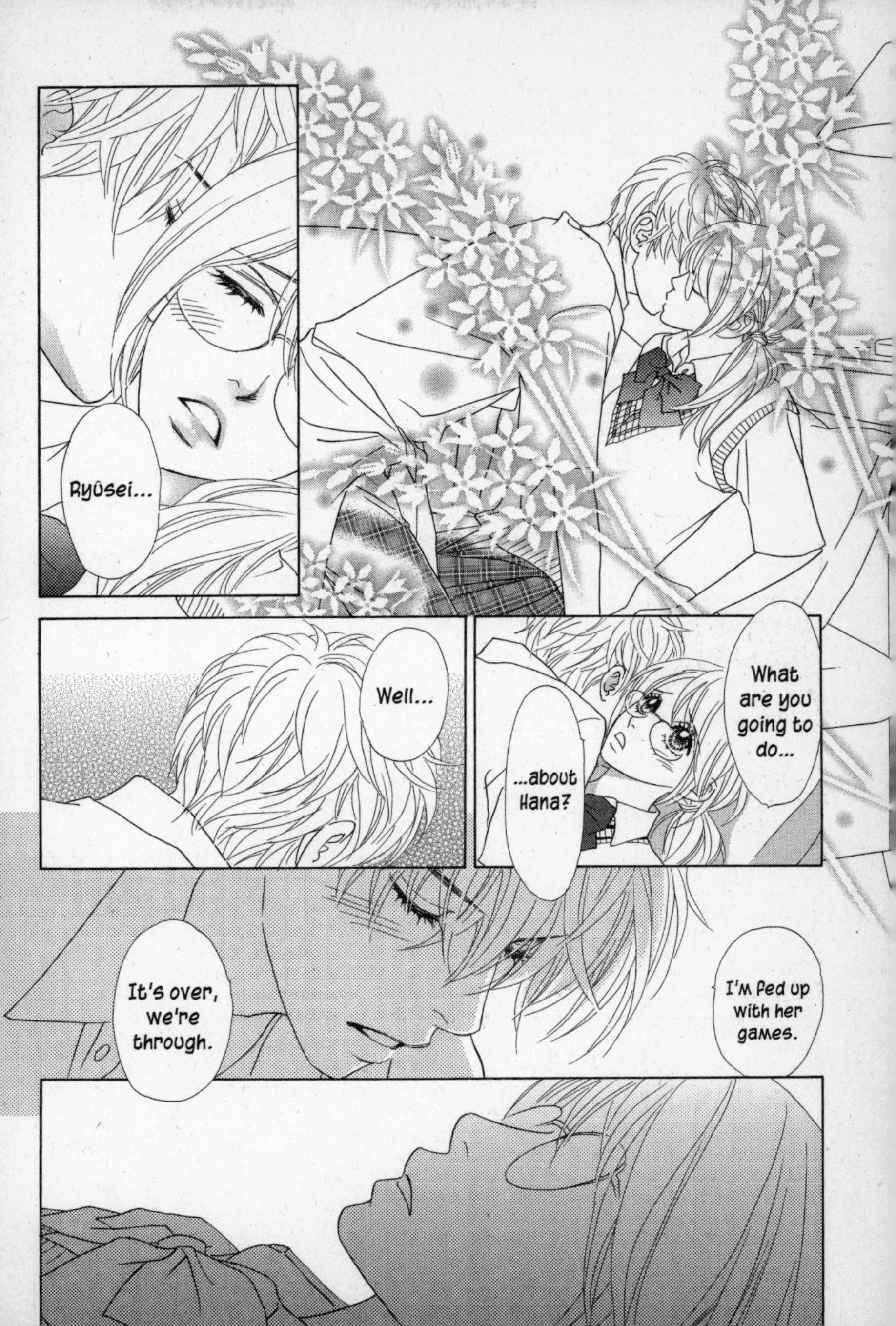
Ryûsei...
What are you going to do...
...about Hana?
Well...
I'm fed up with her games.
It's over, we're through.

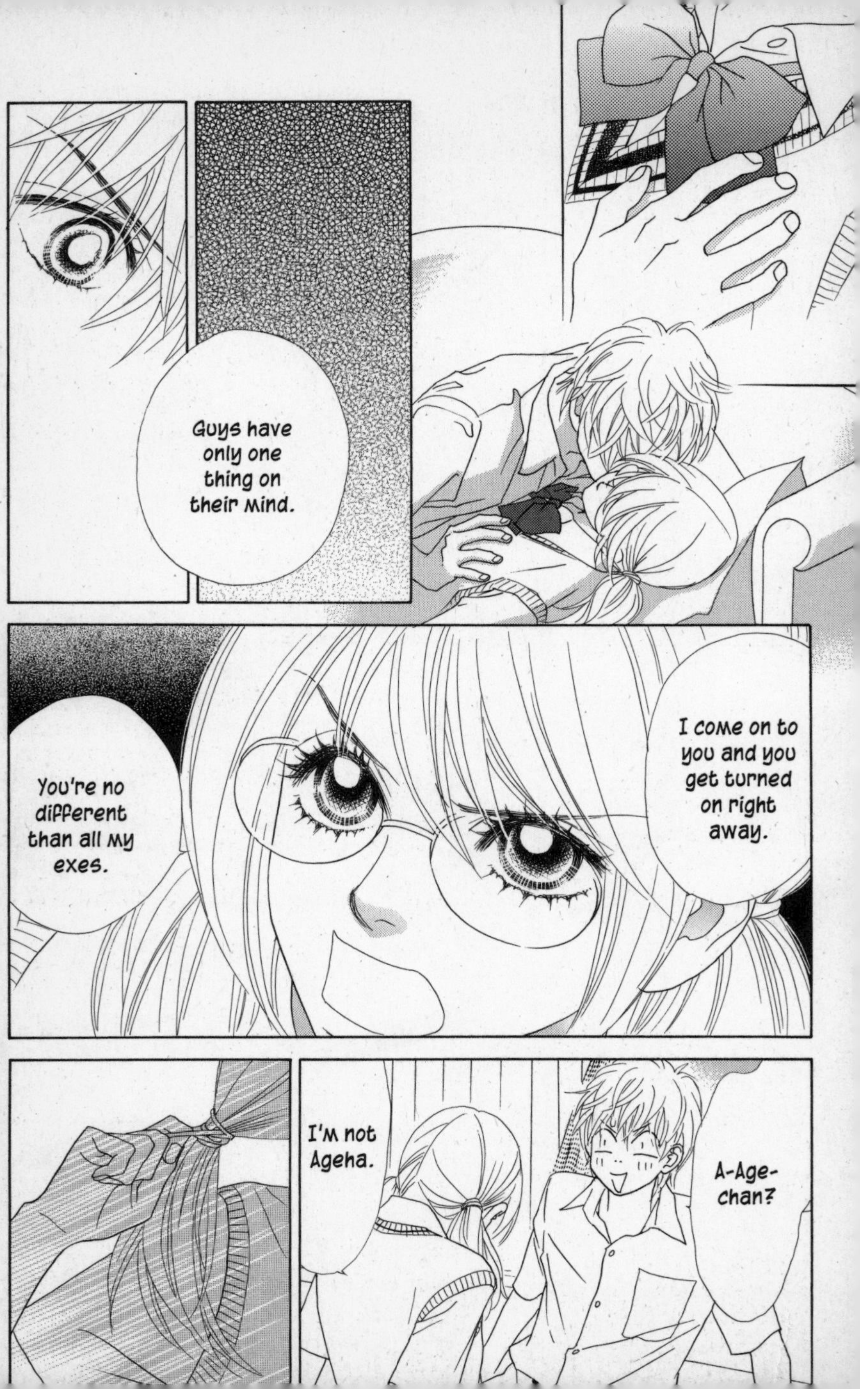
Guys have only one thing on their mind.
I come on to you and you get turned on right away.
You're no different than all my exes.
A-Age-chan?
I'm not Ageha.

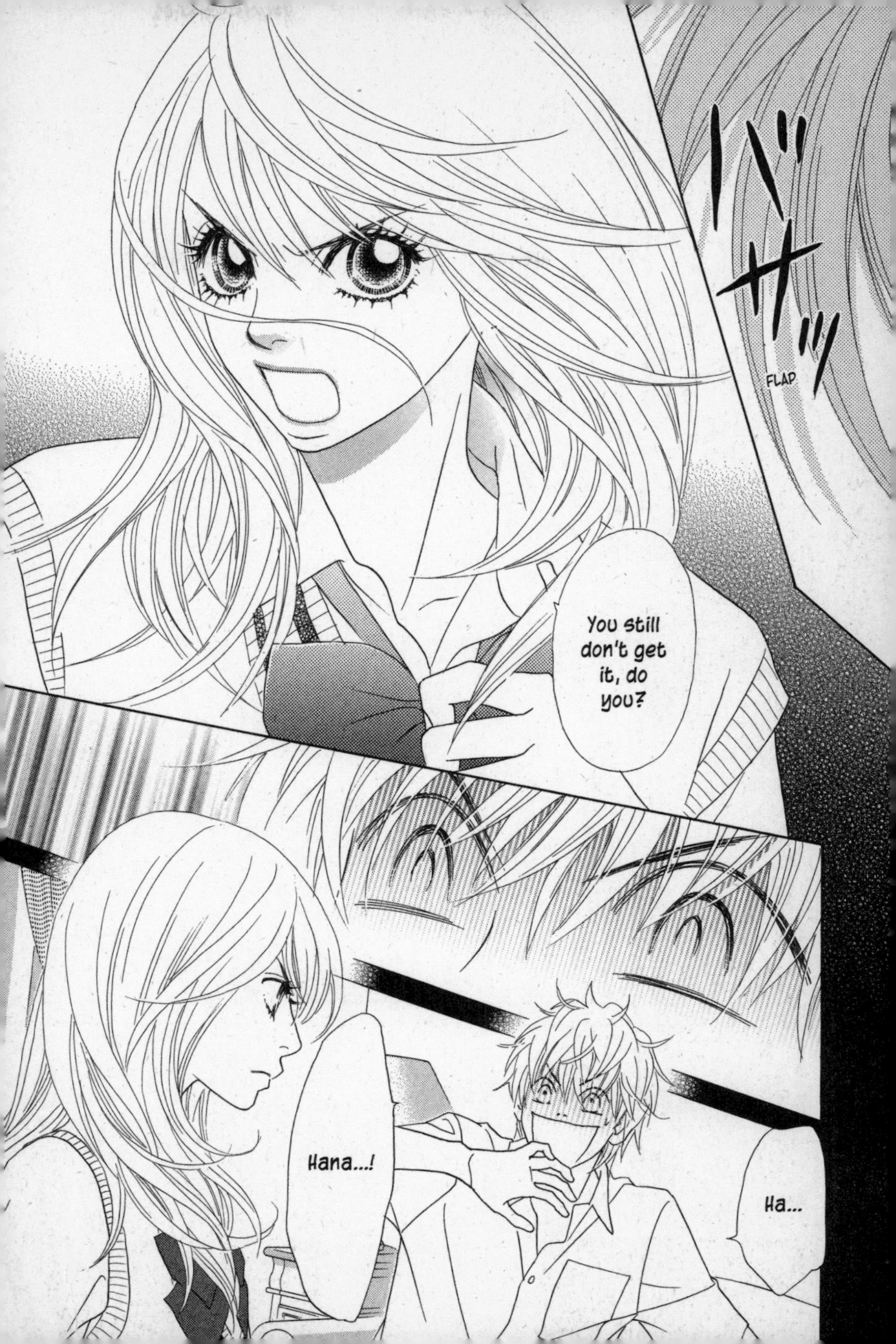
バサッ
FLAP
You still don't get it, do you?
Ha...
Hana...!

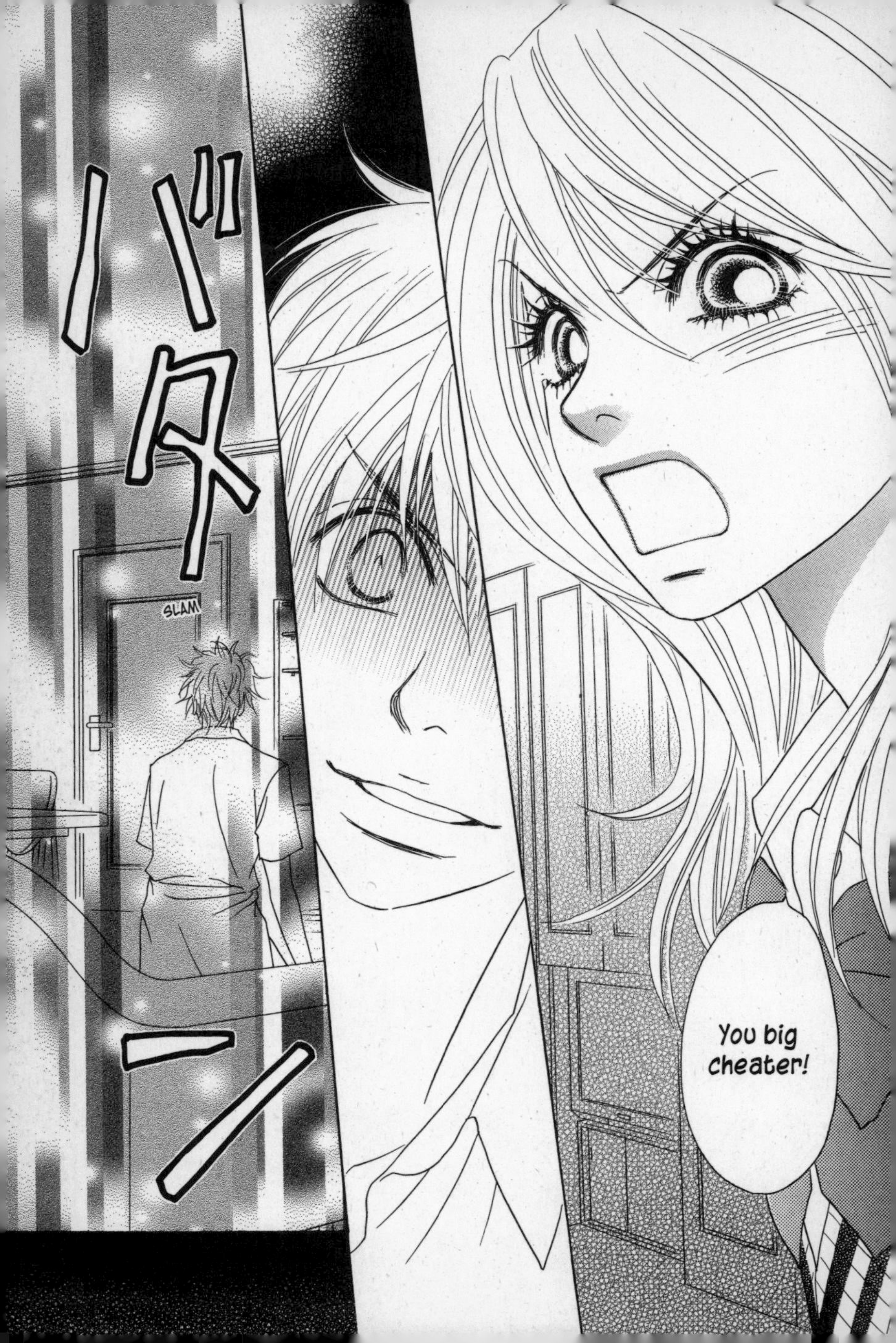
You big cheater!
バタン
SLAM

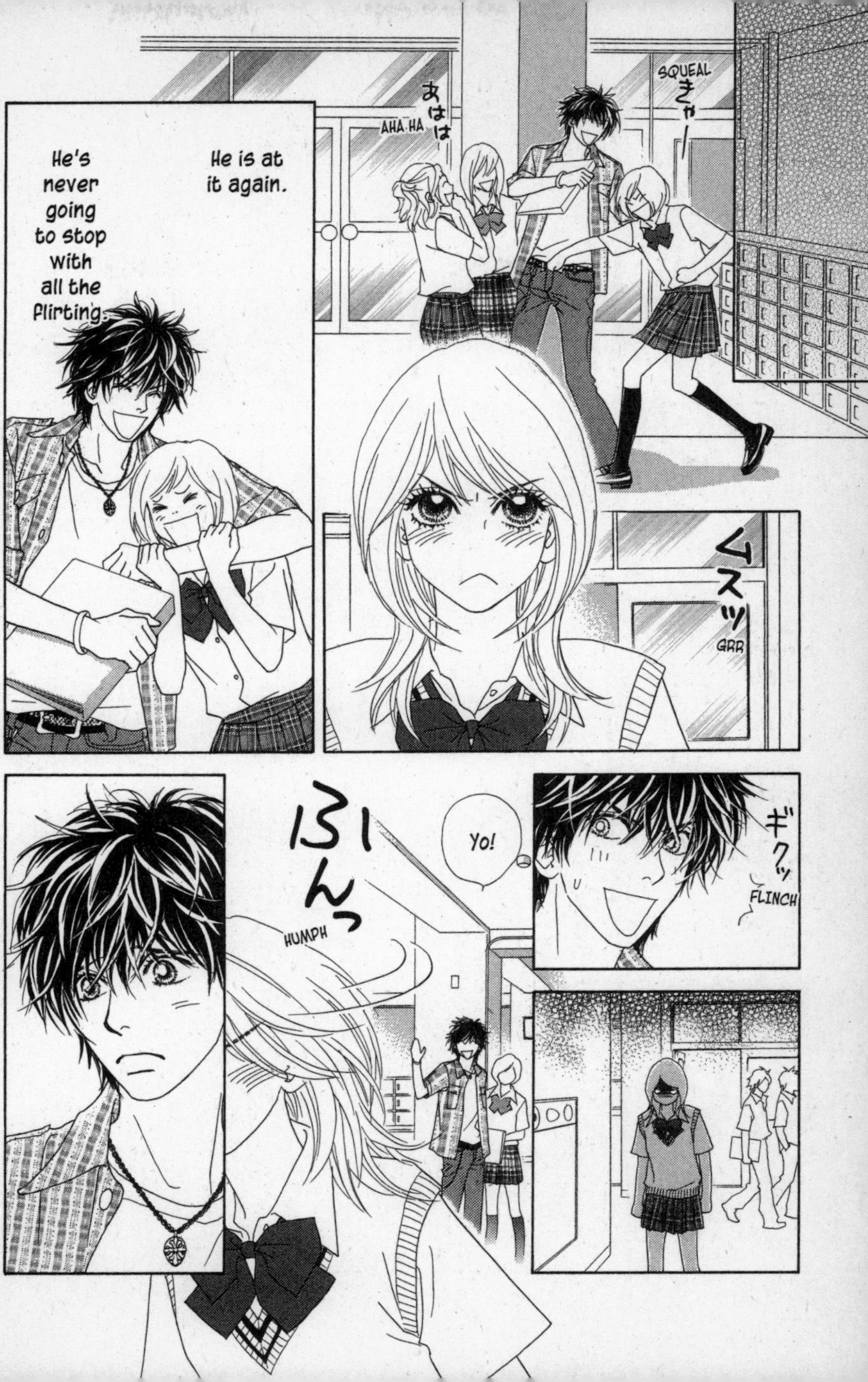
SQUEAL
きゃー
AHA HA
あはは
ムスッ
GRR
He is at it again.
He's never going to stop with all the flirting.
ギクッ
FLINCH
Yo!
ふんっ
HUMPH

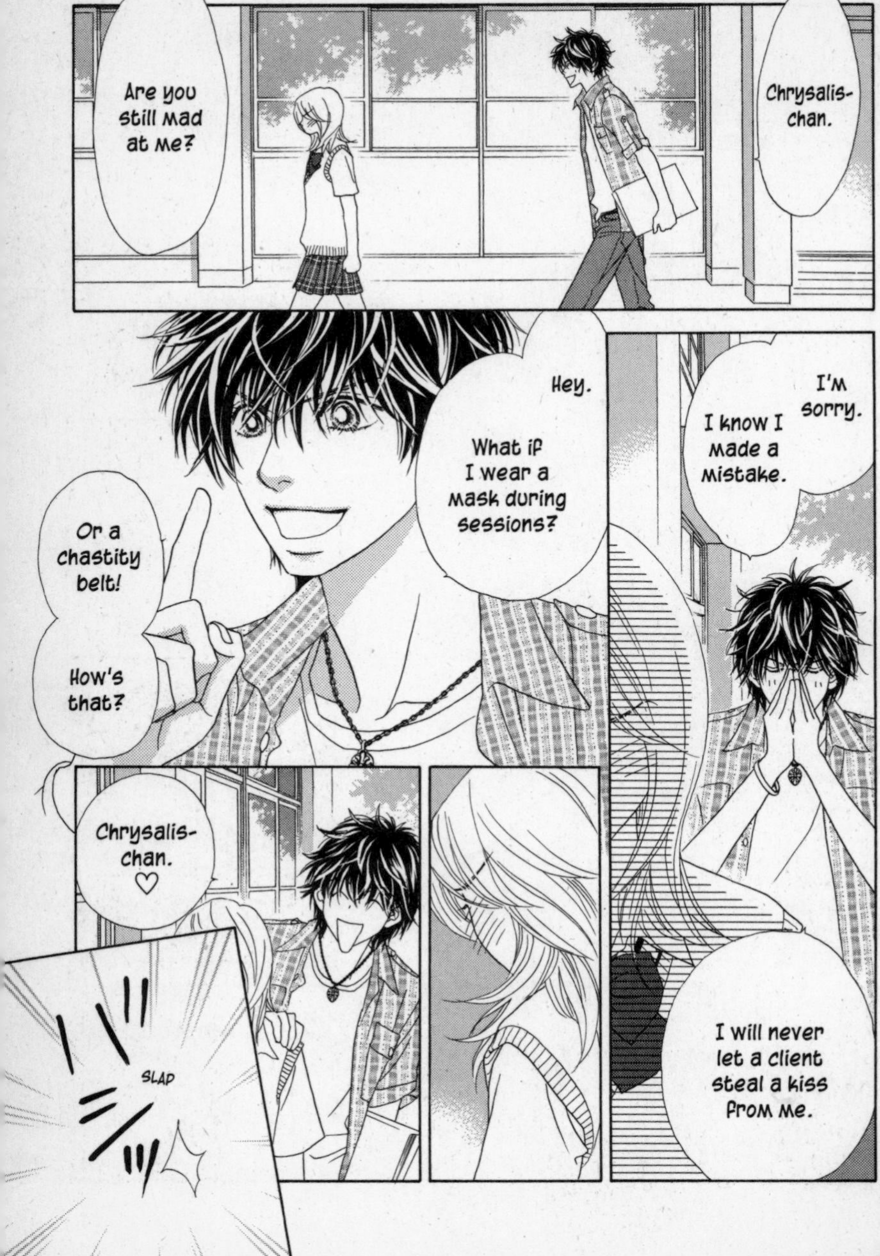
Chrysalis-chan.
Are you still mad at me?
I'm sorry.
I know I made a mistake.
I will never let a client steal a kiss from me.
Hey.
What if I wear a mask during sessions?
Or a chastity belt!
How's that?
Chrysalis-chan. ♡
SLAP

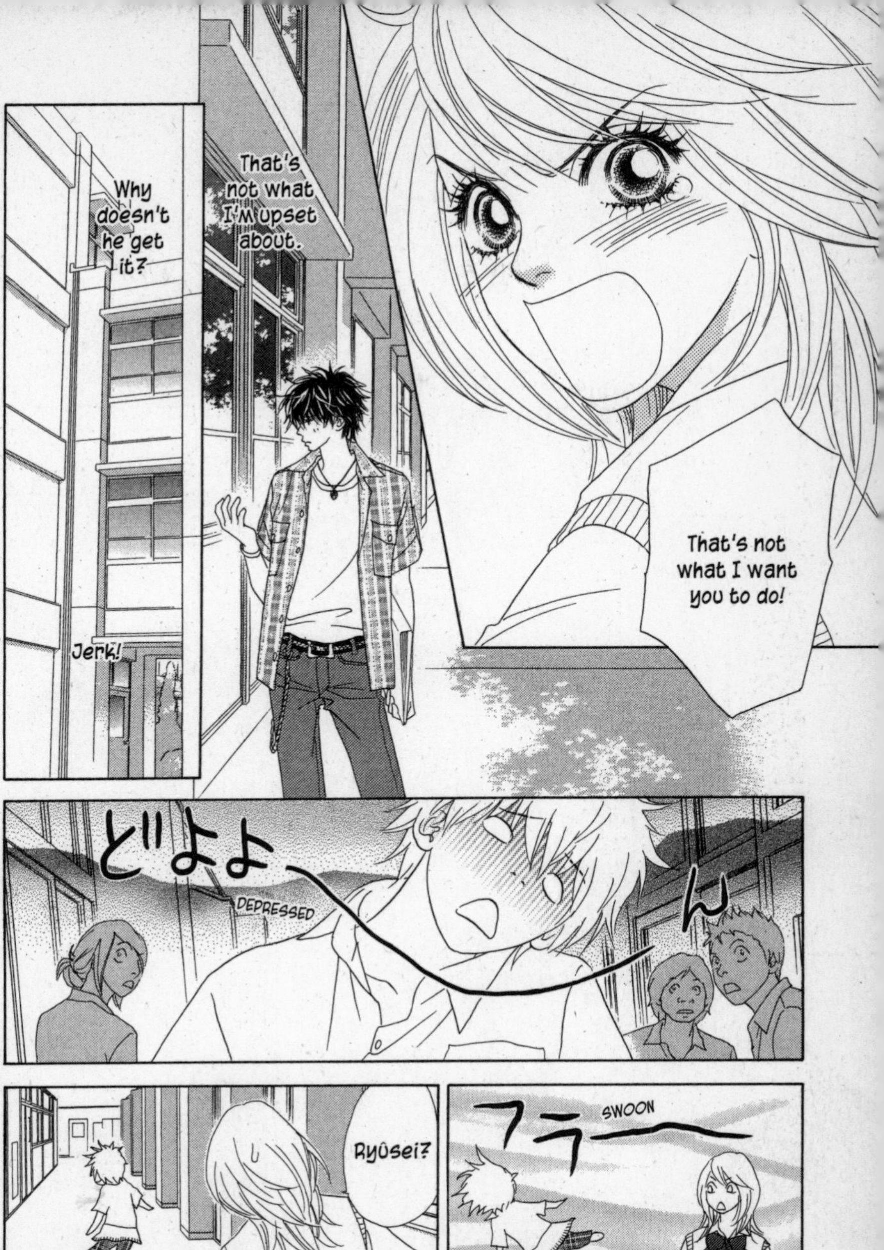
That's not what I want you to do!
That's not what I'm upset about.
Why doesn't he get it?
Jerk!
どよよ〜ん
DEPRESSED
フラ〜〜
SWOON
Ryûsei?

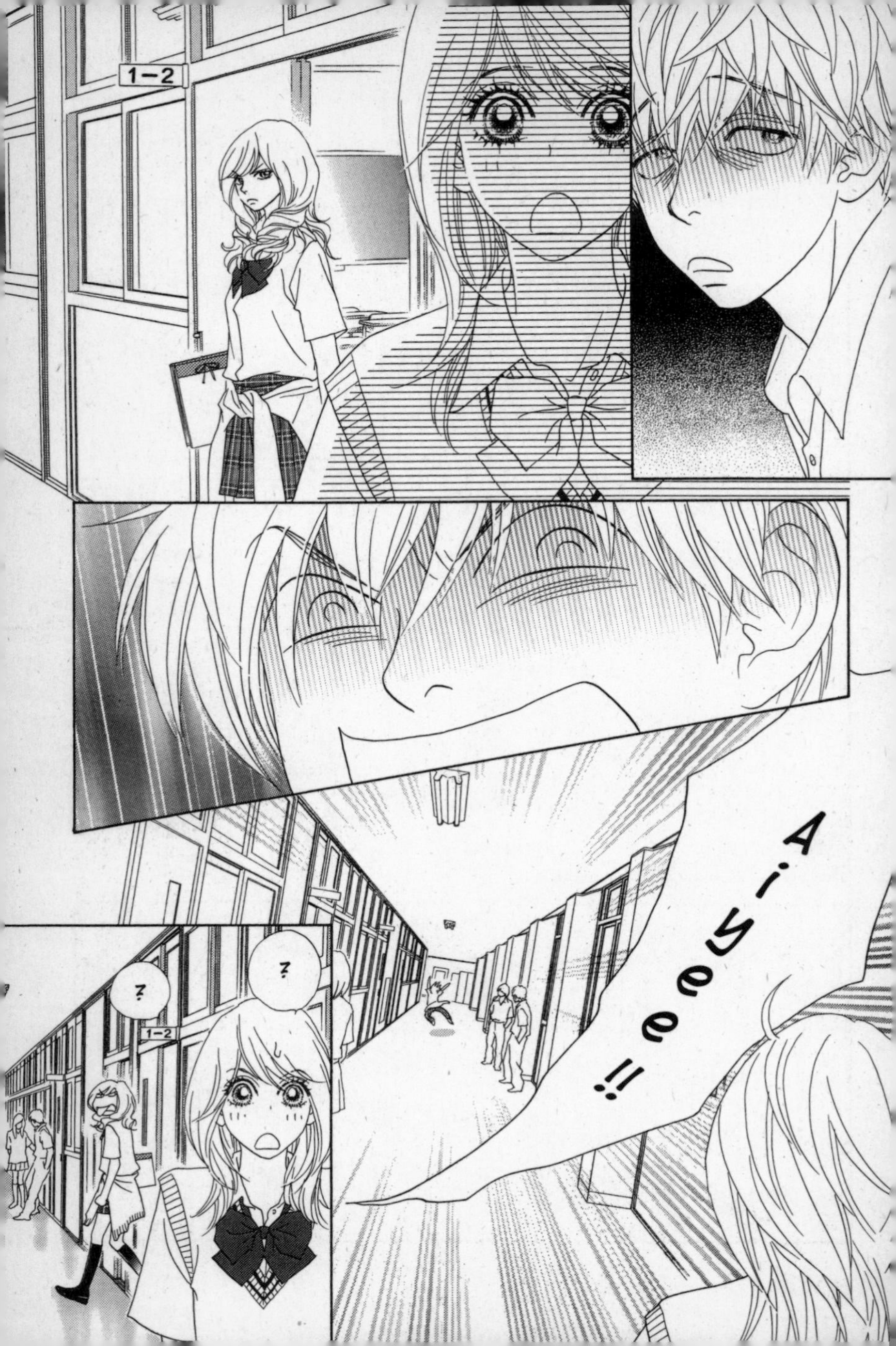
1-2
A-yee!!
?
?
1-2

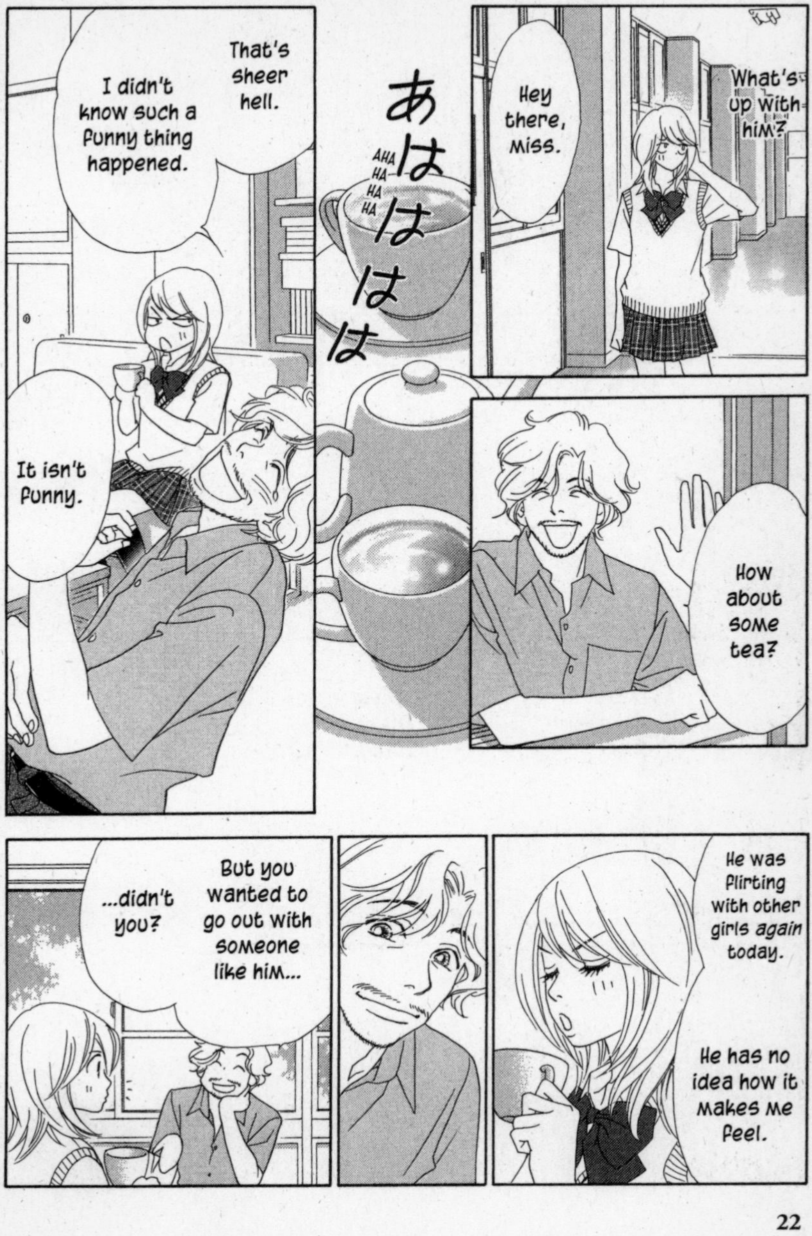
What's up with him?
Hey there, miss.
How about some tea?
あははははは
AHA HA HA HA
That's sheer hell.
I didn't know such a funny thing happened.
It isn't funny.
He was flirting with other girls *again* today.
He has no idea how it makes me feel.
But you wanted to go out with someone like him...
...didn't you?

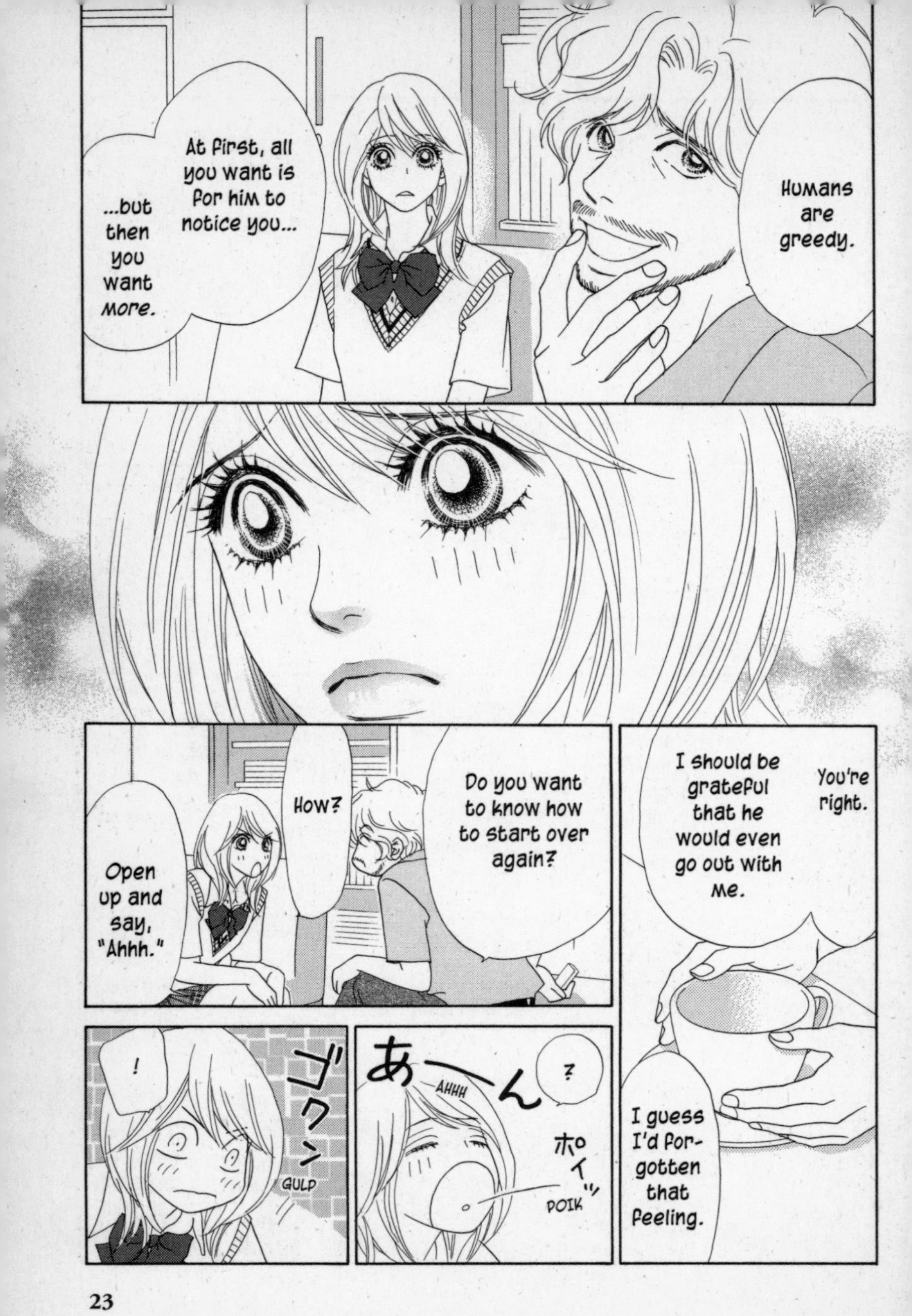
Humans are greedy.
At first, all you want is for him to notice you...
...but then you want more.
You're right.
I should be grateful that he would even go out with me.
I guess I'd forgotten that feeling.
Do you want to know how to start over again?
How?
Open up and say, "Ahhh."
あーん
AHHH
?
ポイッ
POIK
ゴクン
GULP
!

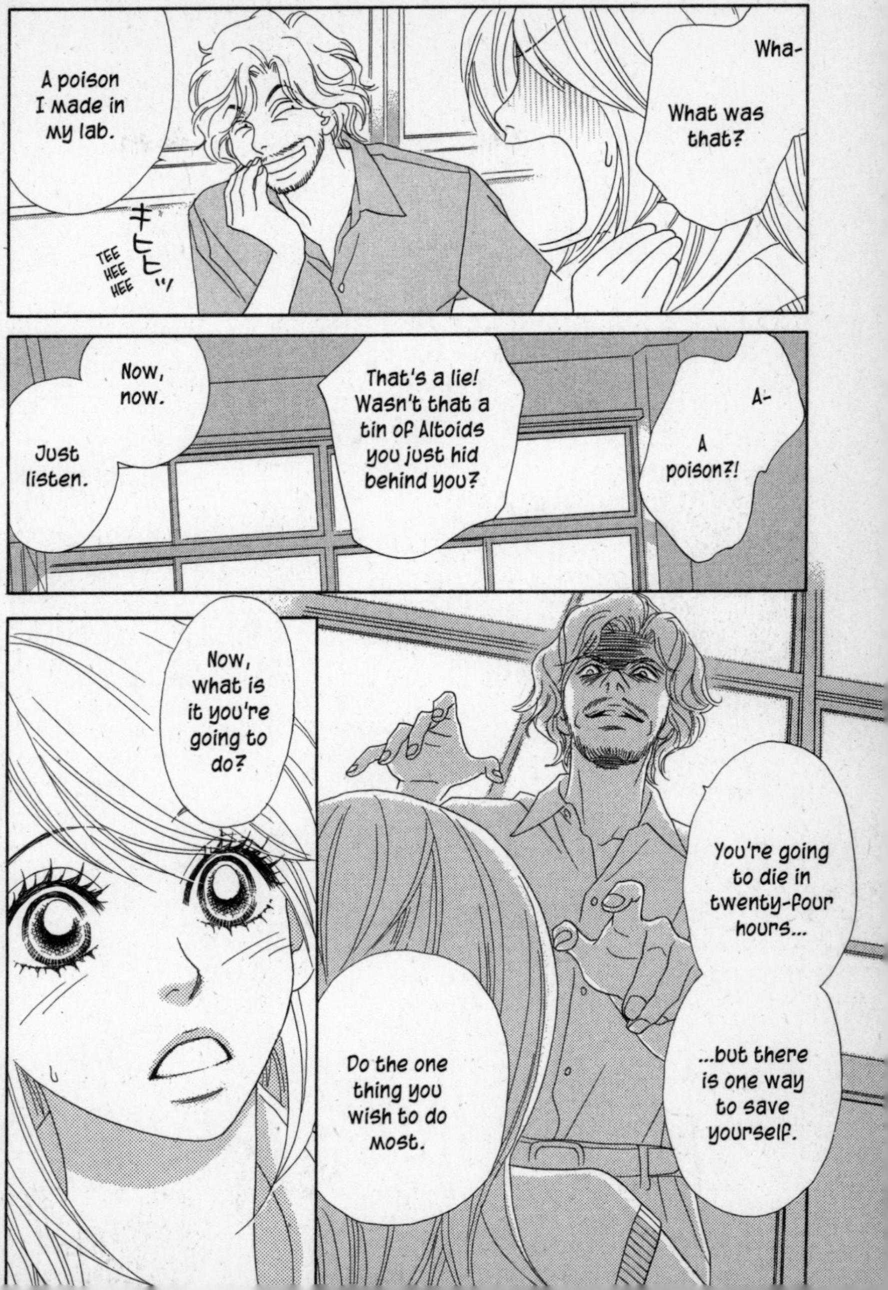
Wha-
What was that?
A poison I made in my lab.
キヒヒッ
TEE HEE HEE
A-
A poison?!
That's a lie! Wasn't that a tin of Altoids you just hid behind you?
Now, now.
Just listen.
You're going to die in twenty-four hours...
...but there is one way to save yourself.
Do the one thing you wish to do most.
Now, what is it you're going to do?

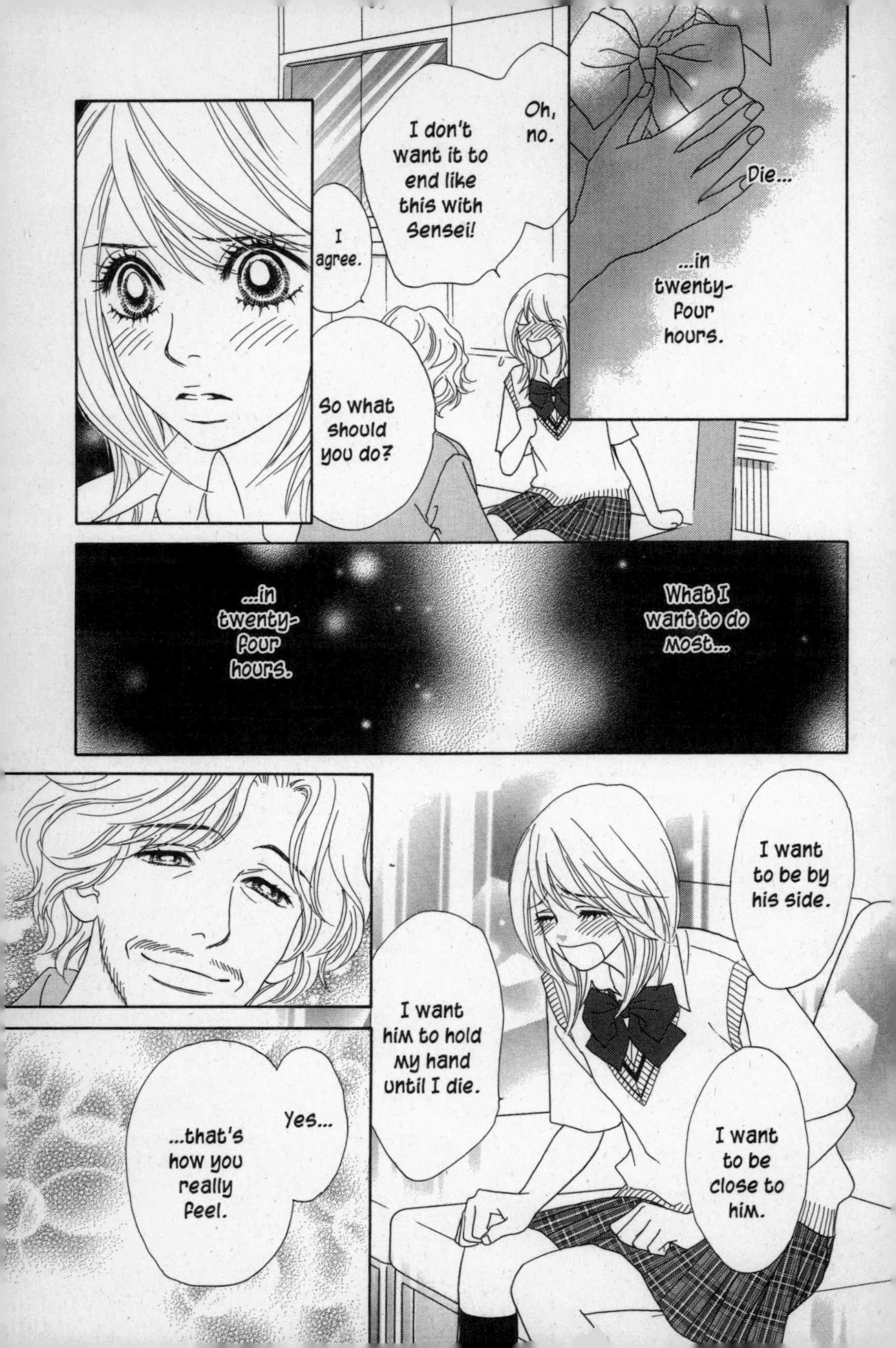
Die...
...in twenty-four hours.
Oh, no.
I don't want it to end like this with Sensei!
I agree.
So what should you do?
What I want to do most...
...in twenty-four hours.
I want to be by his side.
I want to be close to him.
I want him to hold my hand until I die.
Yes...
...that's how you really feel.

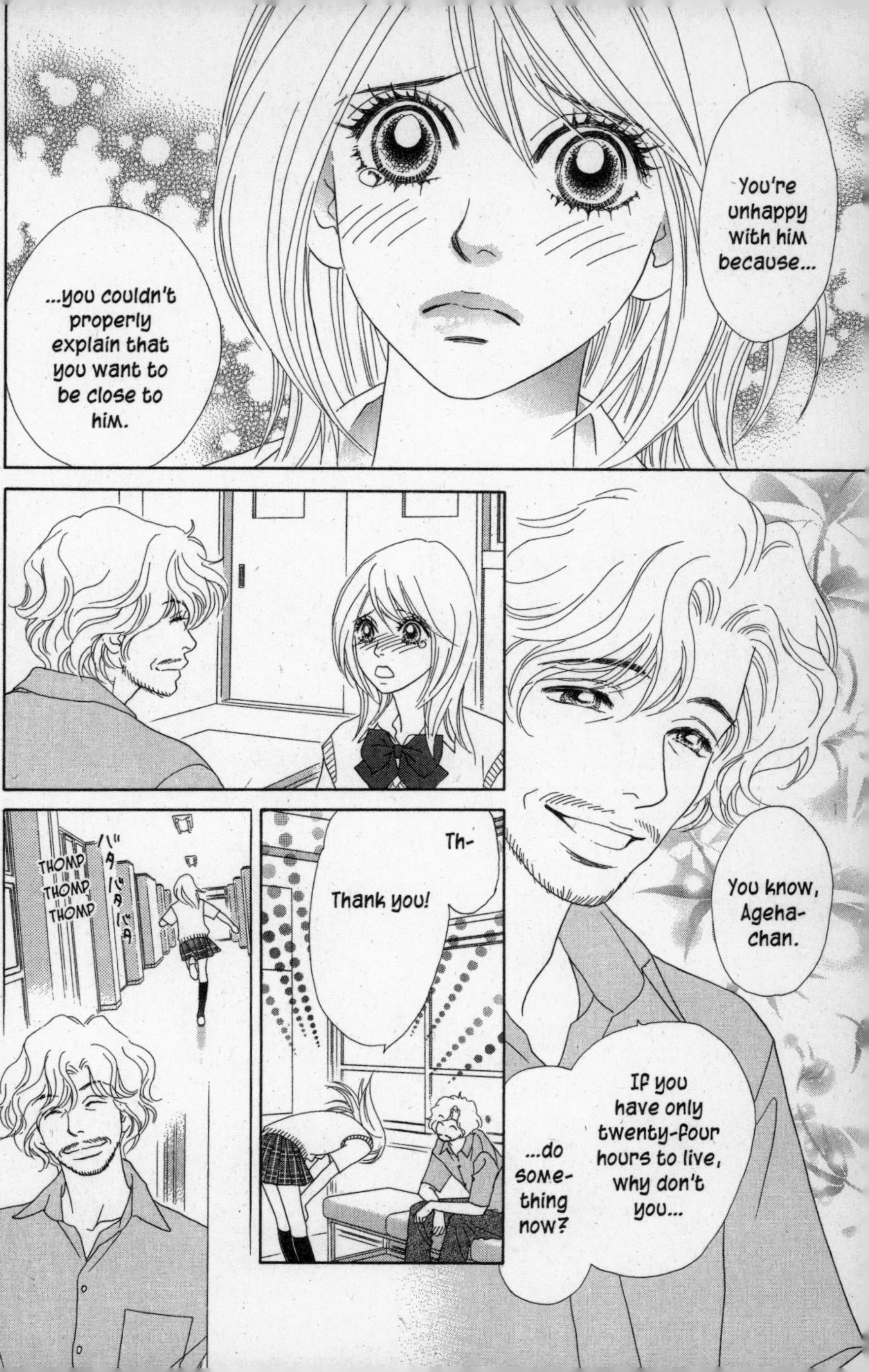
You're unhappy with him because...
...you couldn't properly explain that you want to be close to him.
You know, Ageha-chan.
If you have only twenty-four hours to live, why don't you...
...do something now?
Th-
Thank you!
バタバタバタ
THOMP THOMP THOMP

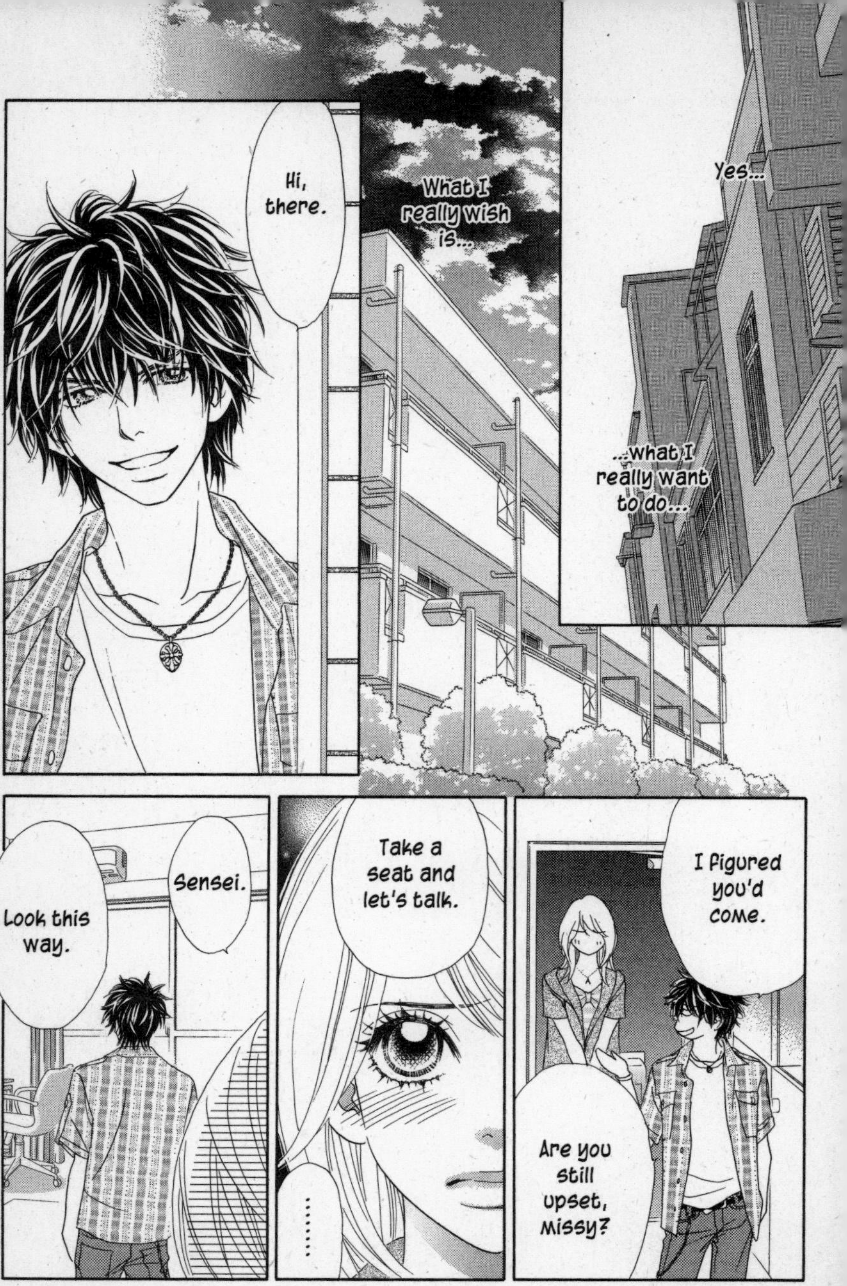
Yes...
...what I really want to do...
What I really wish is...
Hi, there.
I figured you'd come.
Are you still upset, Missy?
Take a seat and let's talk.
......
Sensei.
Look this way.

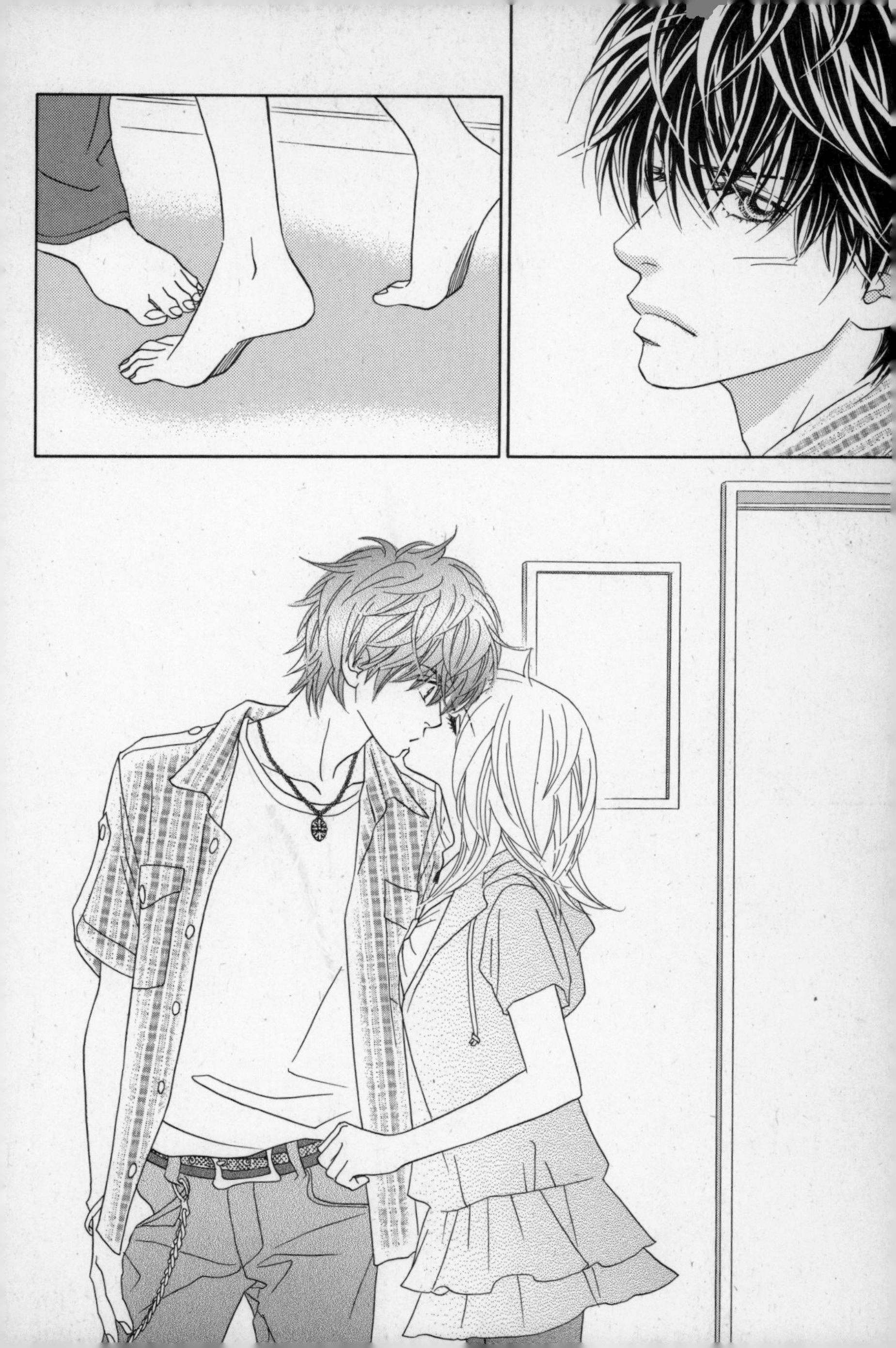

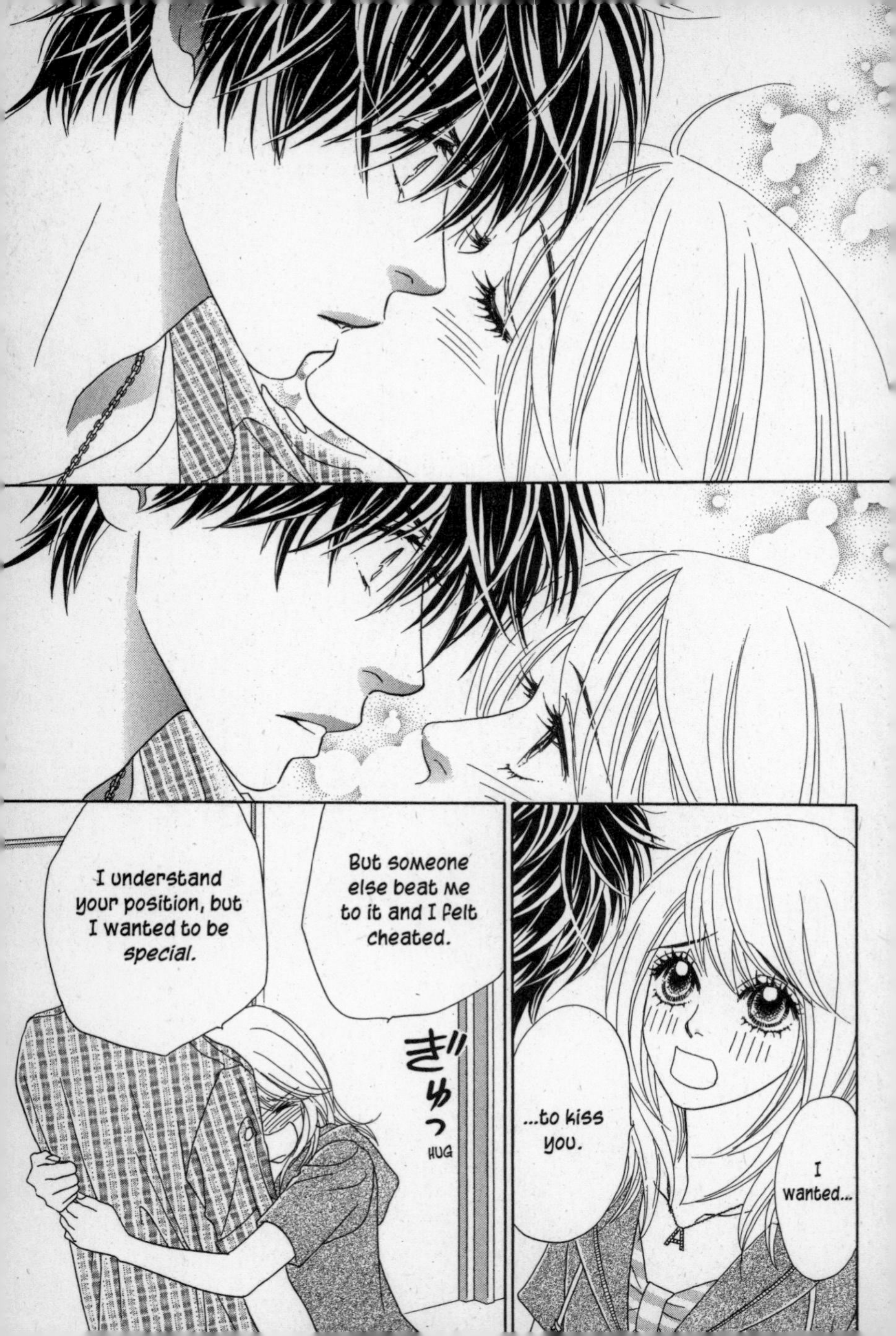
I wanted...
...to kiss you.
But someone else beat me to it and I felt cheated.
I understand your position, but I wanted to be special.
ぎゅっ
HUG

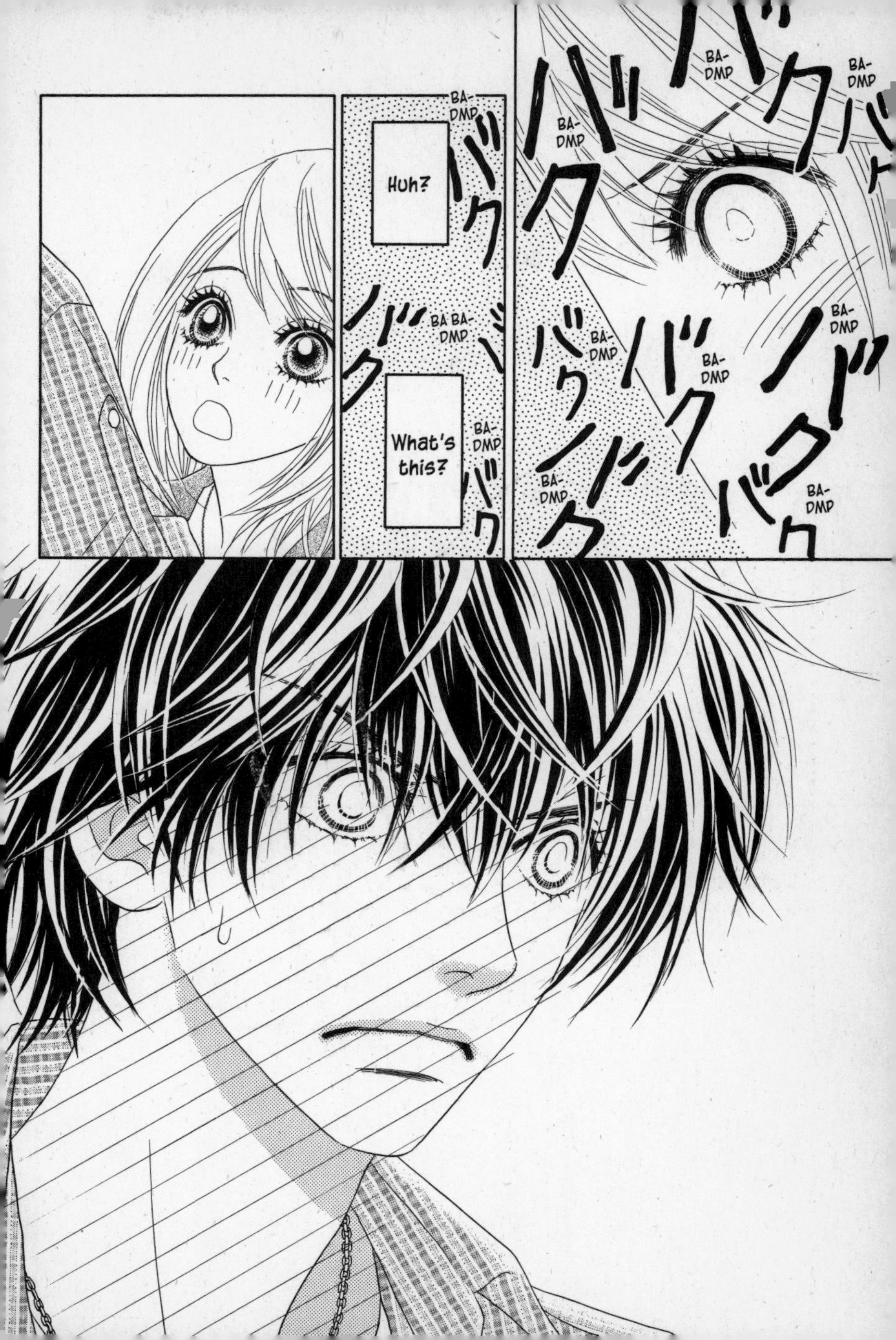

BA-DMP
BA-DMP
BA-DMP
BA-DMP
BA-DMP
BA-DMP
BA-DMP
BA-DMP
BA-DMP
Huh?
BA BA-DMP
What's this?
BA-DMP

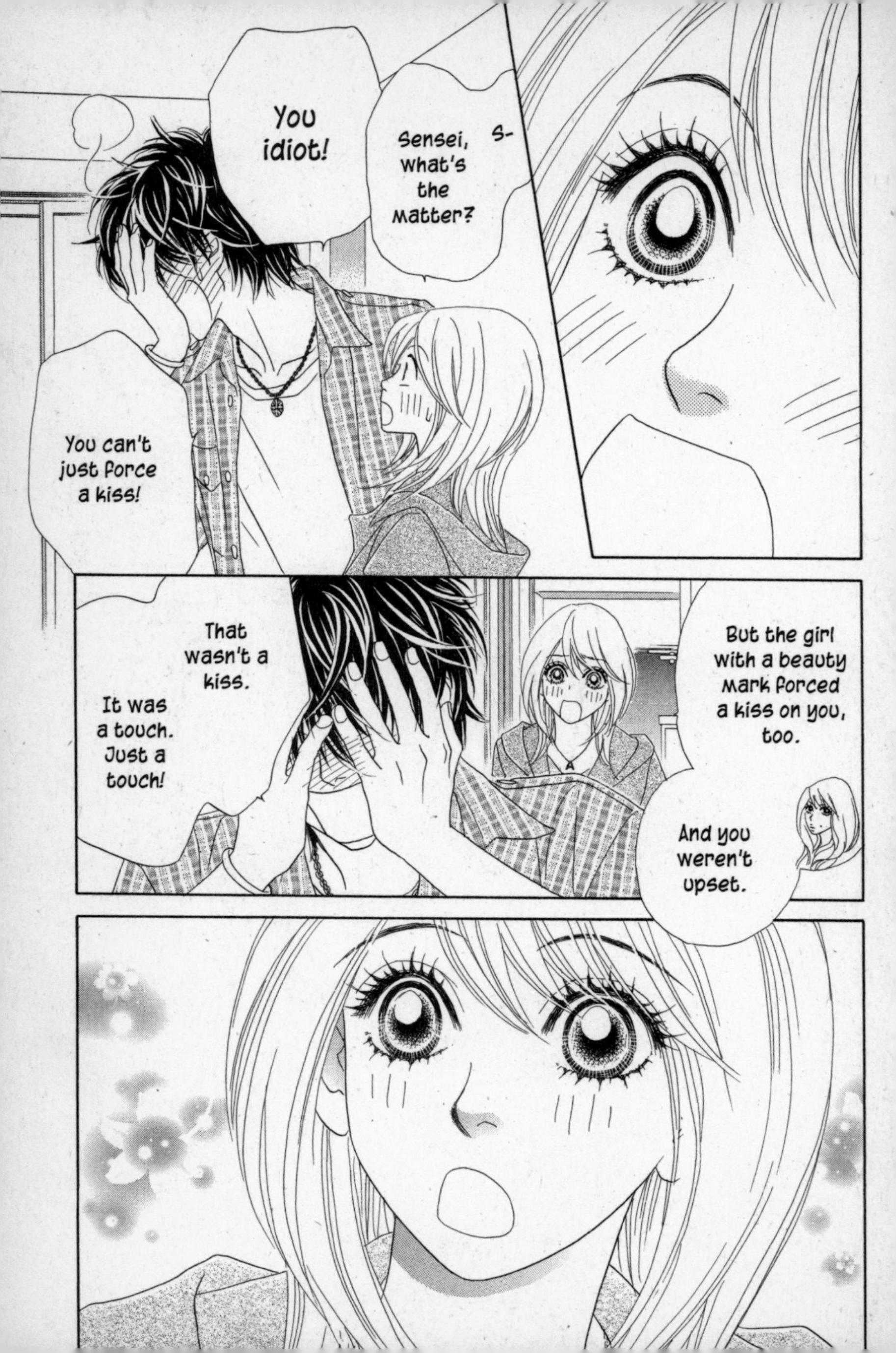
S- Sensei, what's the matter?
You idiot!
You can't just force a kiss!
But the girl with a beauty mark forced a kiss on you, too.
And you weren't upset.
That wasn't a kiss.
It was a touch. Just a touch!

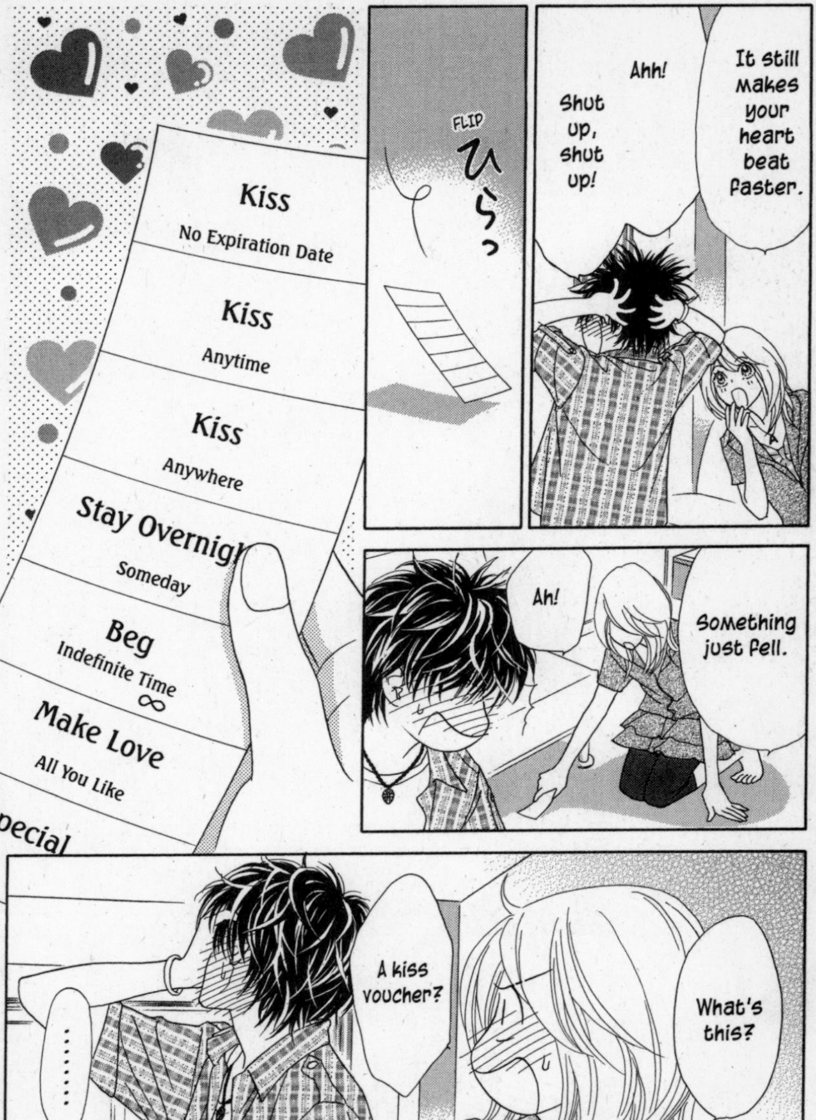
It still makes your heart beat faster.
Ahh!
Shut up, shut up!
FLIP
ひらっ
Something just fell.
Ah!
Kiss
No Expiration Date
Kiss
Anytime
Kiss
Anywhere
Stay Overnigh
Someday
Beg
Indefinite Time
∞
Make Love
All You Like
Special
What's this?
A kiss voucher?
......

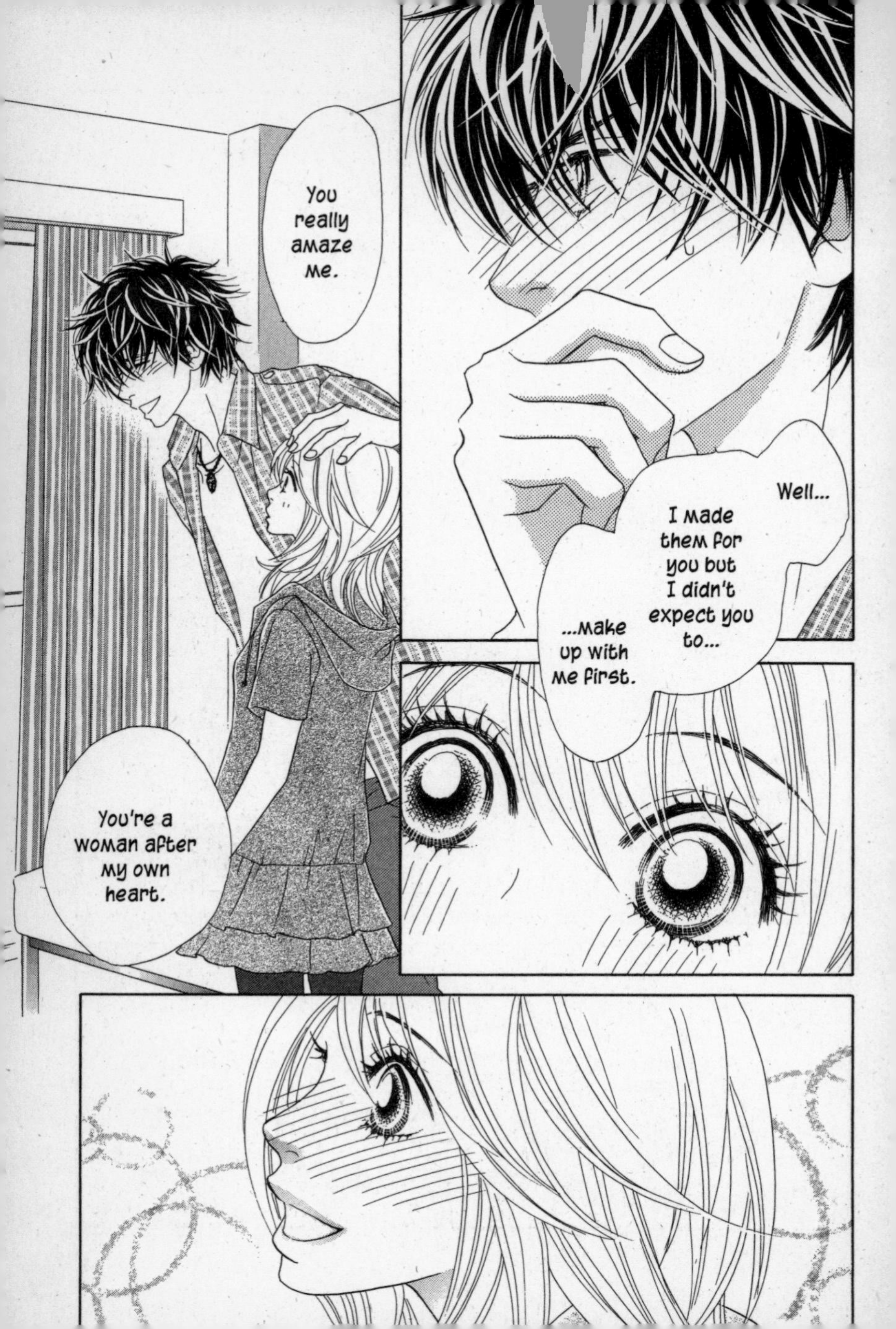
Well...
I made them for you but I didn't expect you to...
...make up with me first.
You really amaze me.
You're a woman after my own heart.

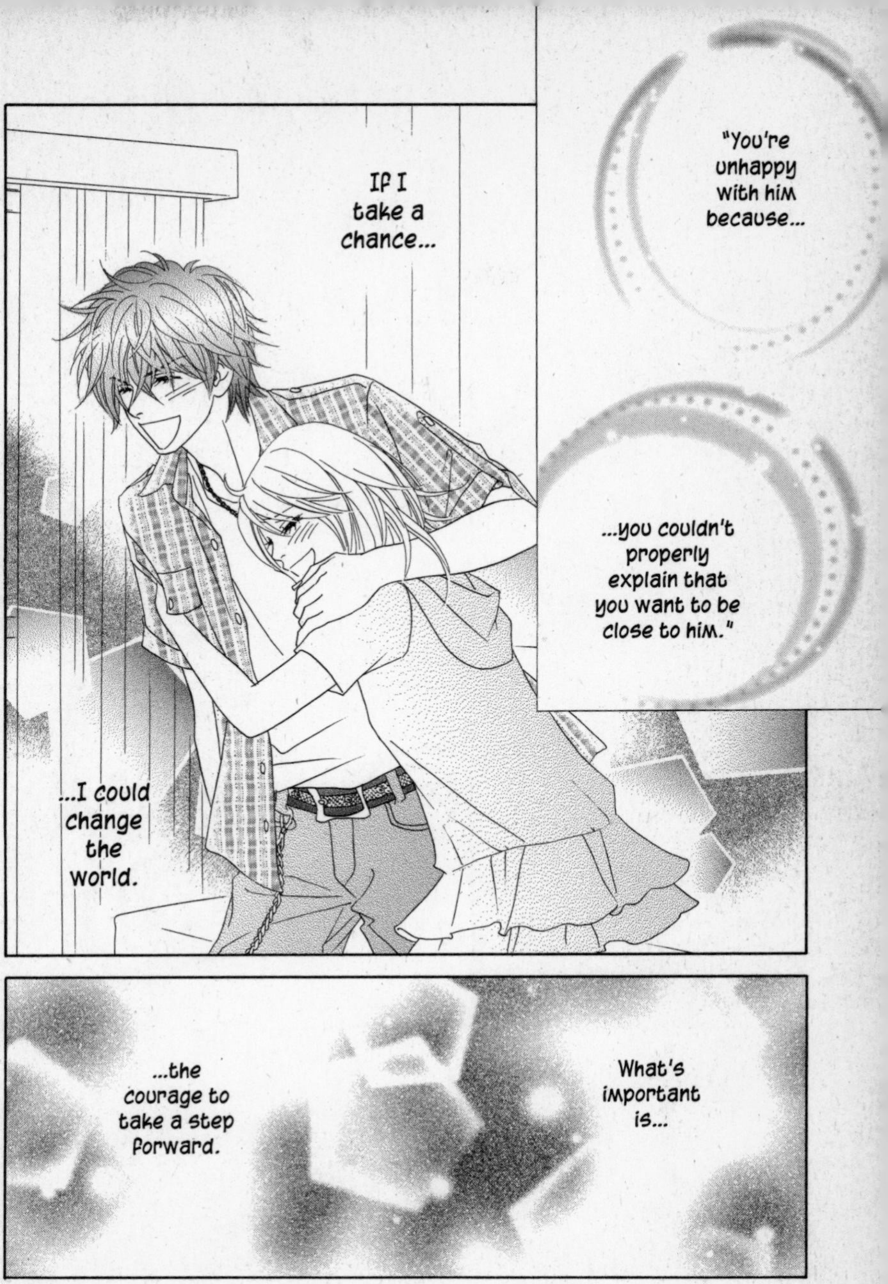
"You're unhappy with him because...
...you couldn't properly explain that you want to be close to him."
If I take a chance...
...I could change the world.
What's important is...
...the courage to take a step forward.

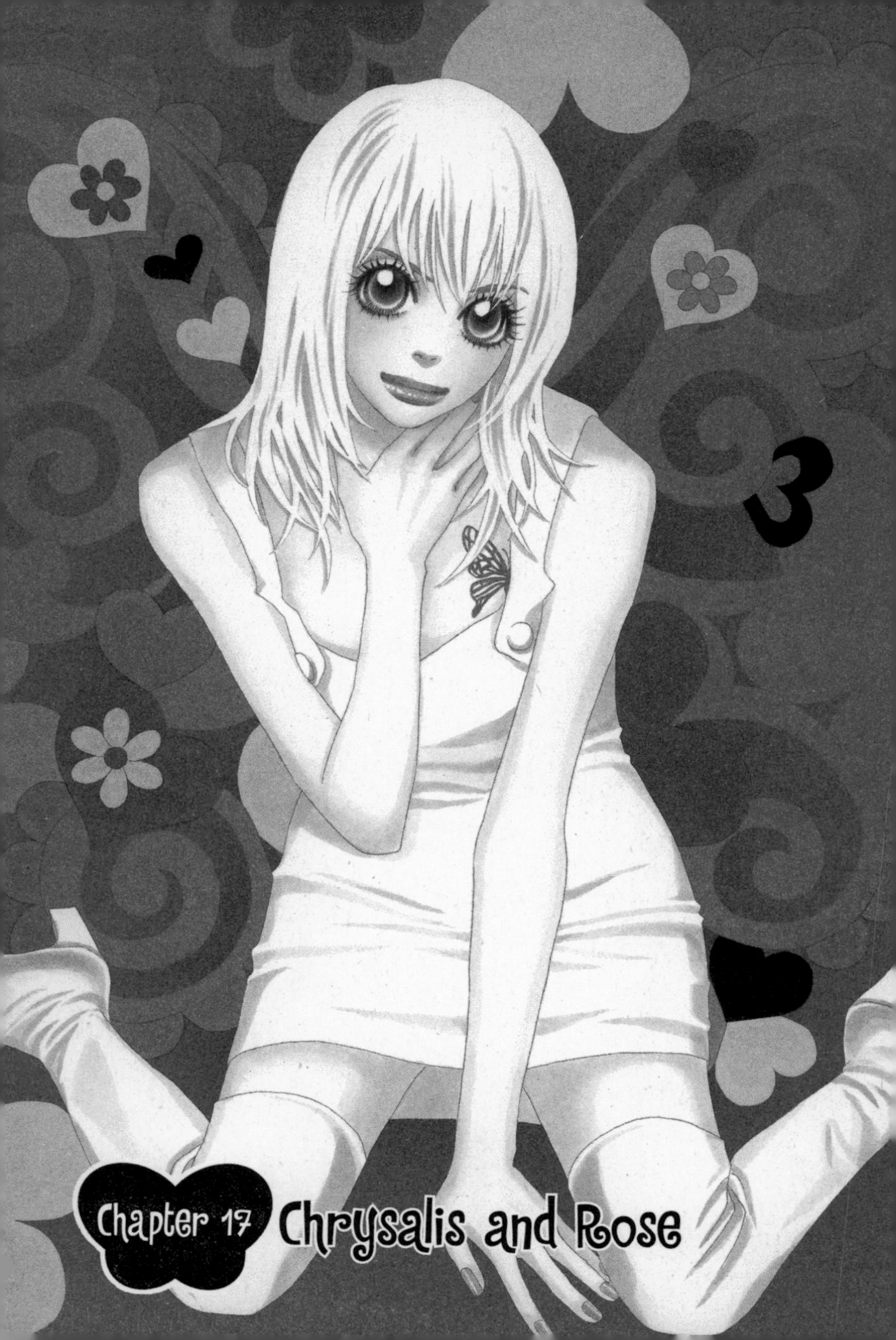
Chapter 17
Chrysalis and Rose

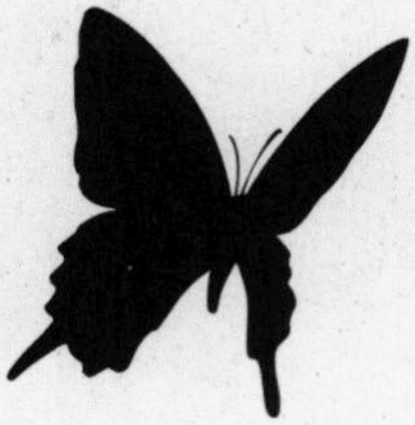

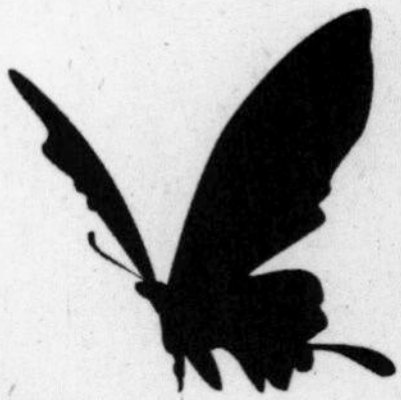

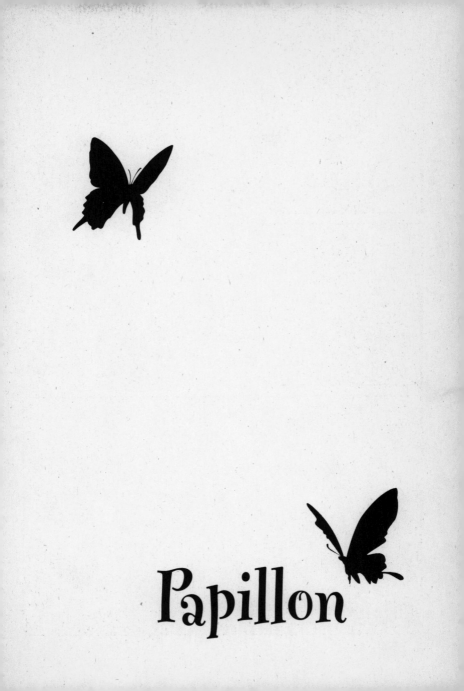

Papillon

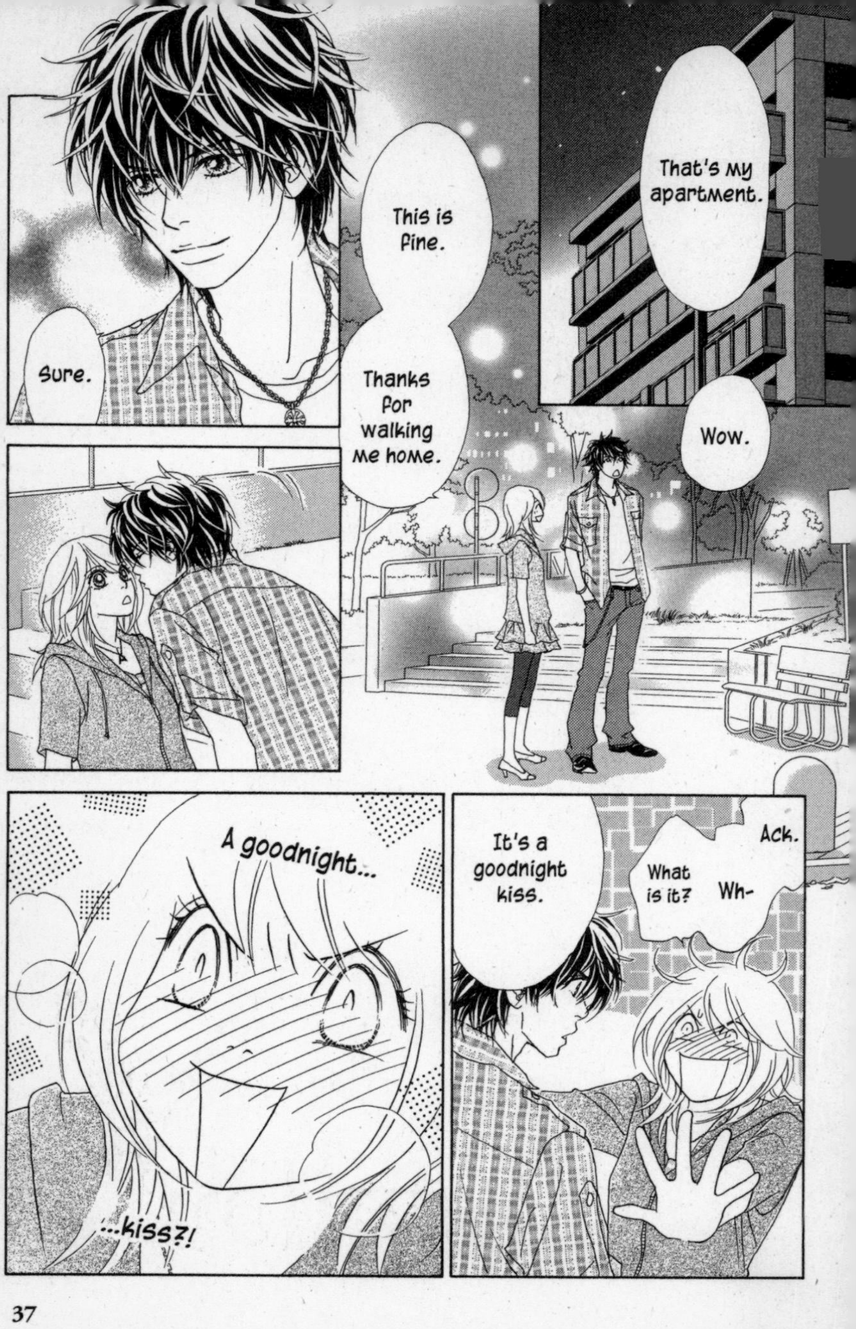
That's my apartment.
Wow.
Thanks for walking me home.
This is fine.
Sure.
Ack.
Wh-
What is it?
It's a goodnight kiss.
A goodnight...
...kiss?!

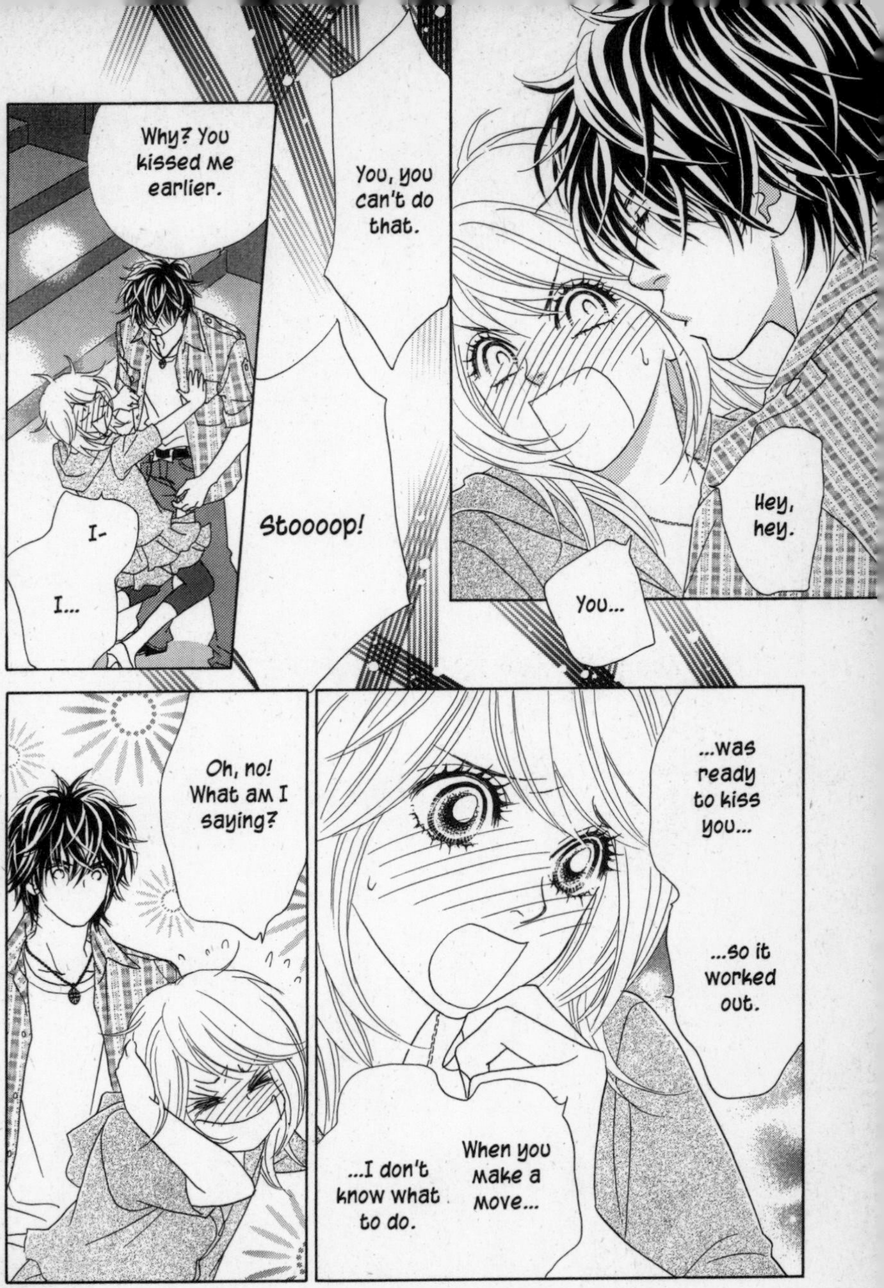
Hey, hey.
You...
You, you can't do that.
Stoooop!
Why? You kissed me earlier.
I-
I...
...was ready to kiss you...
...so it worked out.
When you make a move...
...I don't know what to do.
Oh, no! What am I saying?

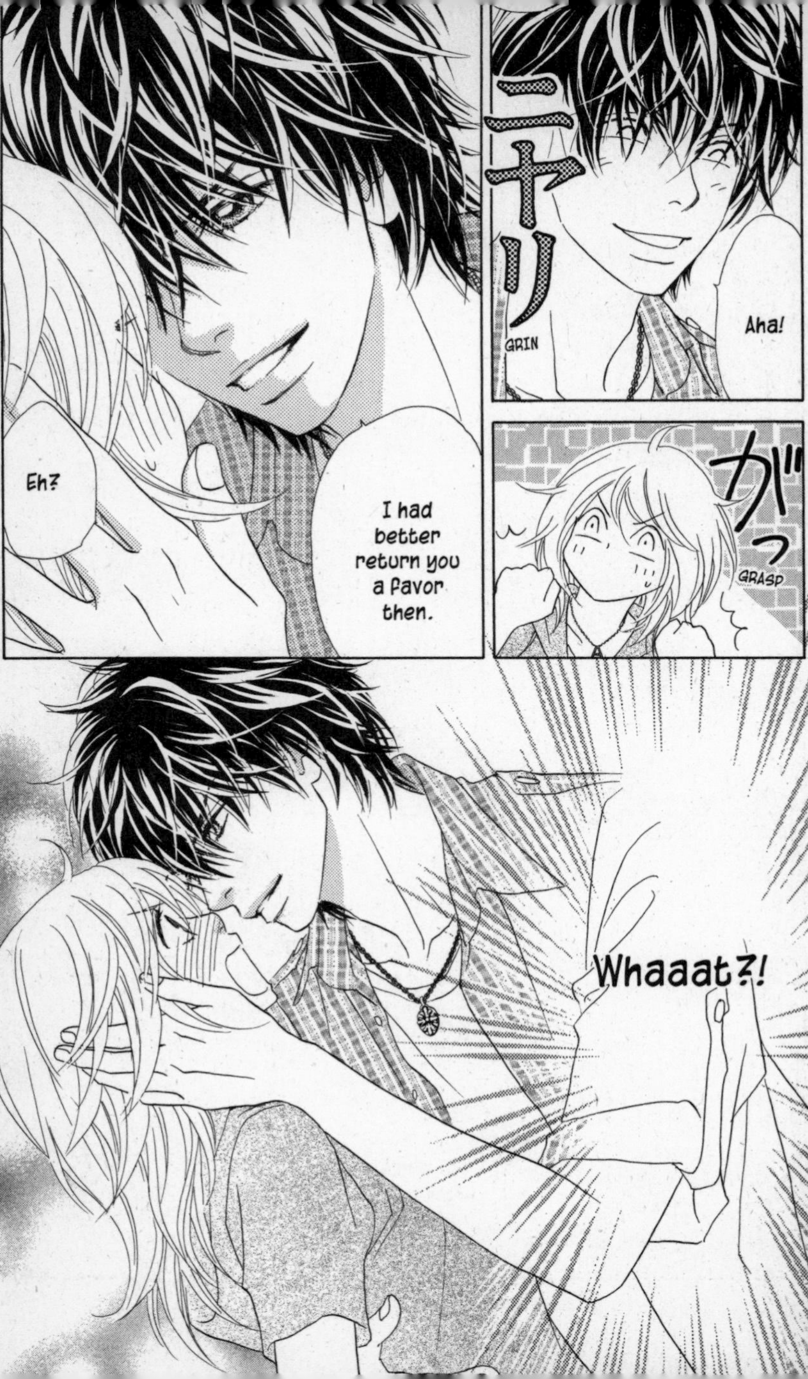
ニヤリ
GRIN
Aha!
がっ
GRASP
I had better return you a favor then.
Eh?
Whaaat?!

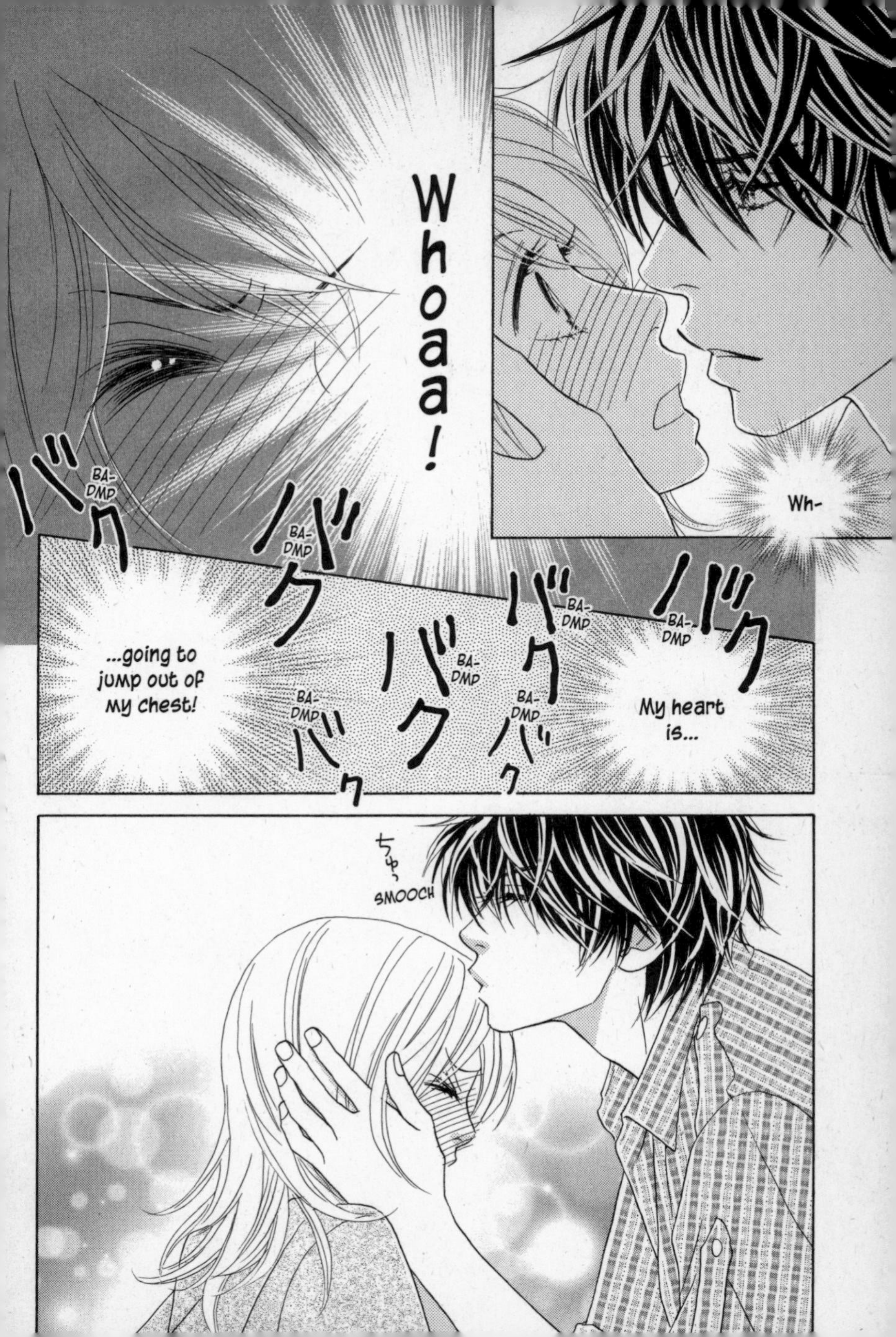
Wh-
Whoaa!
BA-DMP
BA-DMP
My heart is...
BA-DMP
BA-DMP
BA-DMP
BA-DMP
...going to jump out of my chest!
SMOOCH

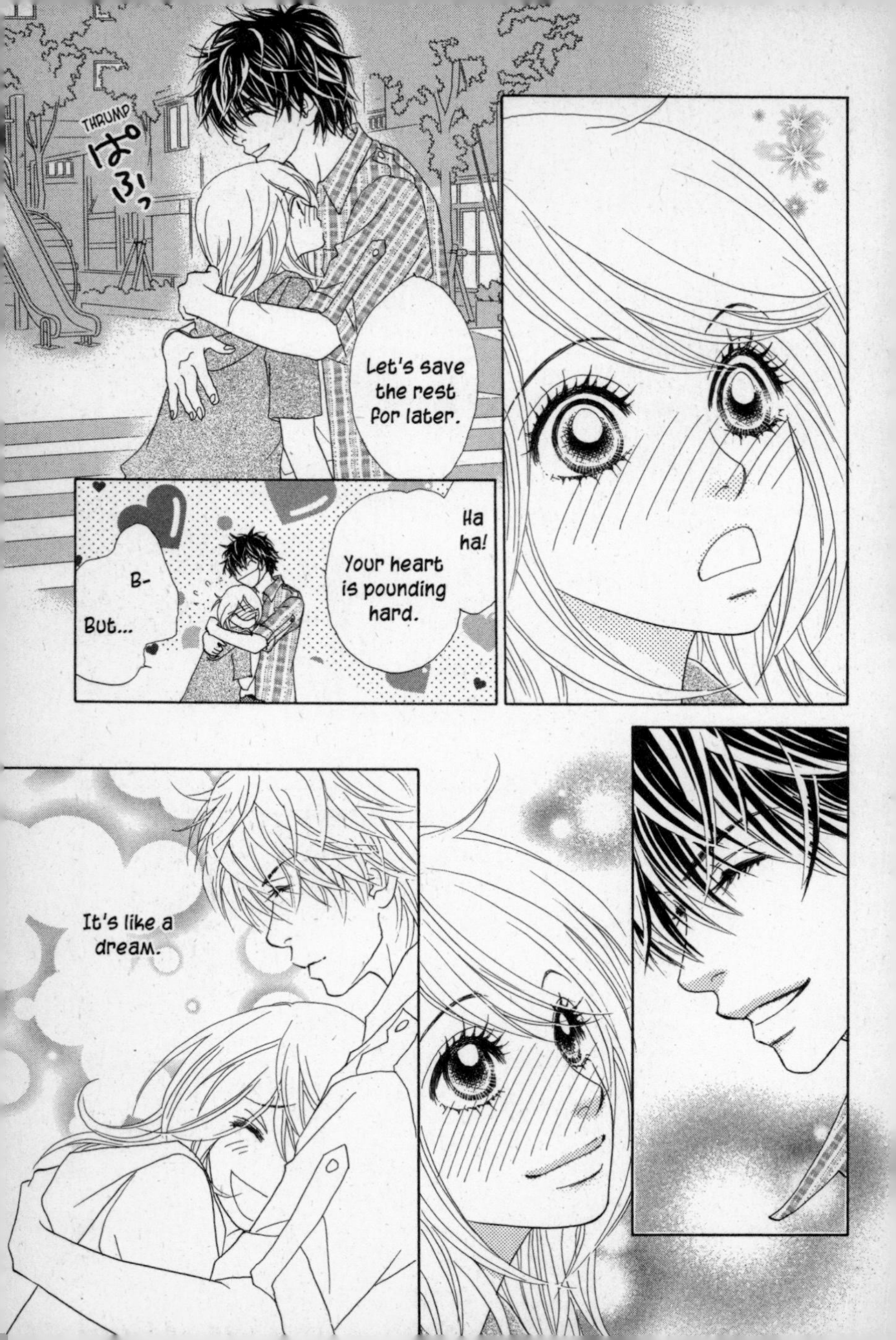
THRUMP
ぱふっ
Let's save the rest for later.
Ha ha!
Your heart is pounding hard.
B-
But...
It's like a dream.

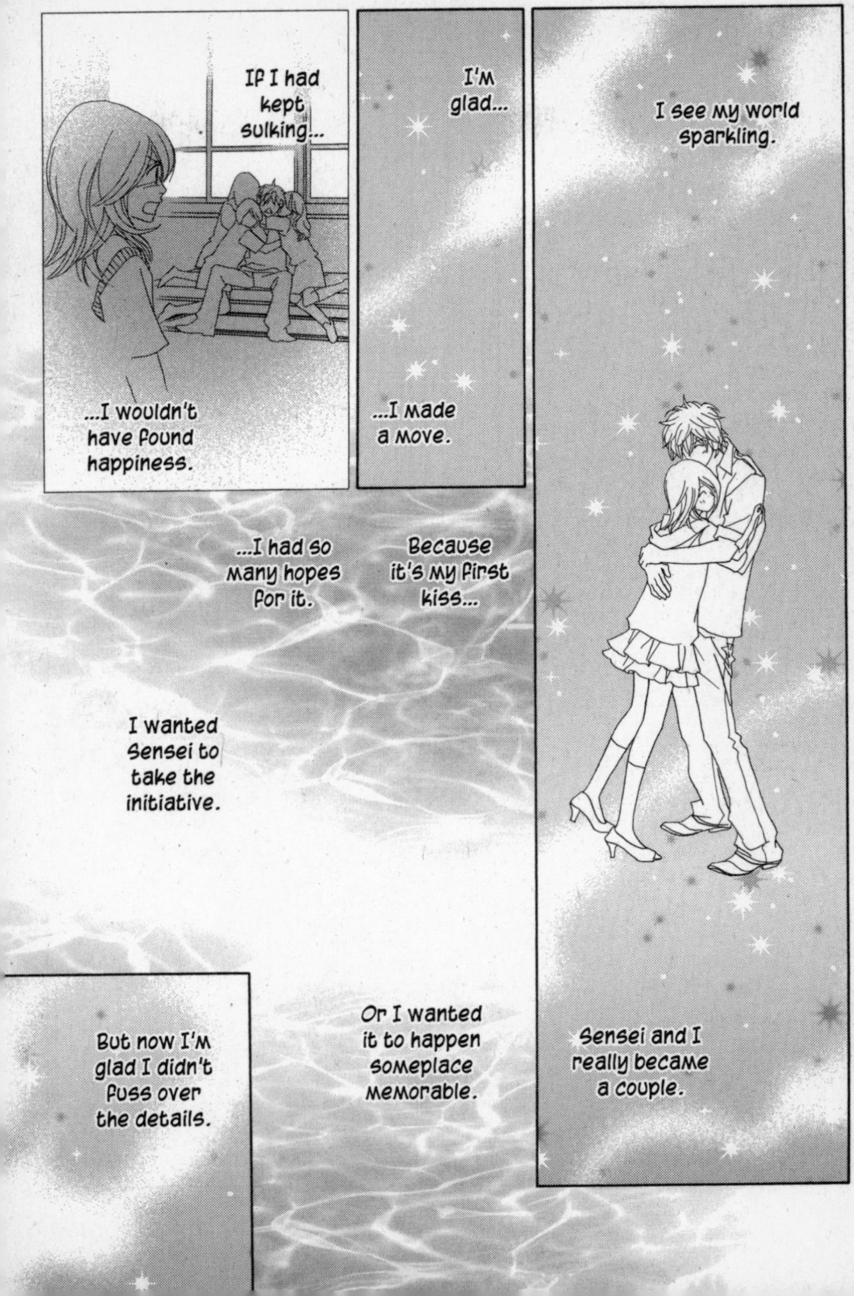
I see my world sparkling.
Sensei and I really became a couple.
I'm glad...
...I made a move.
If I had kept sulking...
...I wouldn't have found happiness.
Because it's my first kiss...
...I had so many hopes for it.
I wanted Sensei to take the initiative.
Or I wanted it to happen someplace memorable.
But now I'm glad I didn't fuss over the details.

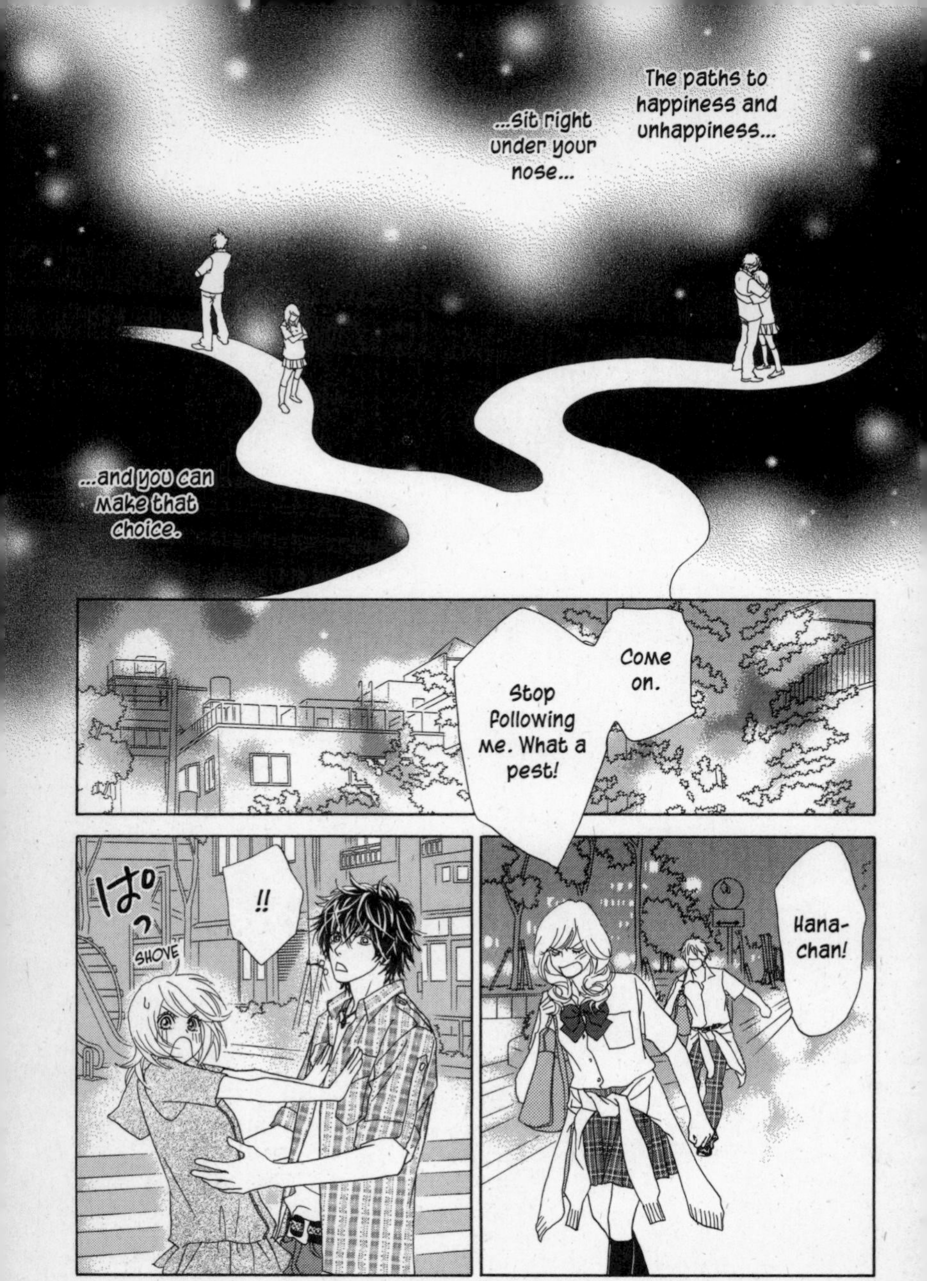
The paths to happiness and unhappiness...
...sit right under your nose...
...and you can make that choice.
Come on.
Stop following me. What a pest!
Hana-chan!
!!
ぱっ
SHOVE

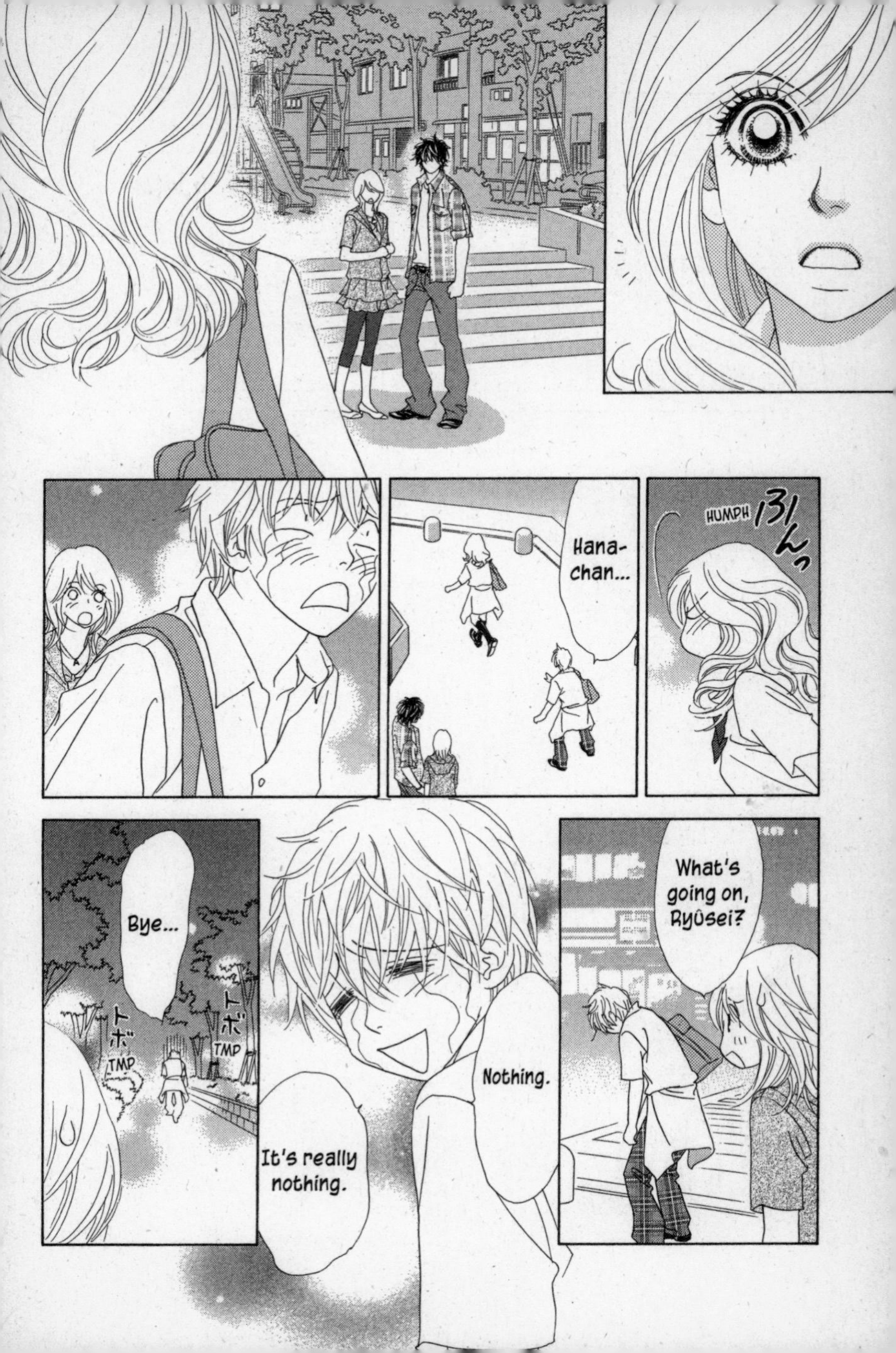
HUMPH
ふんっ
Hana-chan...
What's going on, Ryûsei?
Nothing.
It's really nothing.
Bye...
トボ
TMP
トボ
TMP

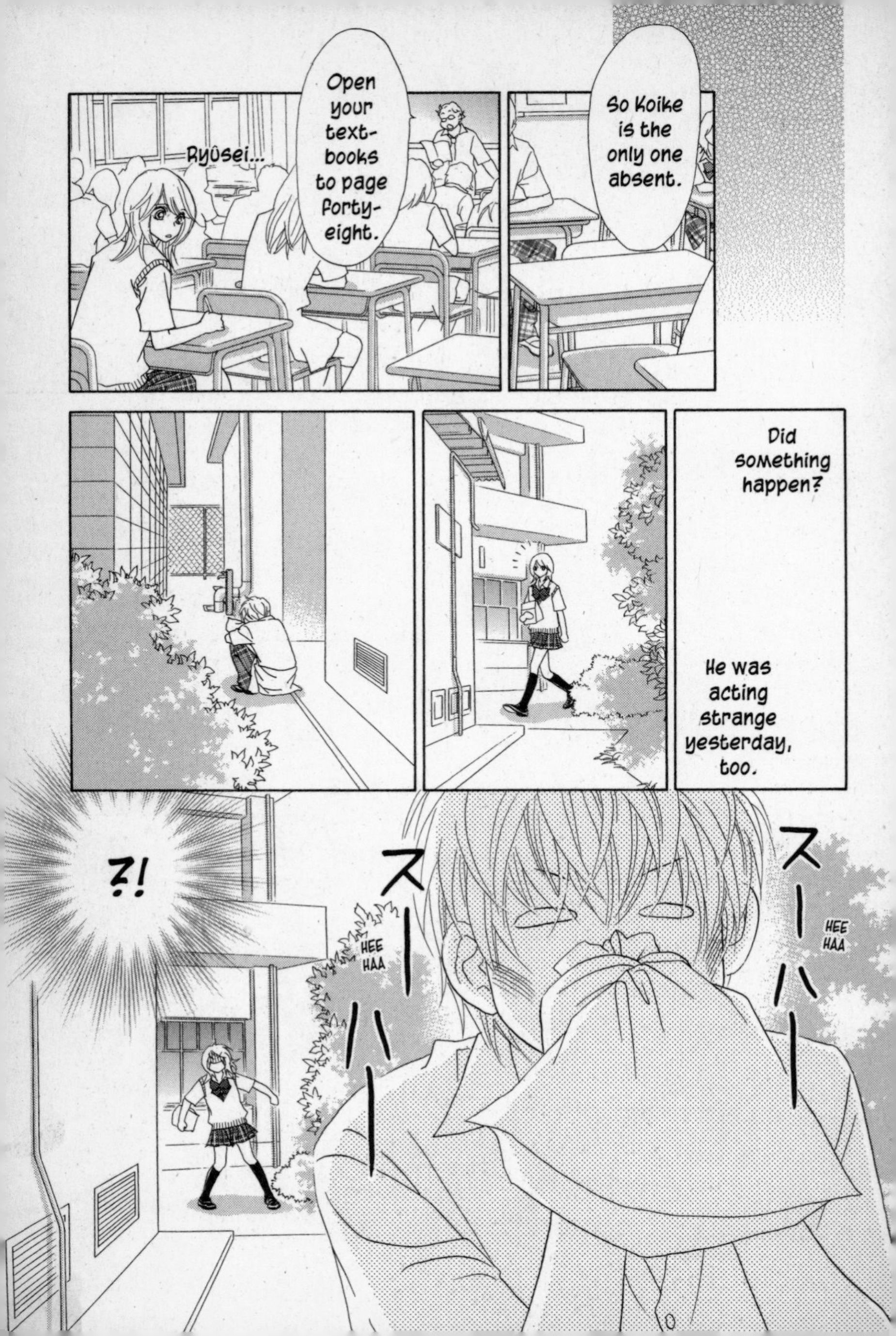
So Koike is the only one absent.
Open your text-books to page forty-eight.
Ryûsei...
Did something happen?
He was acting strange yesterday, too.
スーハー
HEE HAA
スーハー
HEE HAA
?!

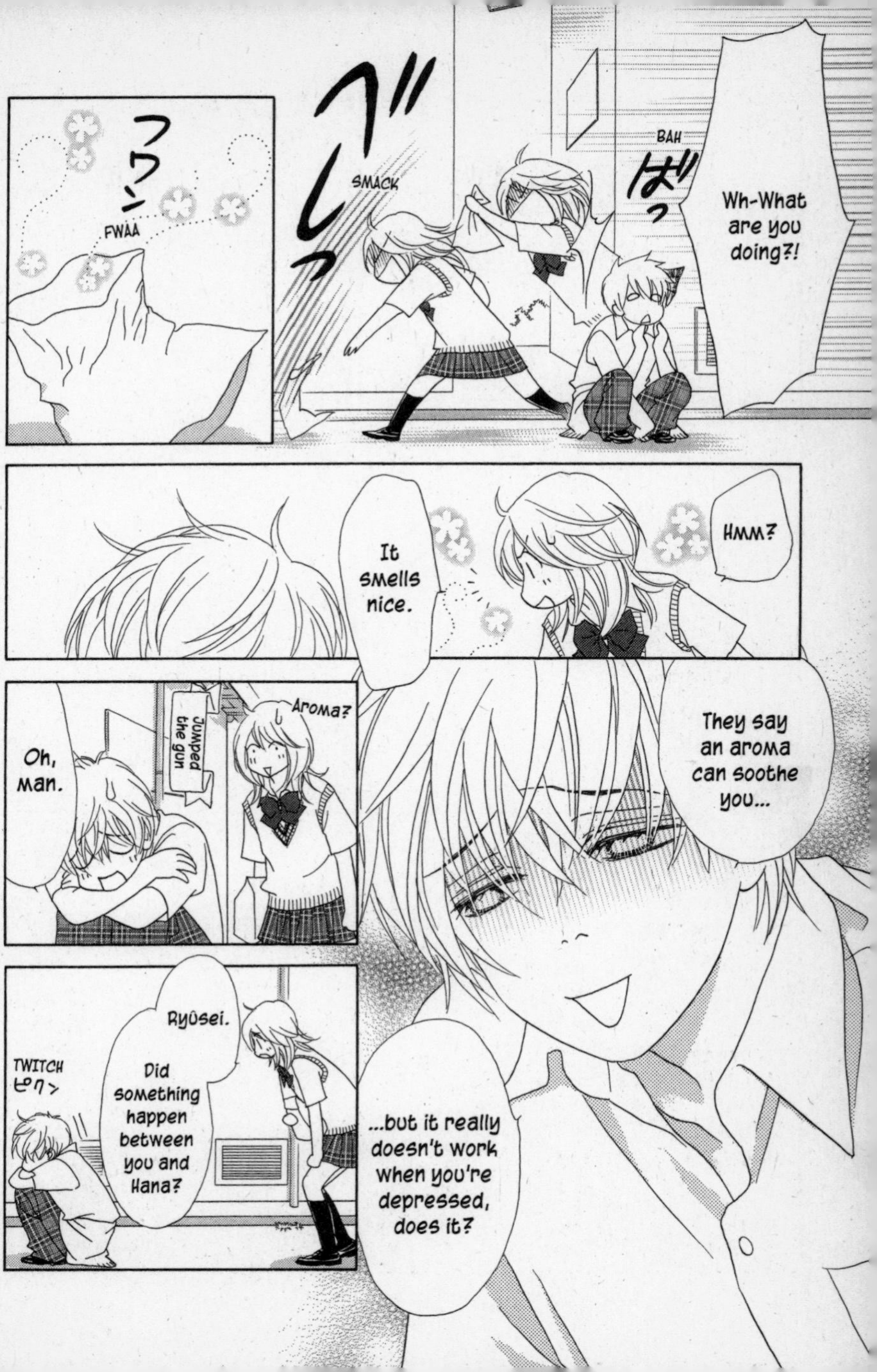
Wh-What are you doing?!
BAH
SMACK
FWAA
HMM?
It smells nice.
They say an aroma can soothe you...
...but it really doesn't work when you're depressed, does it?
Aroma?
Jumped the gun
Oh, man.
Ryûsei.
Did something happen between you and Hana?
TWITCH

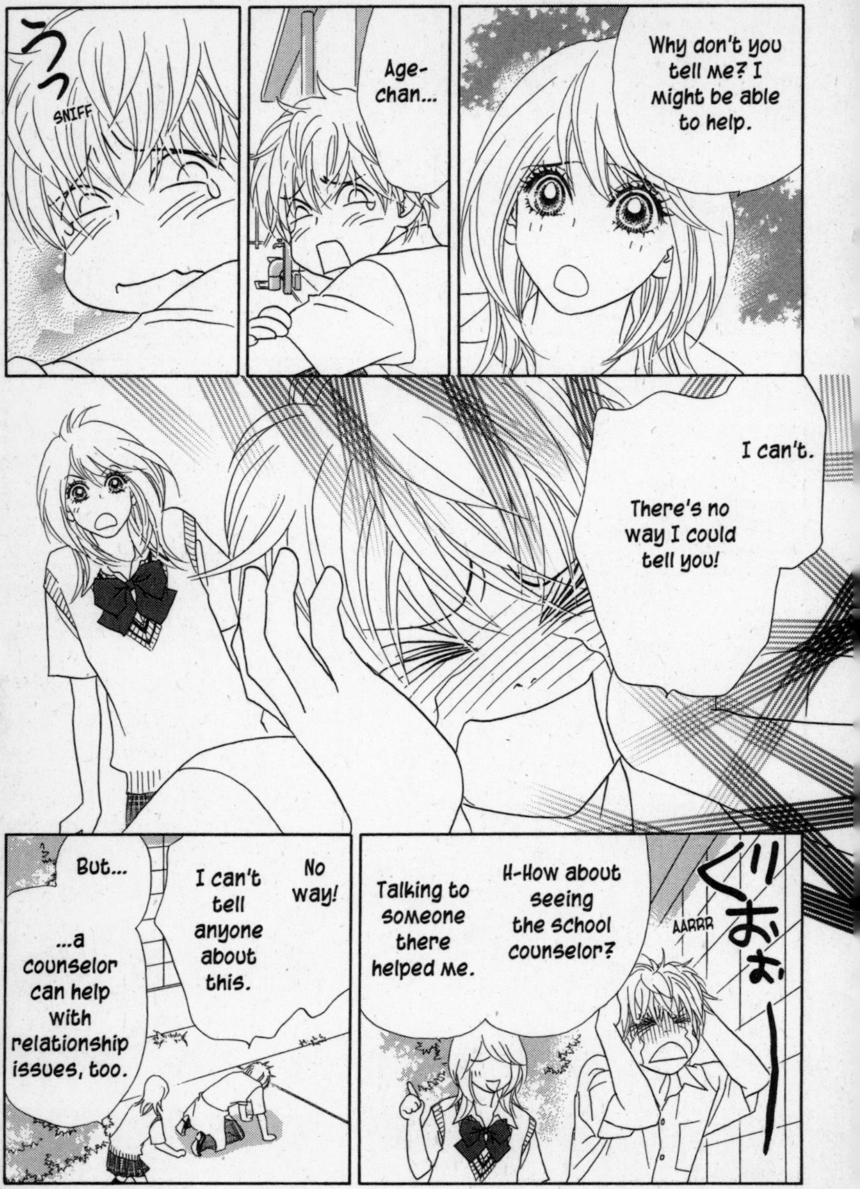
Why don't you tell me? I might be able to help.
Age-chan...
うっ
SNIFF
I can't.
There's no way I could tell you!
くりぉー
AARRR
H-How about seeing the school counselor?
Talking to someone there helped me.
No way!
I can't tell anyone about this.
But...
...a counselor can help with relationship issues, too.

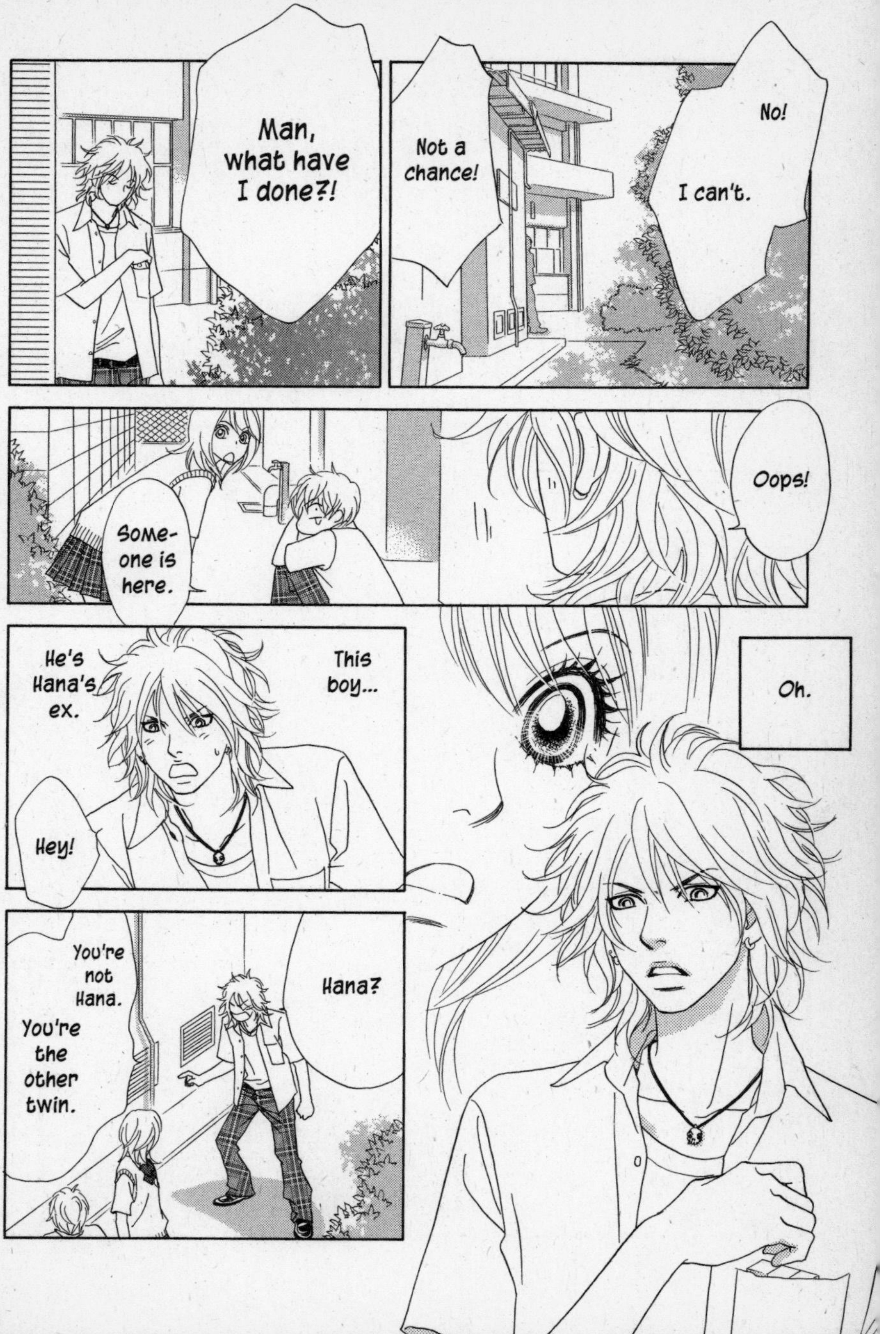

No!
I can't.
Not a chance!
Man, what have I done?!
Oops!
Some-one is here.
Oh.
This boy...
He's Hana's ex.
Hey!
Hana?
You're not Hana.
You're the other twin.

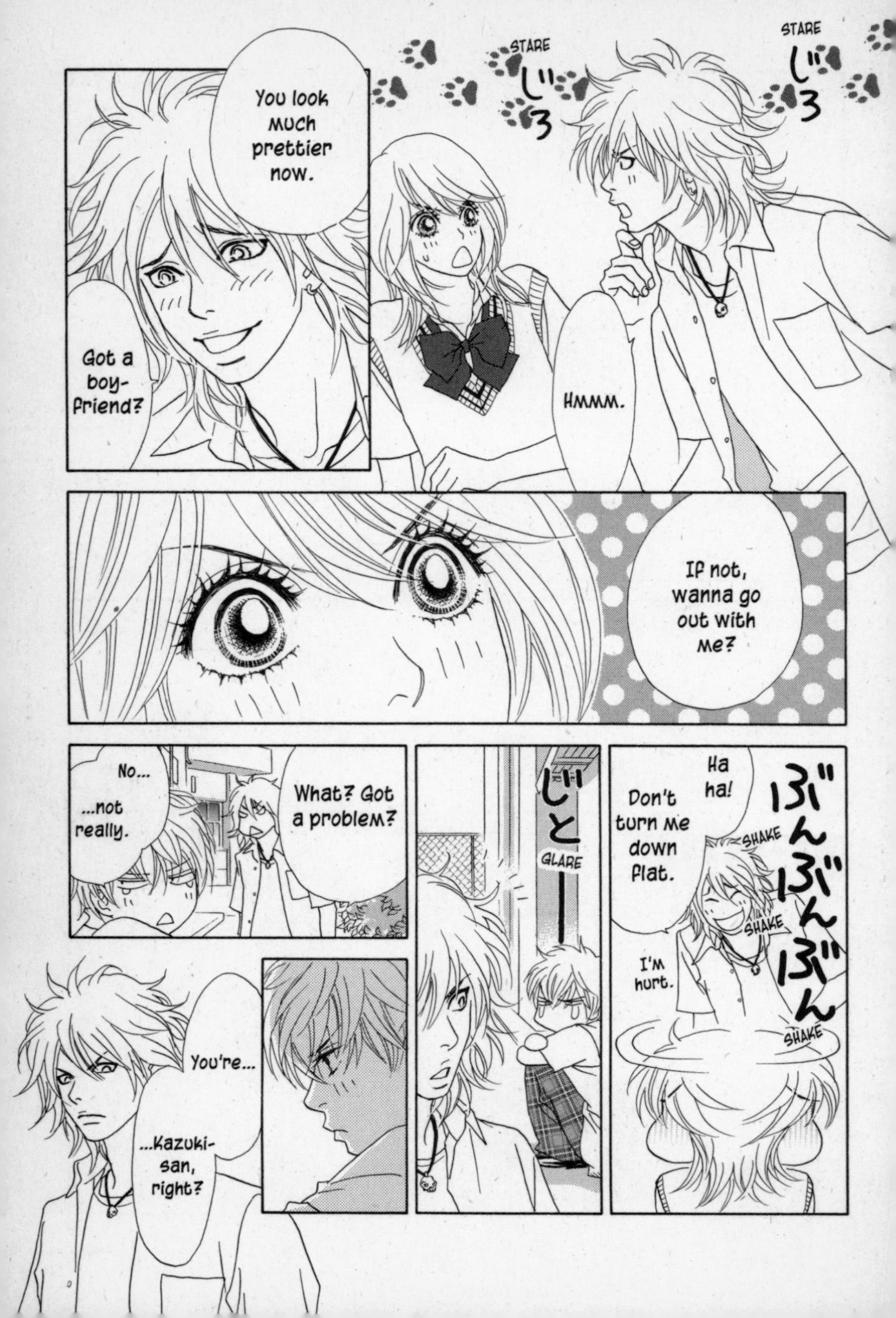

STARE
じろ
STARE
じろ
HMMM.
You look much prettier now.
Got a boyfriend?
If not, wanna go out with me?
ぶんぶんぶん
SHAKE
Ha ha!
Don't turn me down flat.
SHAKE
I'm hurt.
SHAKE
じとーー
GLARE
What? Got a problem?
No... ...not really.
You're...
...Kazuki-san, right?

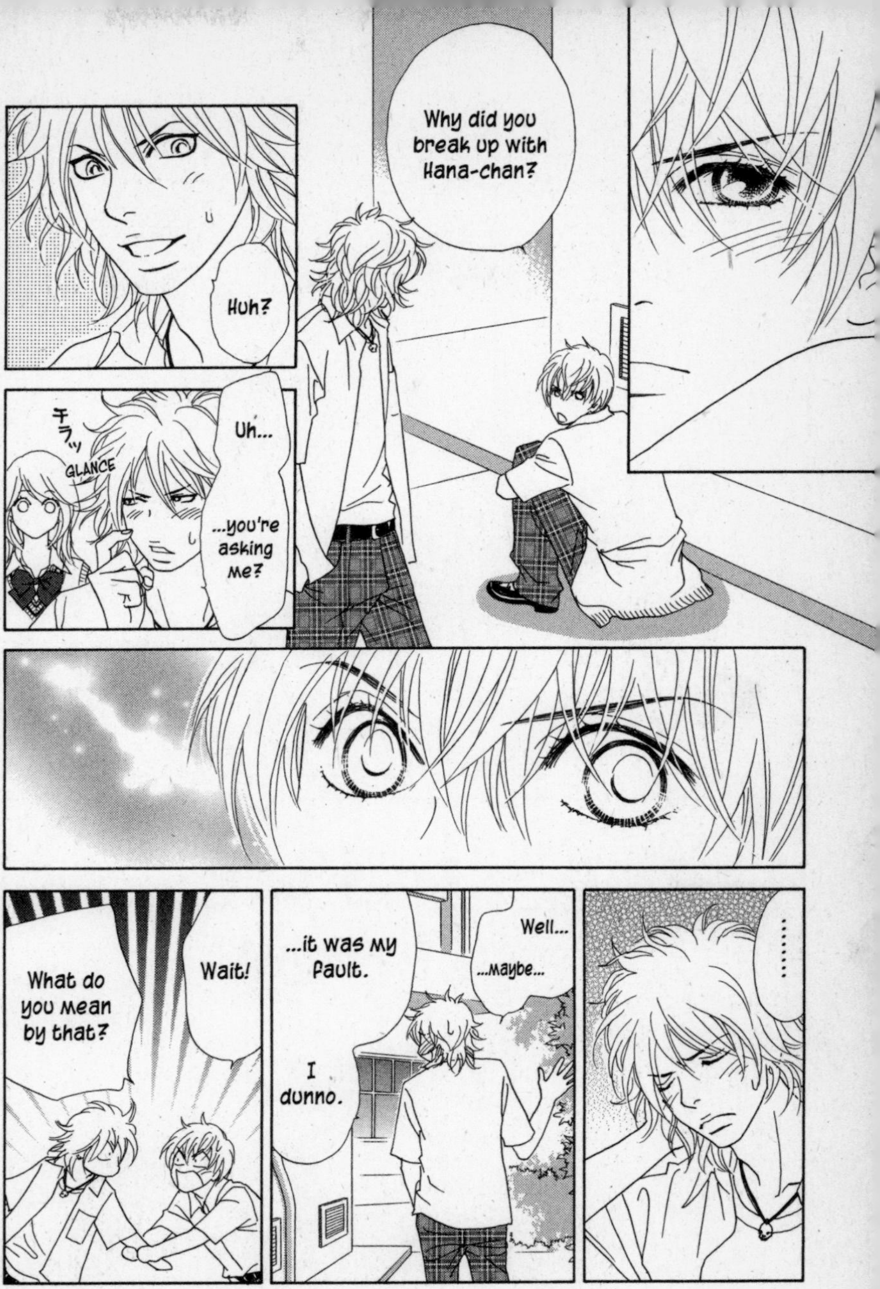

Why did you break up with Hana-chan?
Huh?
チラッ
GLANCE
Uh...
...you're asking me?
......
Well...
...maybe...
...it was my fault.
I dunno.
Wait!
What do you mean by that?

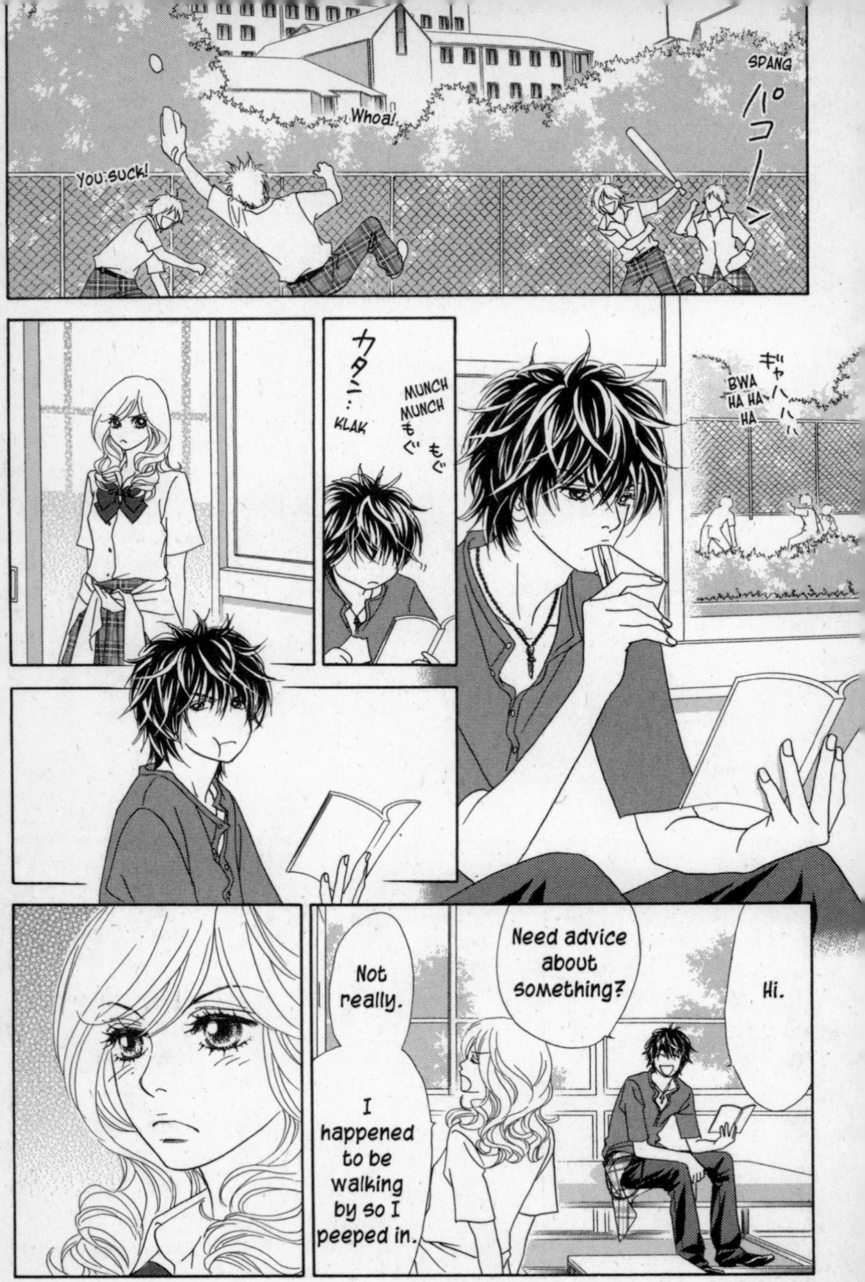
SPANG
パコーン
Whoa!
YOU SUCK!
ギャハハハ
BWA HA HA HA
カタン
KLAK
MUNCH MUNCH
もぐもぐ
Hi.
Need advice about something?
Not really.
I happened to be walking by so I peeped in.

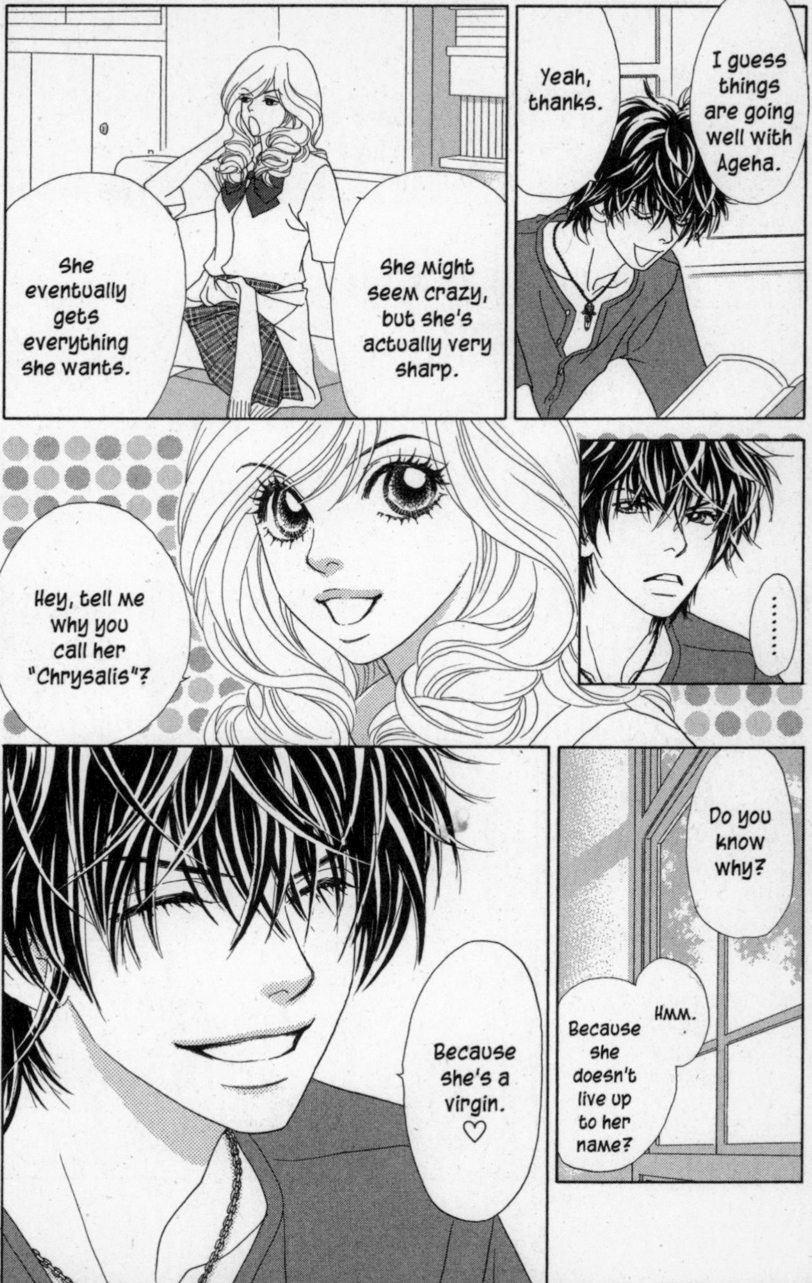
I guess things are going well with Ageha.
Yeah, thanks.
She might seem crazy, but she's actually very sharp.
She eventually gets everything she wants.
......
Hey, tell me why you call her "Chrysalis"?
Do you know why?
HMM.
Because she doesn't live up to her name?
Because she's a virgin. ♡

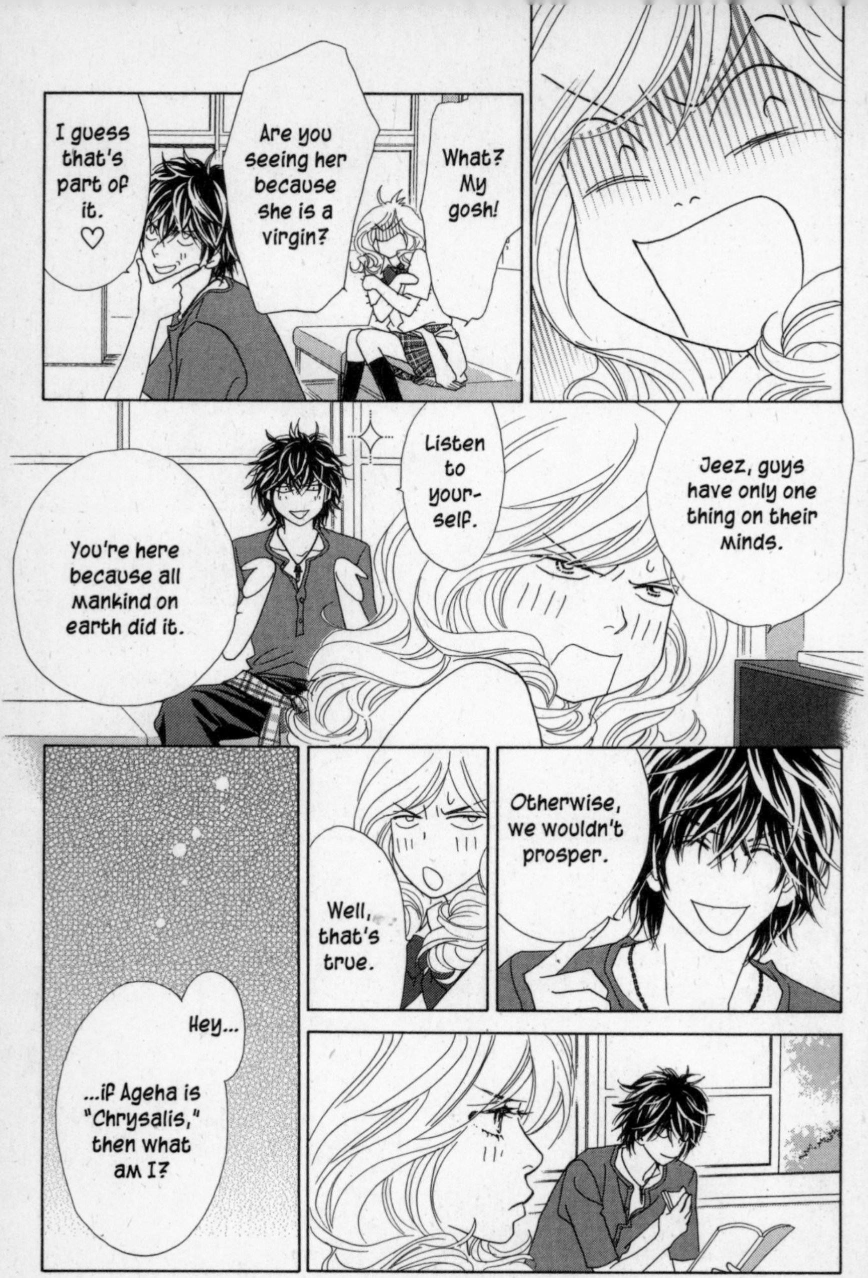
What? My gosh!
Are you seeing her because she is a virgin?
I guess that's part of it. ♡
Jeez, guys have only one thing on their minds.
Listen to your-self.
You're here because all mankind on earth did it.
Otherwise, we wouldn't prosper.
Well, that's true.
Hey...
...if Ageha is "Chrysalis," then what am I?

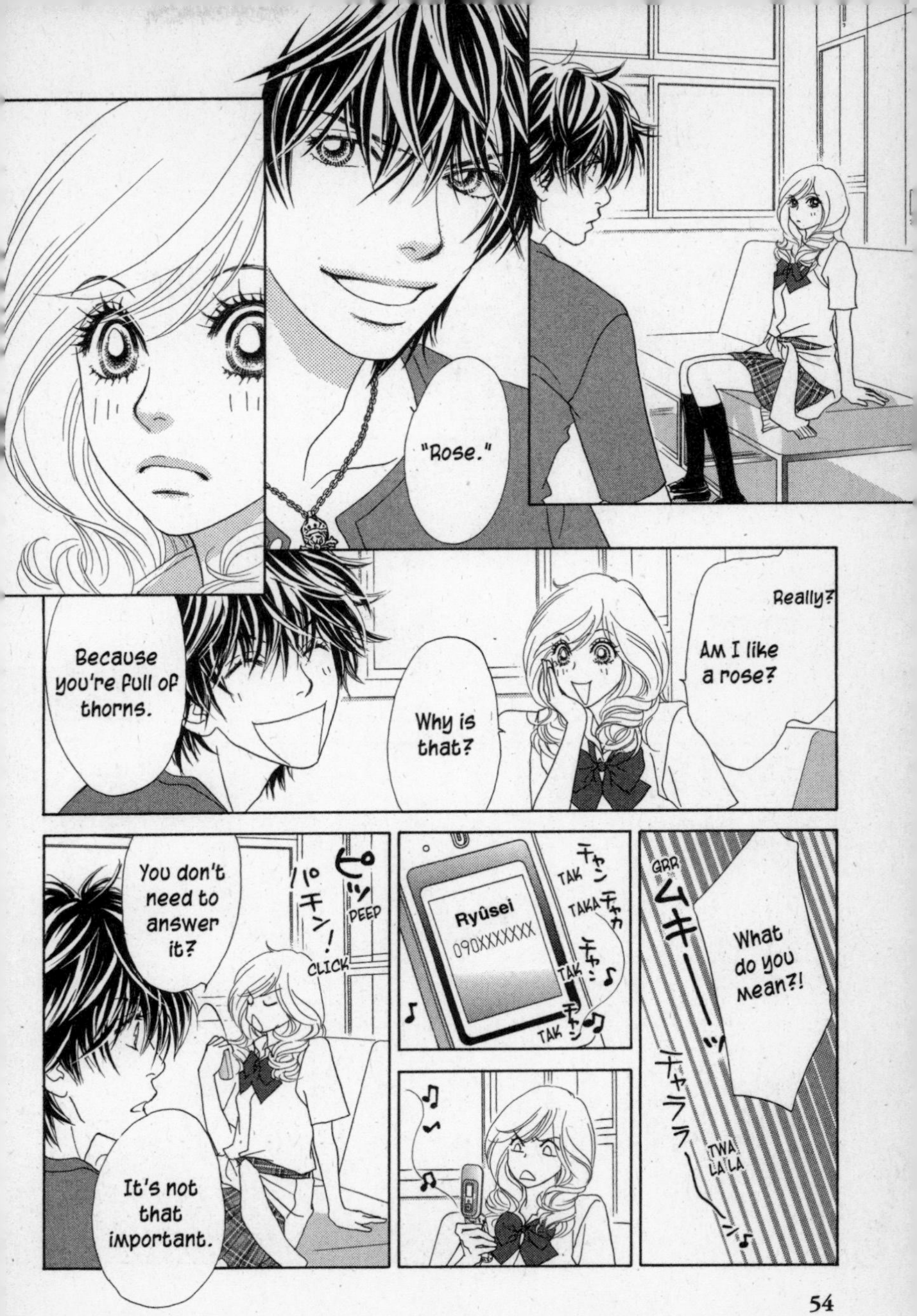
"Rose."
Really?
Am I like a rose?
Why is that?
Because you're full of thorns.
GRR
ムキーーッ
What do you mean?!
チャラララ
TWA LA LA
Ryûsei
090XXXXXXX
チャンチャカチャンチャン
TAK TAKA TAK TAK
ピッ
PEEP
パチン!
CLICK
You don't need to answer it?
It's not that important.

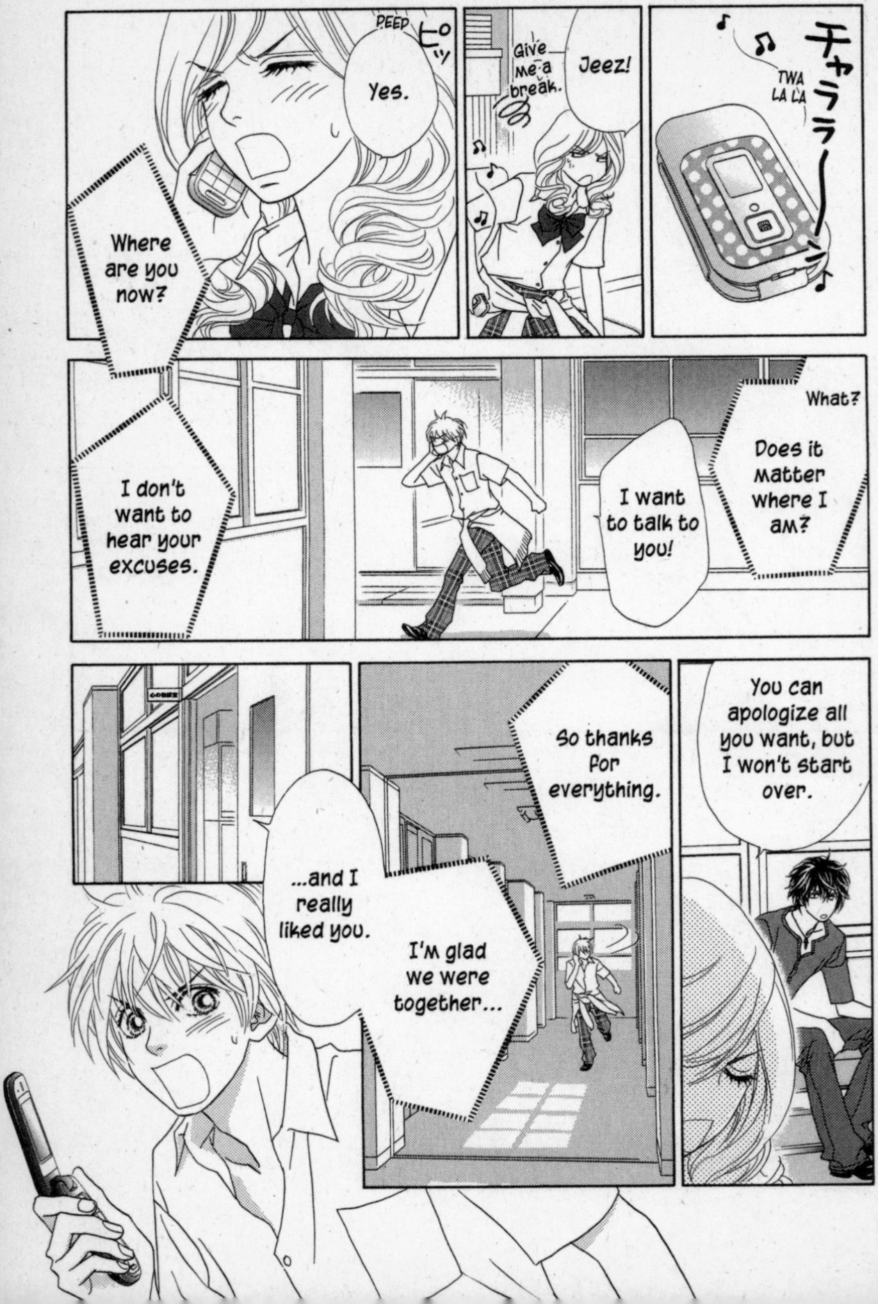
チャララーン
TWA LA LA
Jeez!
Give me a break.
ピッ
PEEP
Yes.
Where are you now?
What?
Does it matter where I am?
I want to talk to you!
I don't want to hear your excuses.
You can apologize all you want, but I won't start over.
So thanks for everything.
I'm glad we were together...
...and I really liked you.

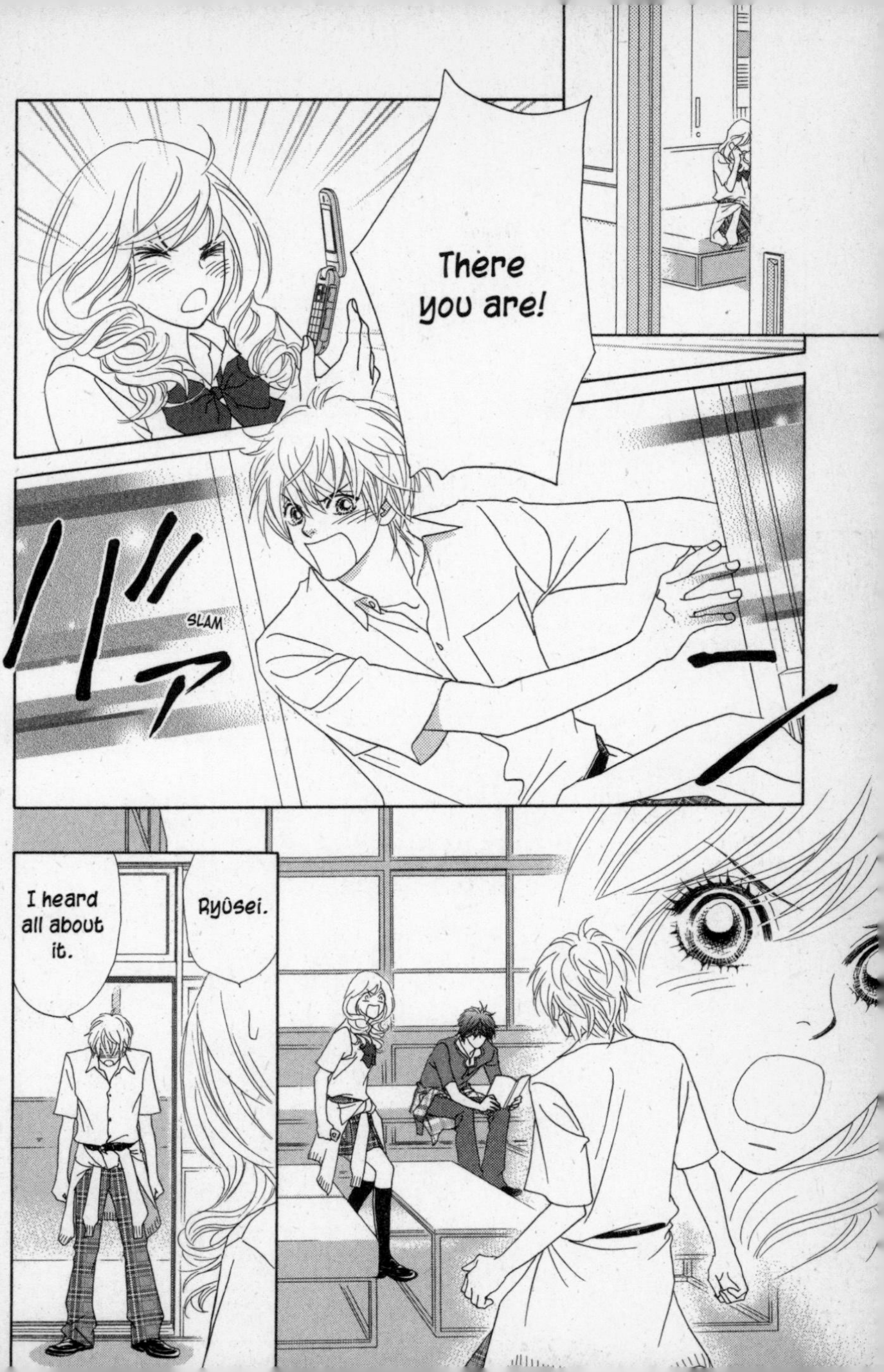
There you are!
SLAM
Ryûsei.
I heard all about it.

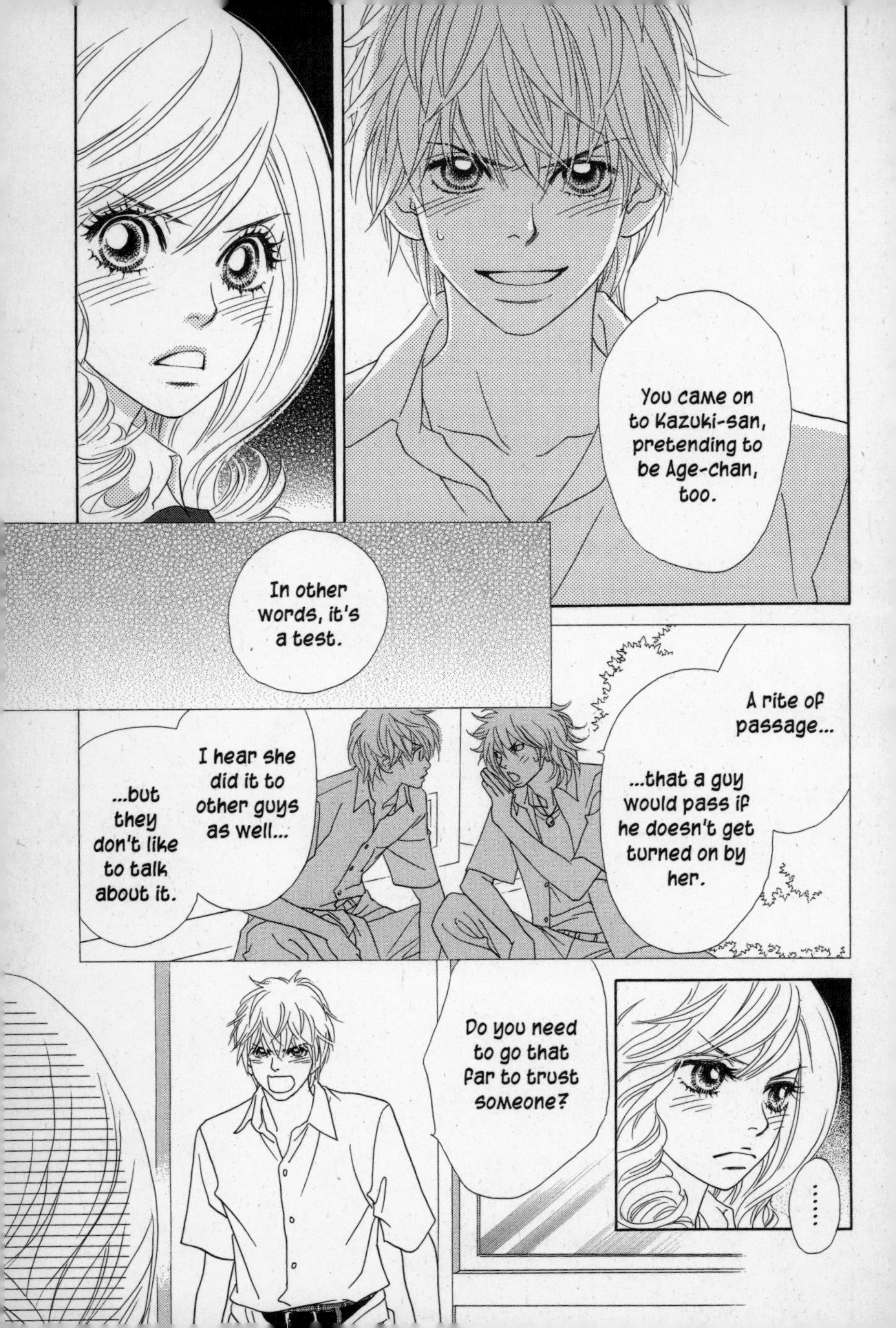
You came on to Kazuki-san, pretending to be Age-chan, too.
In other words, it's a test.
A rite of passage...
...that a guy would pass if he doesn't get turned on by her.
I hear she did it to other guys as well...
...but they don't like to talk about it.
Do you need to go that far to trust someone?
......

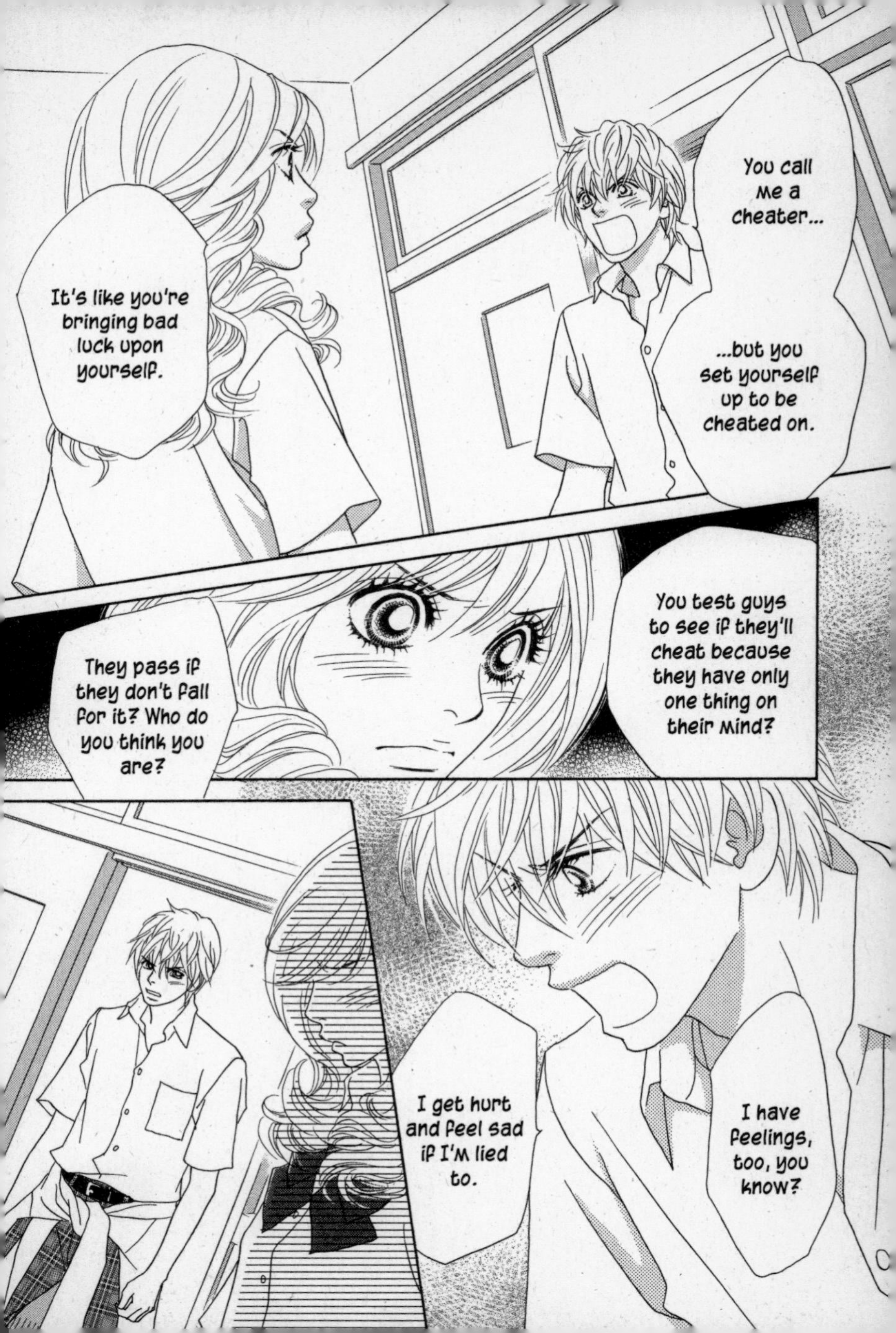
You call me a cheater... ...but you set yourself up to be cheated on.
It's like you're bringing bad luck upon yourself.
You test guys to see if they'll cheat because they have only one thing on their mind?
They pass if they don't fall for it? Who do you think you are?
I have feelings, too, you know?
I get hurt and feel sad if I'm lied to.

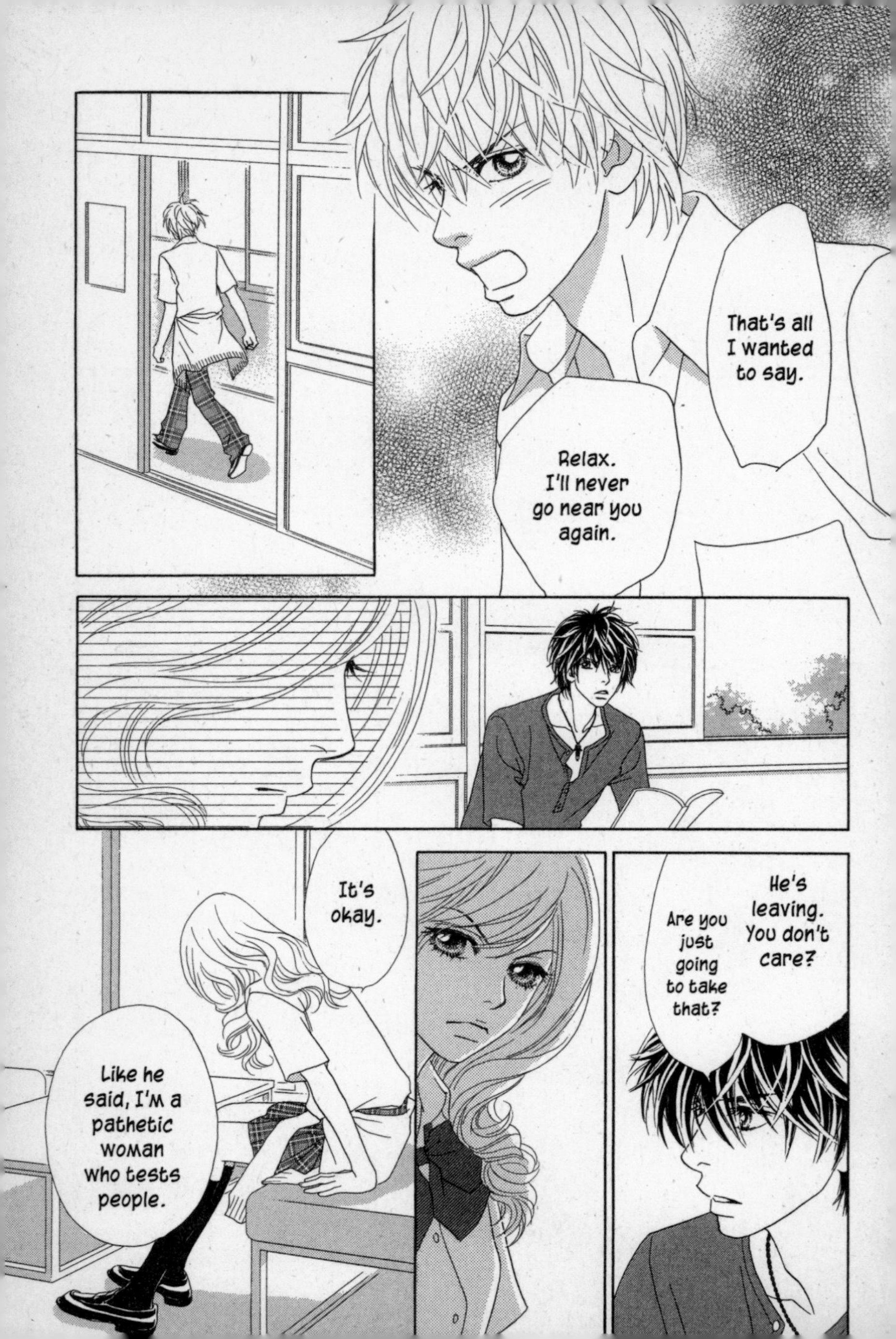
That's all I wanted to say.
Relax. I'll never go near you again.
He's leaving. You don't care?
Are you just going to take that?
It's okay.
Like he said, I'm a pathetic woman who tests people.

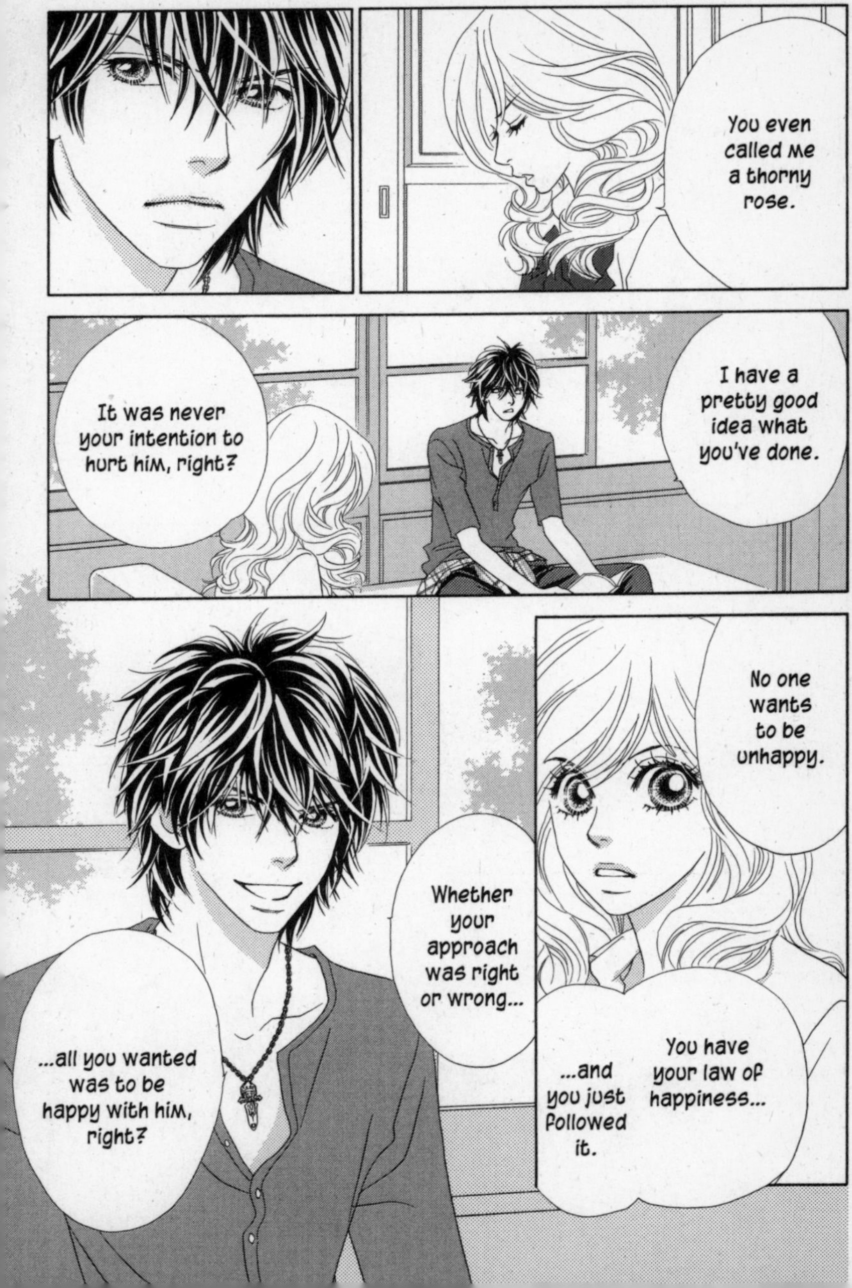
You even called me a thorny rose.
I have a pretty good idea what you've done.
It was never your intention to hurt him, right?
No one wants to be unhappy.
You have your law of happiness...
...and you just followed it.
Whether your approach was right or wrong...
...all you wanted was to be happy with him, right?

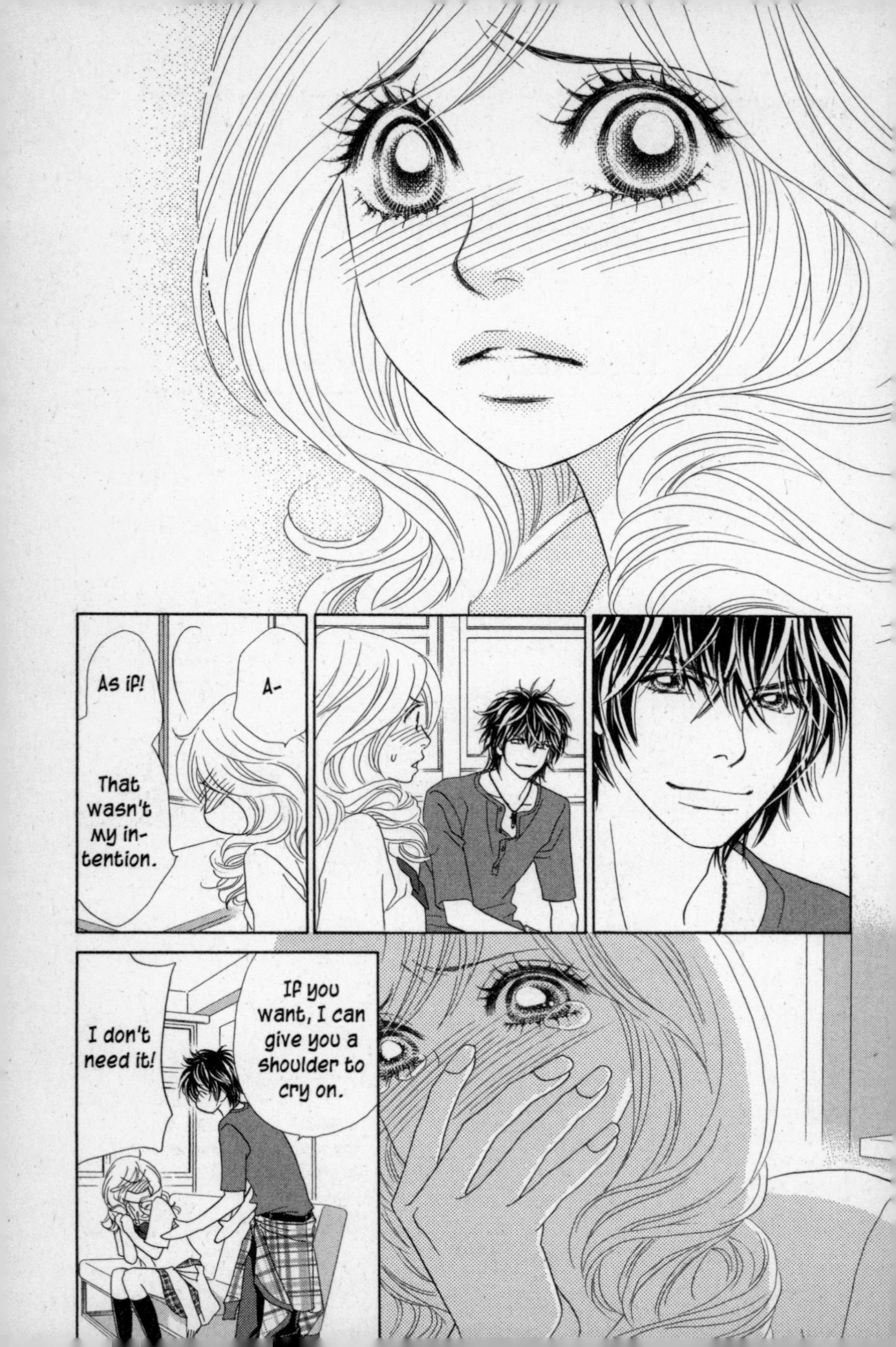
A-
As if!
That wasn't my in-tention.
If you want, I can give you a shoulder to cry on.
I don't need it!

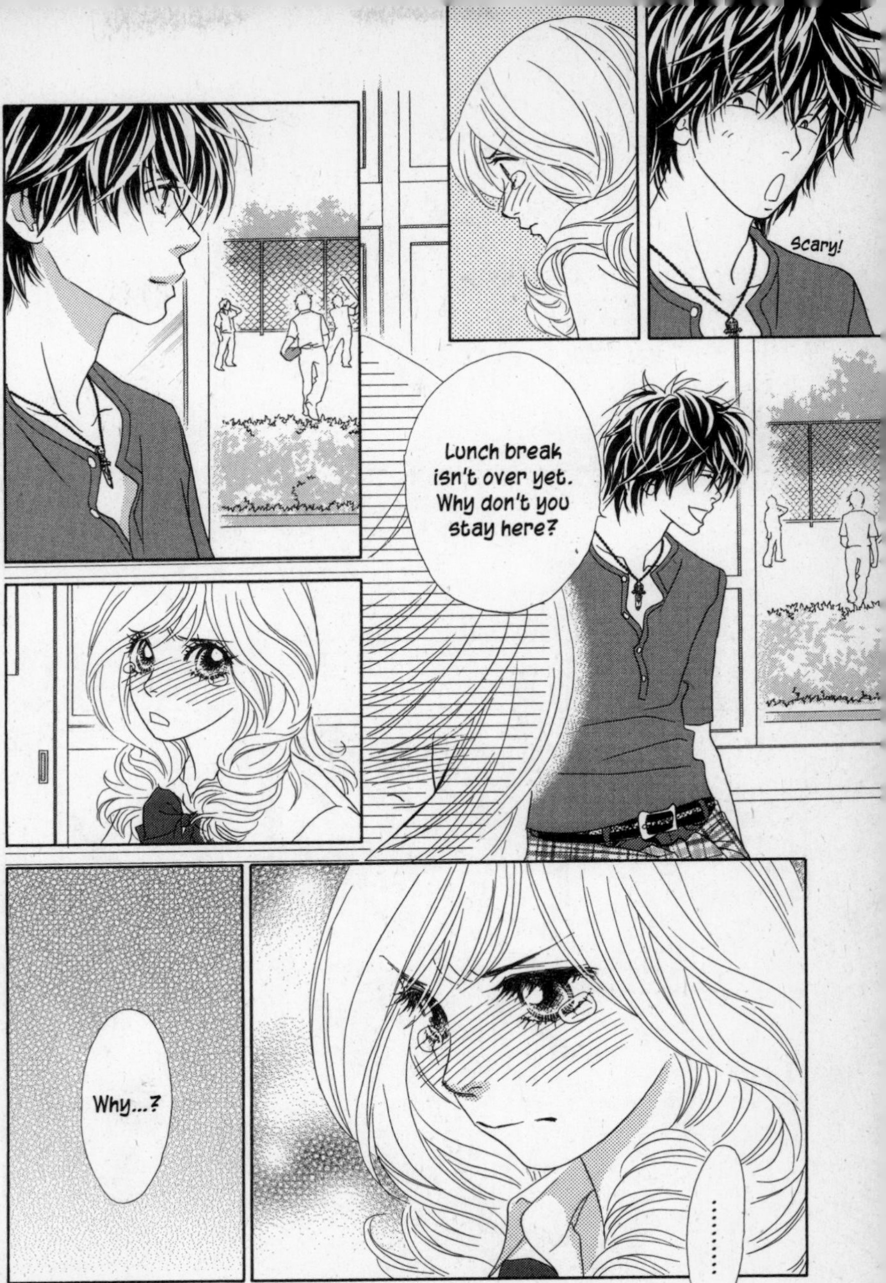
Scary!
Lunch break isn't over yet. Why don't you stay here?
....
Why...?

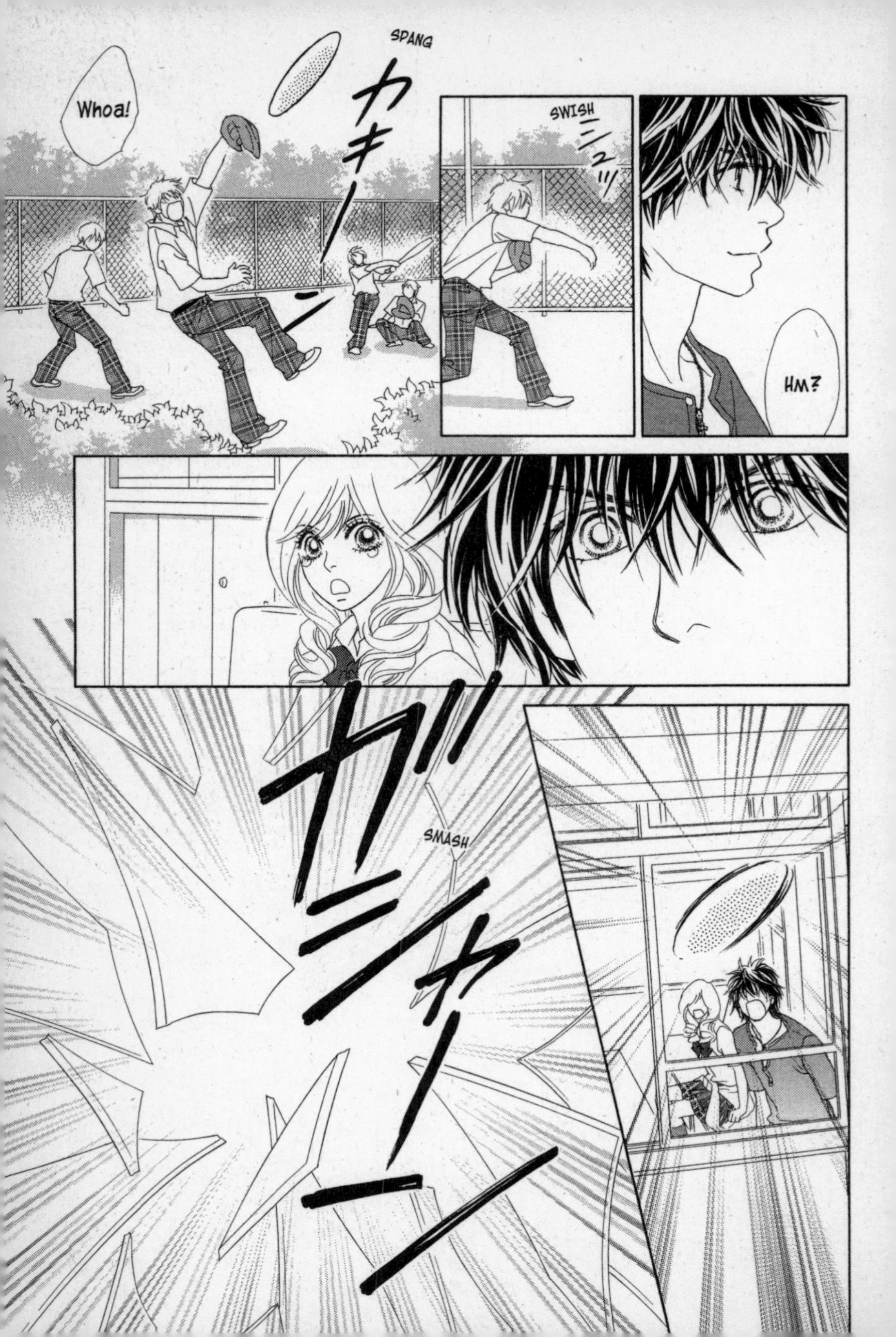
Hm?
SWISH
SPANG
Whoa!
SMASH

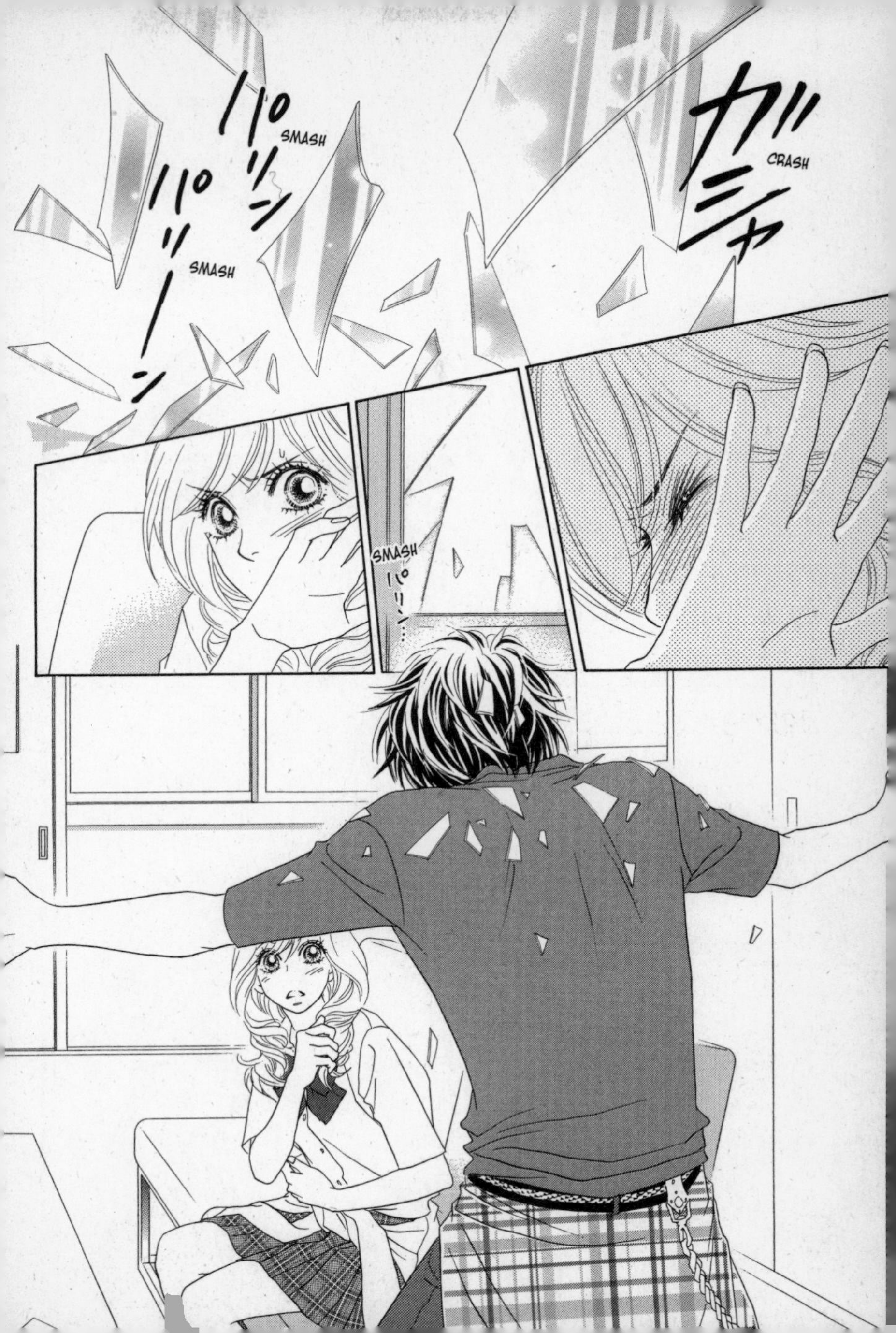
ガシャ
CRASH
パリン
SMASH
パリーン
SMASH
SMASH
パリ…

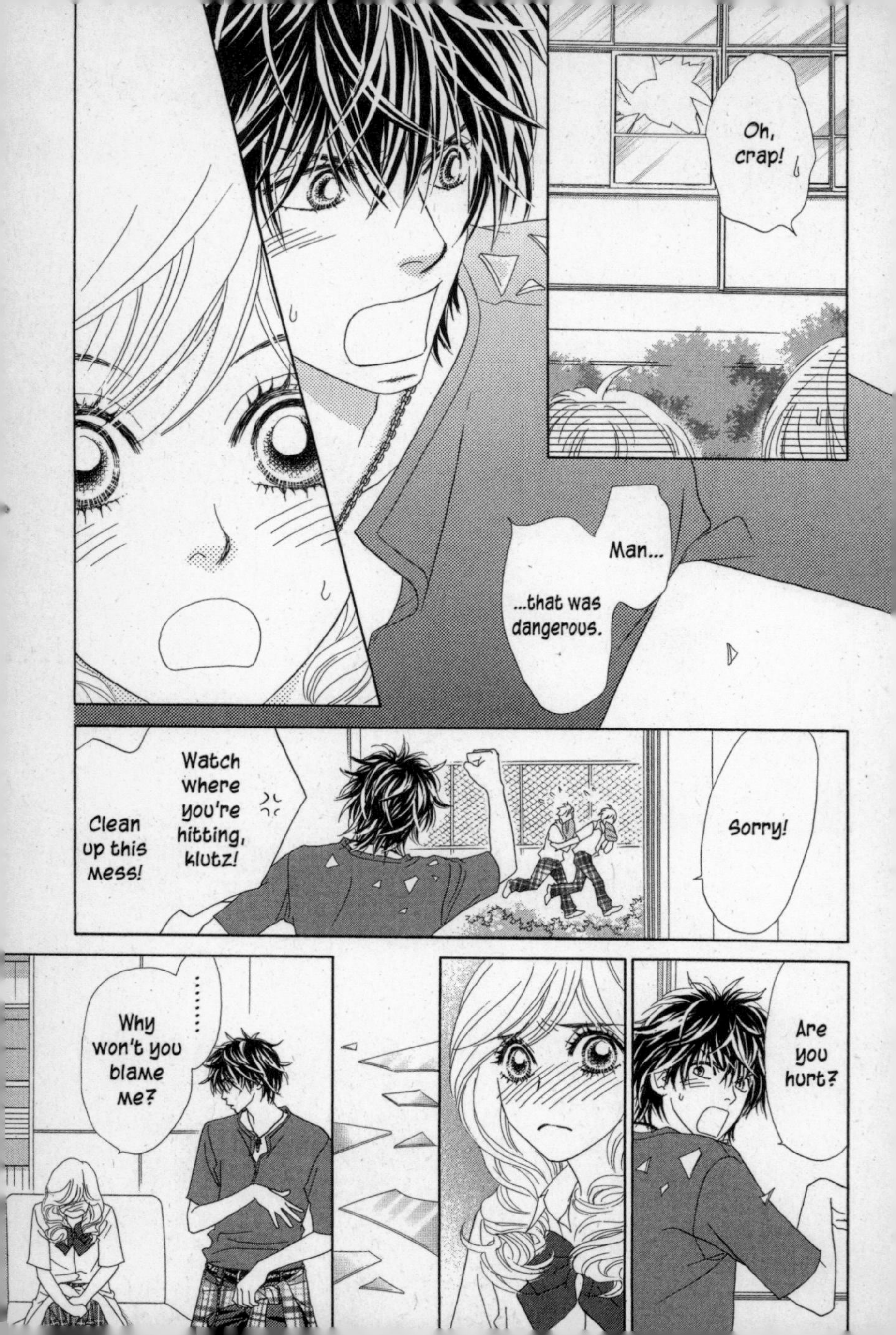
Oh, crap!
Man...
...that was dangerous.
Sorry!
Watch where you're hitting, klutz!
Clean up this mess!
Are you hurt?
......
Why won't you blame me?

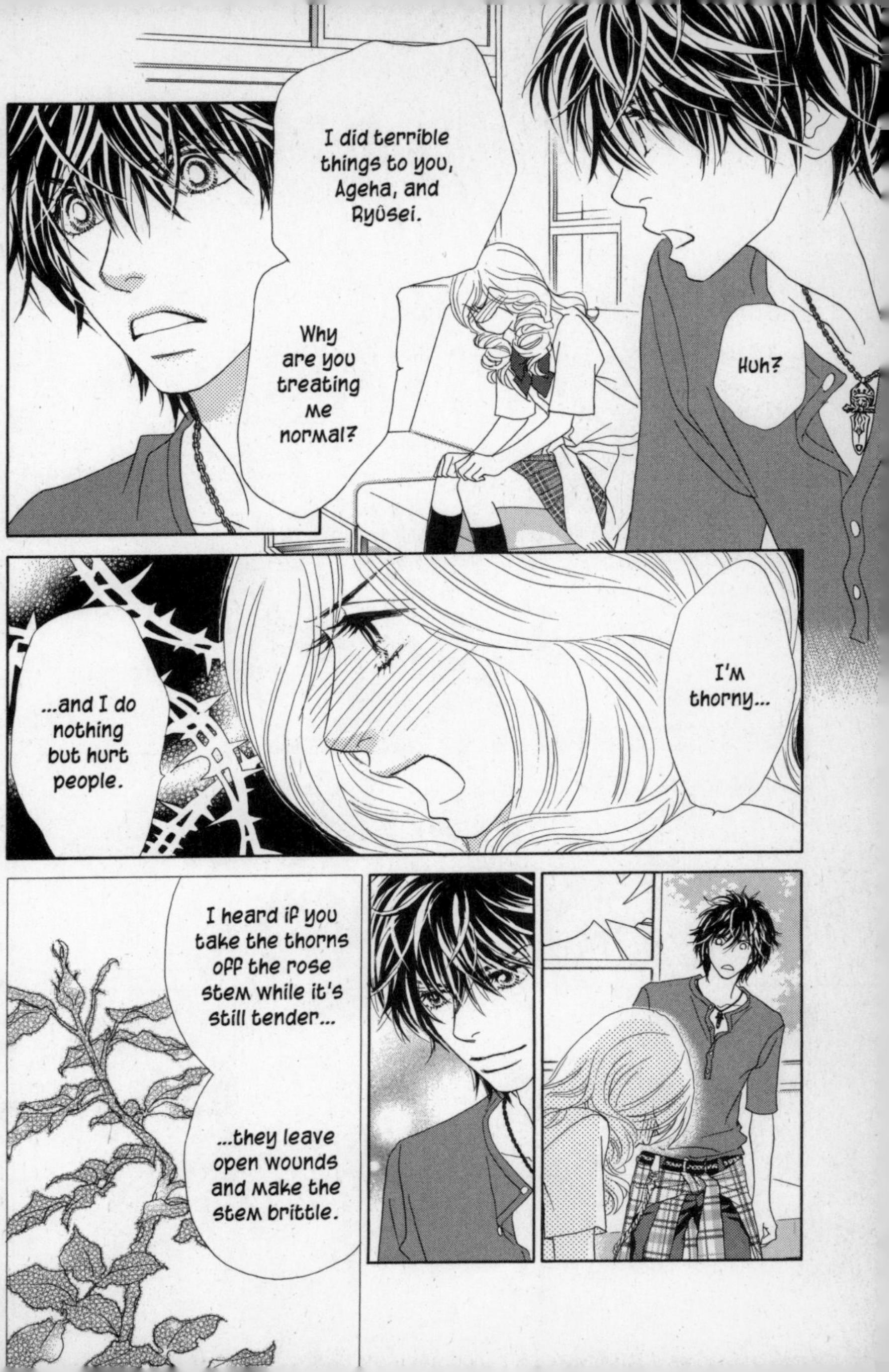
Huh?
I did terrible things to you, Ageha, and Ryûsei.
Why are you treating me normal?
I'm thorny...
...and I do nothing but hurt people.
I heard if you take the thorns off the rose stem while it's still tender...
...they leave open wounds and make the stem brittle.

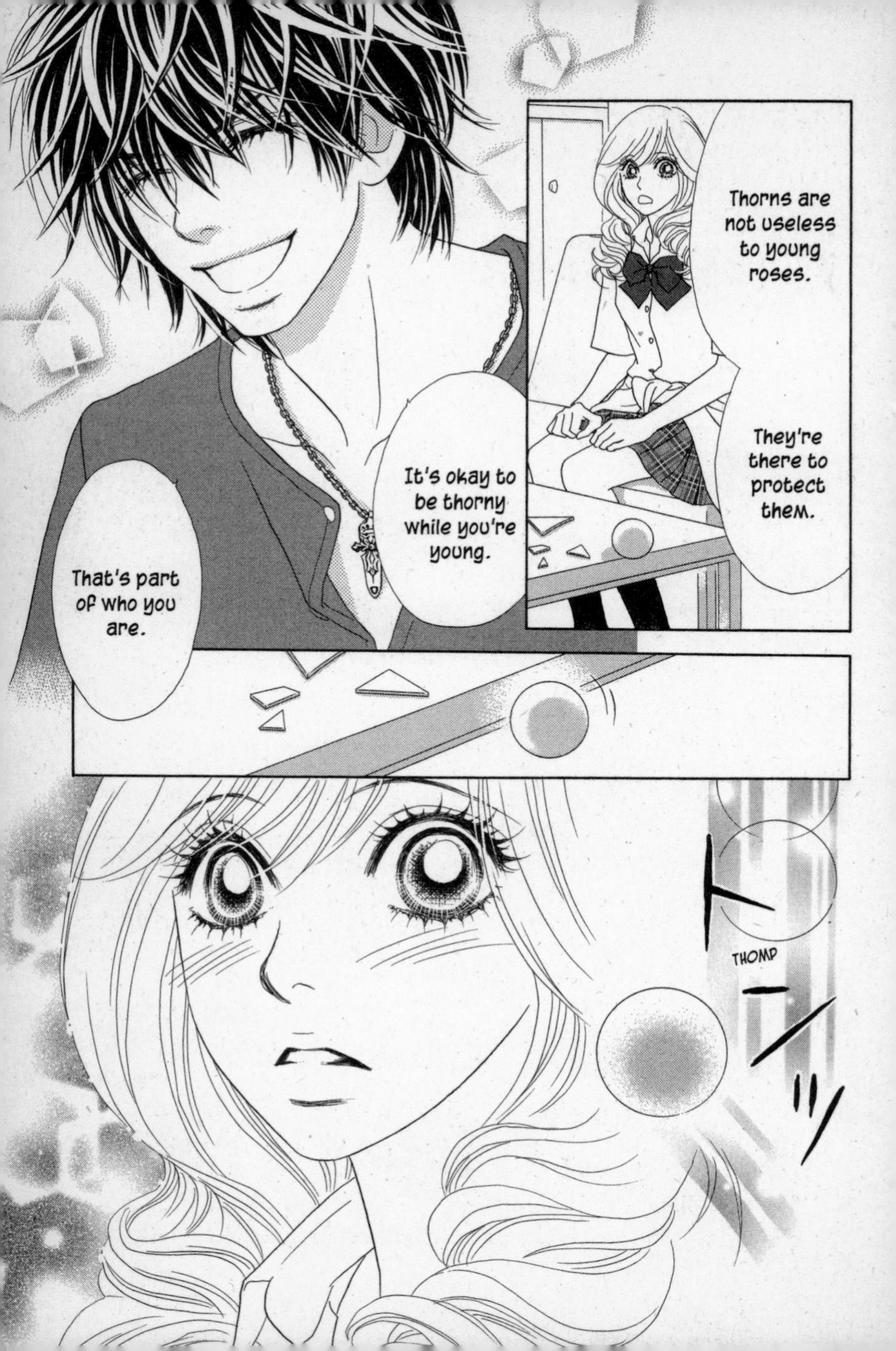
Thorns are not useless to young roses.
They're there to protect them.
It's okay to be thorny while you're young.
That's part of who you are.
THOMP

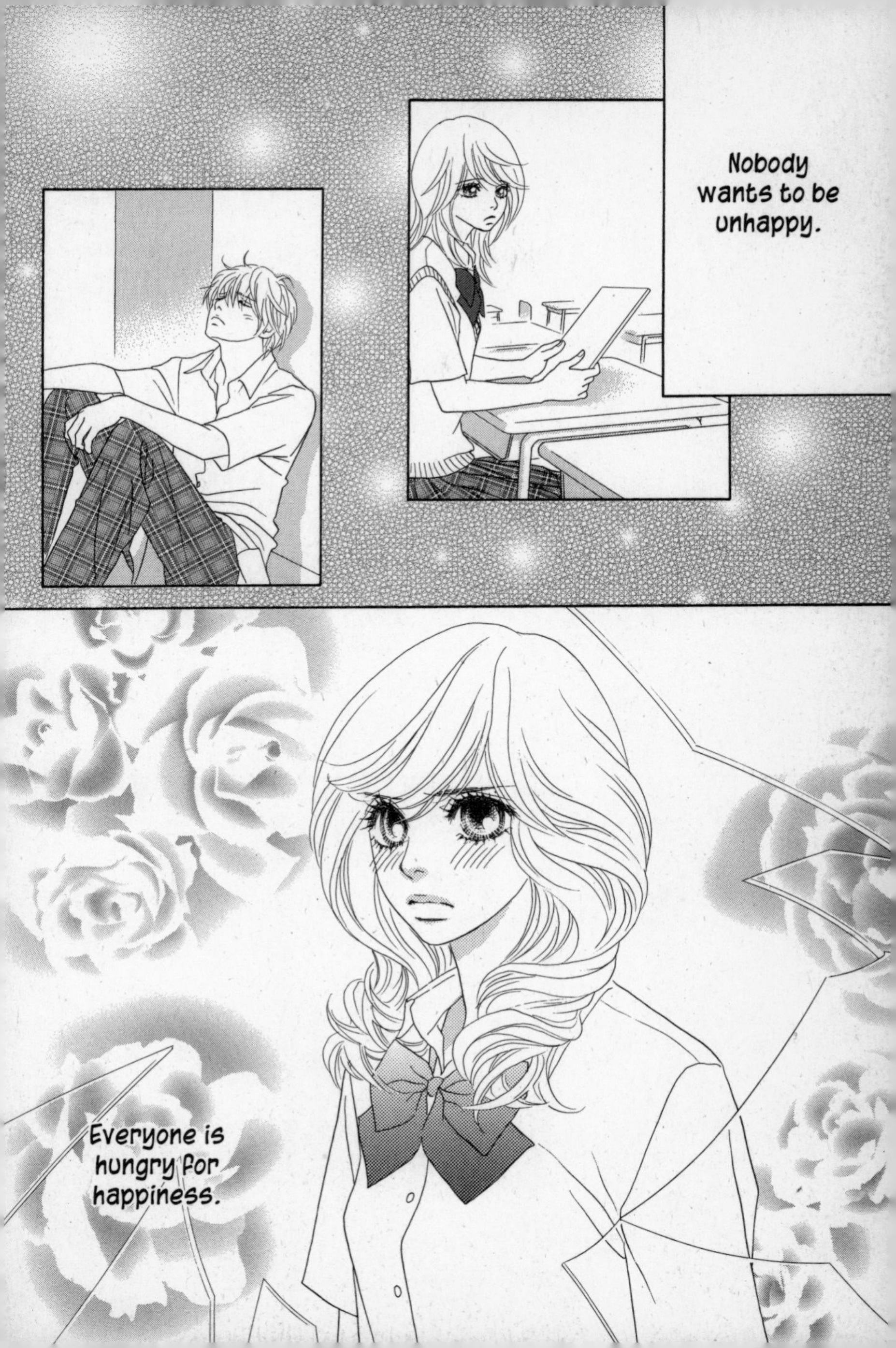
Nobody wants to be unhappy.
Everyone is hungry for happiness.

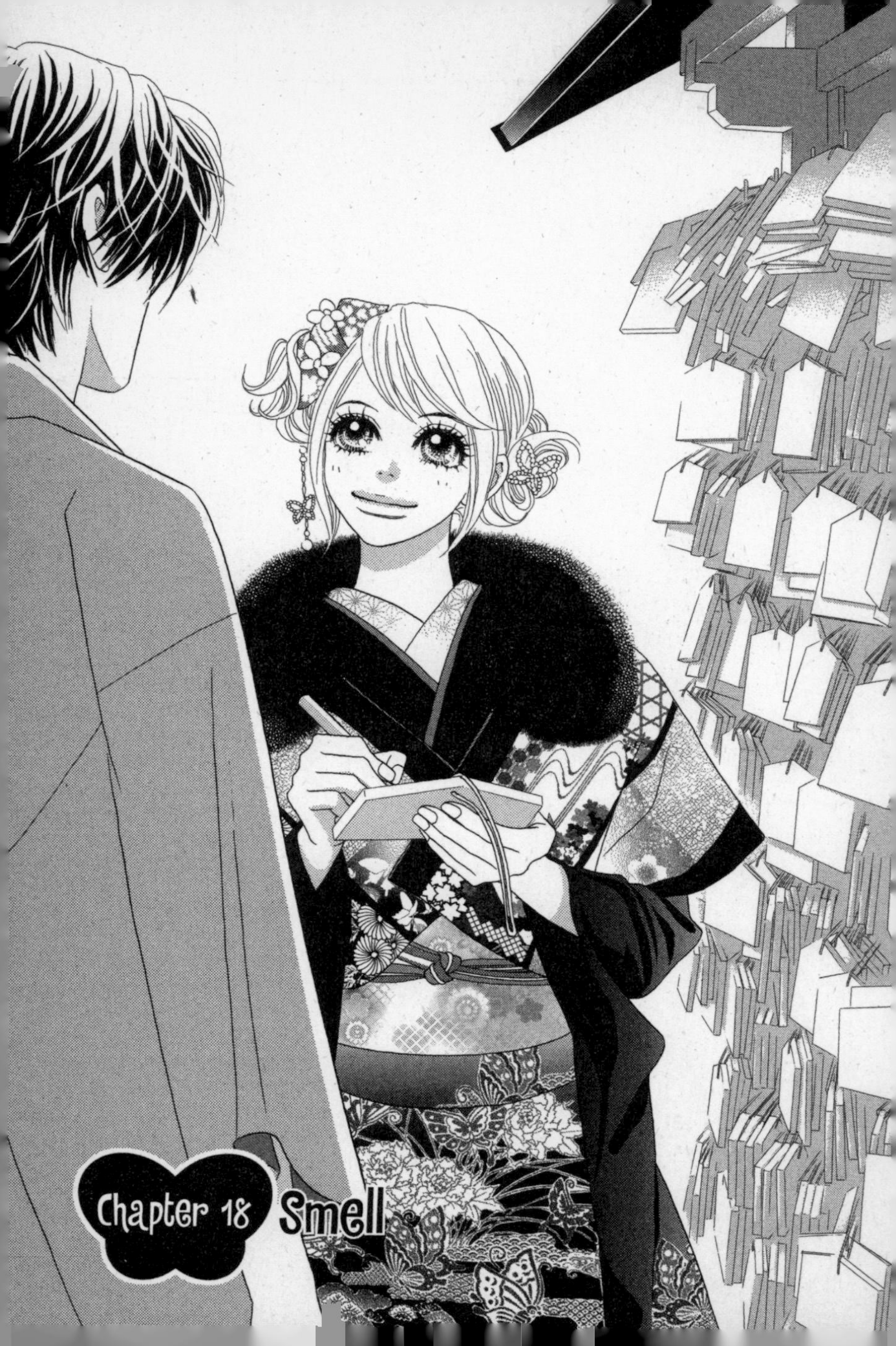
Chapter 18 Smell

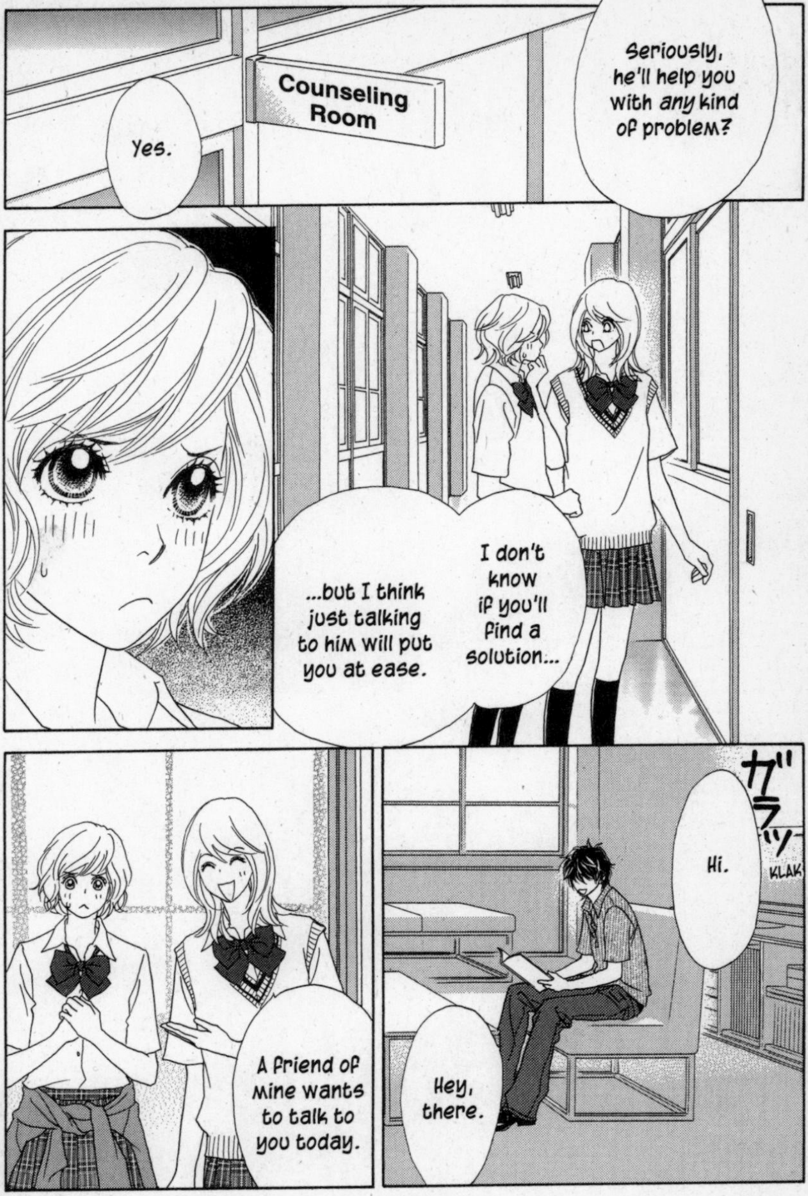
Seriously, he'll help you with *any* kind of problem?
Counseling Room
Yes.
I don't know if you'll find a solution...
...but I think just talking to him will put you at ease.
ガラッ
KLAK
Hi.
Hey, there.
A friend of mine wants to talk to you today.

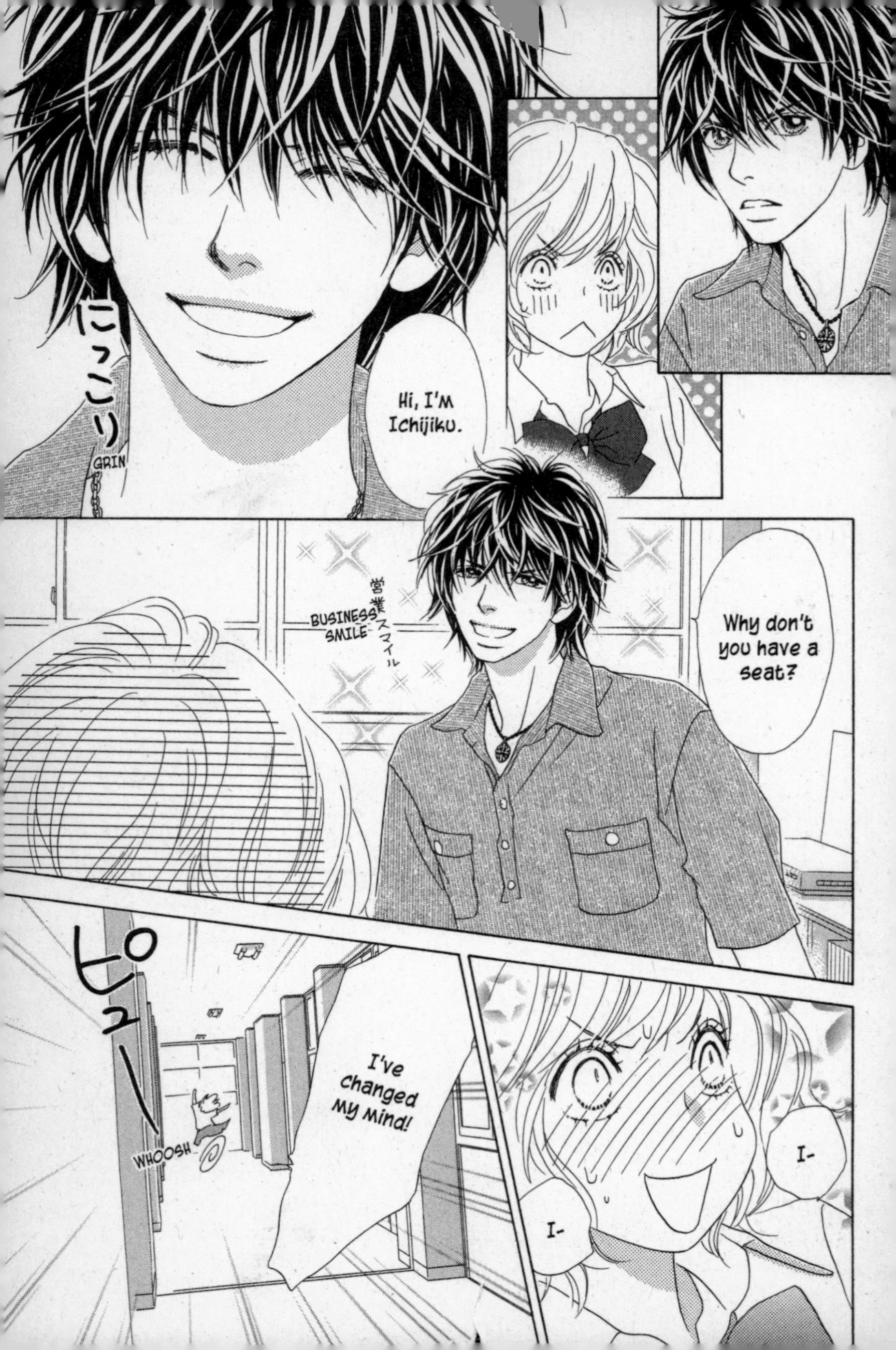

Hi, I'm Ichijiku.
にっこり
GRIN
Why don't you have a seat?
営業スマイル
BUSINESS SMILE
I-
I-
I've changed my mind!
ピュー
WHOOSH

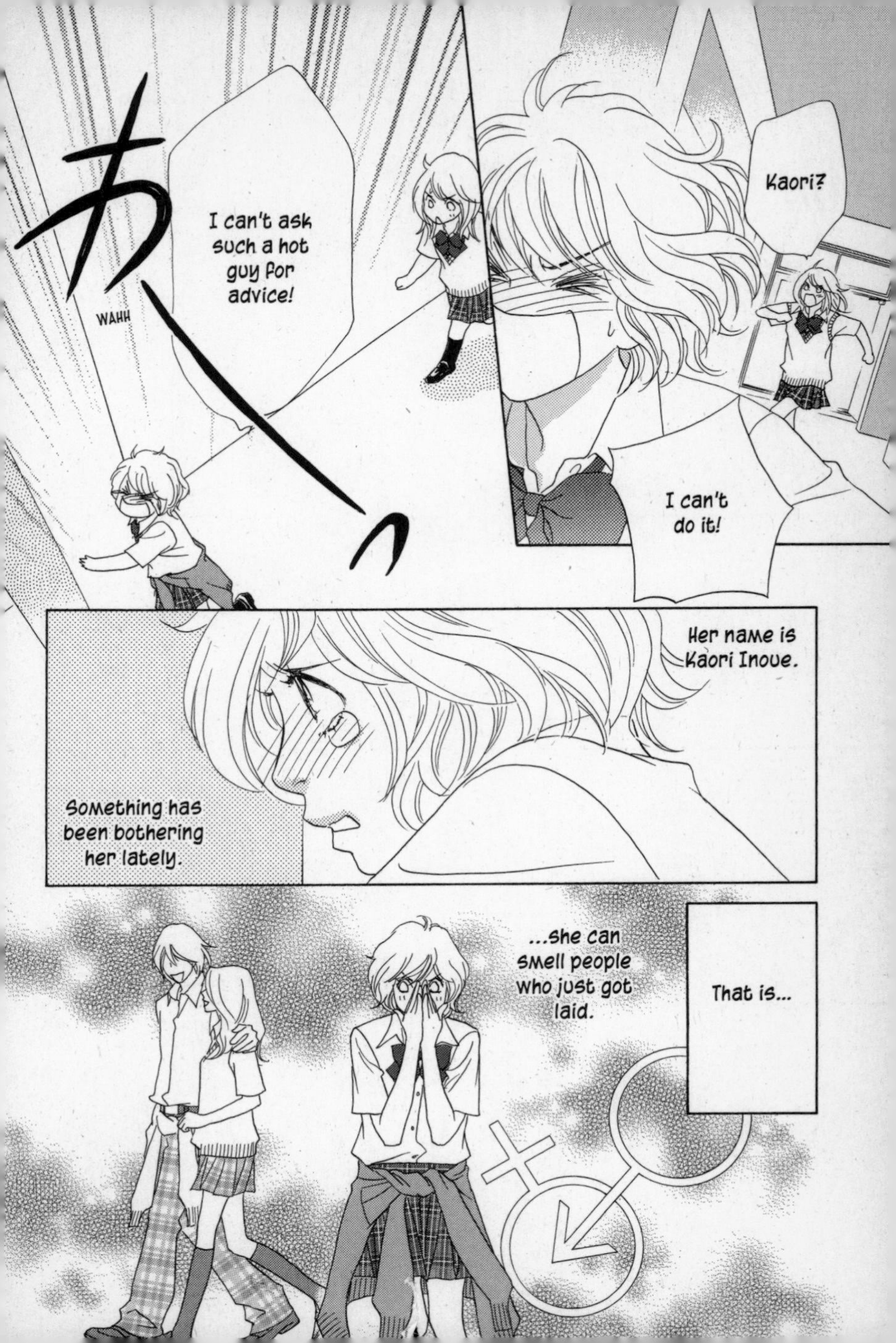
Kaori?
I can't do it!
I can't ask such a hot guy for advice!
WAHH
Her name is Kaori Inoue.
Something has been bothering her lately.
That is...
...she can smell people who just got laid.

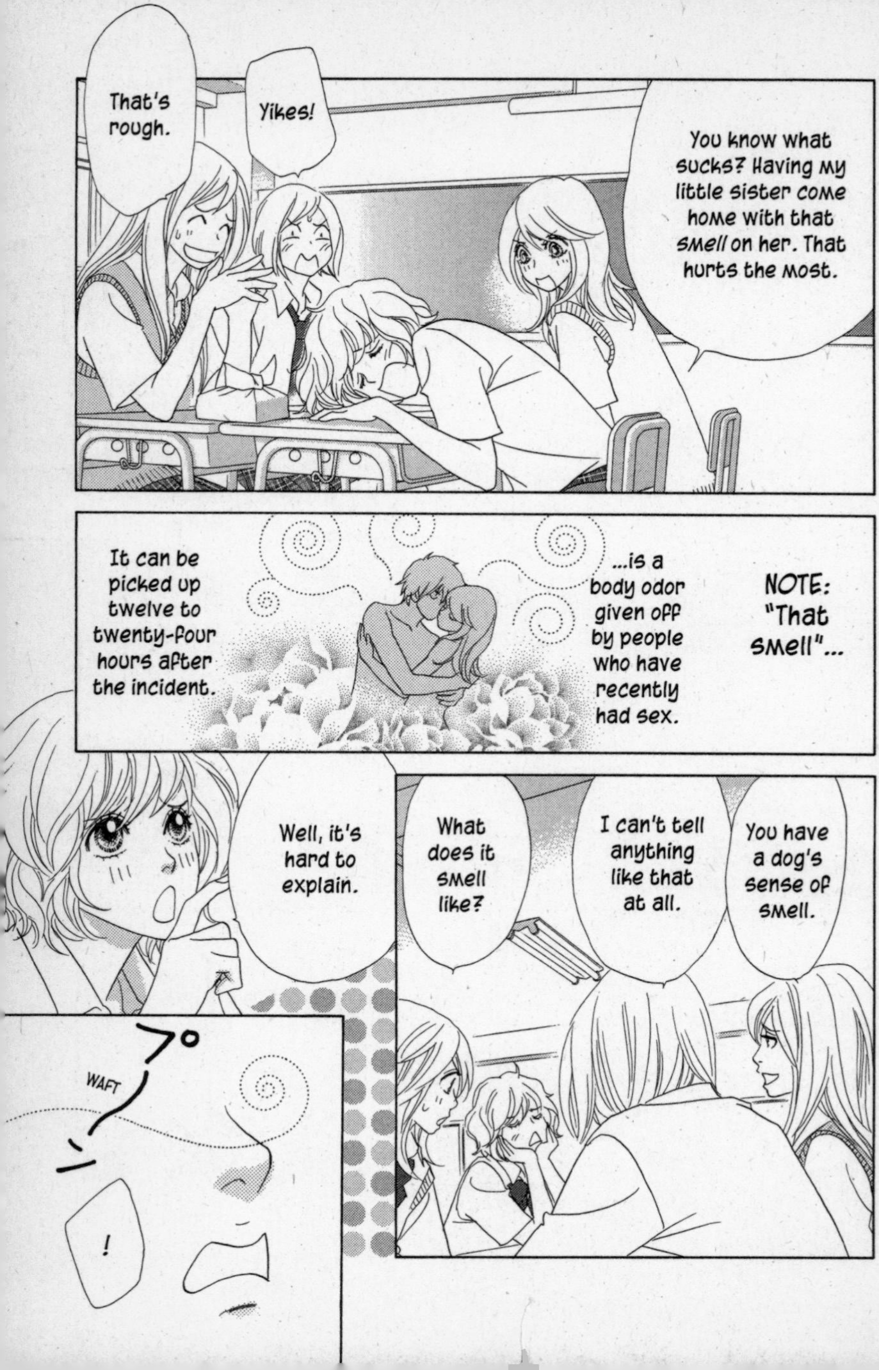
You know what sucks? Having my little sister come home with that *smell* on her. That hurts the most.
Yikes!
That's rough.
NOTE: "That smell"...
...is a body odor given off by people who have recently had sex.
It can be picked up twelve to twenty-four hours after the incident.
You have a dog's sense of smell.
I can't tell anything like that at all.
What does it smell like?
Well, it's hard to explain.
WAFT
!

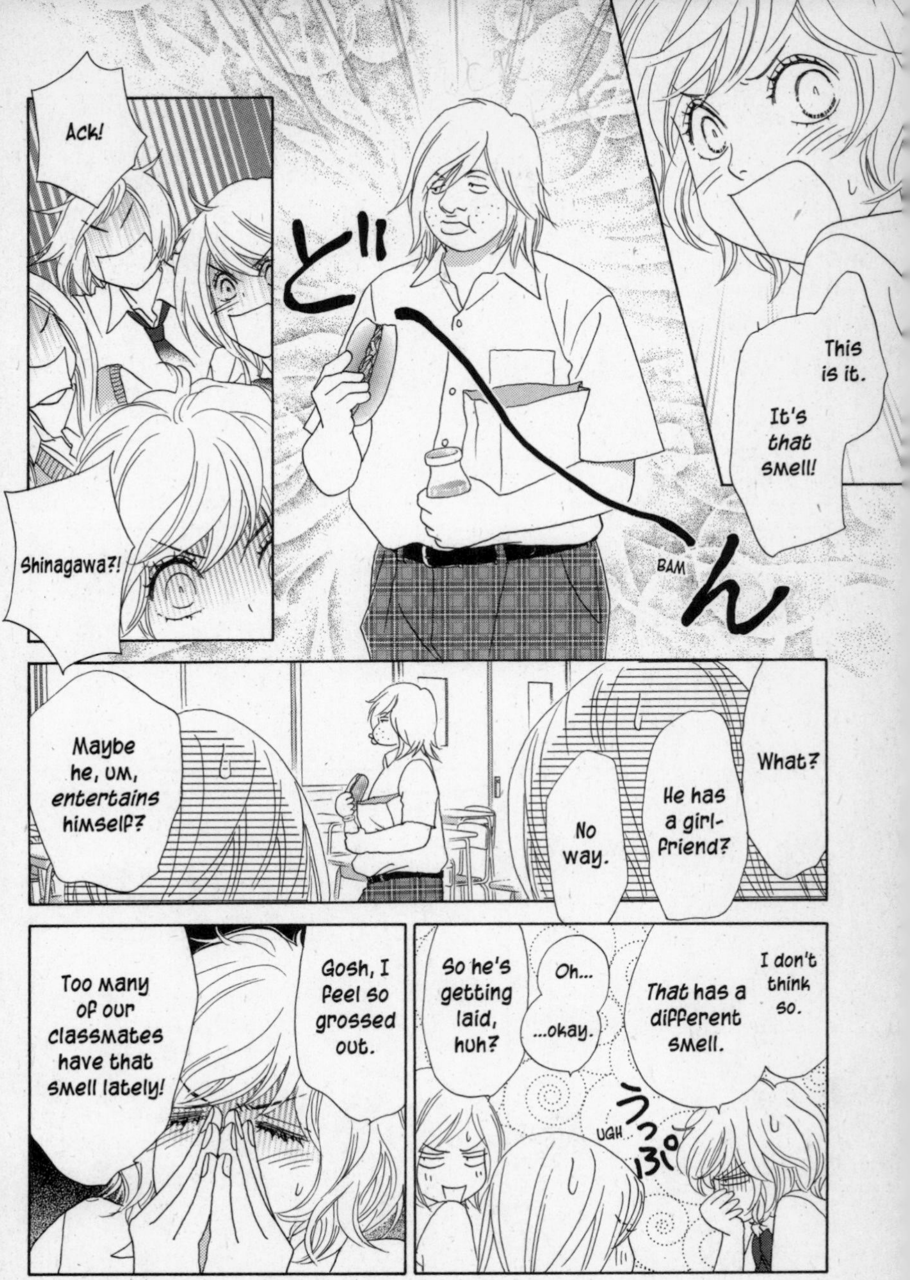
This is it.
It's *that* smell!
BAM
Ack!
Shinagawa?!
What?
He has a girl-friend?
No way.
Maybe he, um, *entertains* himself?
I don't think so.
That has a different smell.
Oh...
...okay.
So he's getting laid, huh?
UGH
Gosh, I feel so grossed out.
Too many of our classmates have that smell lately!

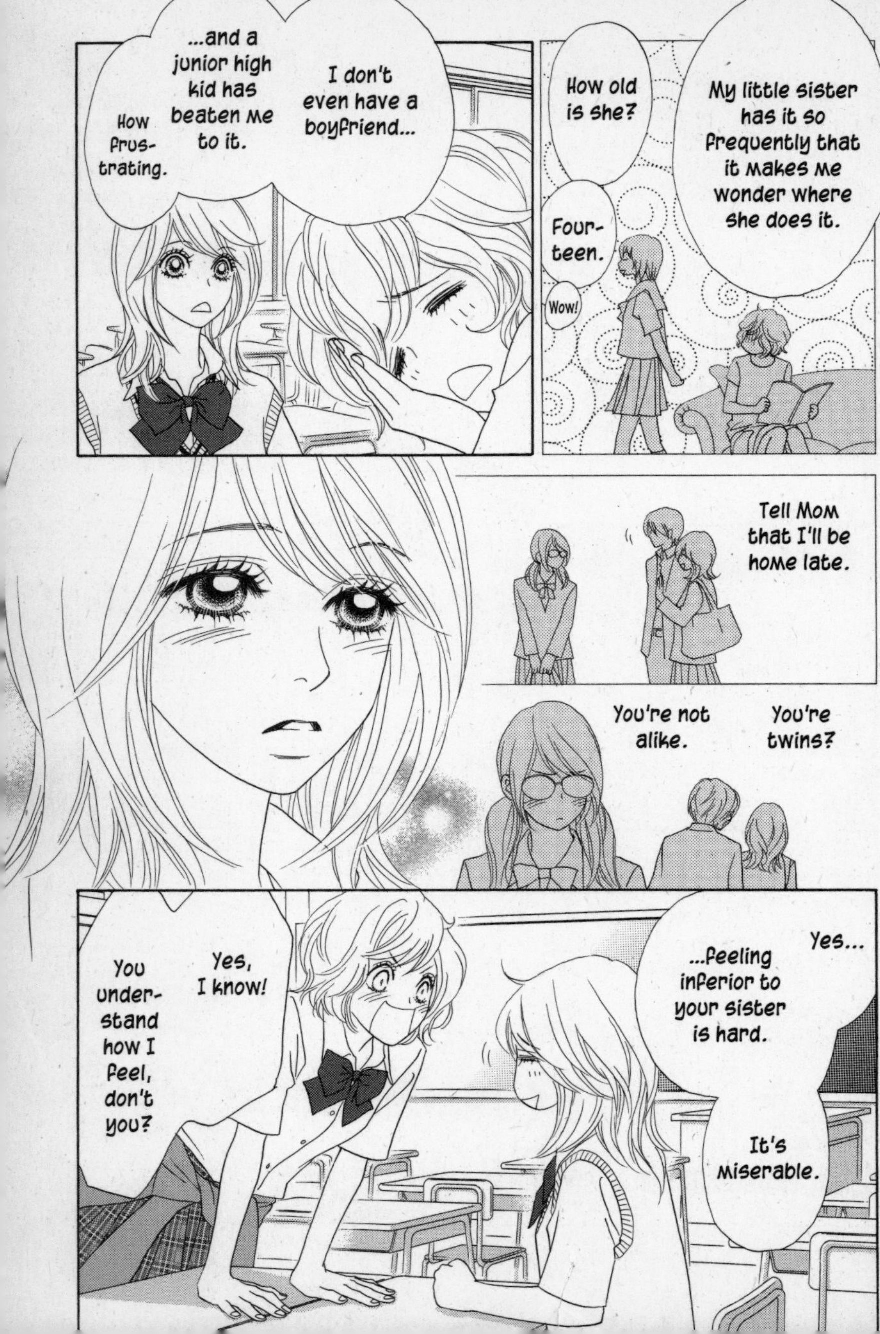
My little sister has it so frequently that it makes me wonder where she does it.
How old is she?
Four-teen.
Wow!
I don't even have a boyfriend...
...and a junior high kid has beaten me to it.
How frus-trating.
Tell Mom that I'll be home late.
You're twins?
You're not alike.
Yes...
...feeling inferior to your sister is hard.
It's miserable.
Yes, I know!
You under-stand how I feel, don't you?

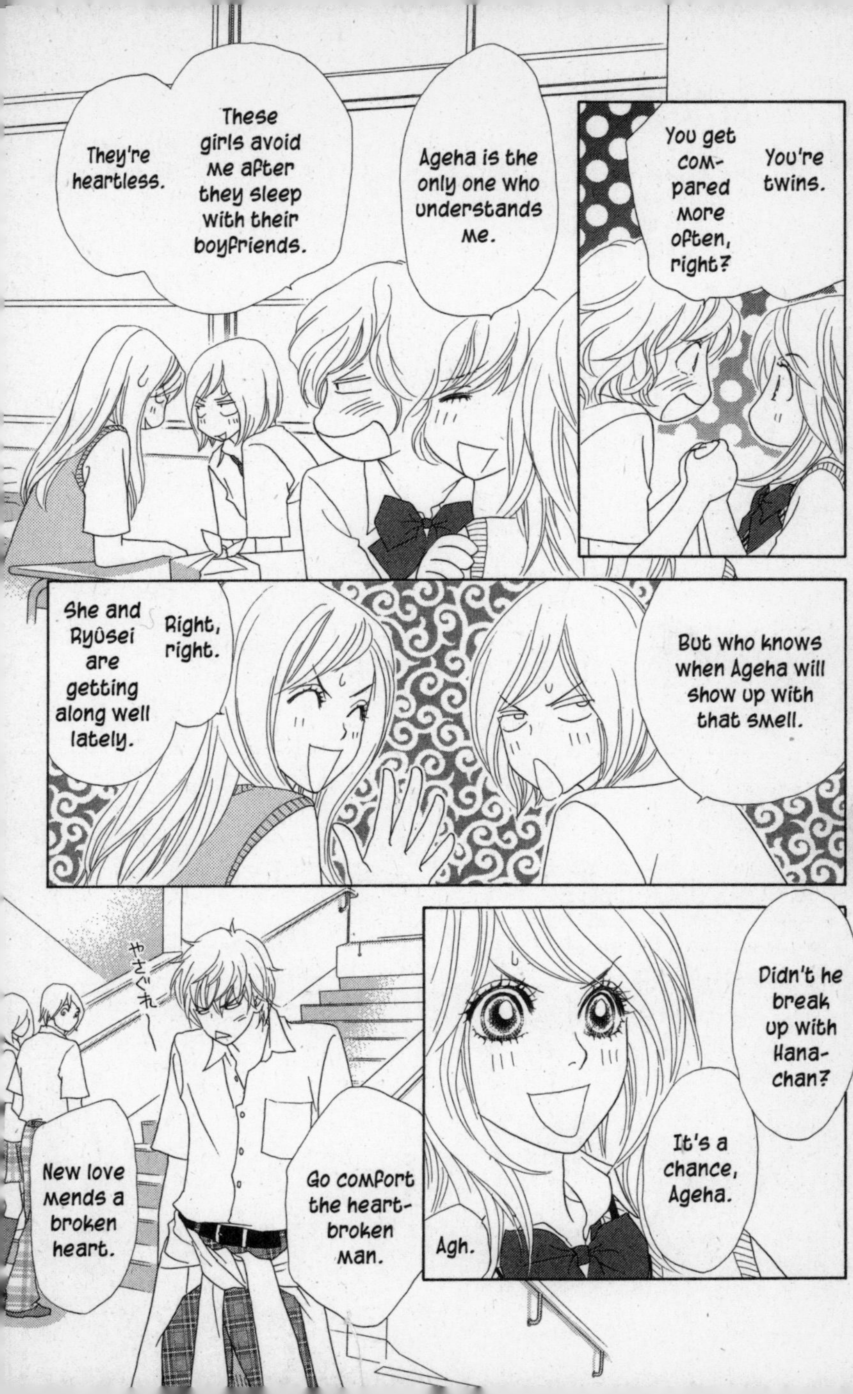
You're twins.
You get com-pared more often, right?
Ageha is the only one who understands me.
These girls avoid me after they sleep with their boyfriends.
They're heartless.
But who knows when Ageha will show up with that smell.
Right, right.
She and Ryûsei are getting along well lately.
Didn't he break up with Hana-chan?
It's a chance, Ageha.
Agh.
Go comfort the heart-broken man.
New love mends a broken heart.
やさぐれ

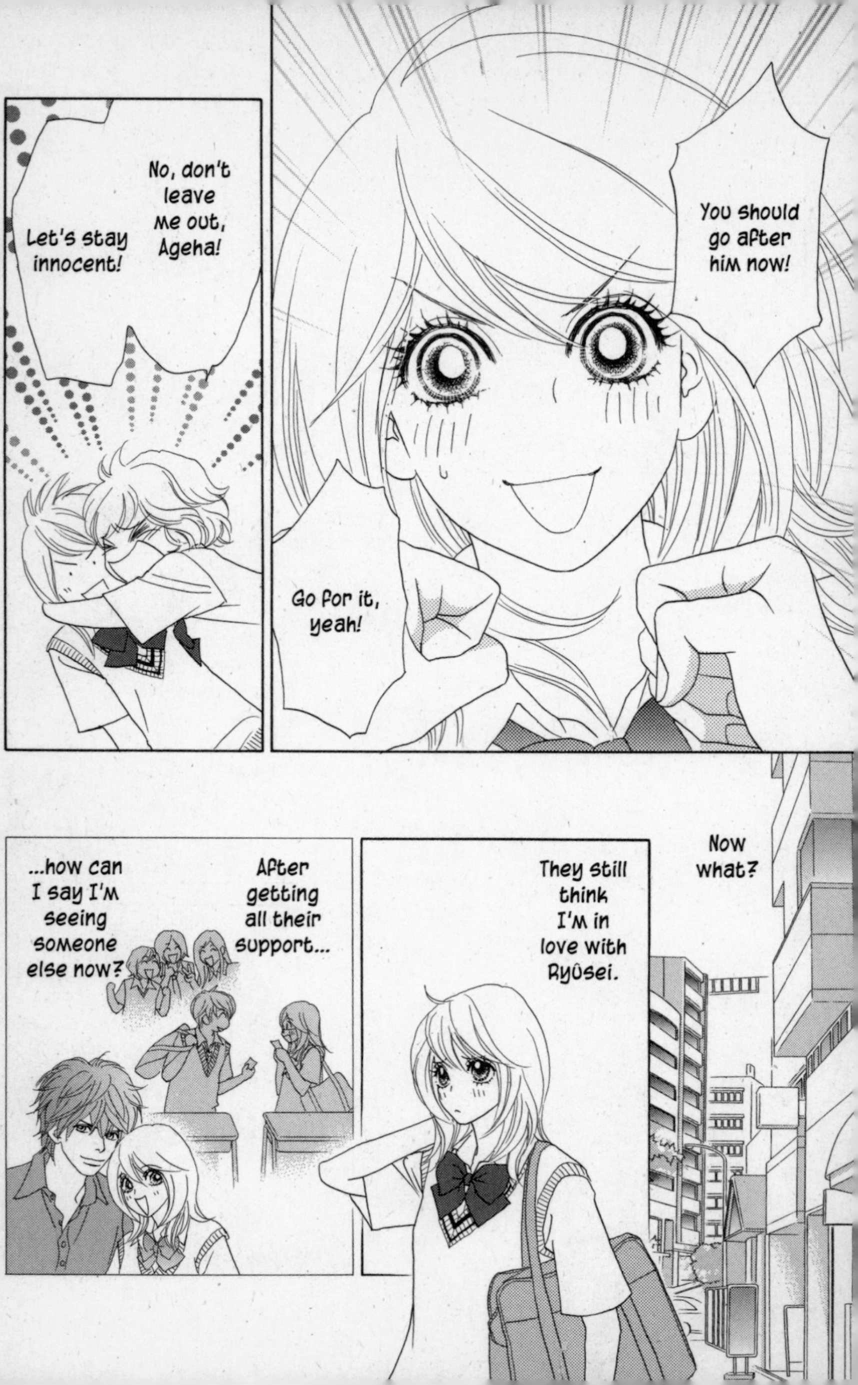
You should go after him now!
Go for it, yeah!
No, don't leave me out, Ageha!
Let's stay innocent!
Now what?
They still think I'm in love with Ryûsei.
After getting all their support...
...how can I say I'm seeing someone else now?

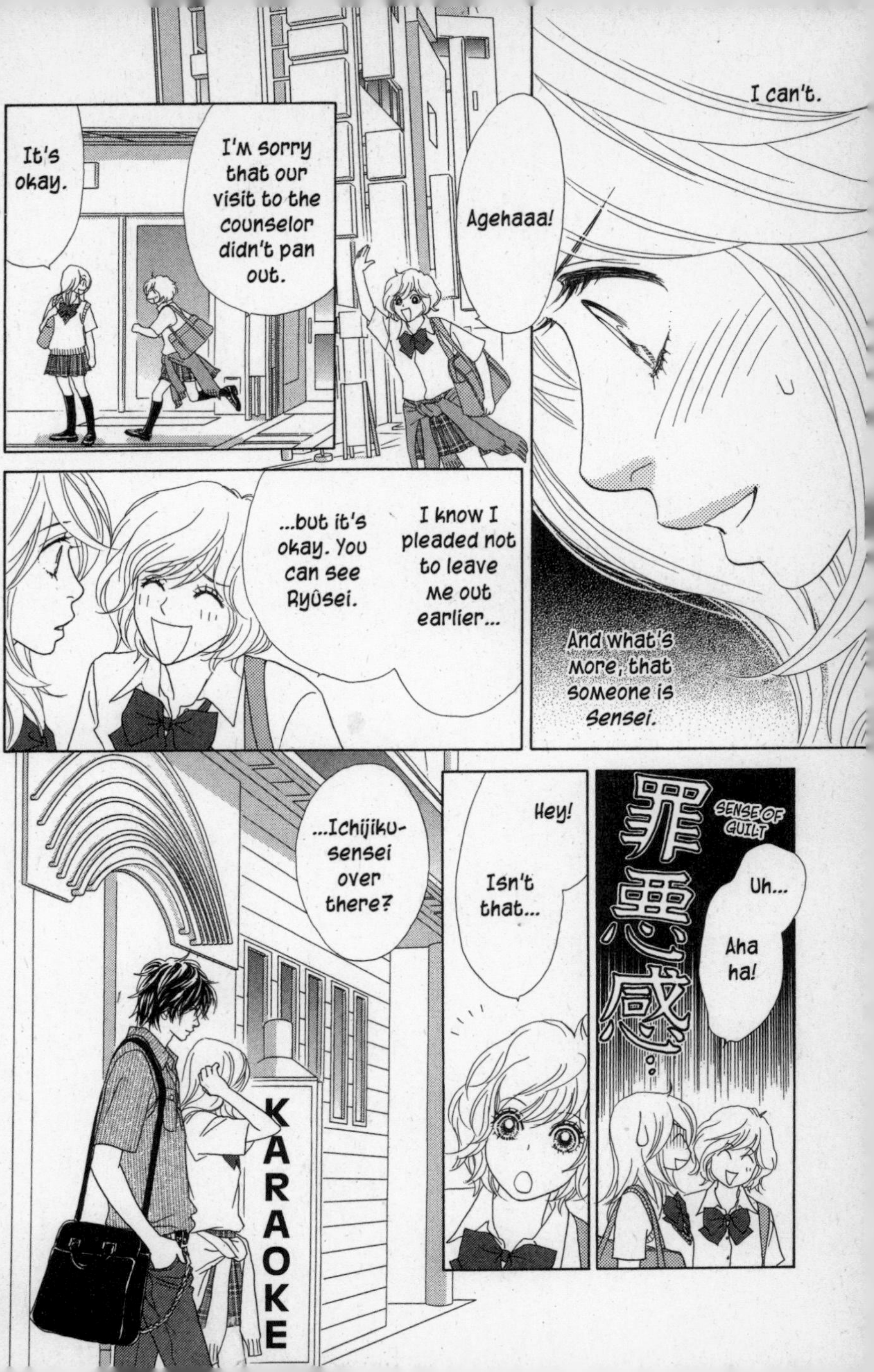
I can't.
And what's more, that someone is Sensei.
Agehaaa!
I'm sorry that our visit to the counselor didn't pan out.
It's okay.
I know I pleaded not to leave me out earlier...
...but it's okay. You can see Ryûsei.
罪悪感。
SENSE OF GUILT
Uh...
Aha ha!
Hey!
Isn't that...
...Ichijiku-sensei over there?
KARAOKE

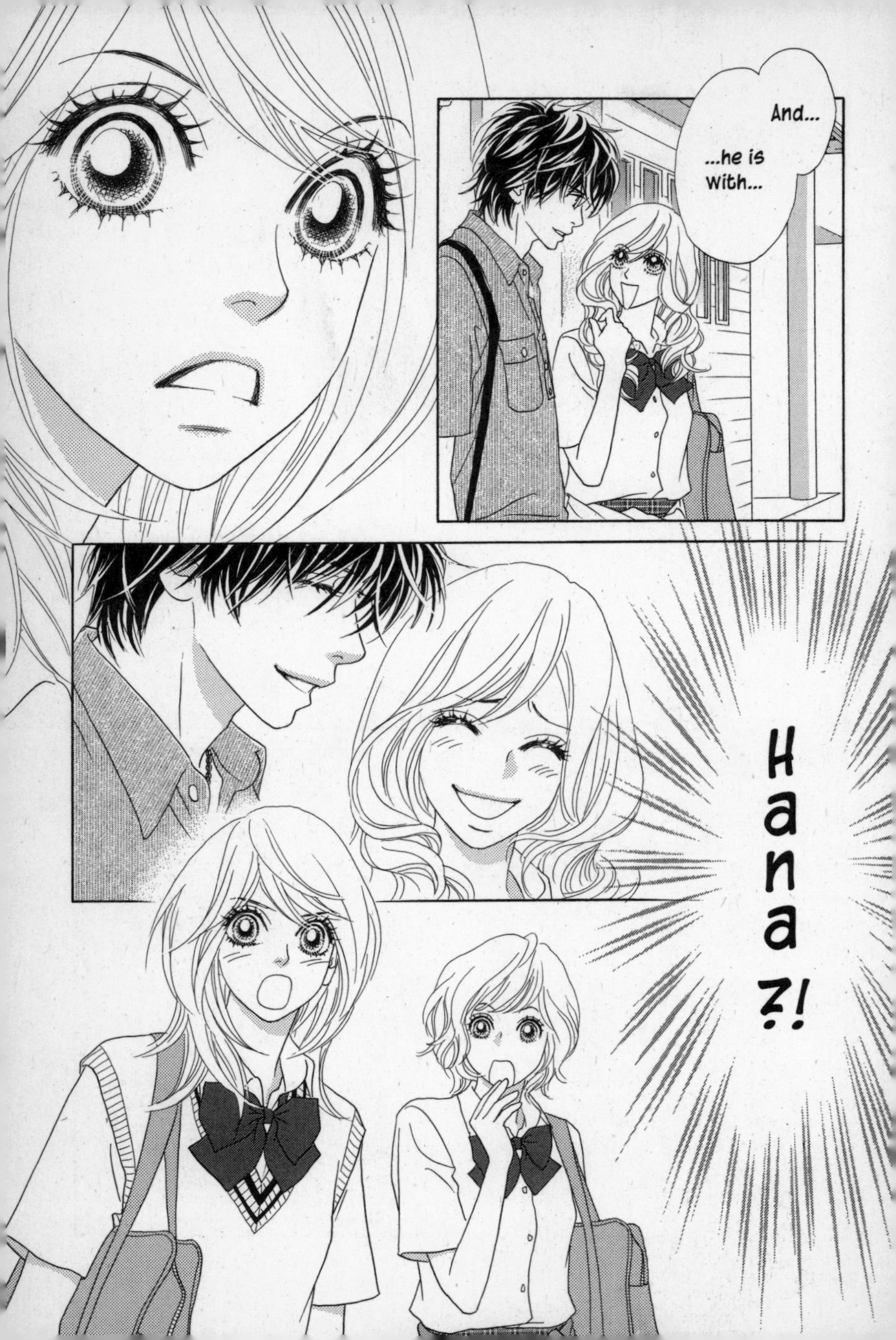
And... ...he is with...
Hana?!

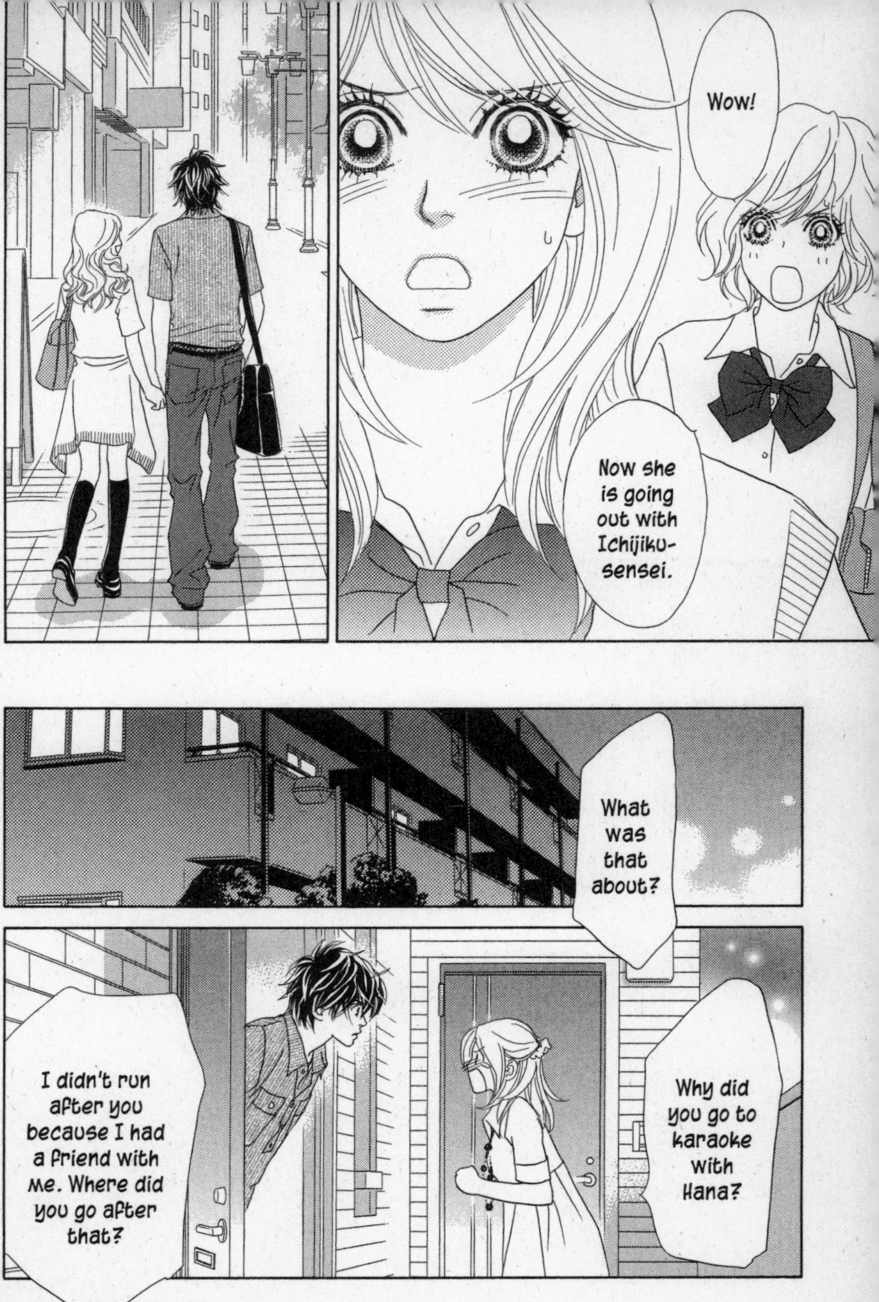
Wow!
Now she is going out with Ichijiku-sensei.
What was that about?
Why did you go to karaoke with Hana?
I didn't run after you because I had a friend with me. Where did you go after that?

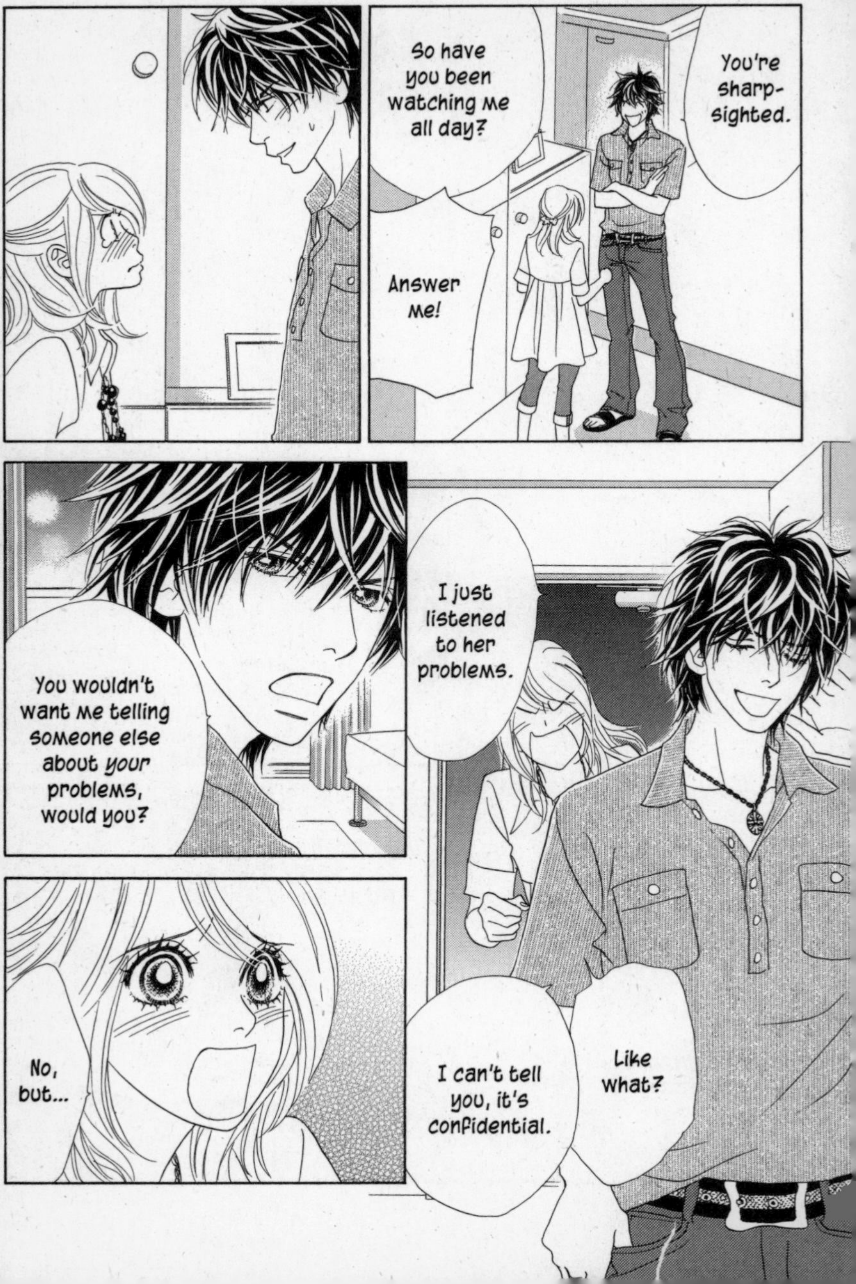
You're sharp-sighted.
So have you been watching me all day?
Answer me!
I just listened to her problems.
Like what?
I can't tell you, it's confidential.
You wouldn't want me telling someone else about *your* problems, would you?
No, but...

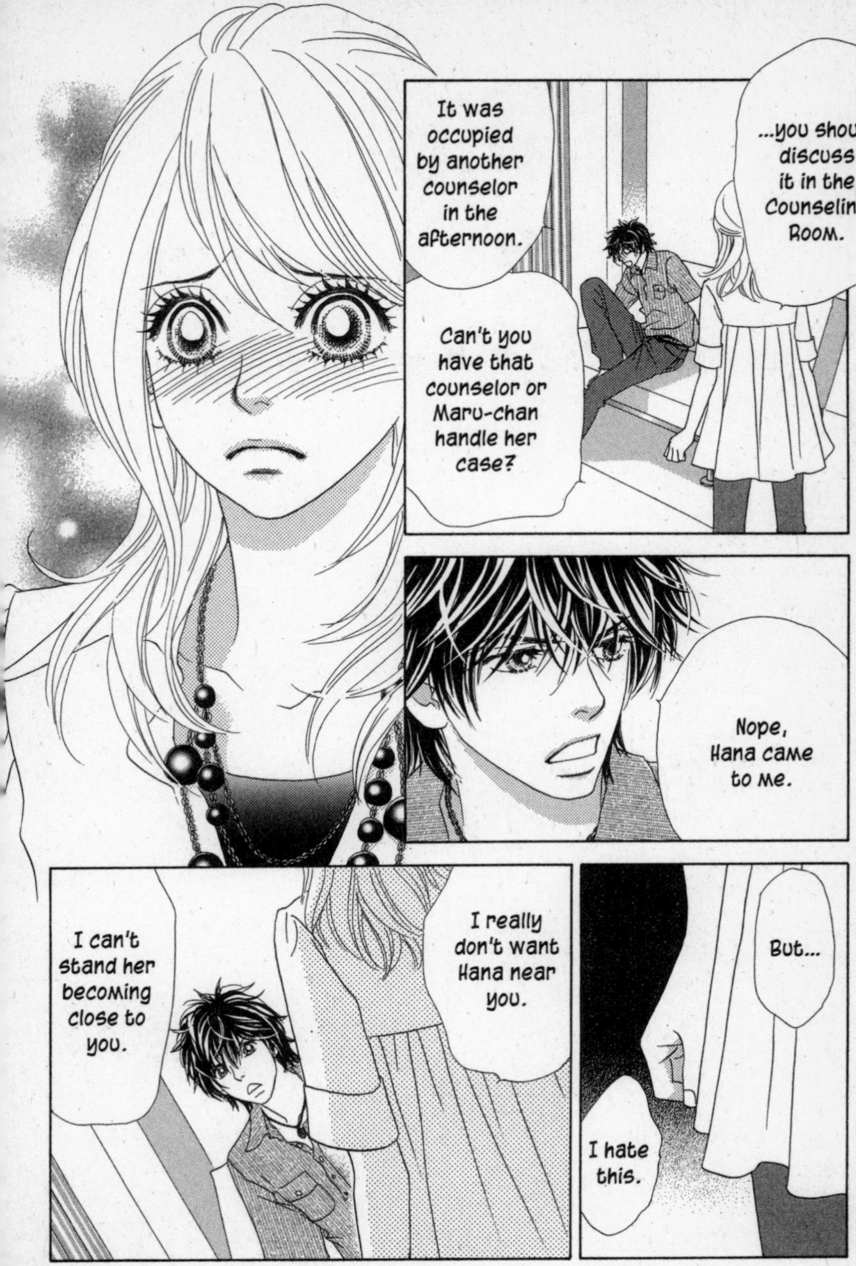
...you should discuss it in the Counseling Room.
It was occupied by another counselor in the afternoon.
Can't you have that counselor or Maru-chan handle her case?
Nope, Hana came to me.
But...
I hate this.
I really don't want Hana near you.
I can't stand her becoming close to you.

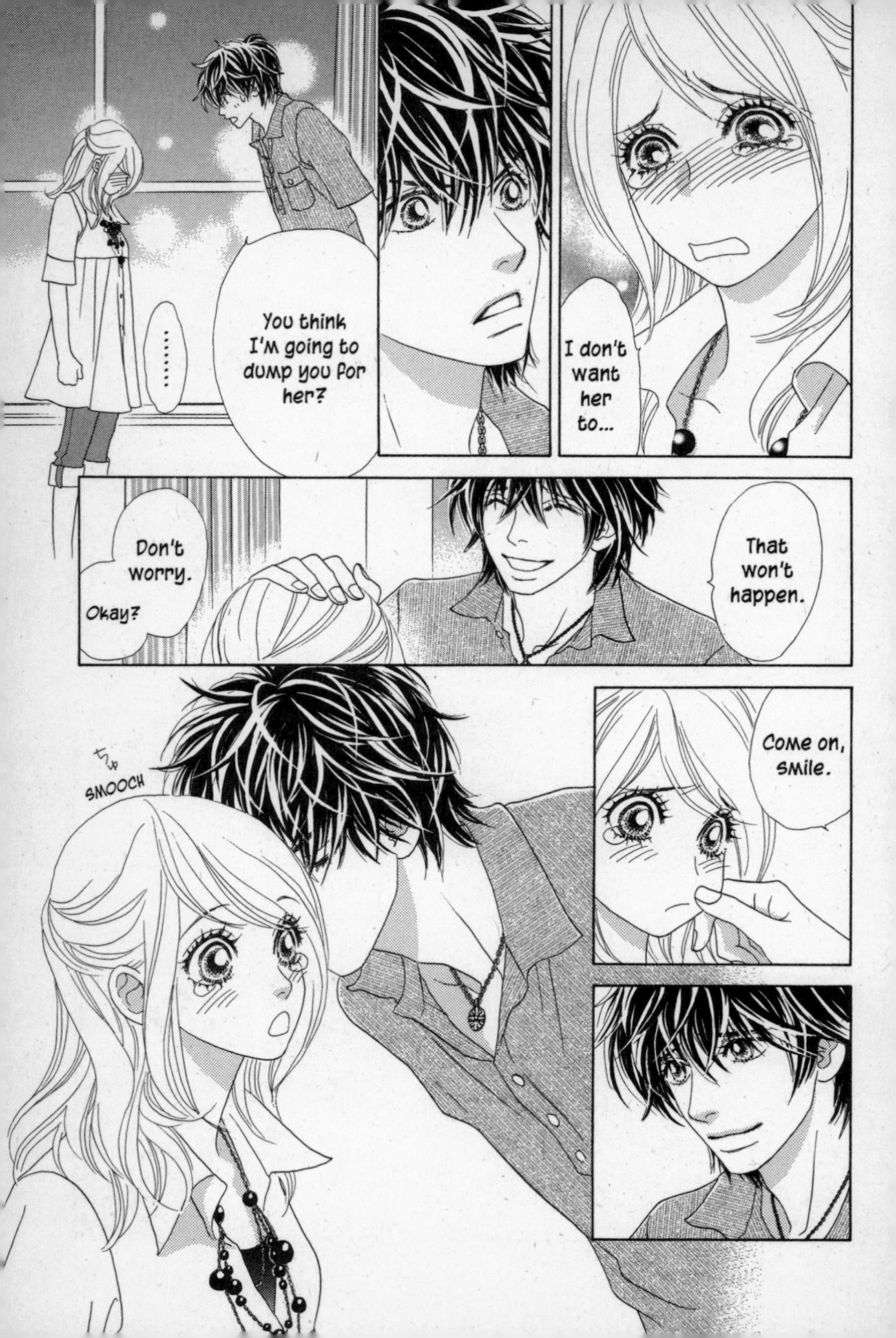
I don't want her to...
You think I'm going to dump you for her?
......
That won't happen.
Don't worry.
Okay?
Come on, smile.
ちゅ
SMOOCH

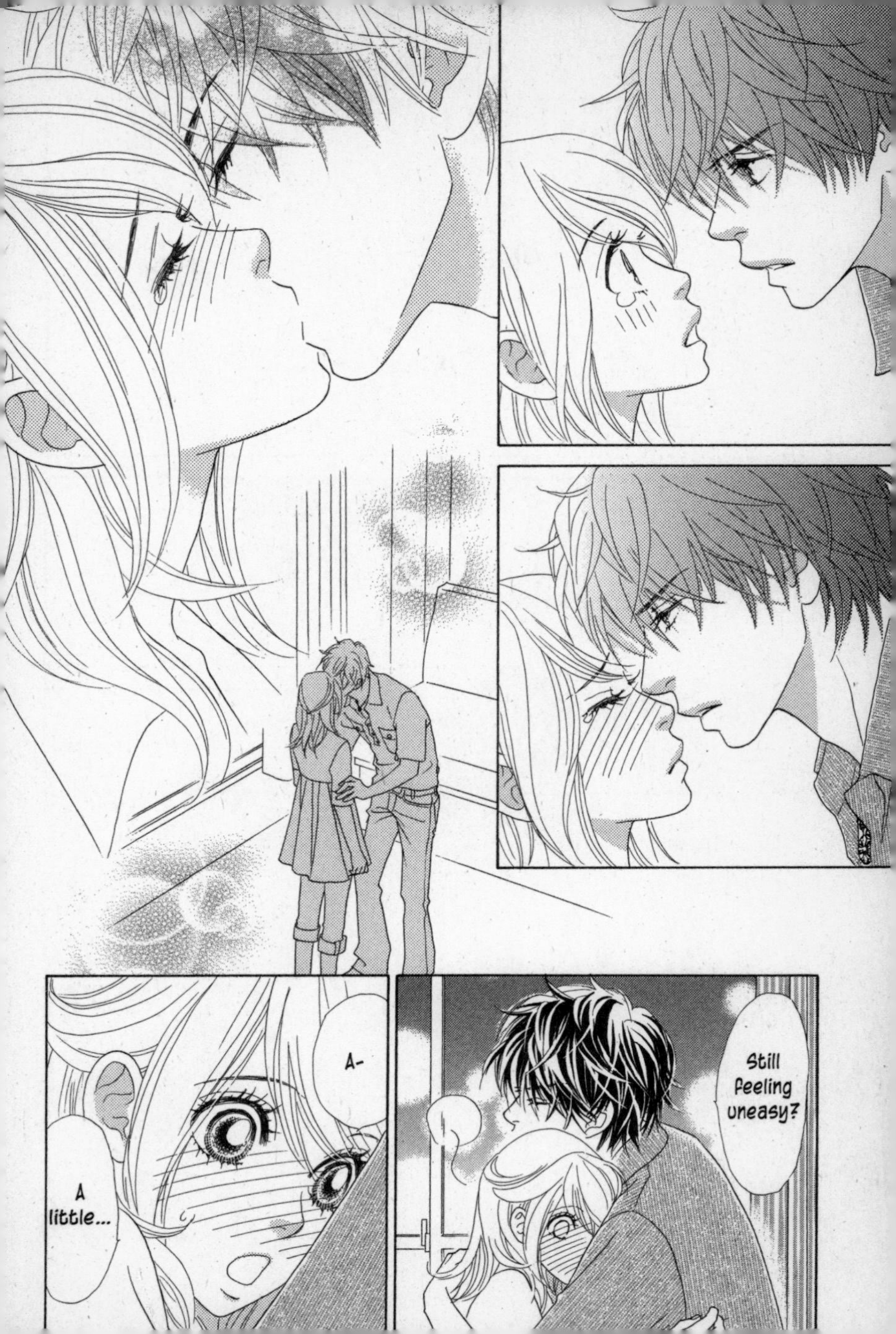
Still feeling uneasy?
A-
A little...

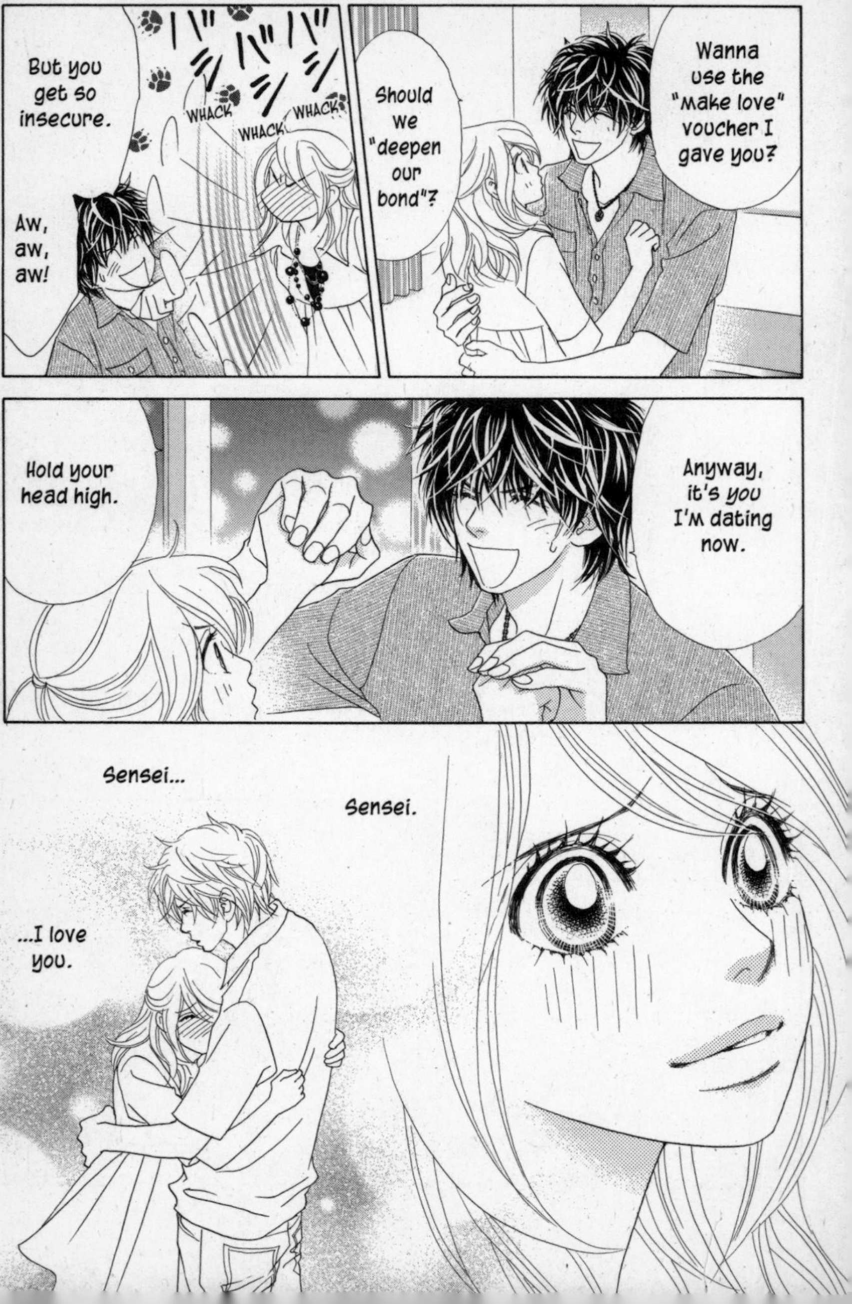

Wanna use the "make love" voucher I gave you?
Should we "deepen our bond"?
But you get so insecure.
WHACK
WHACK
WHACK
Aw, aw, aw!
Anyway, it's *you* I'm dating now.
Hold your head high.
Sensei...
Sensei.
...I love you.

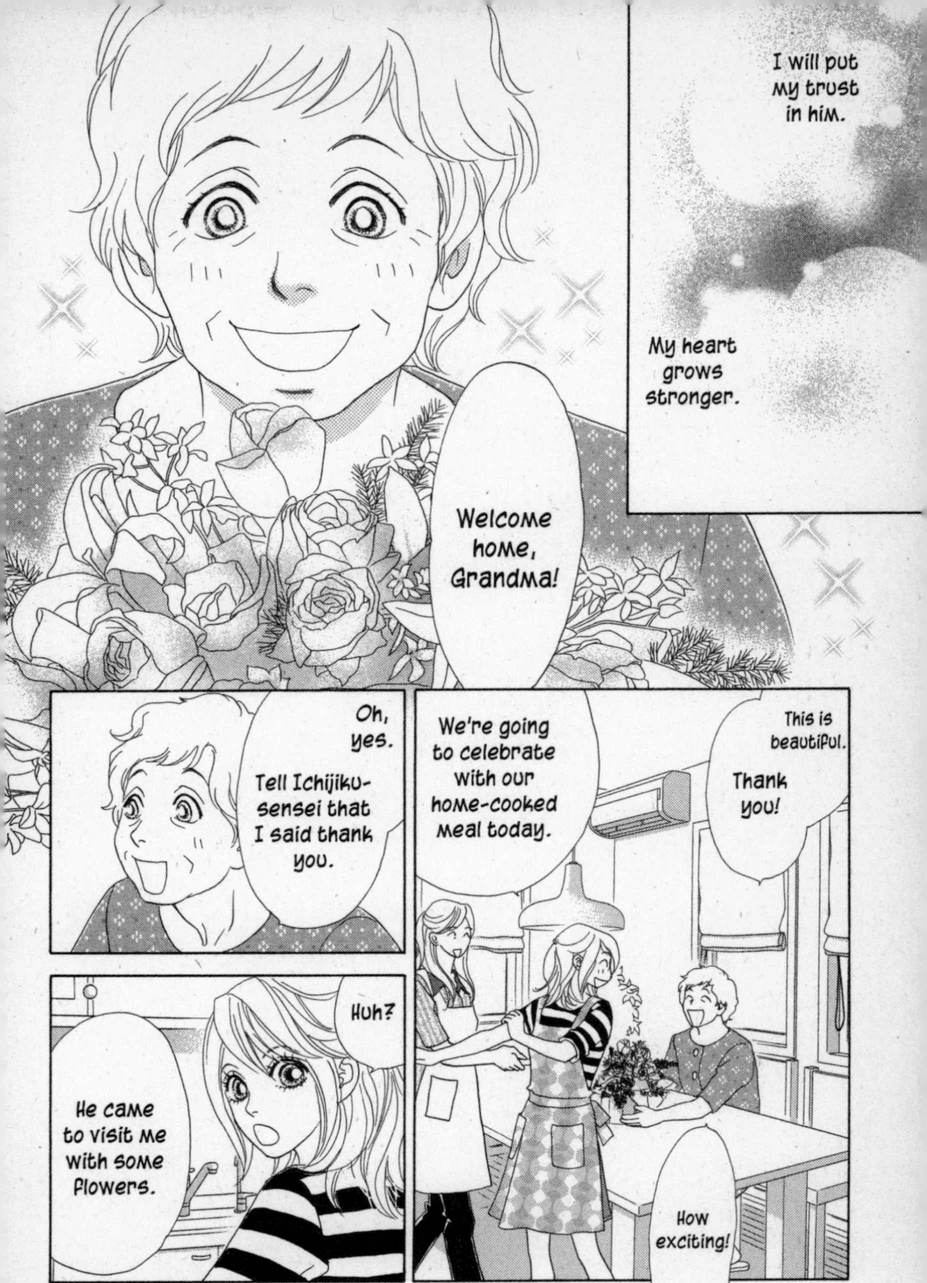
I will put my trust in him.
My heart grows stronger.
Welcome home, Grandma!
This is beautiful.
Thank you!
We're going to celebrate with our home-cooked meal today.
How exciting!
Oh, yes.
Tell Ichijiku-sensei that I said thank you.
Huh?
He came to visit me with some flowers.

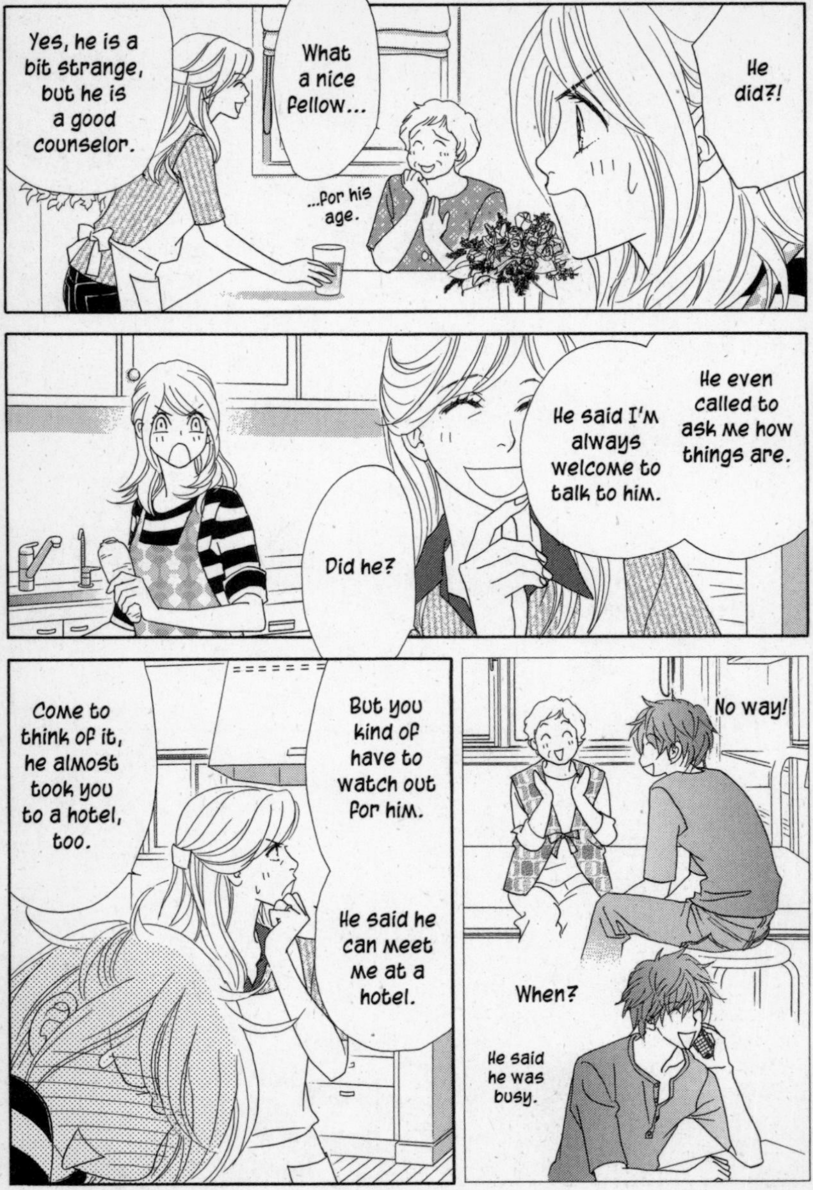
He did?!
What a nice fellow...
...for his age.
Yes, he is a bit strange, but he is a good counselor.
He even called to ask me how things are.
He said I'm always welcome to talk to him.
Did he?
No way!
When?
He said he was busy.
But you kind of have to watch out for him.
He said he can meet me at a hotel.
Come to think of it, he almost took you to a hotel, too.

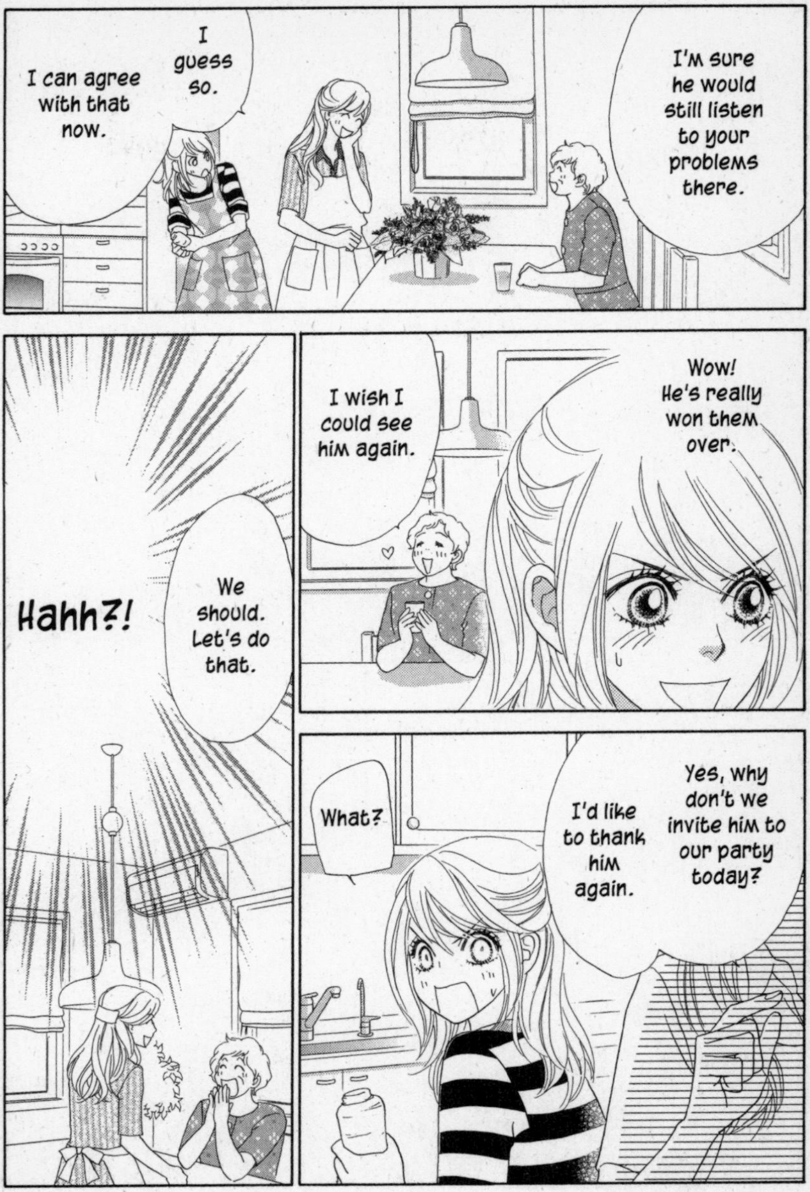
I'm sure he would still listen to your problems there.
I guess so.
I can agree with that now.
Wow! He's really won them over.
I wish I could see him again.
Yes, why don't we invite him to our party today?
I'd like to thank him again.
What?
We should. Let's do that.
Hahh?!

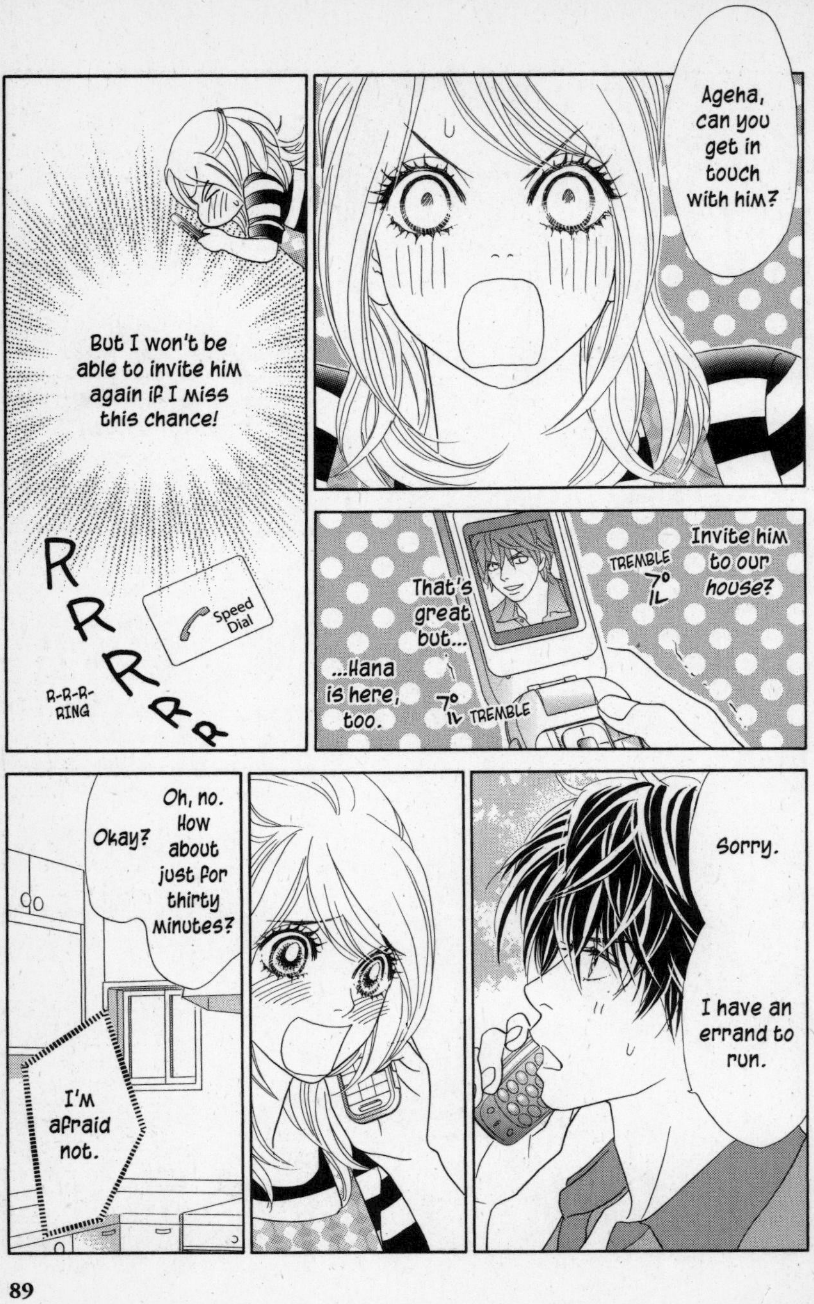
Ageha, can you get in touch with him?
Invite him to our house?
TREMBLE
That's great but...
...Hana is here, too.
TREMBLE
But I won't be able to invite him again if I miss this chance!
Speed Dial
RRRRR
R-R-R-RING
Sorry.
I have an errand to run.
Oh, no. How about just for thirty minutes?
Okay?
I'm afraid not.

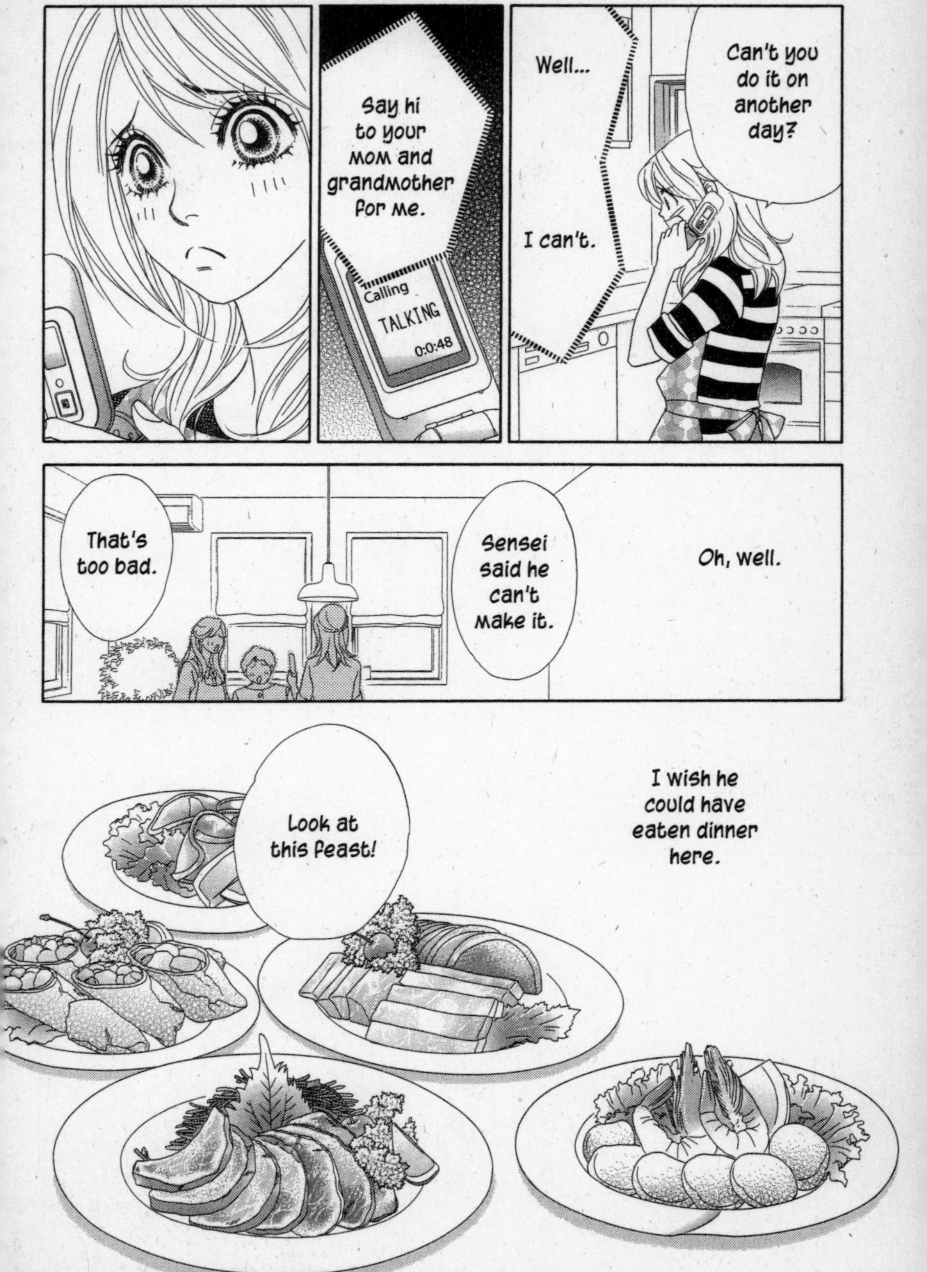

Can't you do it on another day?
Well...
I can't.
Say hi to your mom and grandmother for me.
Calling
TALKING
0:0:48
Oh, well.
Sensei said he can't make it.
That's too bad.
I wish he could have eaten dinner here.
Look at this feast!

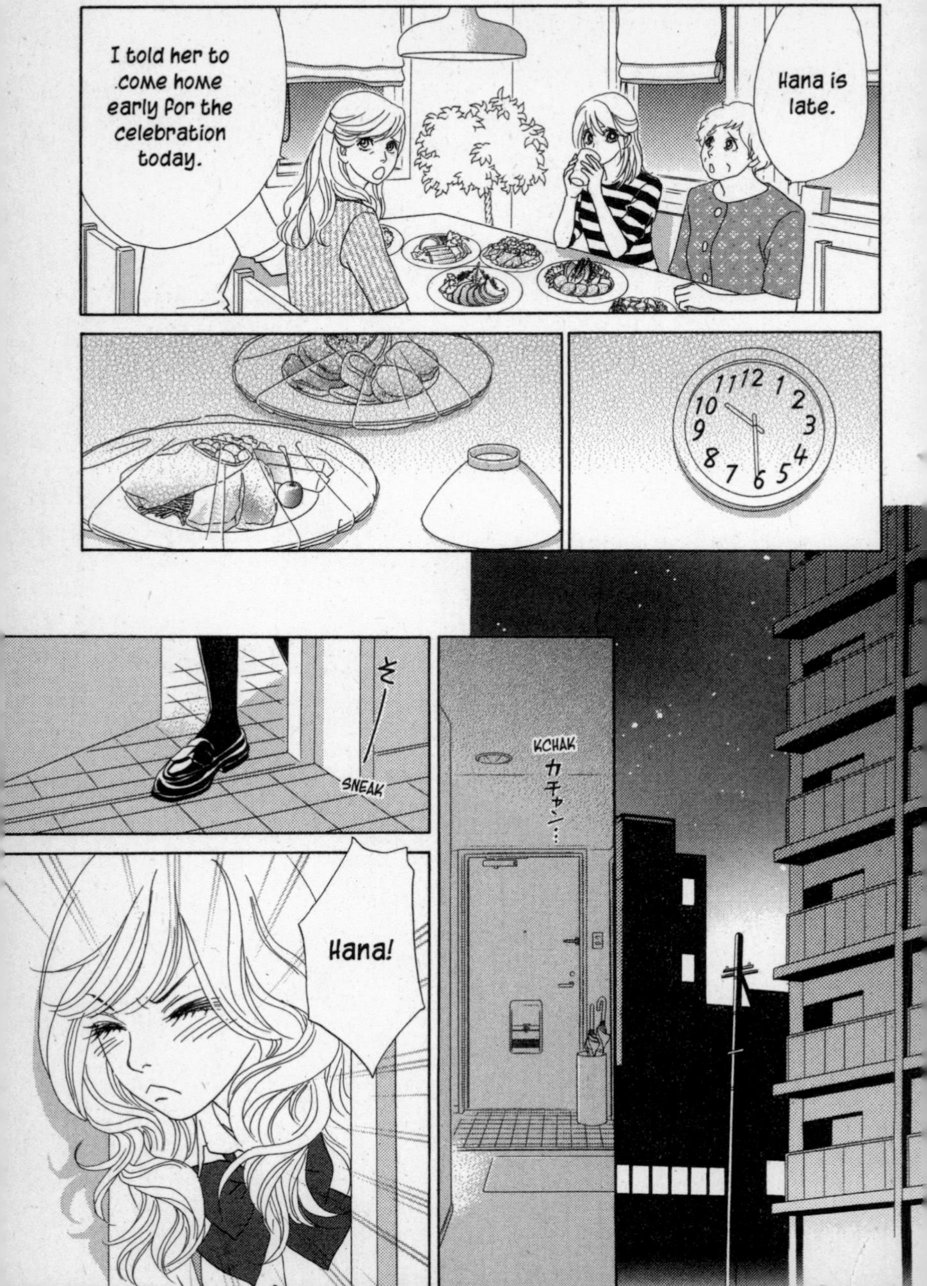
Hana is late.
I told her to come home early for the celebration today.
KCHAK
カチャン…
SNEAK
Hana!

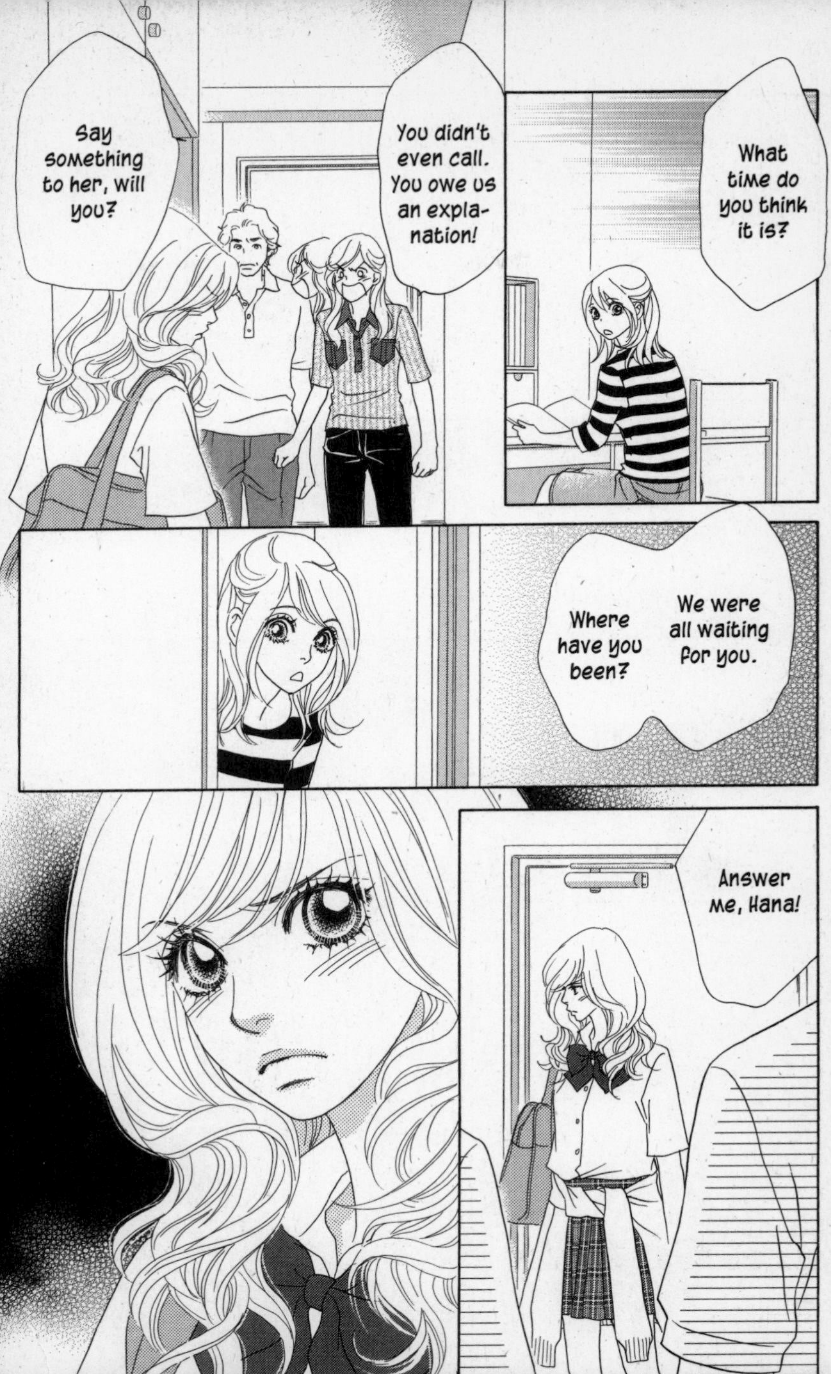
What time do you think it is?
You didn't even call. You owe us an expla-nation!
Say something to her, will you?
We were all waiting for you.
Where have you been?
Answer me, Hana!

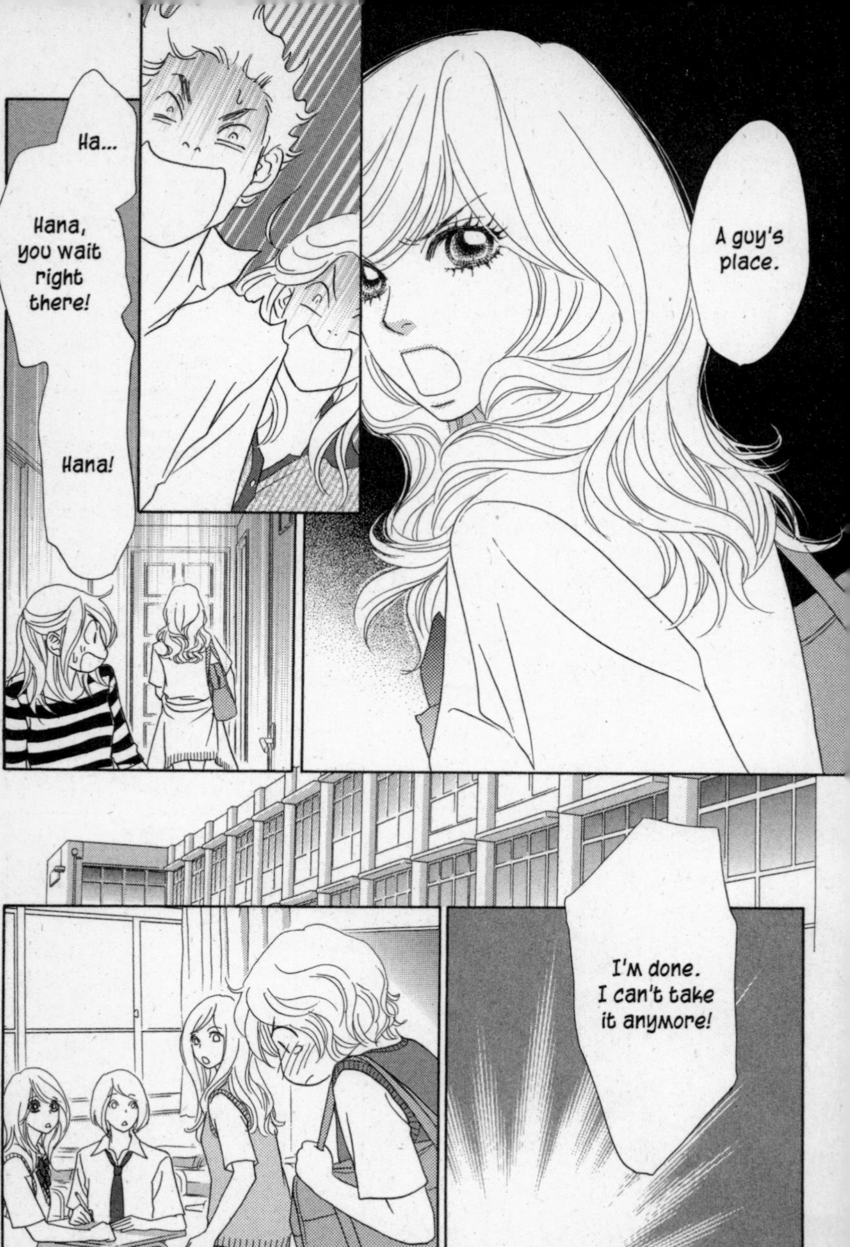
A guy's place.
Ha...
Hana, you wait right there!
Hana!
I'm done. I can't take it anymore!

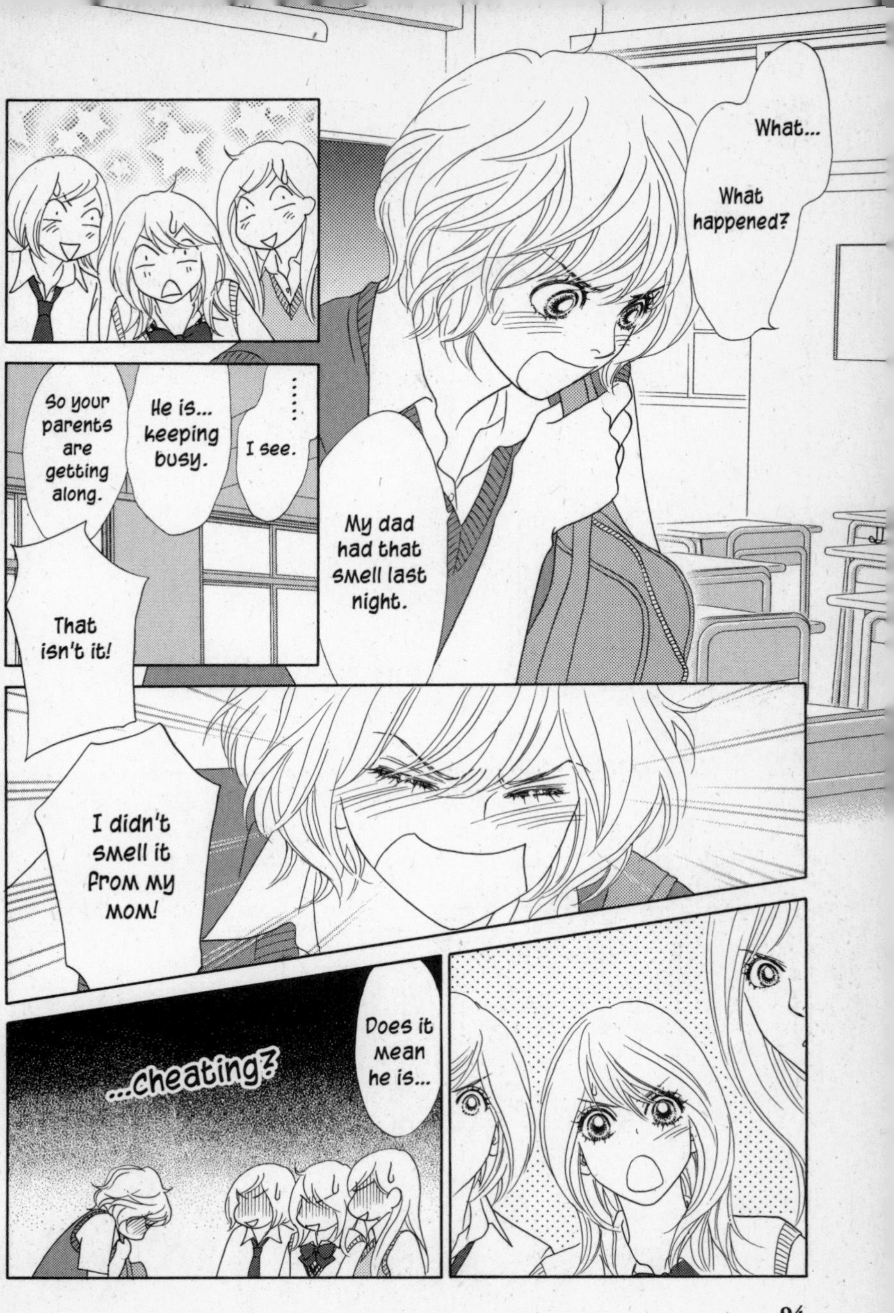

What...
What happened?
My dad had that smell last night.
......
I see.
He is... keeping busy.
So your parents are getting along.
That isn't it!
I didn't smell it from my MOM!
Does it mean he is...
...Cheating?

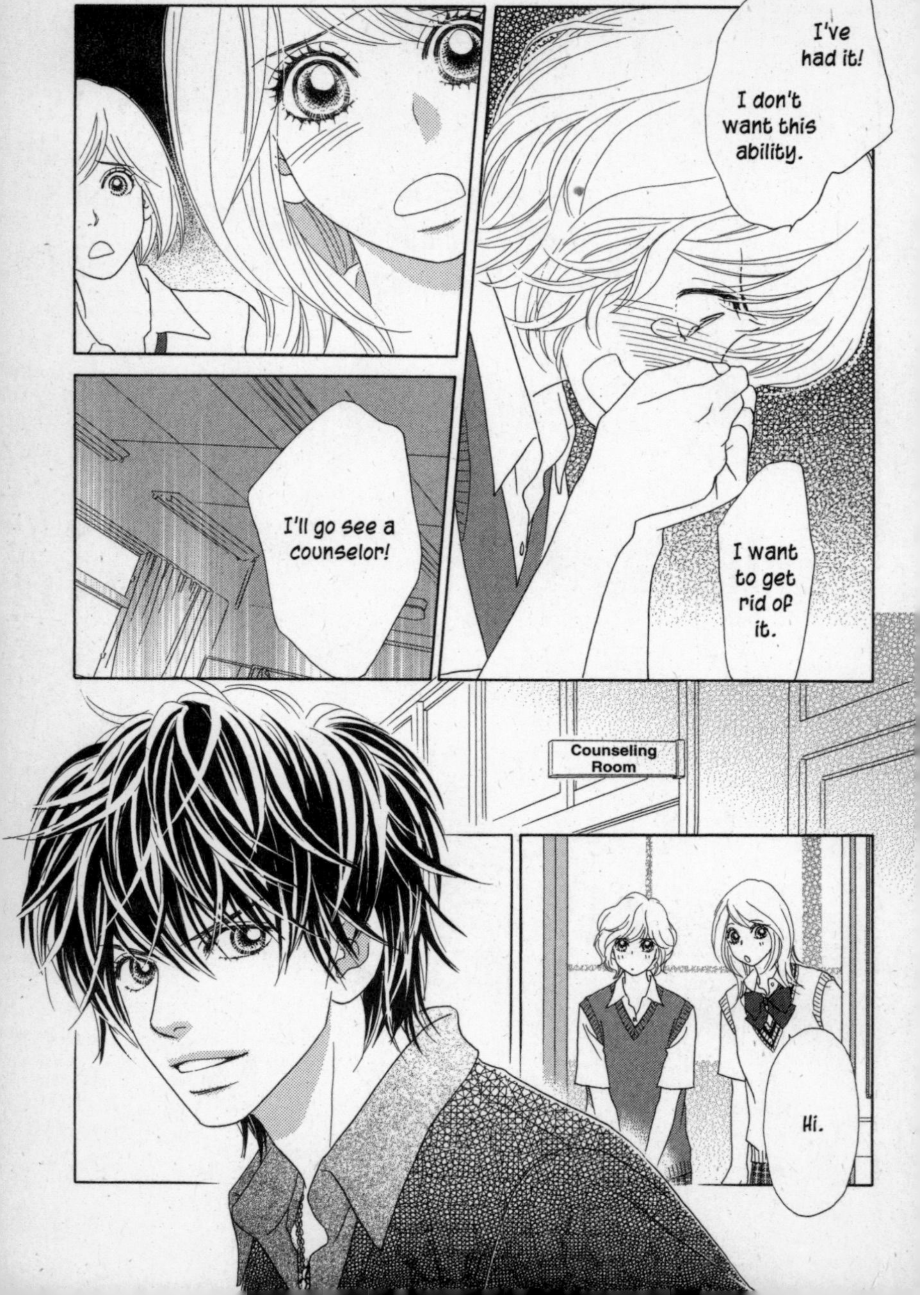

I've had it!
I don't want this ability.
I want to get rid of it.
I'll go see a counselor!
Counseling Room
Hi.

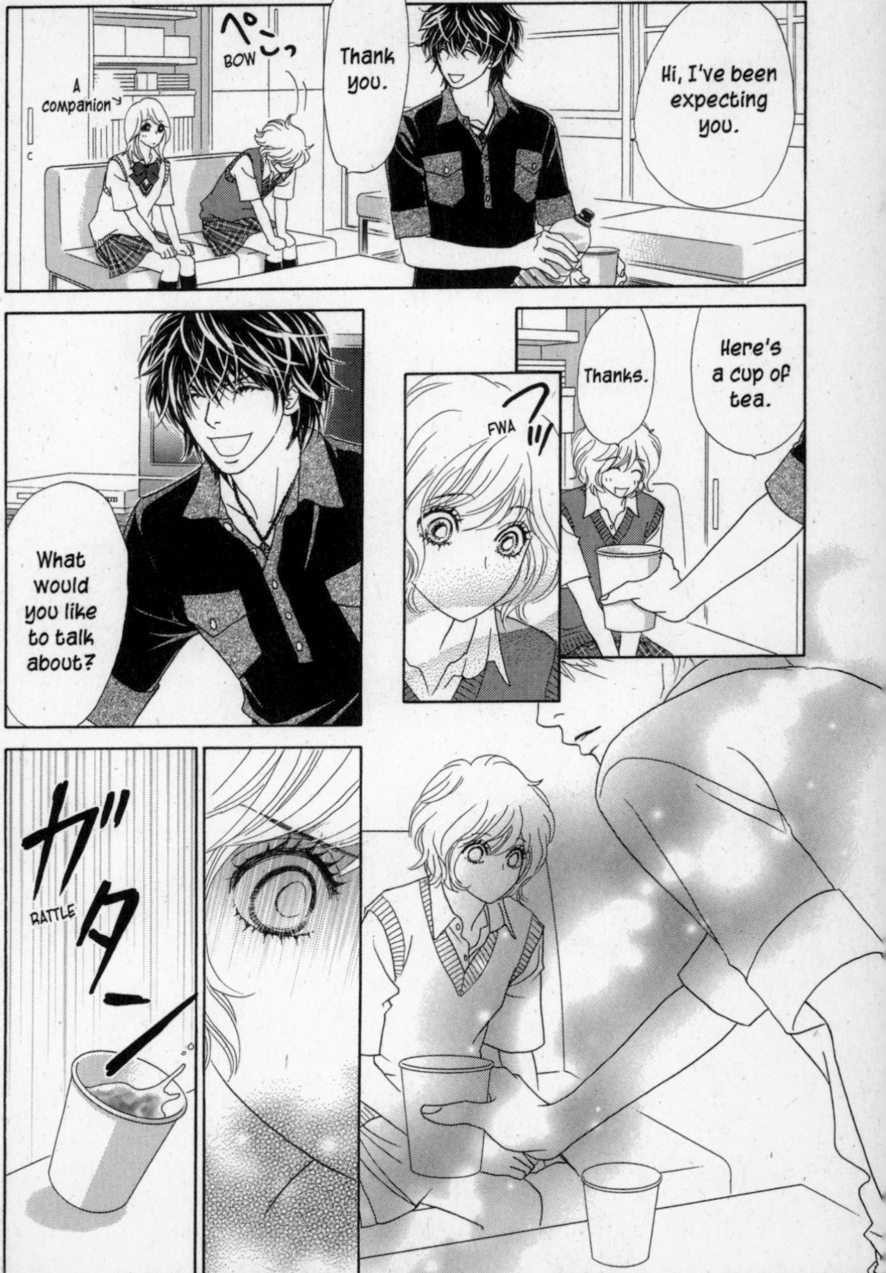
Hi, I've been expecting you.
Thank you.
ぺこっ
BOW
A companion
Here's a cup of tea.
Thanks.
FWA
What would you like to talk about?
ガタ—
RATTLE

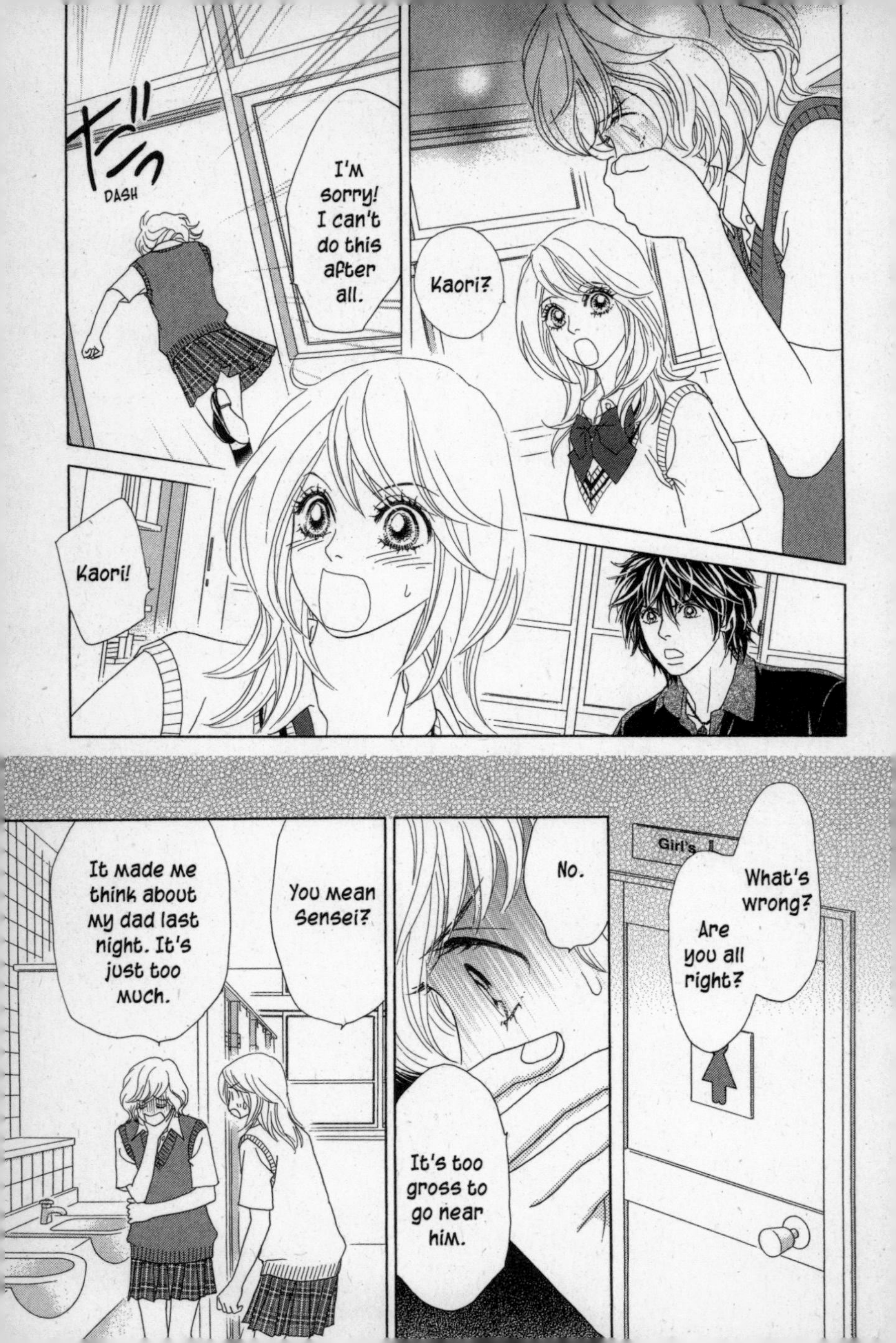
Kaori?
I'm sorry! I can't do this after all.
DASH
Kaori!
Girl's
What's wrong?
Are you all right?
No.
It's too gross to go near him.
You mean Sensei?
It made me think about my dad last night. It's just too much.

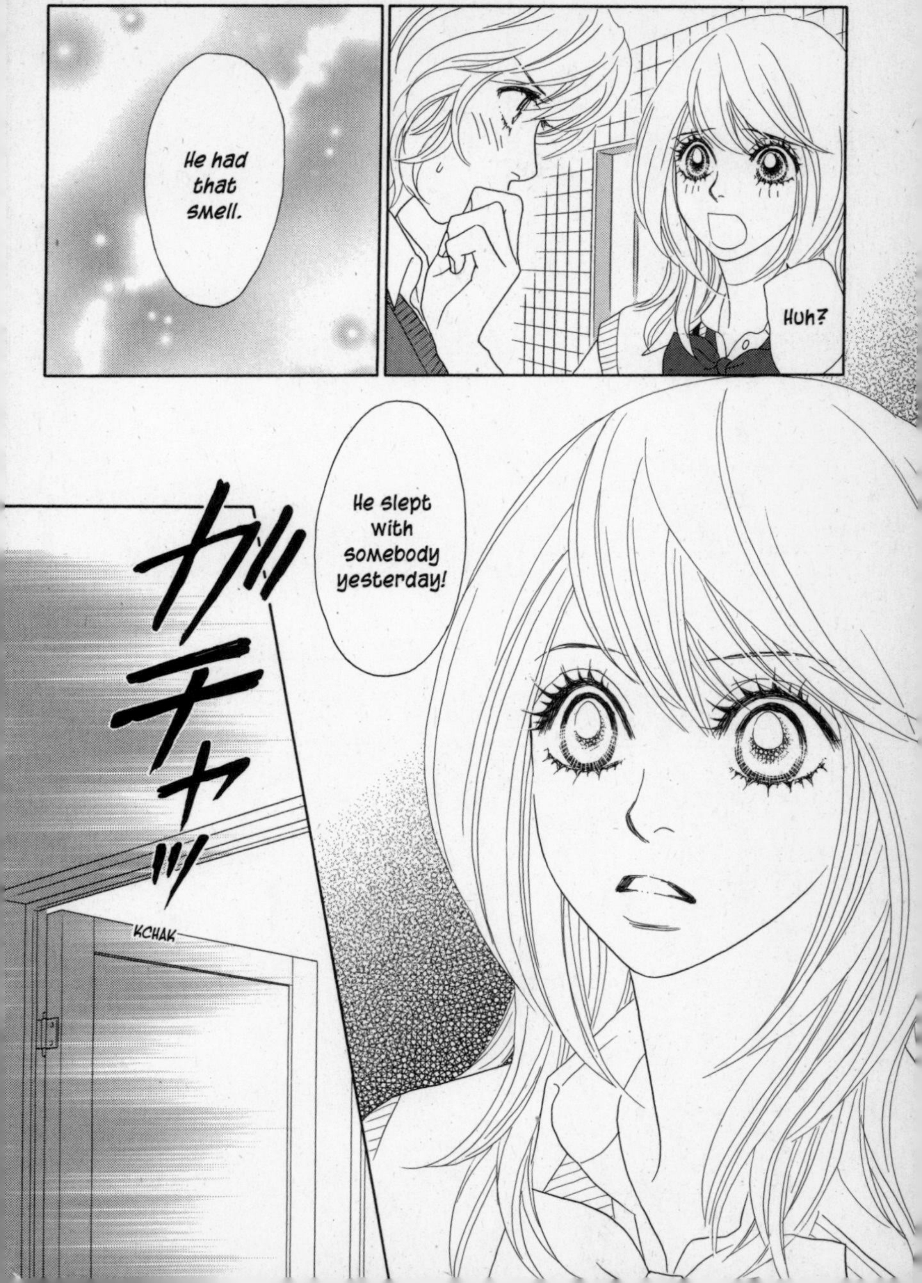
Huh?
He had that smell.
He slept with somebody yesterday!
ガチャッ
KCHAK

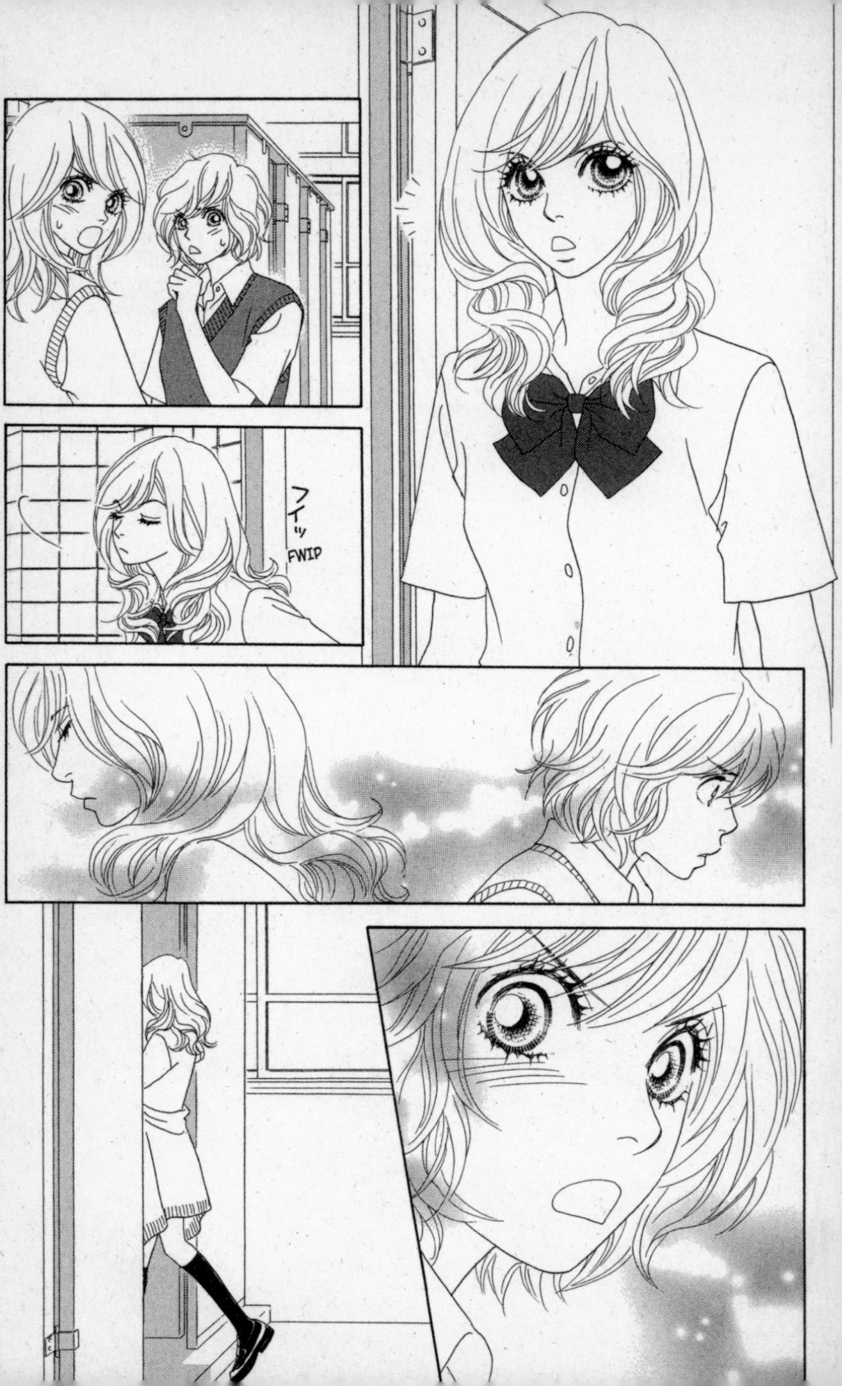
フイッ
FWIP

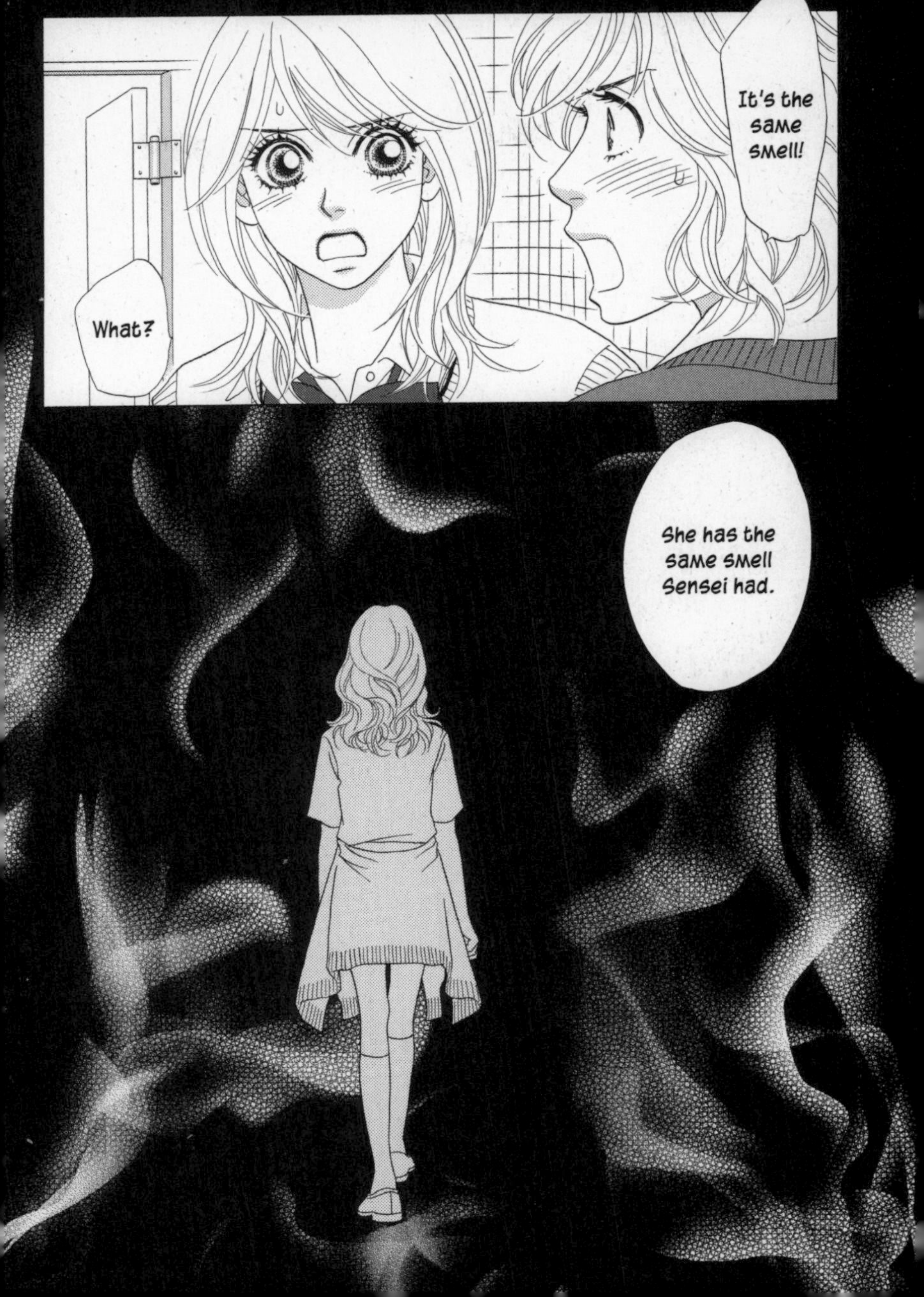
It's the same smell!
What?
She has the same smell Sensei had.

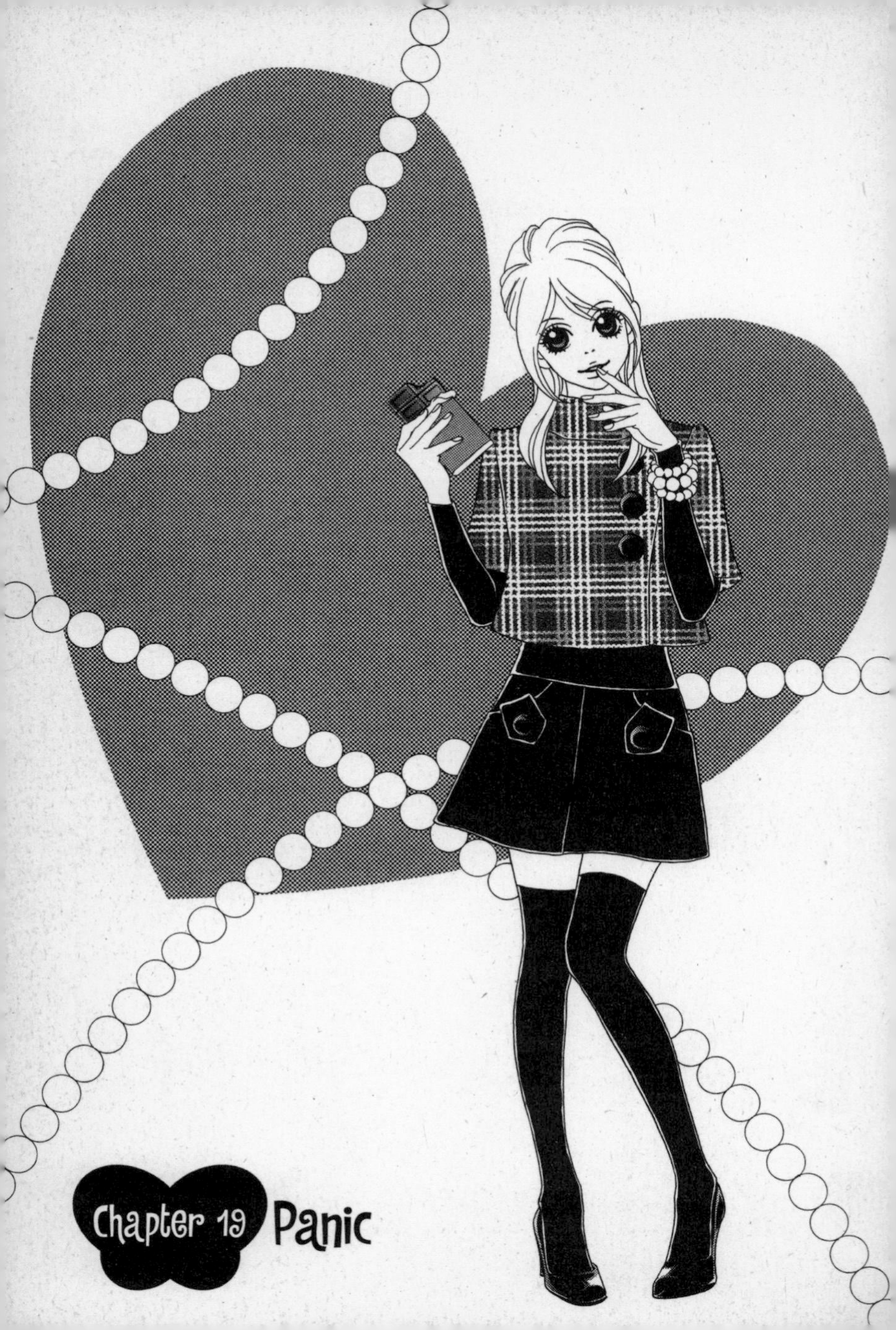

Chapter 19 Panic

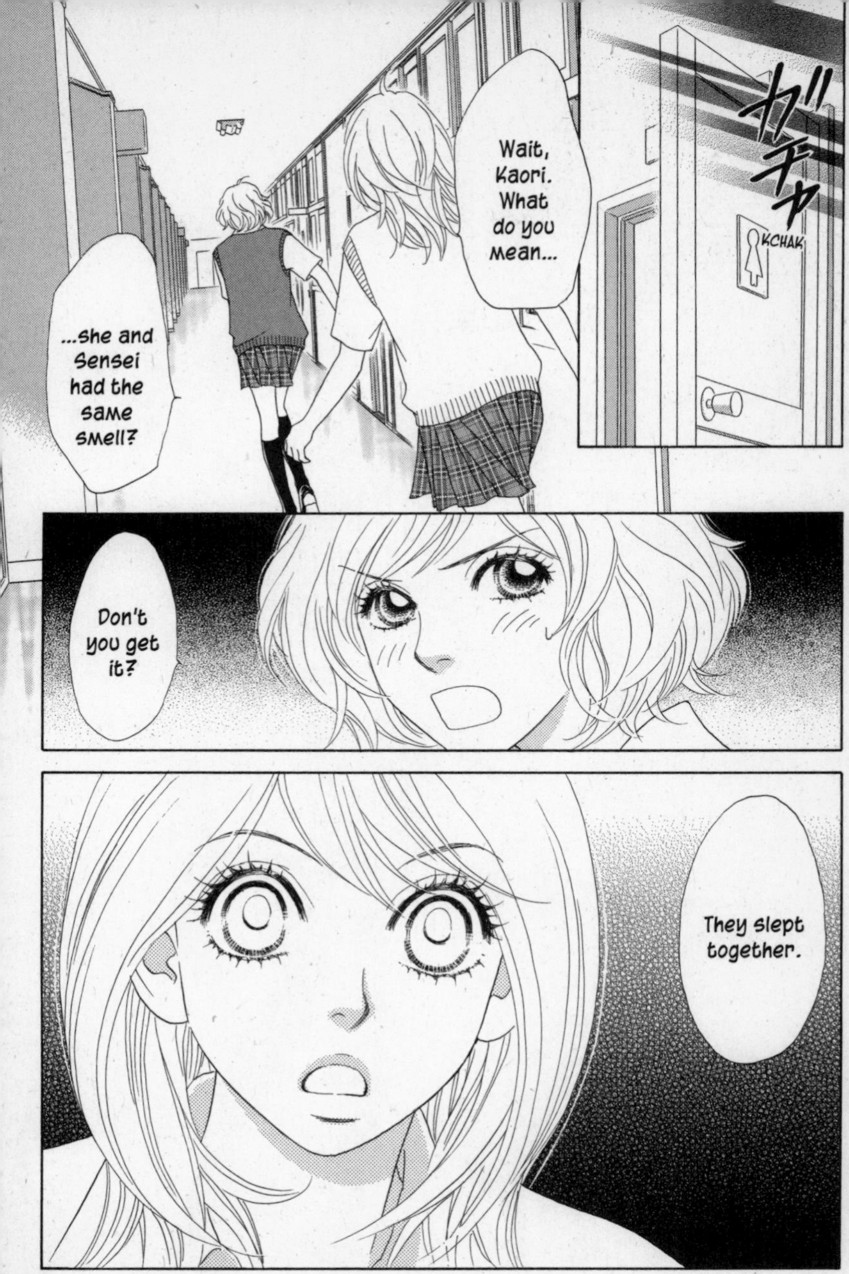
ガチャ
KCHAK
Wait, Kaori. What do you mean...
...she and Sensei had the same smell?
Don't you get it?
They slept together.

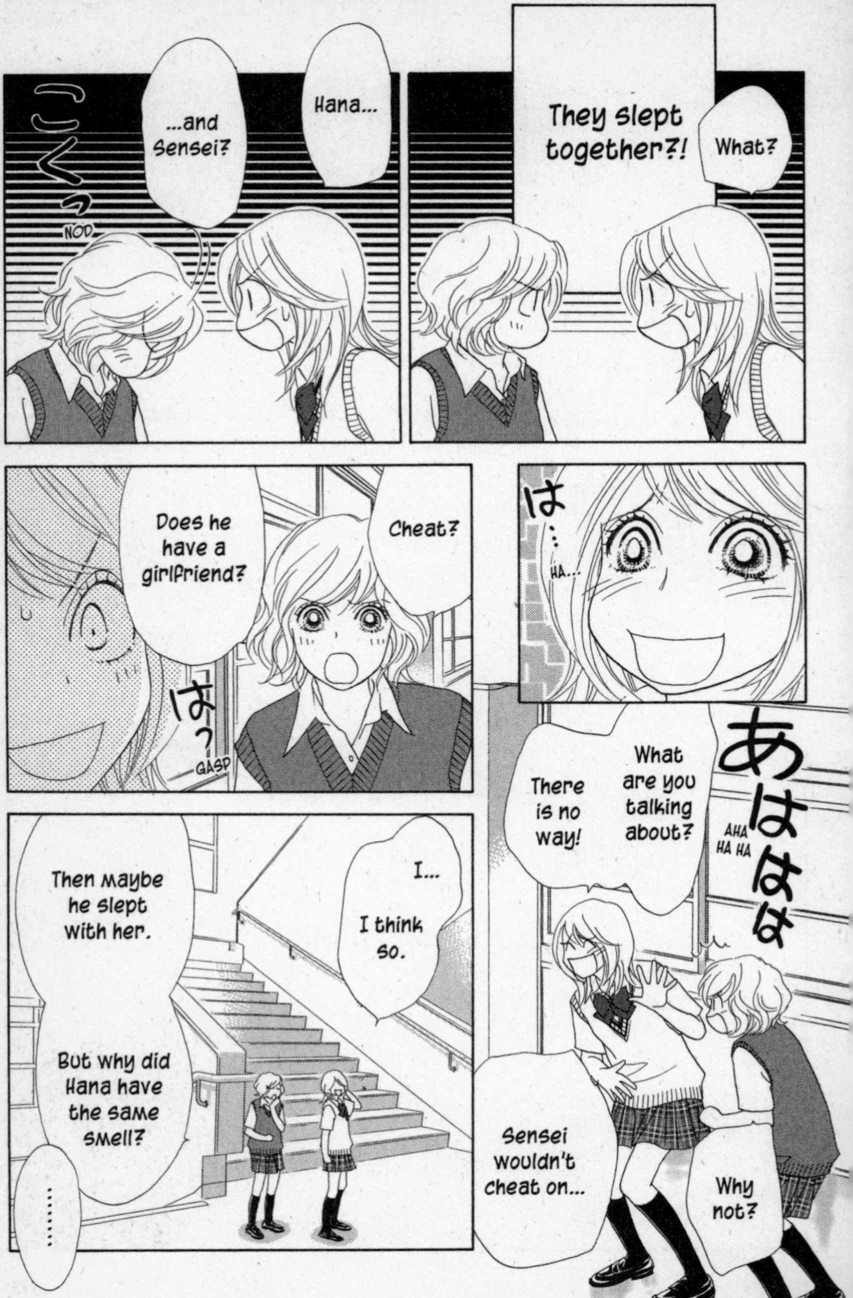
They slept together?!
What?
Hana...
...and Sensei?
こくっ
NOD
は…
HA...
Cheat?
Does he have a girlfriend?
はっ
GASP
あははは
AHA HA HA
What are you talking about?
There is no way!
Sensei wouldn't cheat on...
Why not?
I...
I think so.
Then maybe he slept with her.
But why did Hana have the same smell?
......

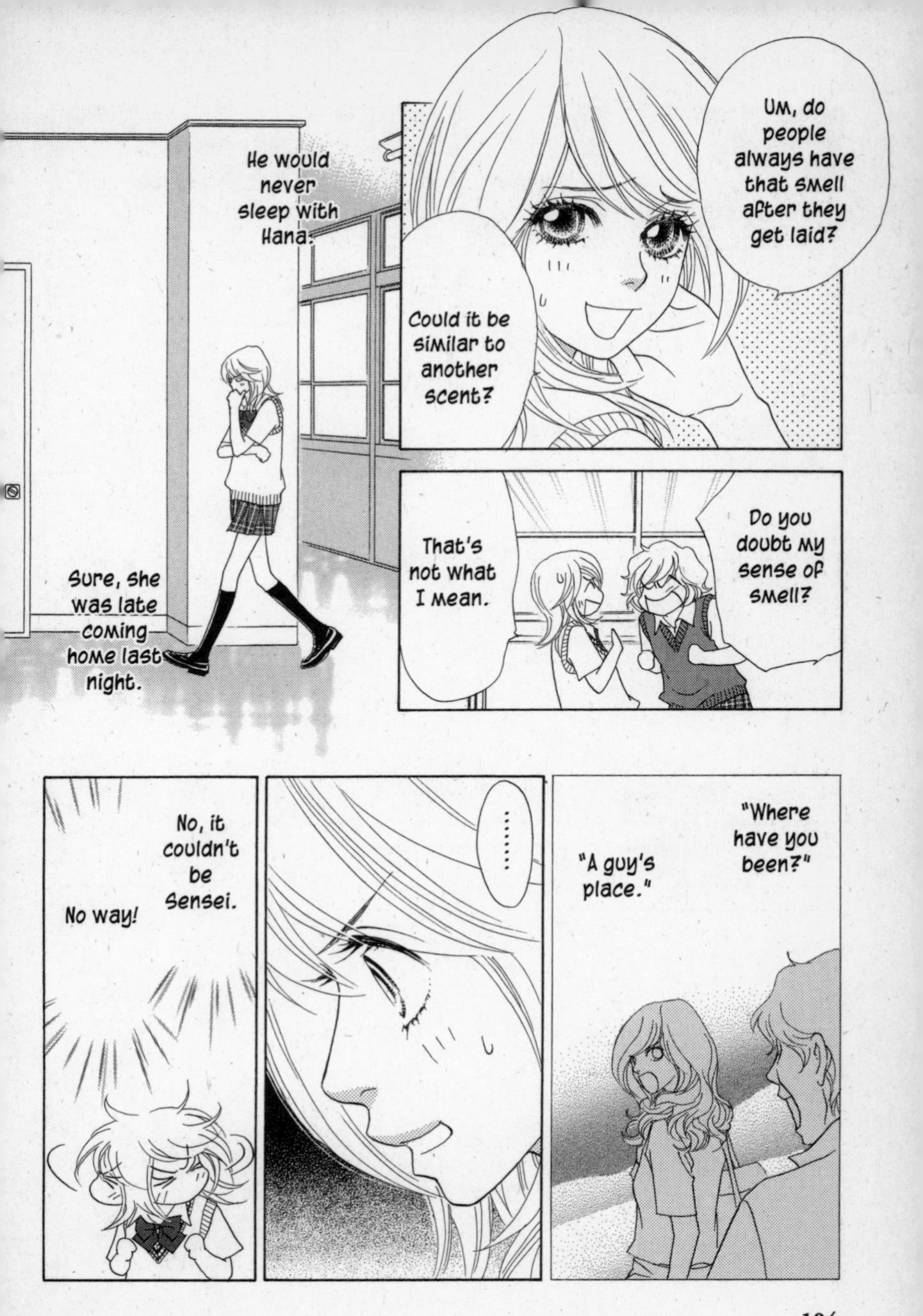

Um, do people always have that smell after they get laid?
Could it be similar to another scent?
Do you doubt my sense of smell?
That's not what I mean.
He would never sleep with Hana.
Sure, she was late coming home last night.
"Where have you been?"
"A guy's place."
......
No, it couldn't be Sensei.
No way!

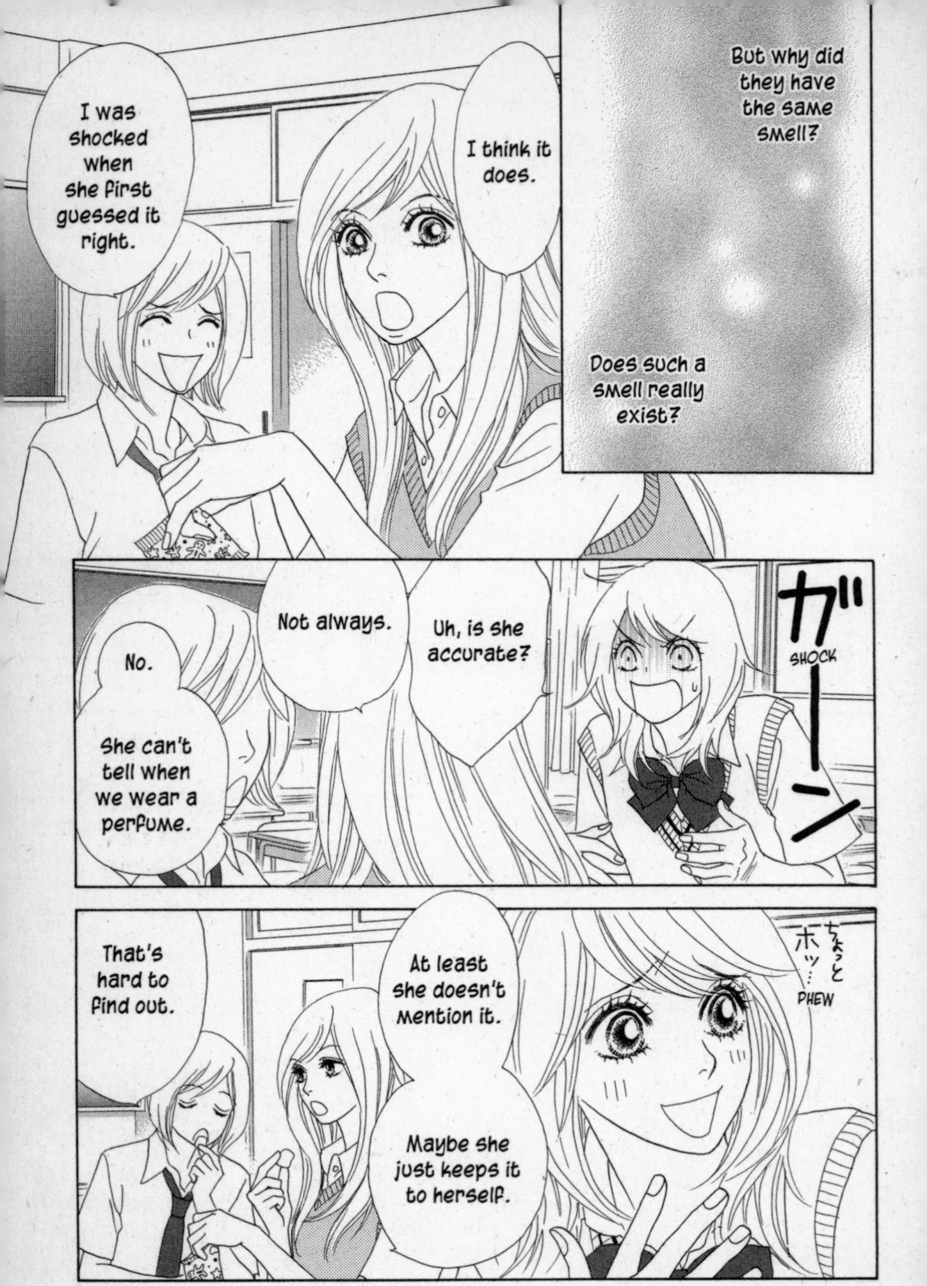
But why did they have the same smell?
Does such a smell really exist?
I think it does.
I was shocked when she first guessed it right.
ガーン
SHOCK
Uh, is she accurate?
Not always.
No.
She can't tell when we wear a perfume.
ちょっとホッ…
PHEW
At least she doesn't mention it.
Maybe she just keeps it to herself.
That's hard to find out.

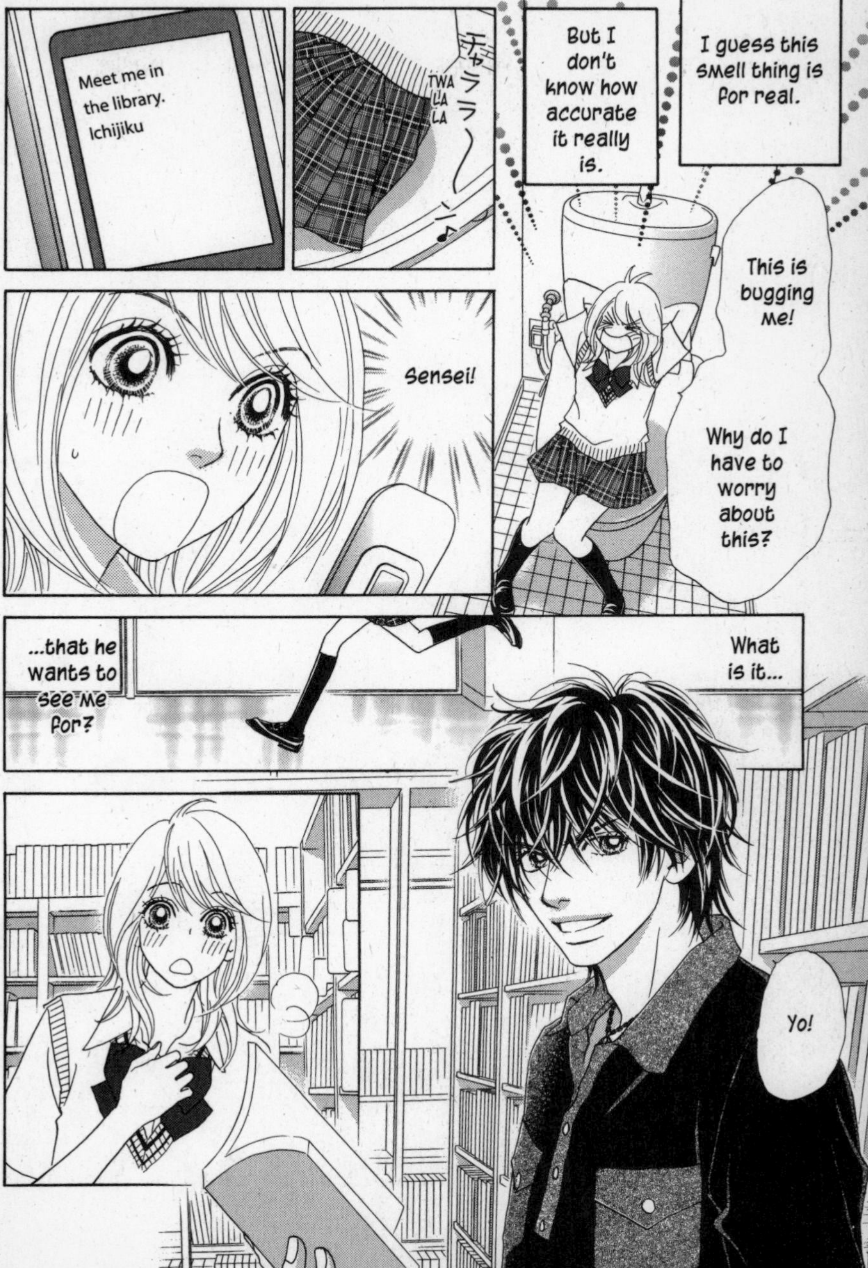
I guess this smell thing is for real.
But I don't know how accurate it really is.
This is bugging me!
Why do I have to worry about this?
チャラ〜♪
TWA LA LA
Meet me in the library.
Ichijiku
Sensei!
What is it...
...that he wants to see me for?
Yo!

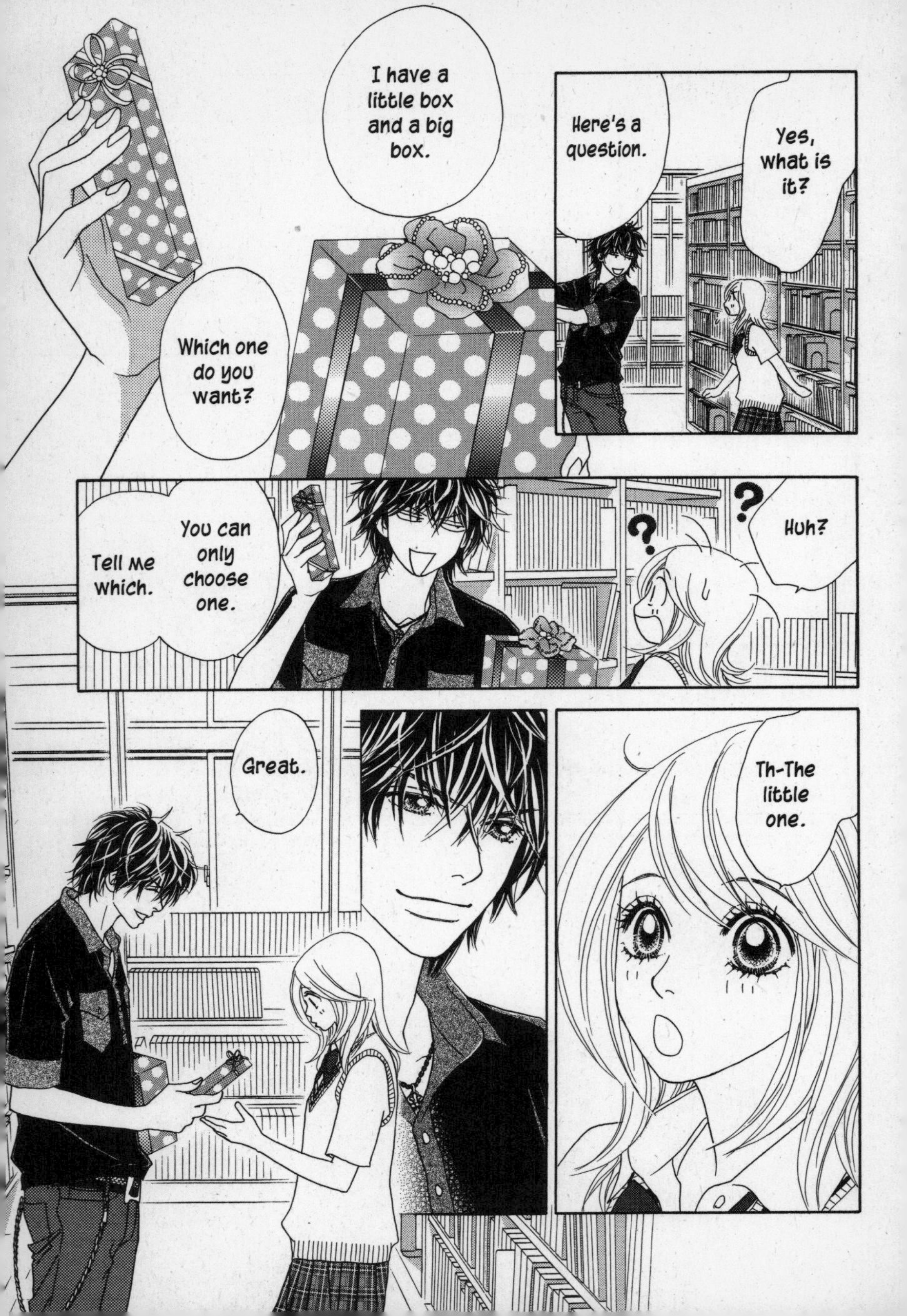

Here's a question.
Yes, what is it?
I have a little box and a big box.
Which one do you want?
Huh?
You can only choose one.
Tell me which.
Th-The little one.
Great.

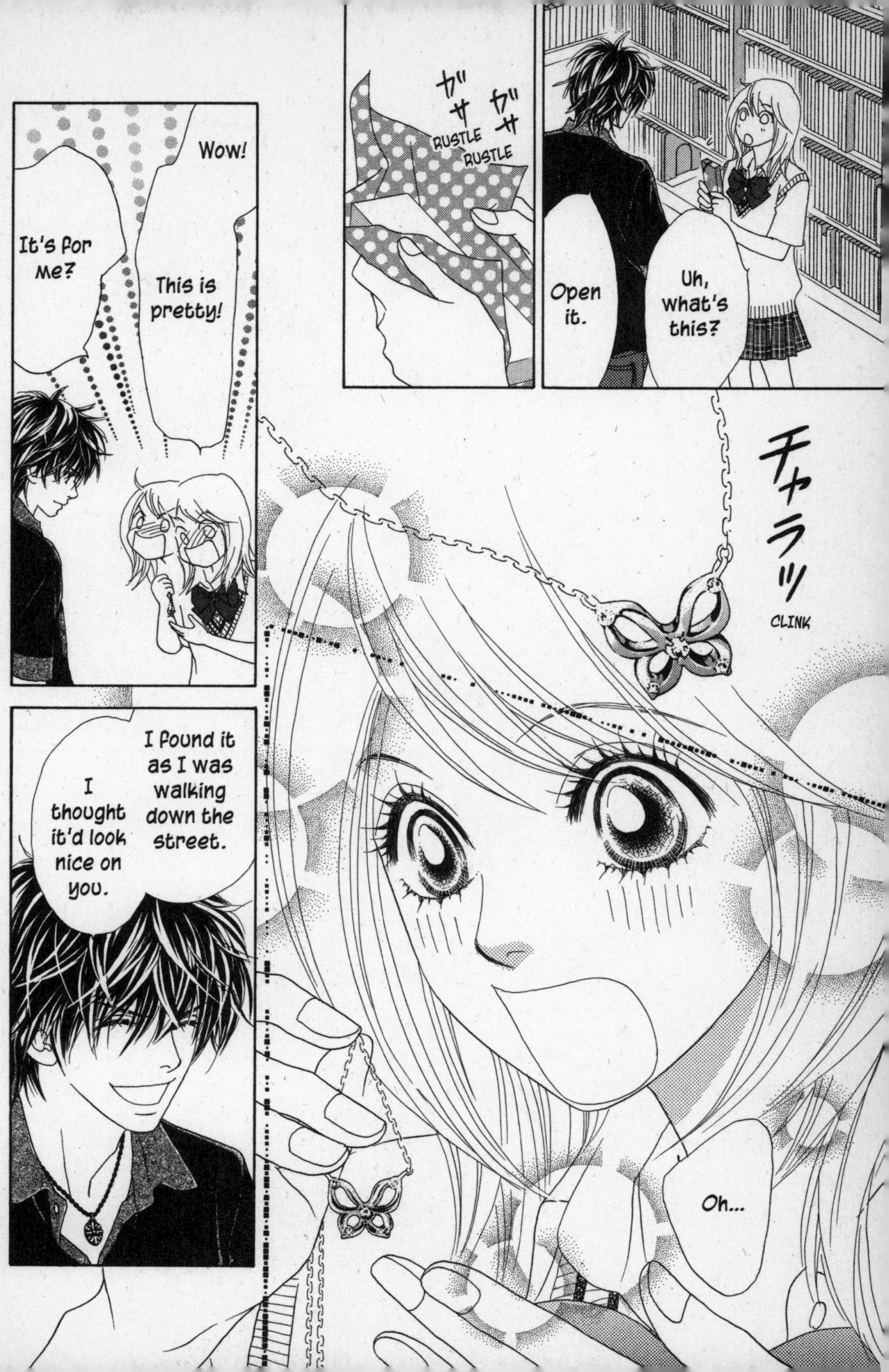
Uh, what's this?
Open it.
ガサ ガサ
RUSTLE RUSTLE
チャラッ
CLINK
Oh...
Wow!
This is pretty!
It's for me?
I found it as I was walking down the street.
I thought it'd look nice on you.

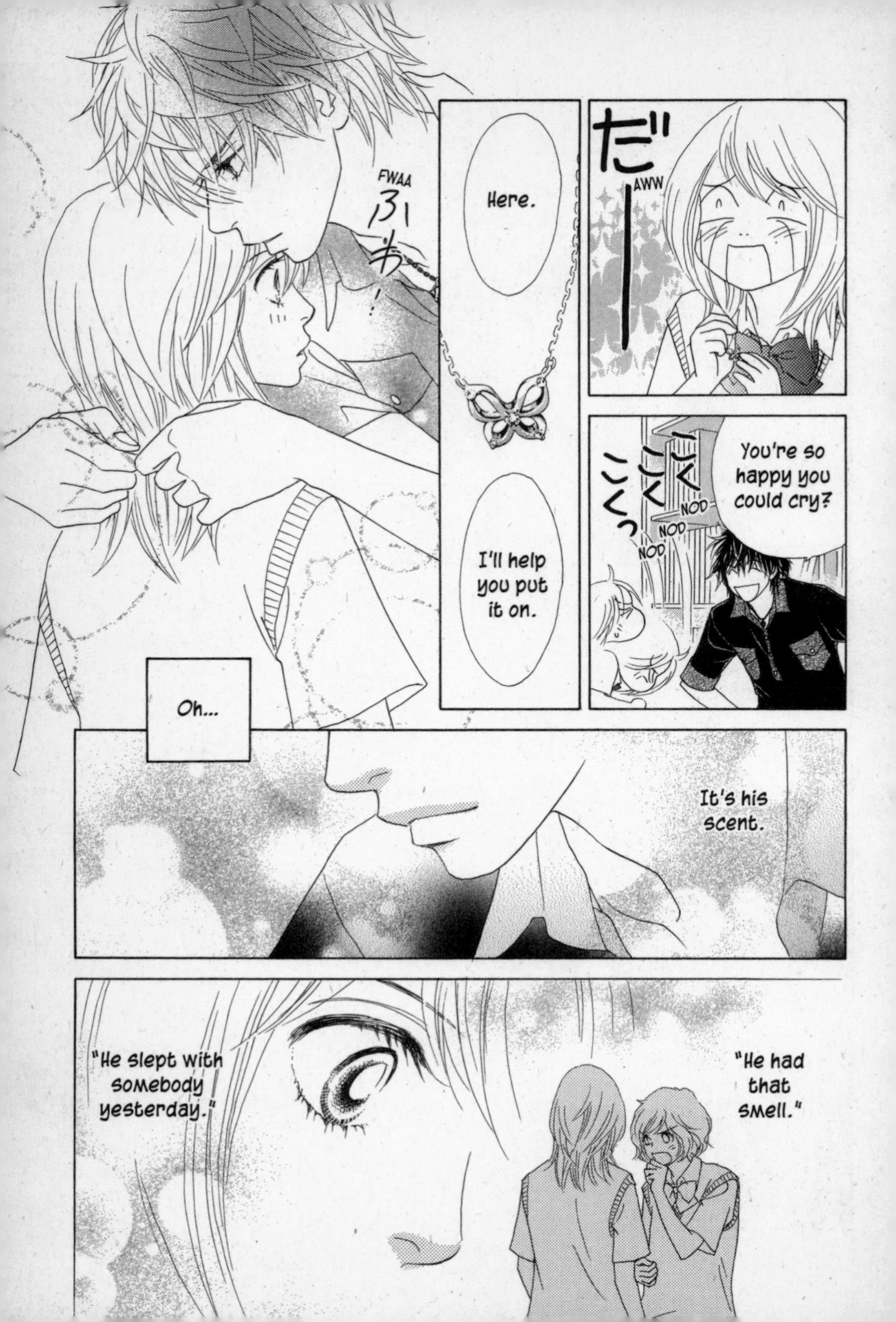
だー
AWW
You're so happy you could cry?
こくこくこくっ
NOD
NOD
NOD
Here.
I'll help you put it on.
FWAA
Oh...
It's his scent.
"He had that smell."
"He slept with somebody yesterday."

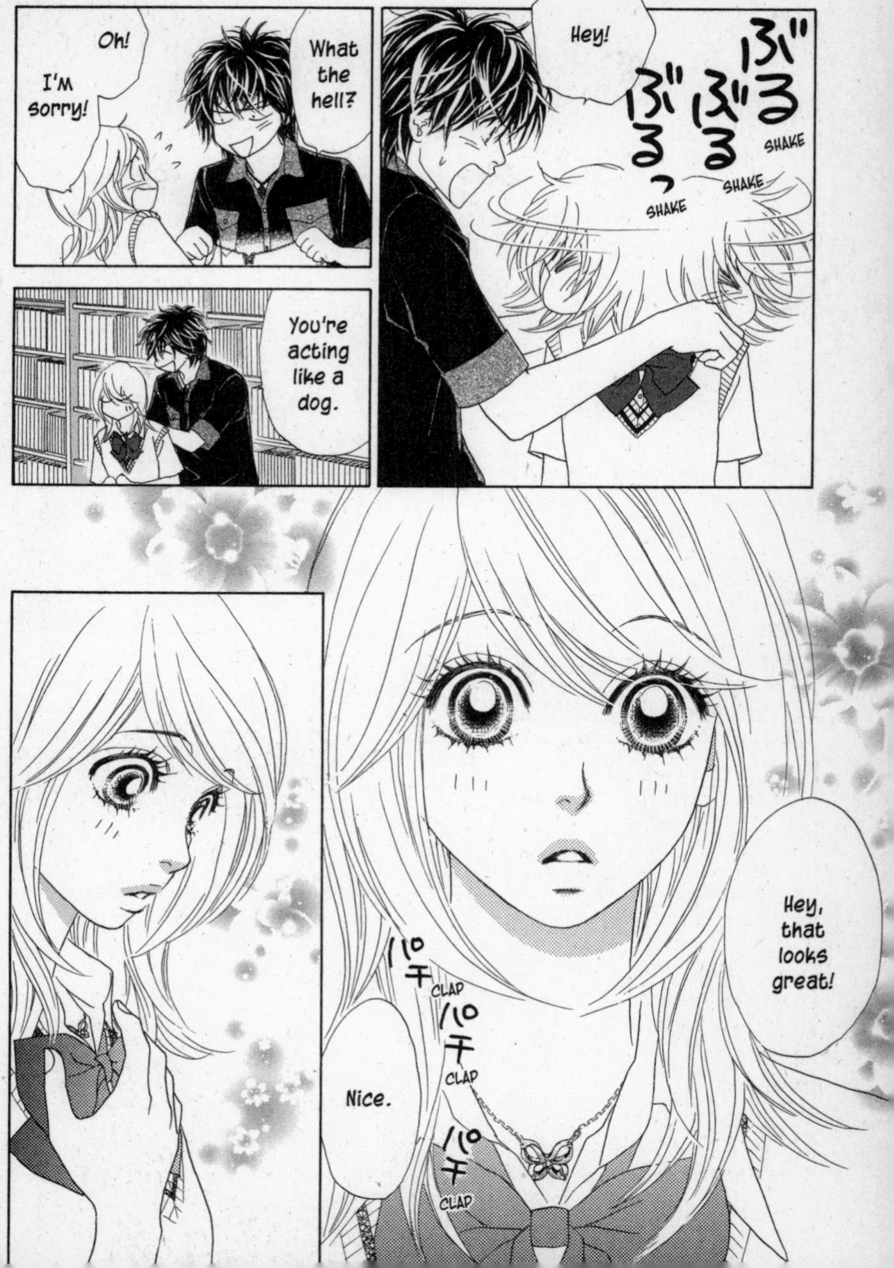
Hey!
ぶるぶるぶるっ
SHAKE
SHAKE
SHAKE
What the hell?
Oh!
I'M sorry!
You're acting like a dog.
Hey, that looks great!
パチ
CLAP
パチ
CLAP
パチ
CLAP
Nice.

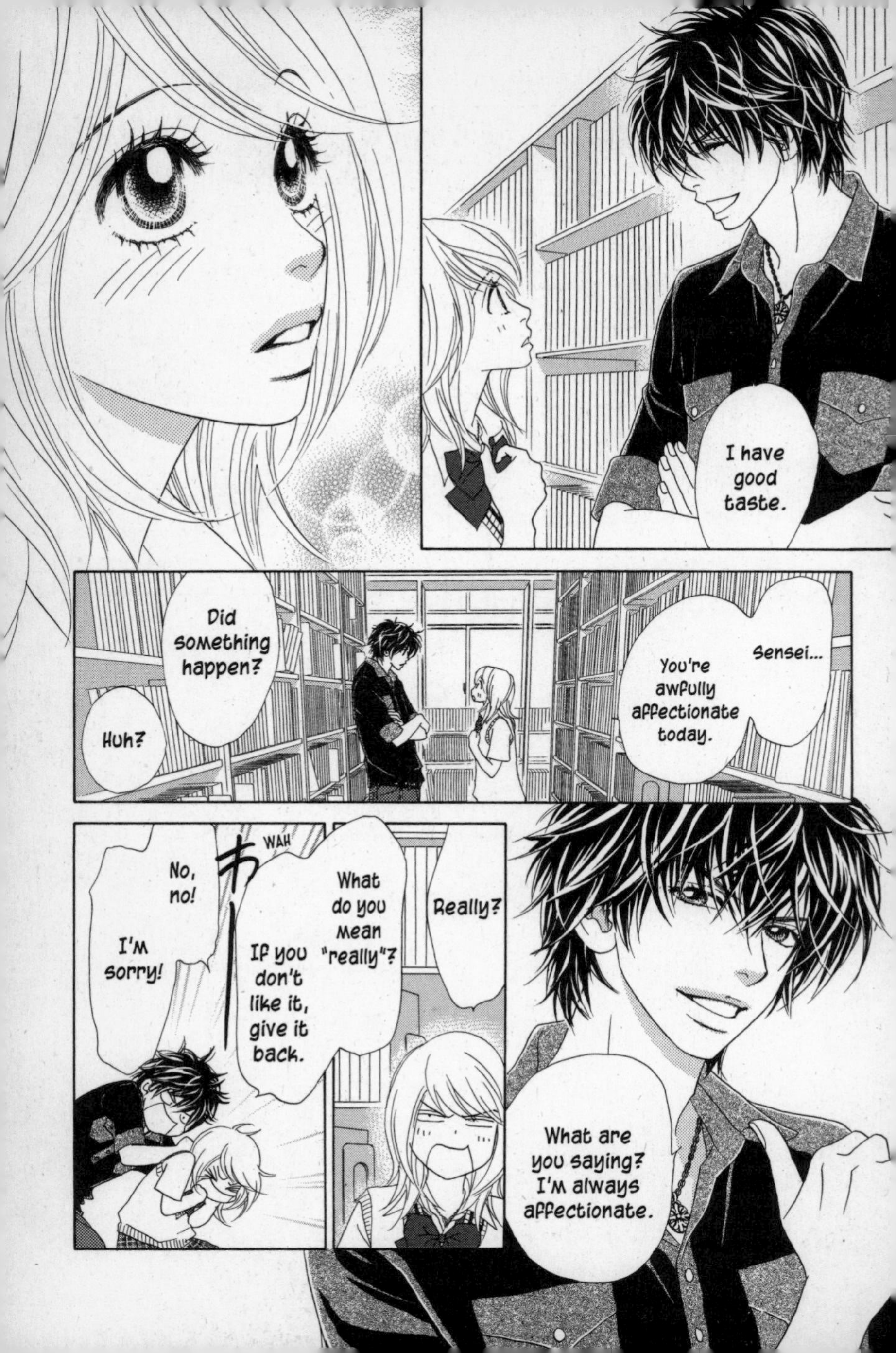
I have good taste.
Sensei...
You're awfully affectionate today.
Did something happen?
Huh?
What are you saying? I'm always affectionate.
Really?
What do you mean "really"?
If you don't like it, give it back.
WAH
No, no!
I'm sorry!

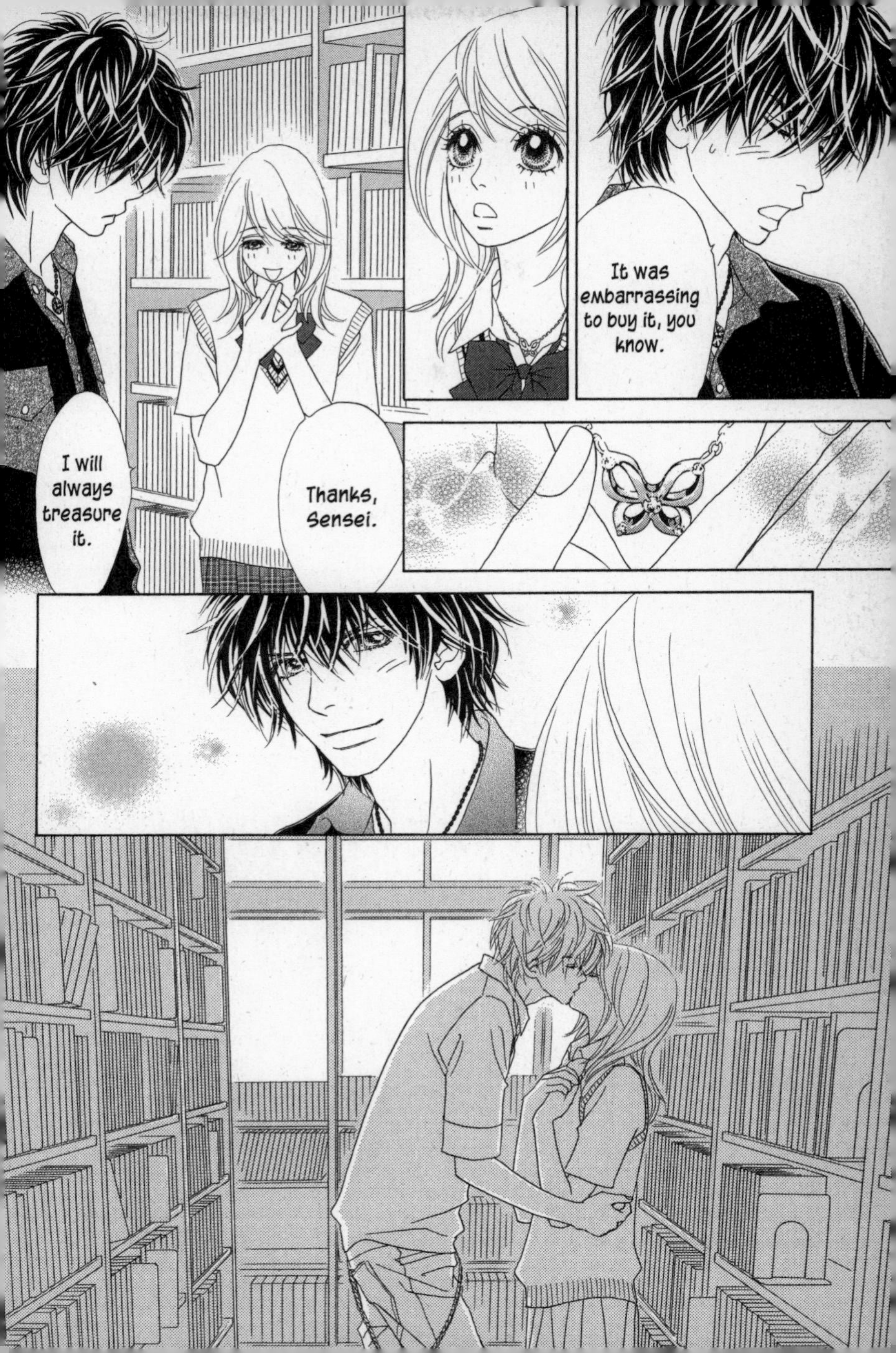
It was embarrassing to buy it, you know.
Thanks, Sensei.
I will always treasure it.

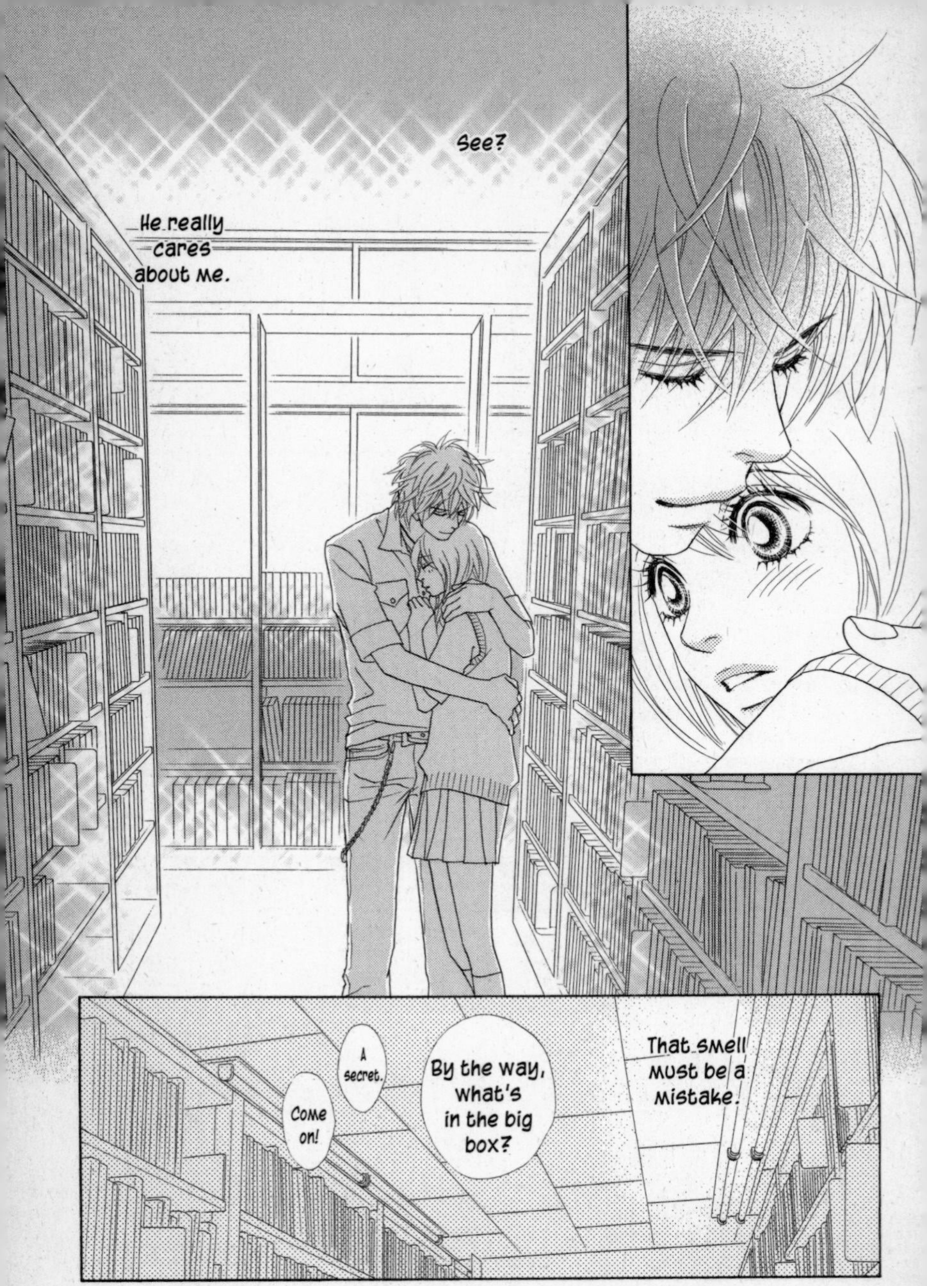
See?
He really cares about me.
That smell must be a mistake.
By the way, what's in the big box?
A secret.
Come on!

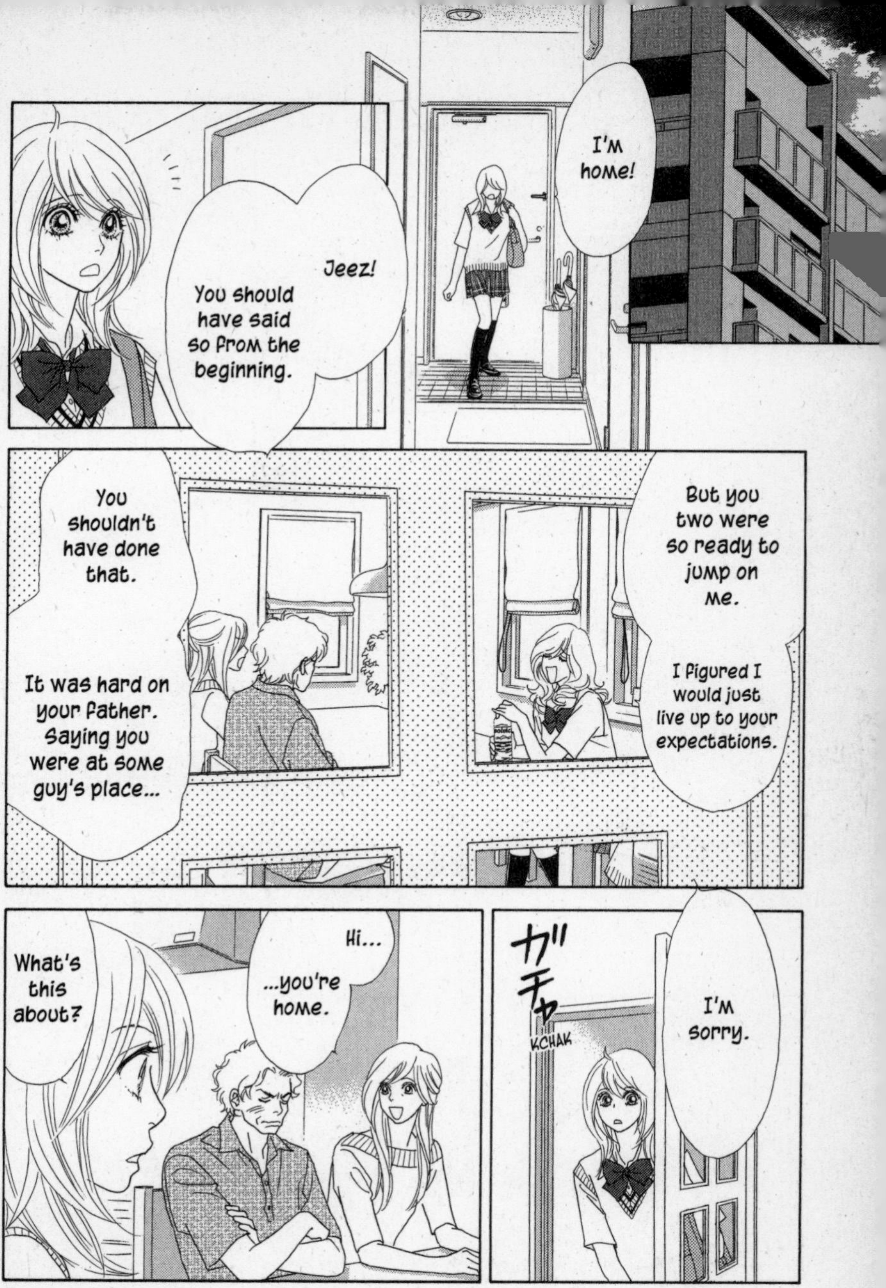
I'm home!
Jeez!
You should have said so from the beginning.
But you two were so ready to jump on me.
I figured I would just live up to your expectations.
You shouldn't have done that.
It was hard on your father. Saying you were at some guy's place...
ガチャ
KCHAK
I'm sorry.
Hi...
...you're home.
What's this about?

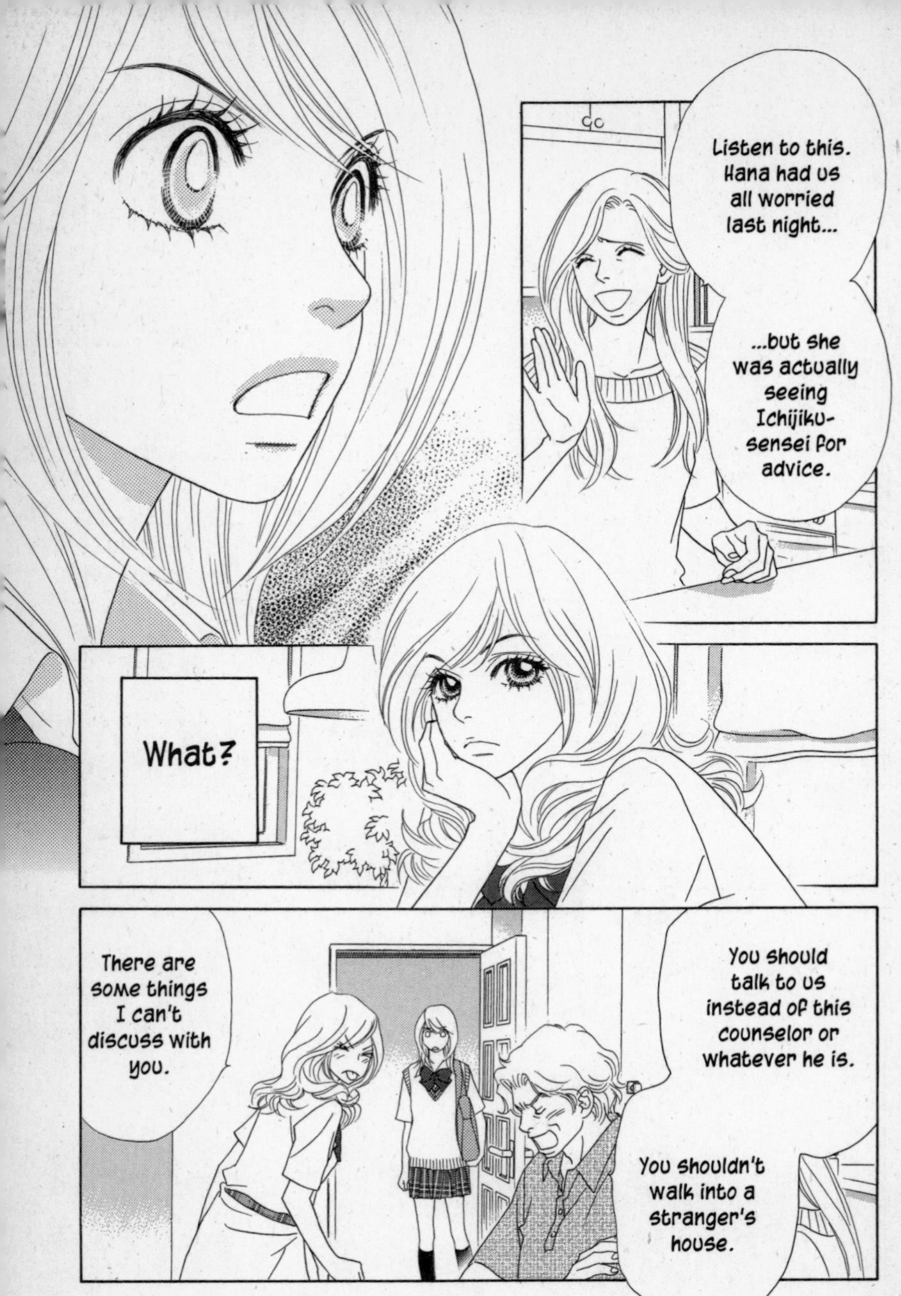
Listen to this. Hana had us all worried last night...
...but she was actually seeing Ichijiku-sensei for advice.
What?
You should talk to us instead of this counselor or whatever he is.
You shouldn't walk into a stranger's house.
There are some things I can't discuss with you.

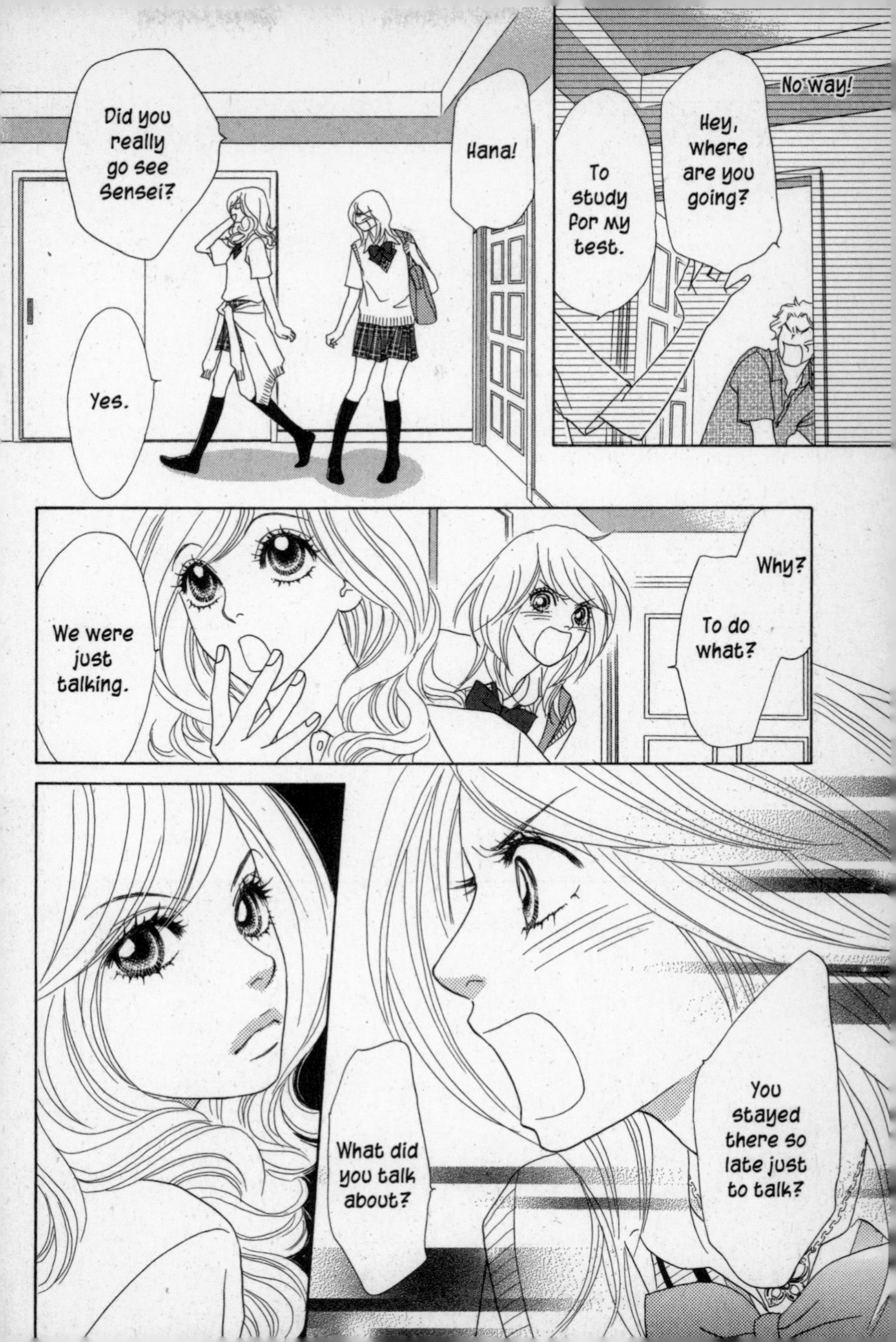
No way!
Hey, where are you going?
To study for my test.
Hana!
Did you really go see Sensei?
Yes.
Why?
To do what?
We were just talking.
You stayed there so late just to talk?
What did you talk about?

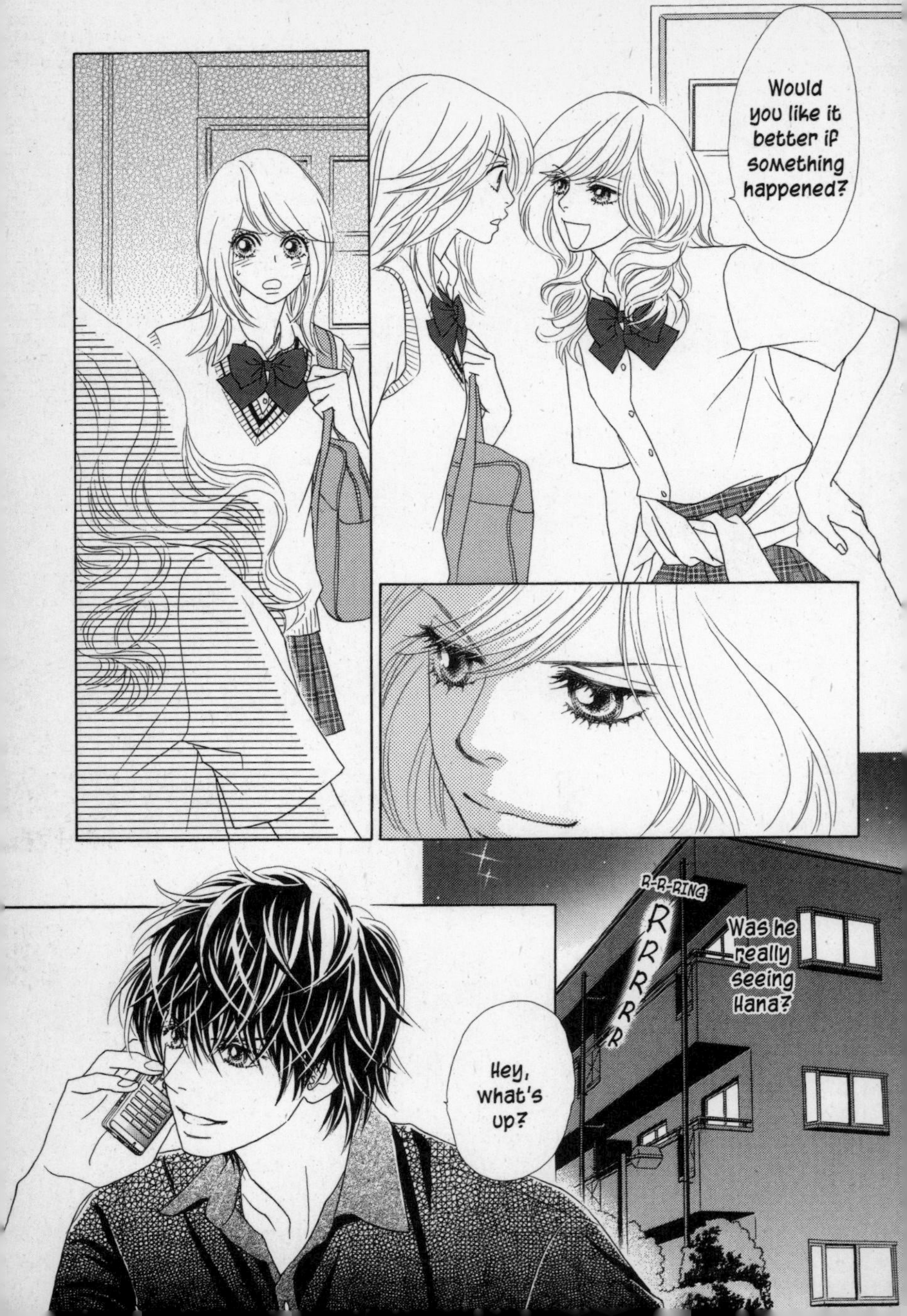
Would you like it better if something happened?
R-R-RING
RRRRR
Was he really seeing Hana?
Hey, what's up?

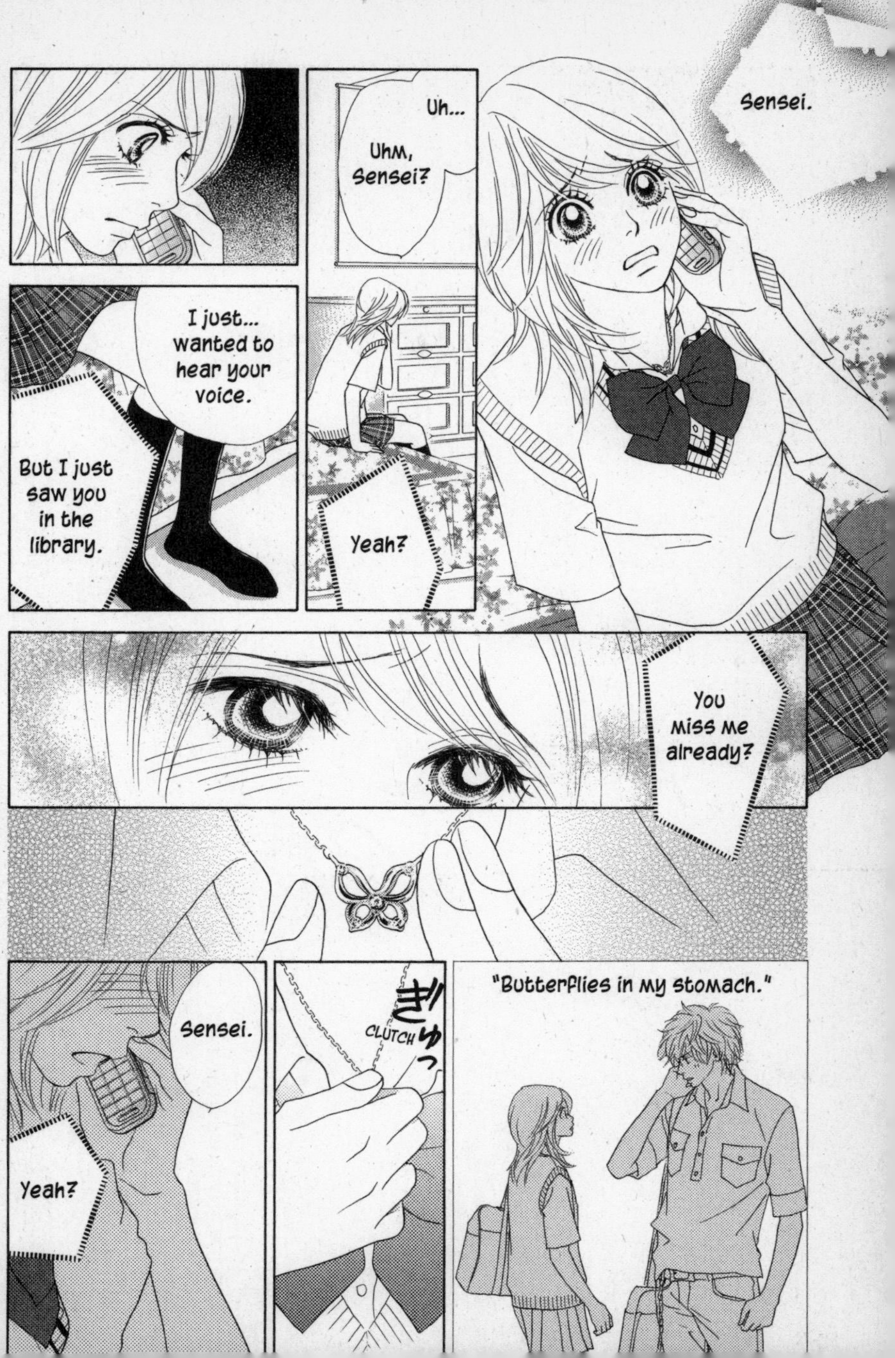
Sensei.
Uh...
Uhm, Sensei?
Yeah?
I just... wanted to hear your voice.
But I just saw you in the library.
You miss me already?
"Butterflies in my stomach."
ぎゅっ
CLUTCH
Sensei.
Yeah?

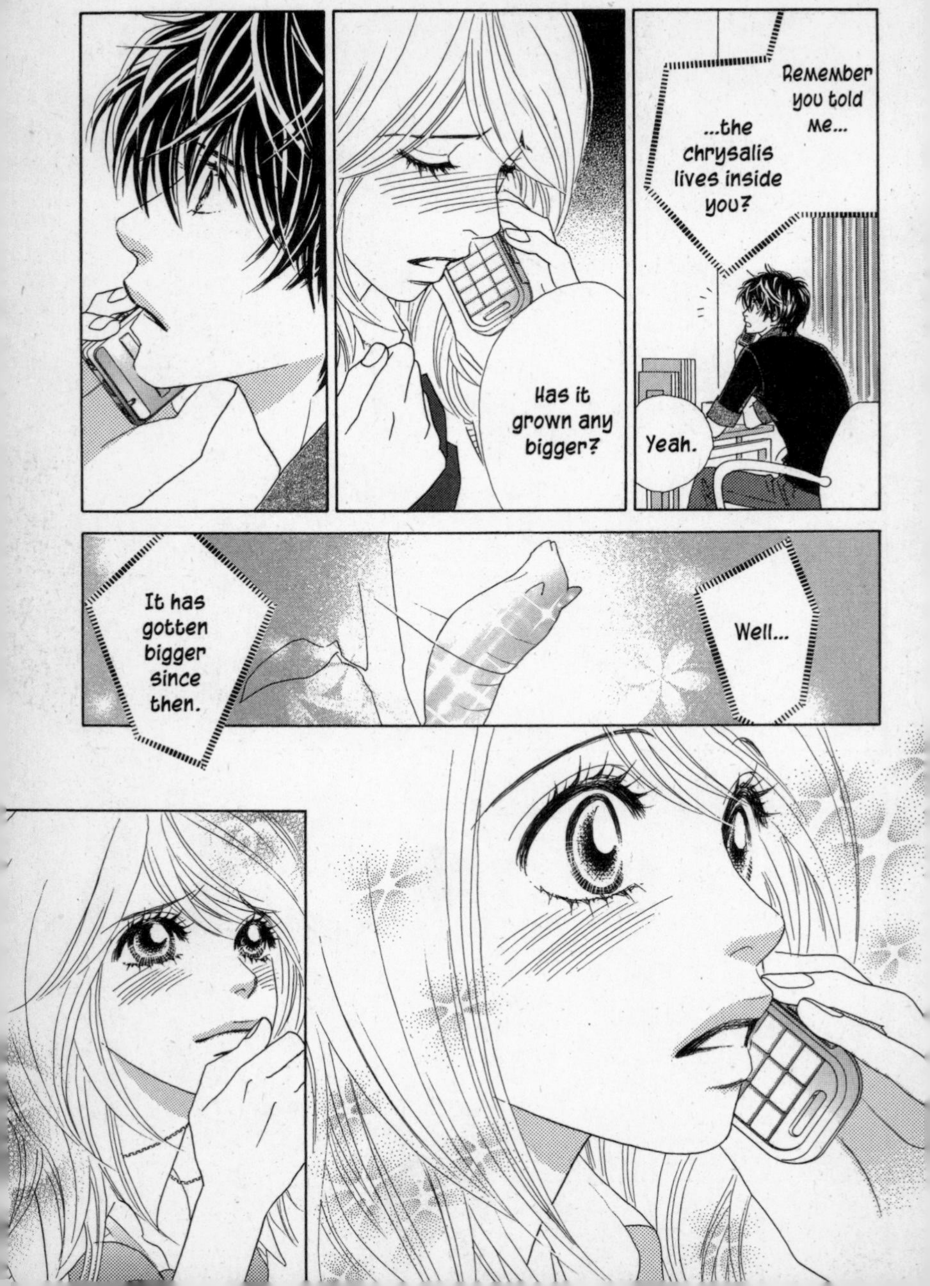
Remember you told me...
...the chrysalis lives inside you?
Yeah.
Has it grown any bigger?
Well...
It has gotten bigger since then.

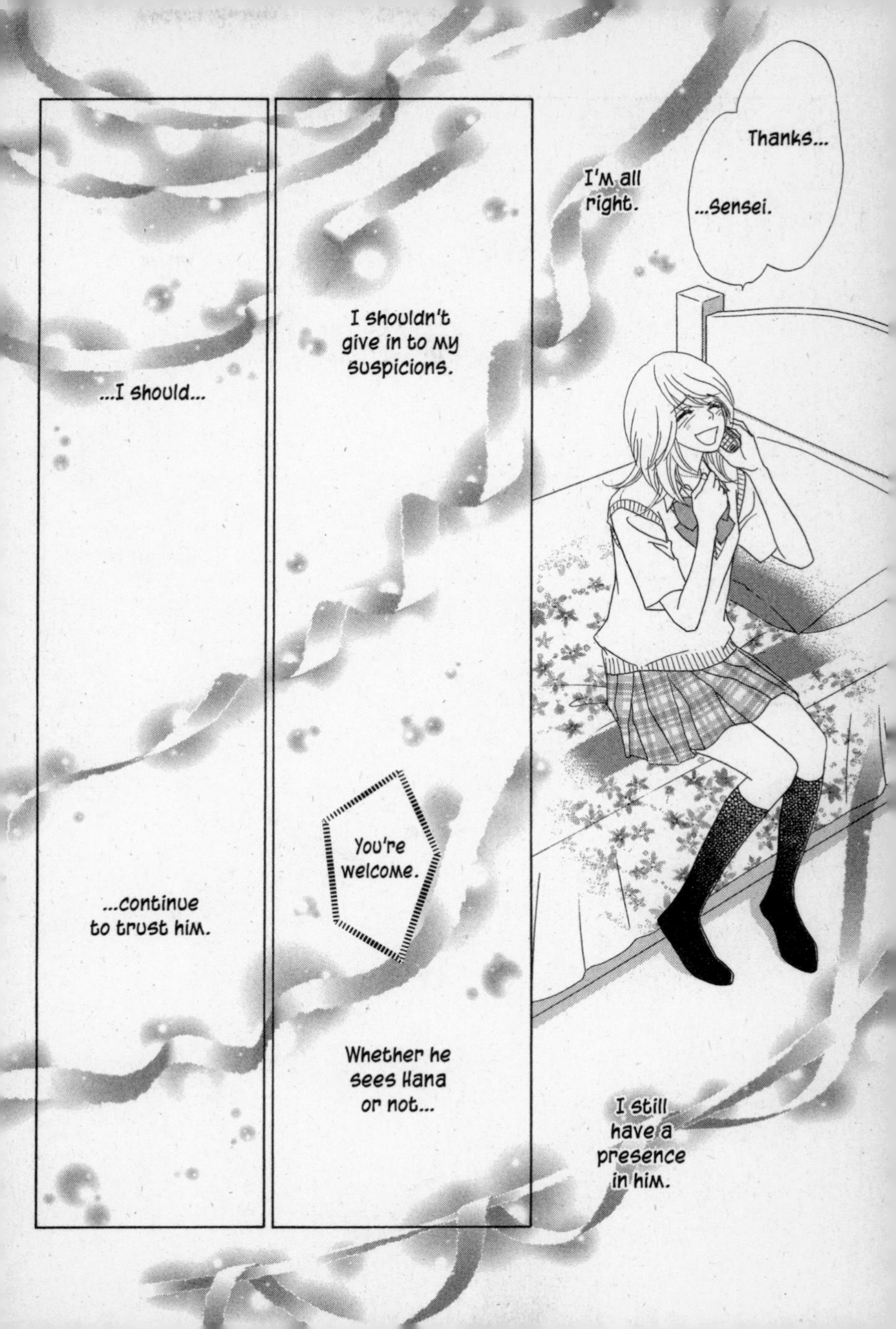
Thanks... ...Sensei.
I'm all right.
I still have a presence in him.
I shouldn't give in to my suspicions.
You're welcome.
Whether he sees Hana or not...
...I should...
...continue to trust him.

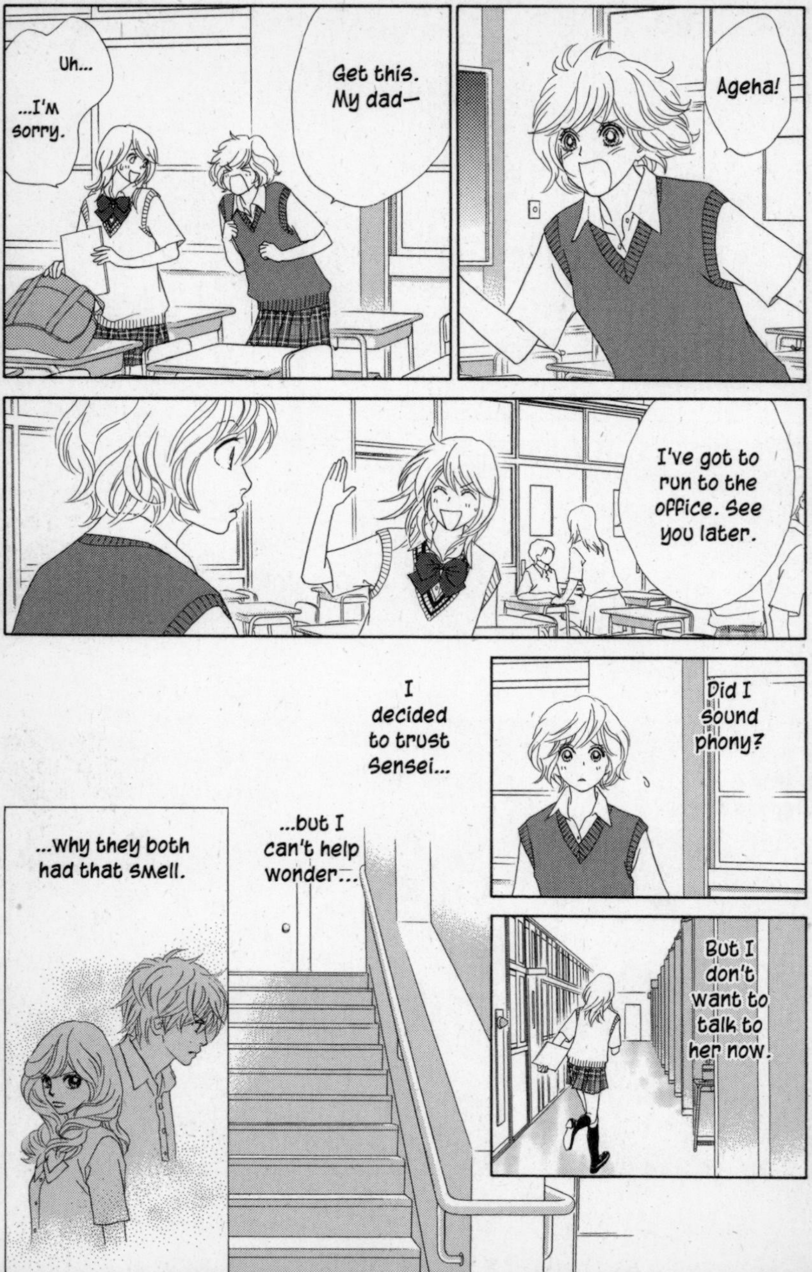
Ageha!
Get this. My dad—
Uh...
...I'm sorry.
I've got to run to the office. See you later.
Did I sound phony?
But I don't want to talk to her now.
I decided to trust Sensei...
...but I can't help wonder...
...why they both had that smell.

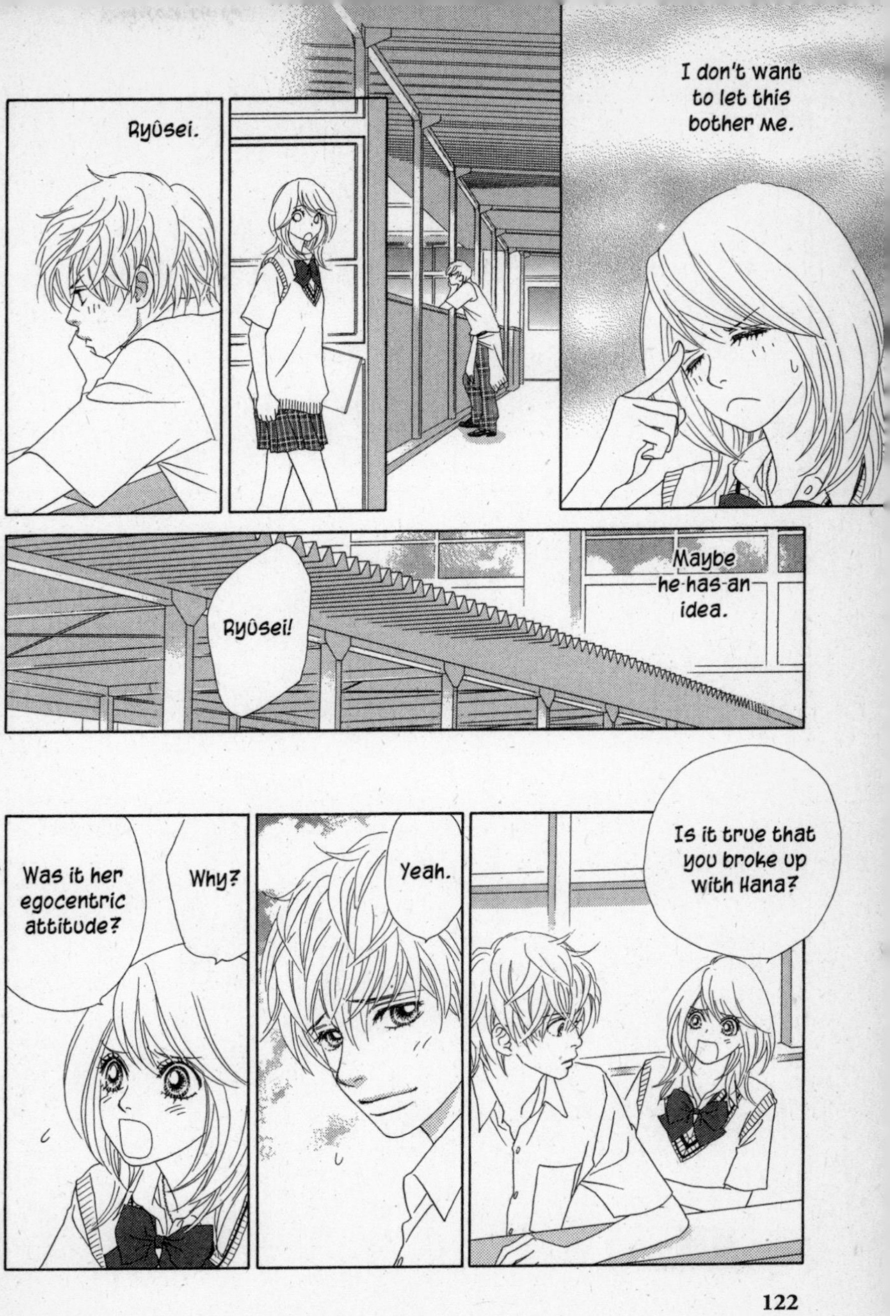
I don't want to let this bother me.
Ryûsei.
Maybe he has an idea.
Ryûsei!
Is it true that you broke up with Hana?
Yeah.
Why?
Was it her egocentric attitude?

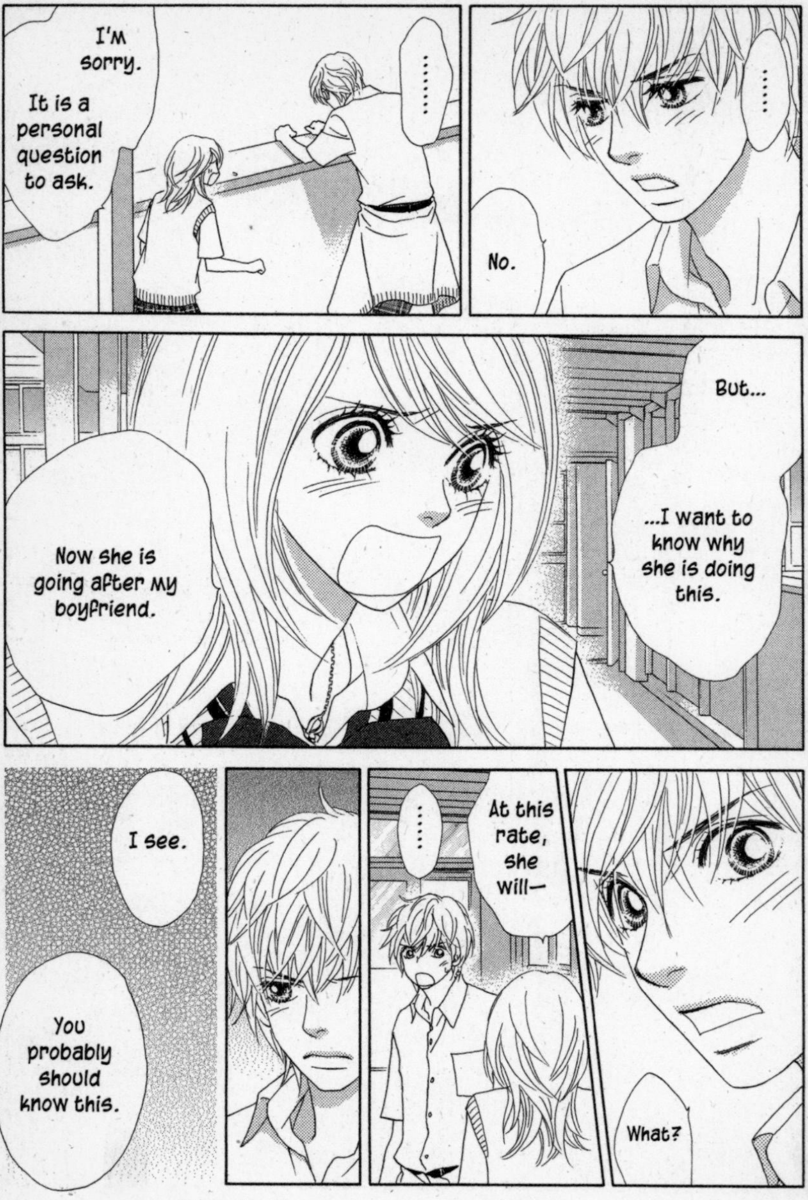
……
No.
……
I'm sorry.
It is a personal question to ask.
But...
...I want to know why she is doing this.
Now she is going after my boyfriend.
What?
At this rate, she will—
……
I see.
You probably should know this.

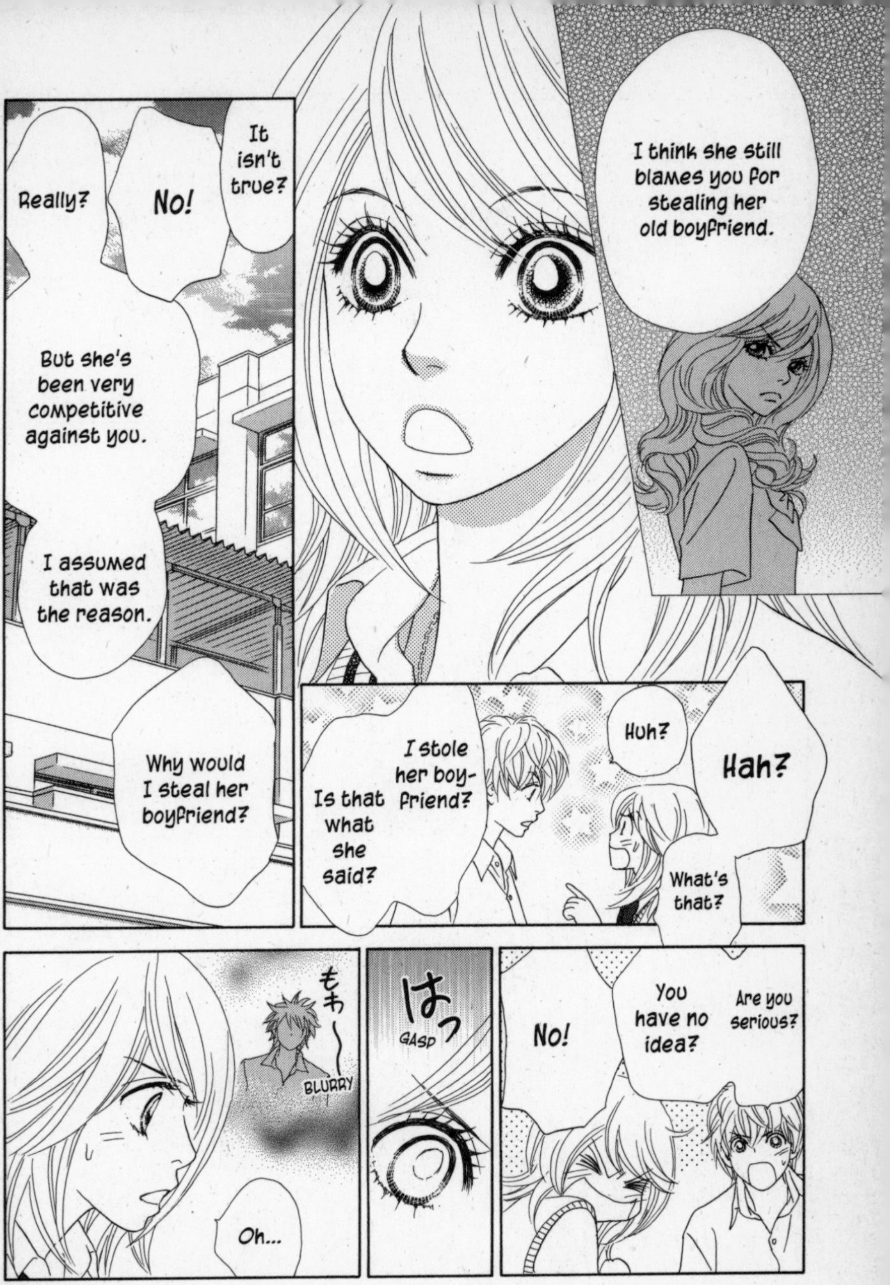
I think she still blames you for stealing her old boyfriend.
It isn't true?
No!
Really?
But she's been very competitive against you.
I assumed that was the reason.
Why would I steal her boyfriend?
I stole her boy-friend?
Is that what she said?
Huh?
Hah?
What's that?
Are you serious?
You have no idea?
No!
はっ
GASP
もわ~
BLURRY
Oh...

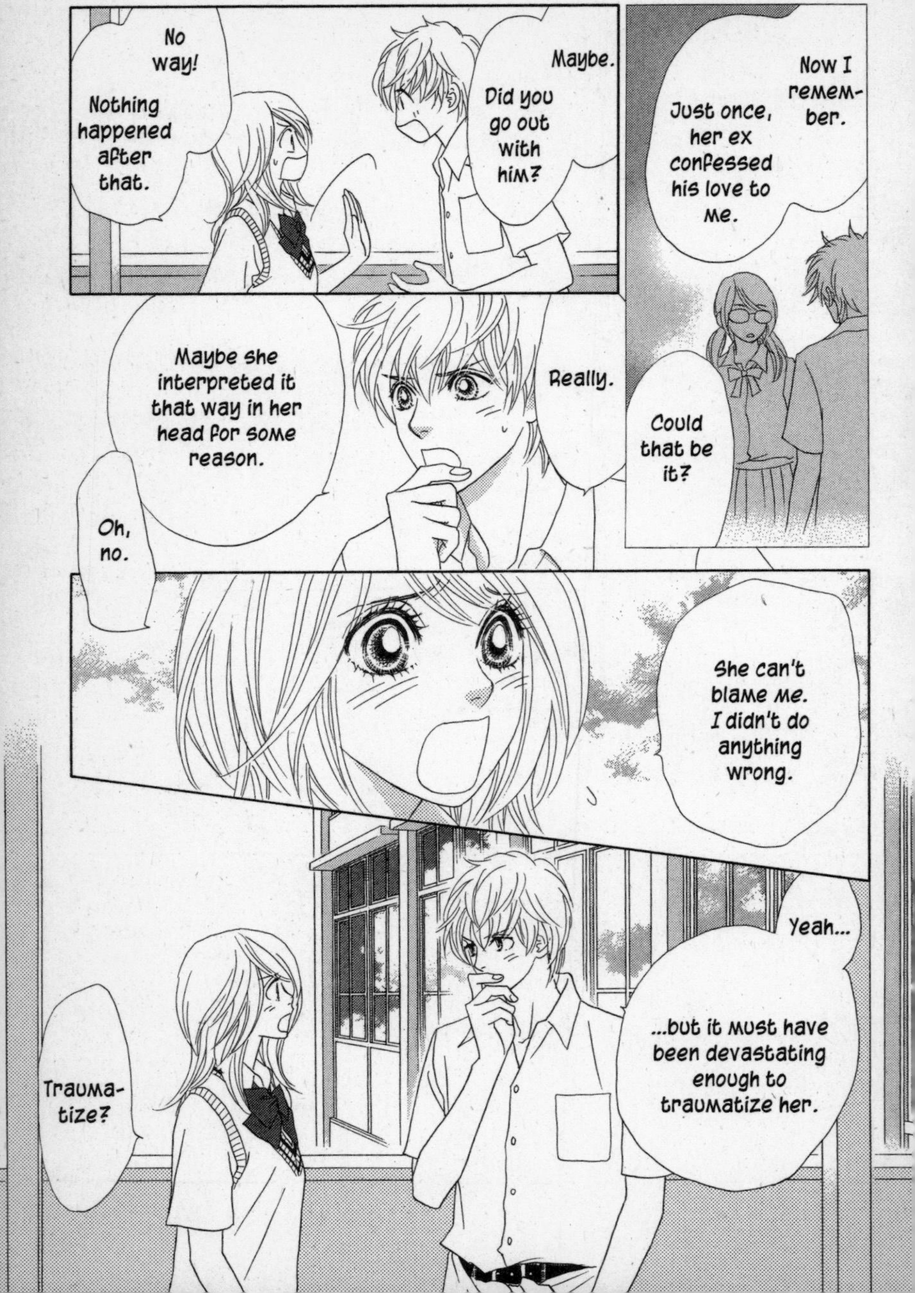
Now I remember.
Just once, her ex confessed his love to me.
Could that be it?
Maybe.
Did you go out with him?
No way!
Nothing happened after that.
Really.
Maybe she interpreted it that way in her head for some reason.
Oh, no.
She can't blame me. I didn't do anything wrong.
Yeah...
...but it must have been devastating enough to traumatize her.
Trauma-tize?

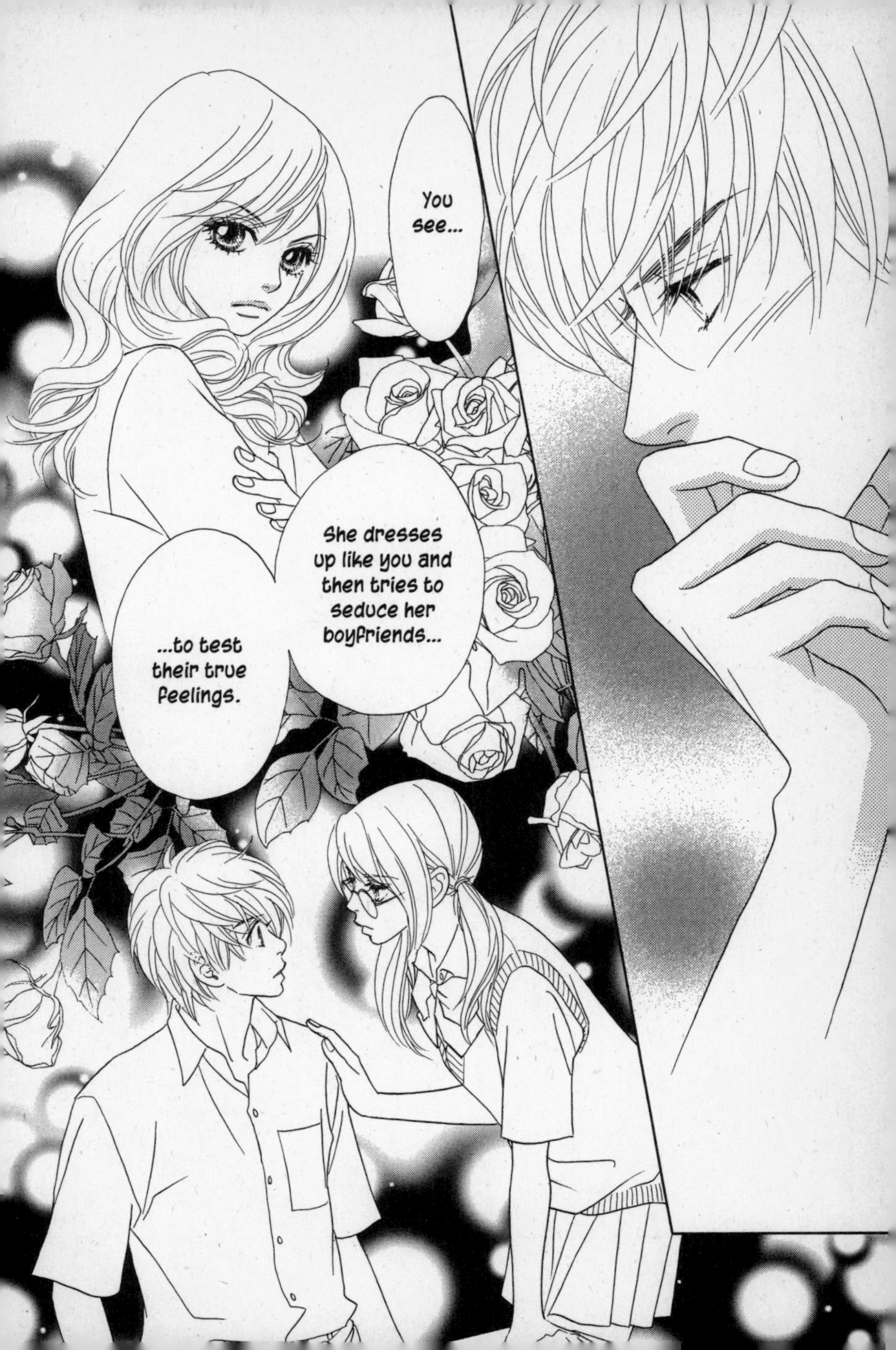
You see...
She dresses up like you and then tries to seduce her boyfriends...
...to test their true feelings.

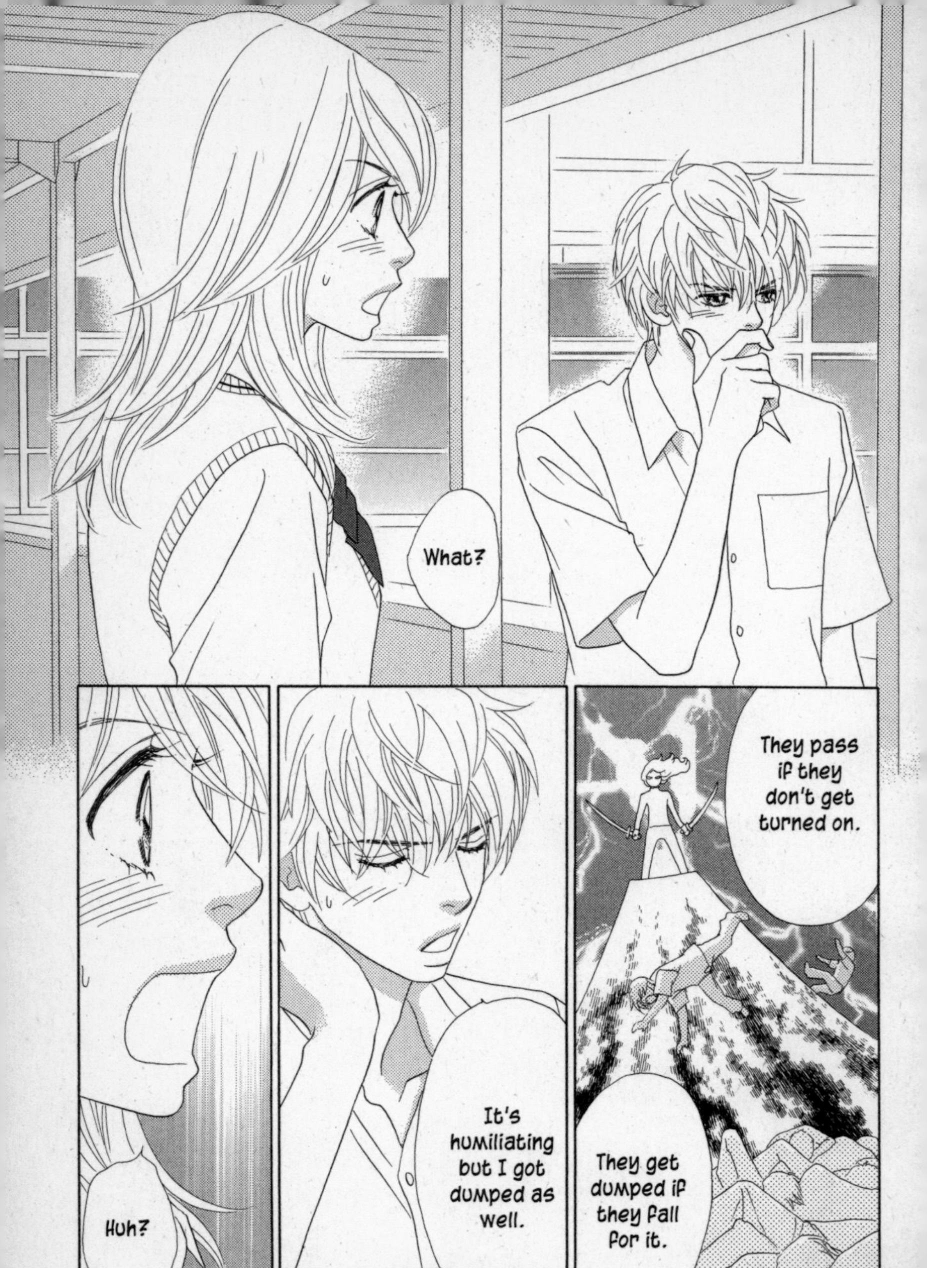
What?
They pass if they don't get turned on.
They get dumped if they fall for it.
It's humiliating but I got dumped as well.
Huh?

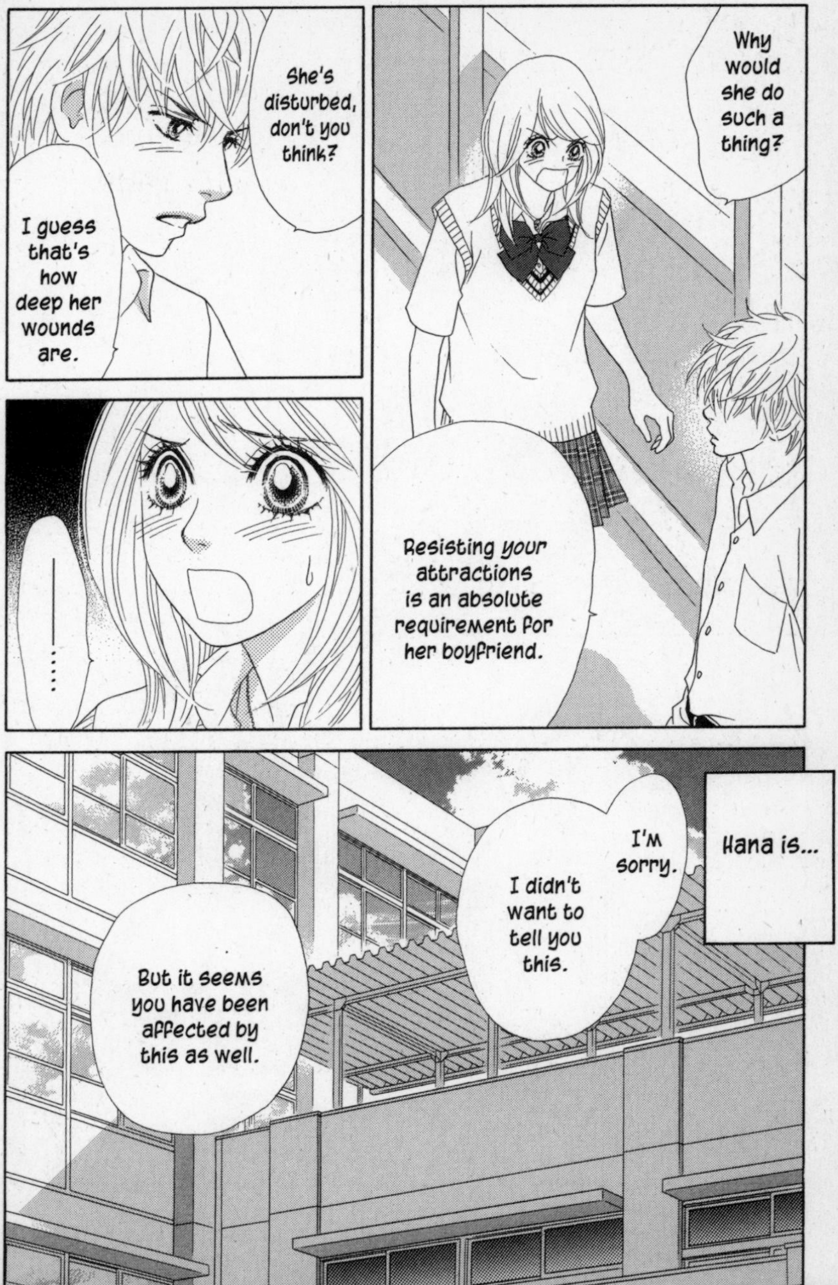
Why would she do such a thing?
Resisting your attractions is an absolute requirement for her boyfriend.
She's disturbed, don't you think?
I guess that's how deep her wounds are.
......
Hana is...
I'm sorry.
I didn't want to tell you this.
But it seems you have been affected by this as well.

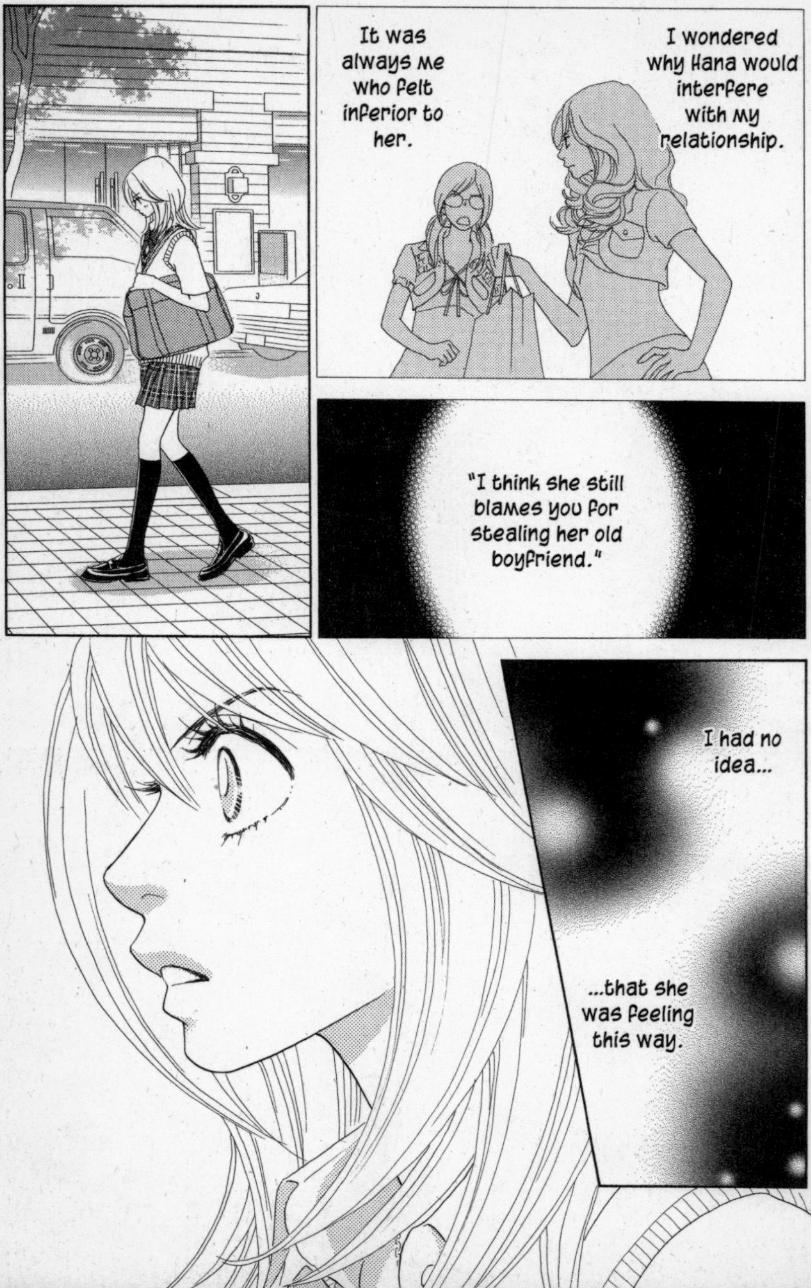
I wondered why Hana would interfere with my relationship.
It was always me who felt inferior to her.
"I think she still blames you for stealing her old boyfriend."
I had no idea...
...that she was feeling this way.

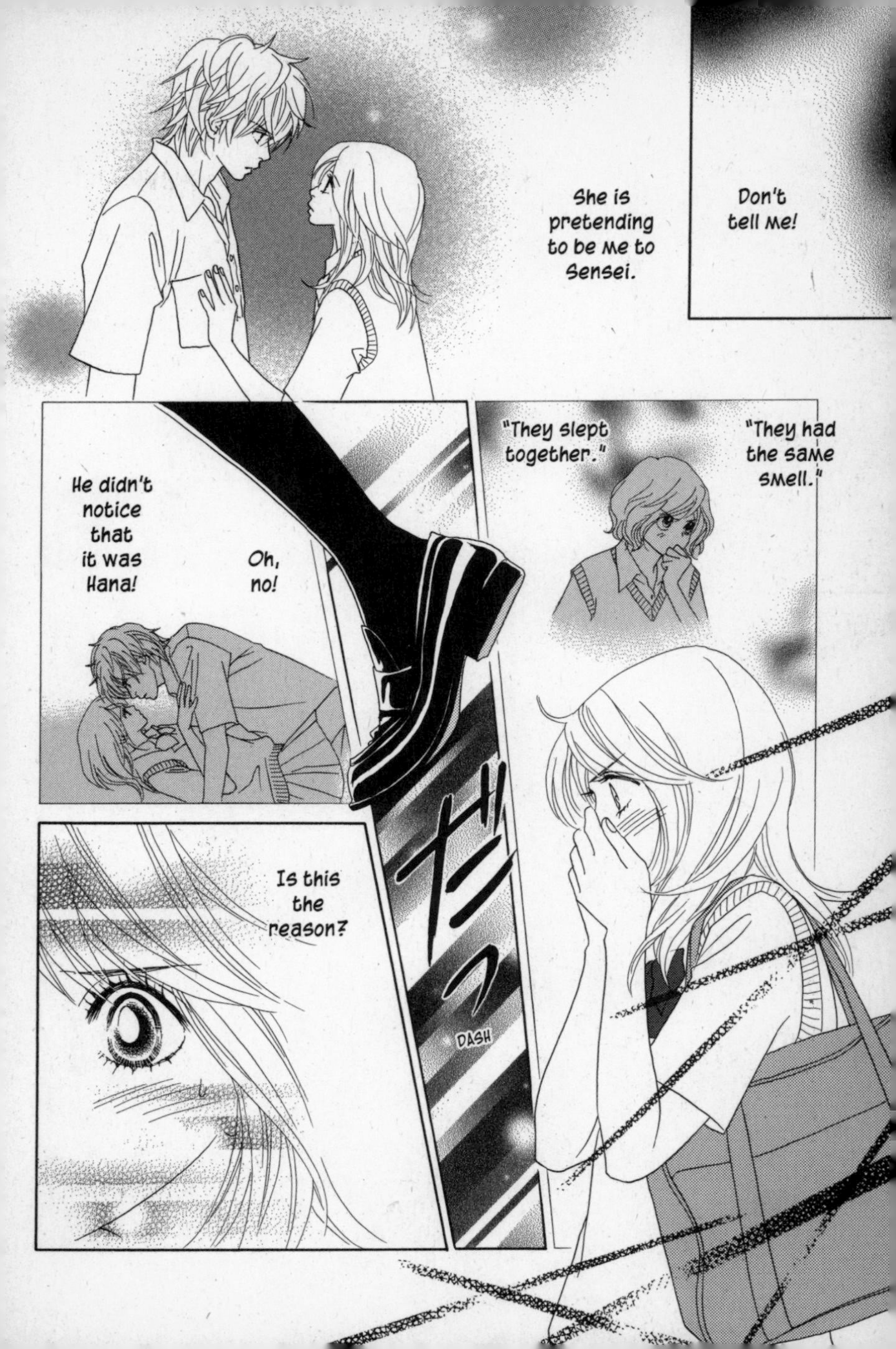
Don't tell me!
She is pretending to be me to Sensei.
"They had the same smell."
"They slept together."
DASH
Oh, no!
He didn't notice that it was Hana!
Is this the reason?

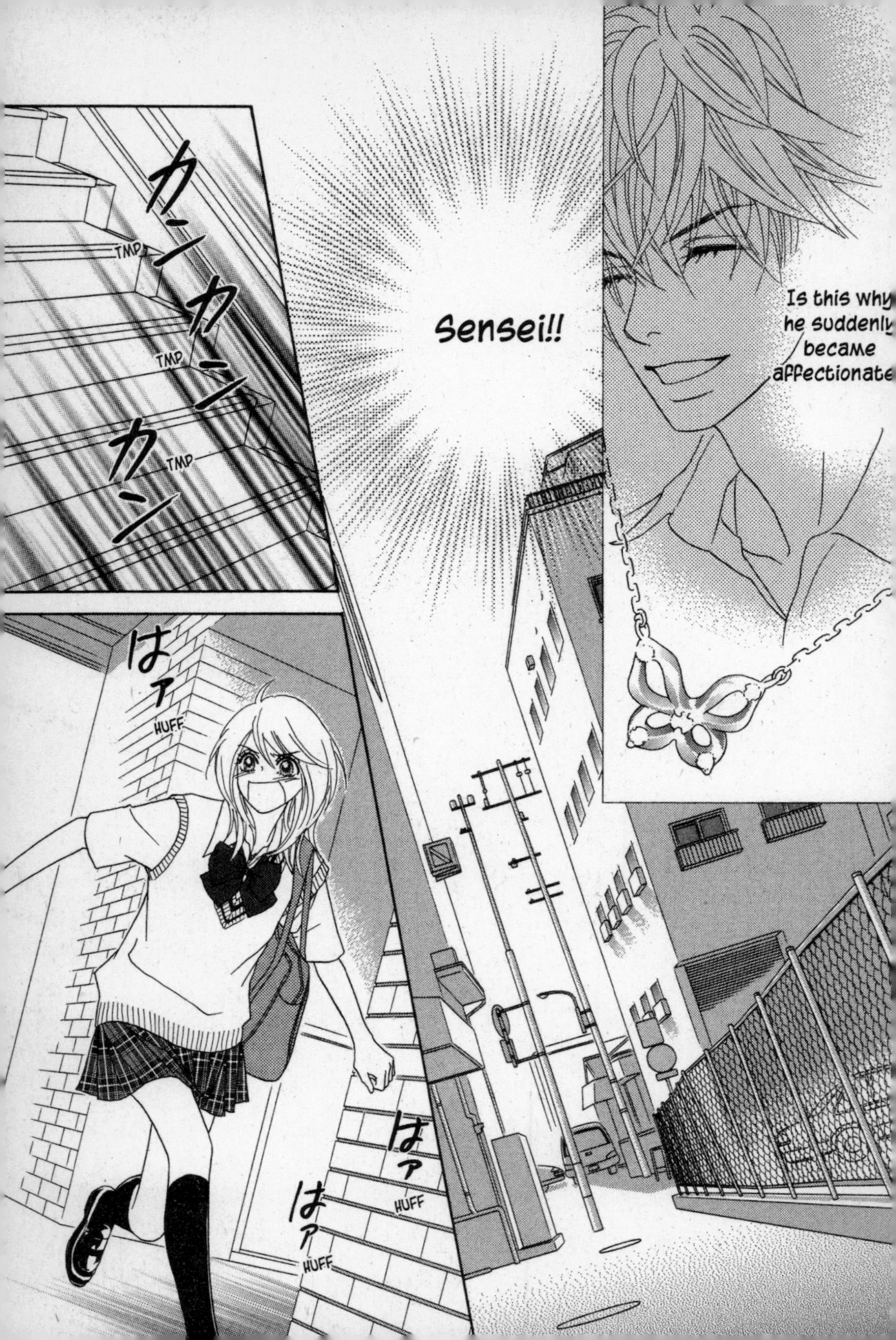
Is this why he suddenly became affectionate
Sensei!!
カーン TMP
カン TMP
カン TMP
はァ HUFF
はァ HUFF
はァ HUFF

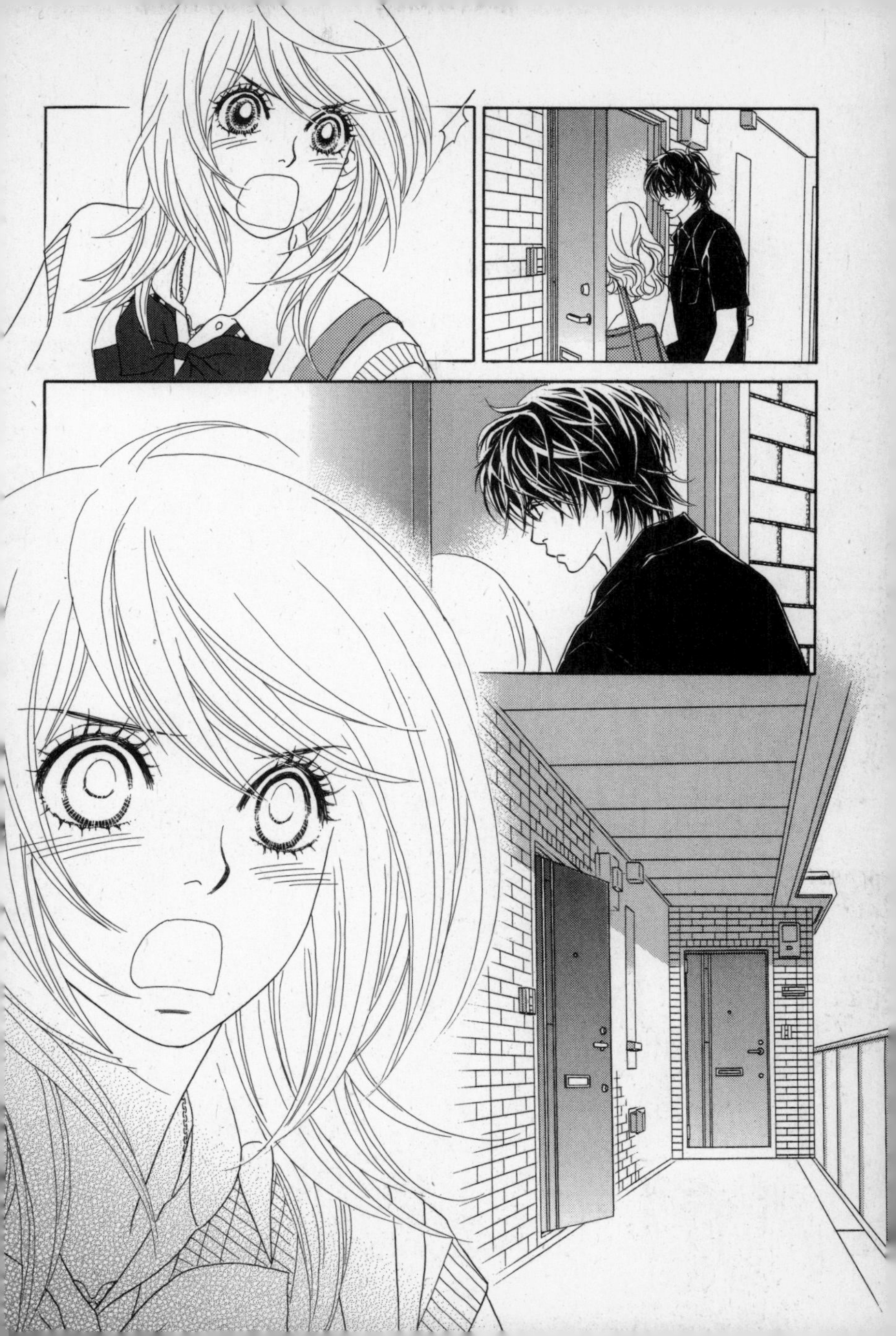

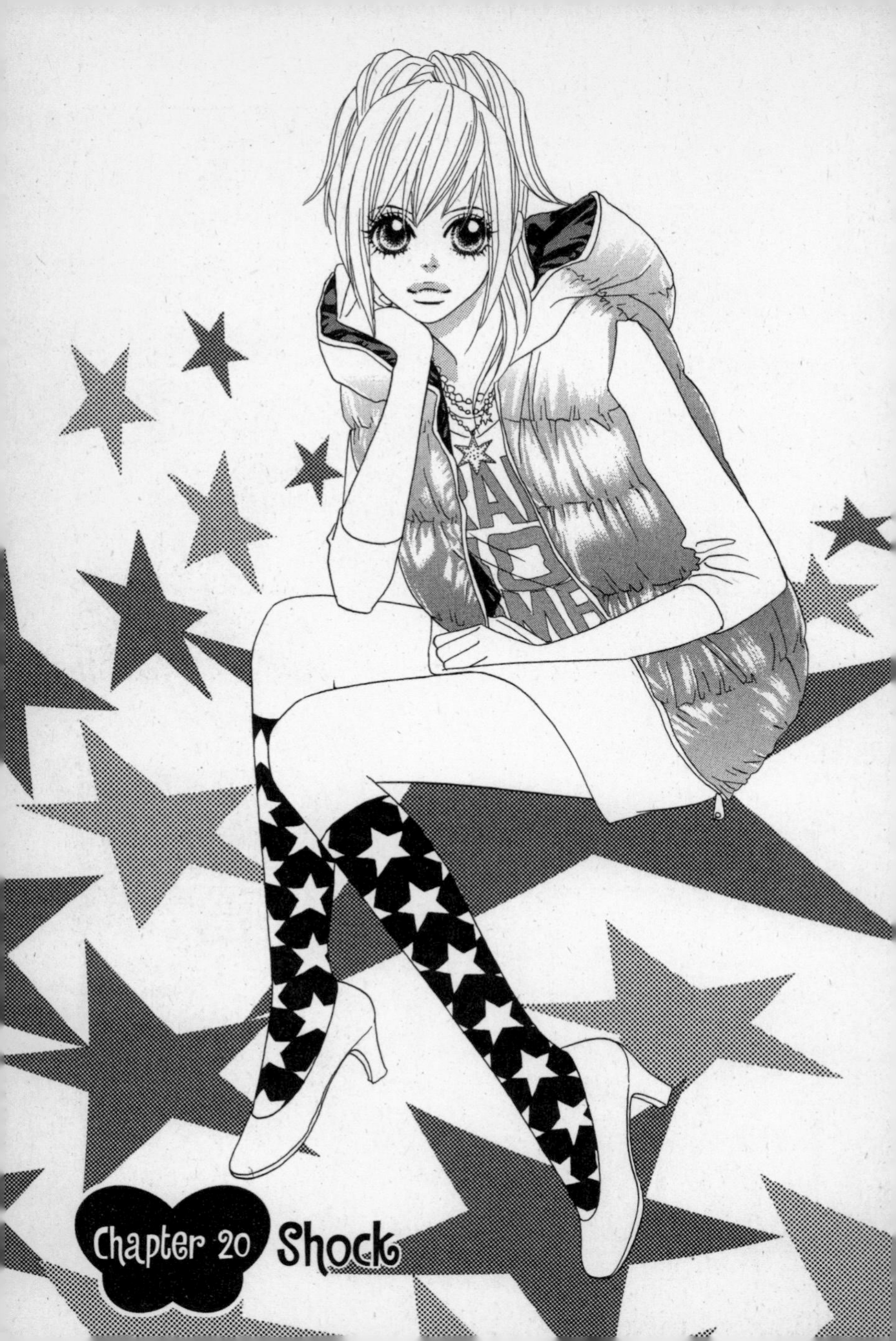
Chapter 20
Shock

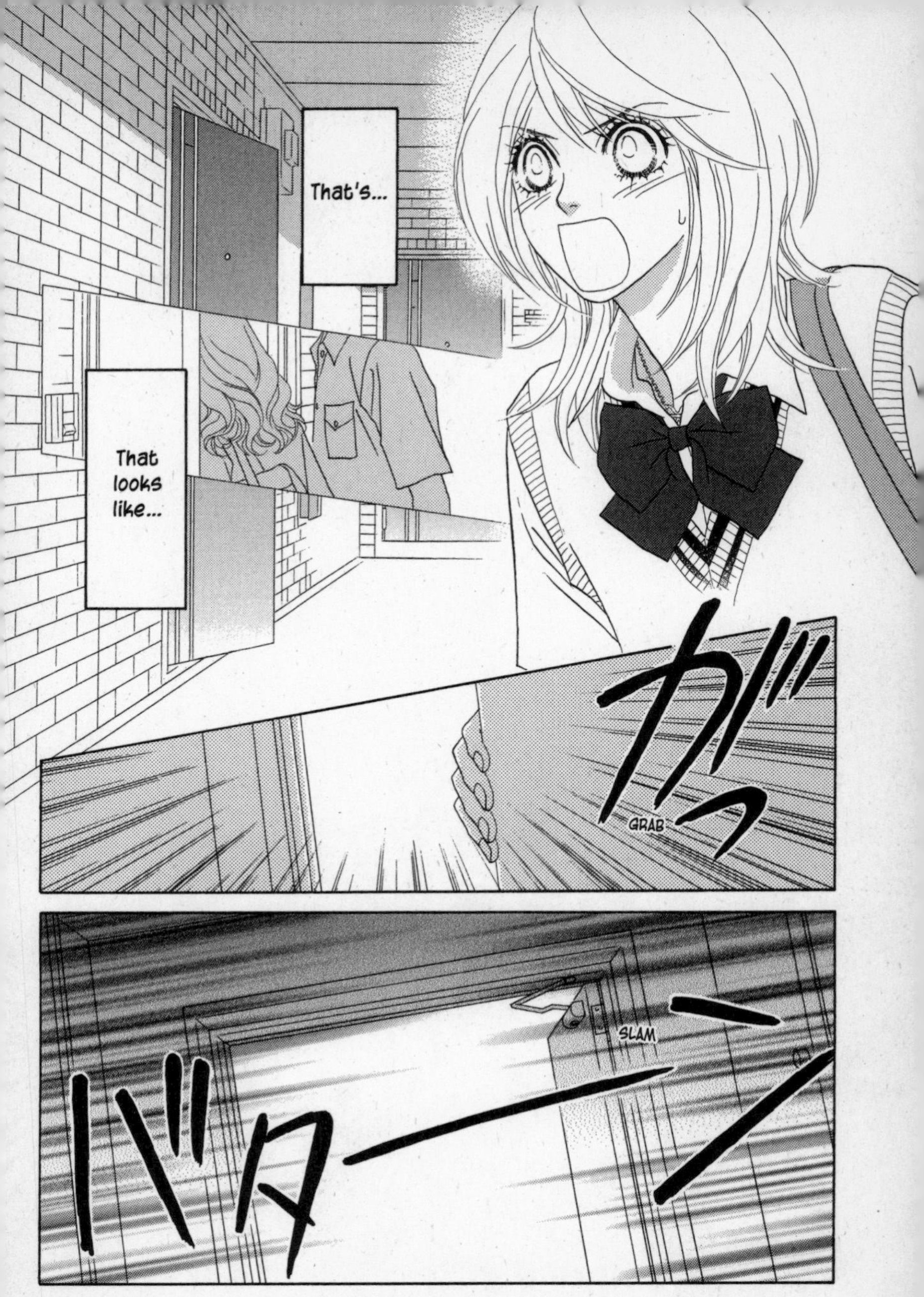
That's...
That looks like...
GRAB
SLAM

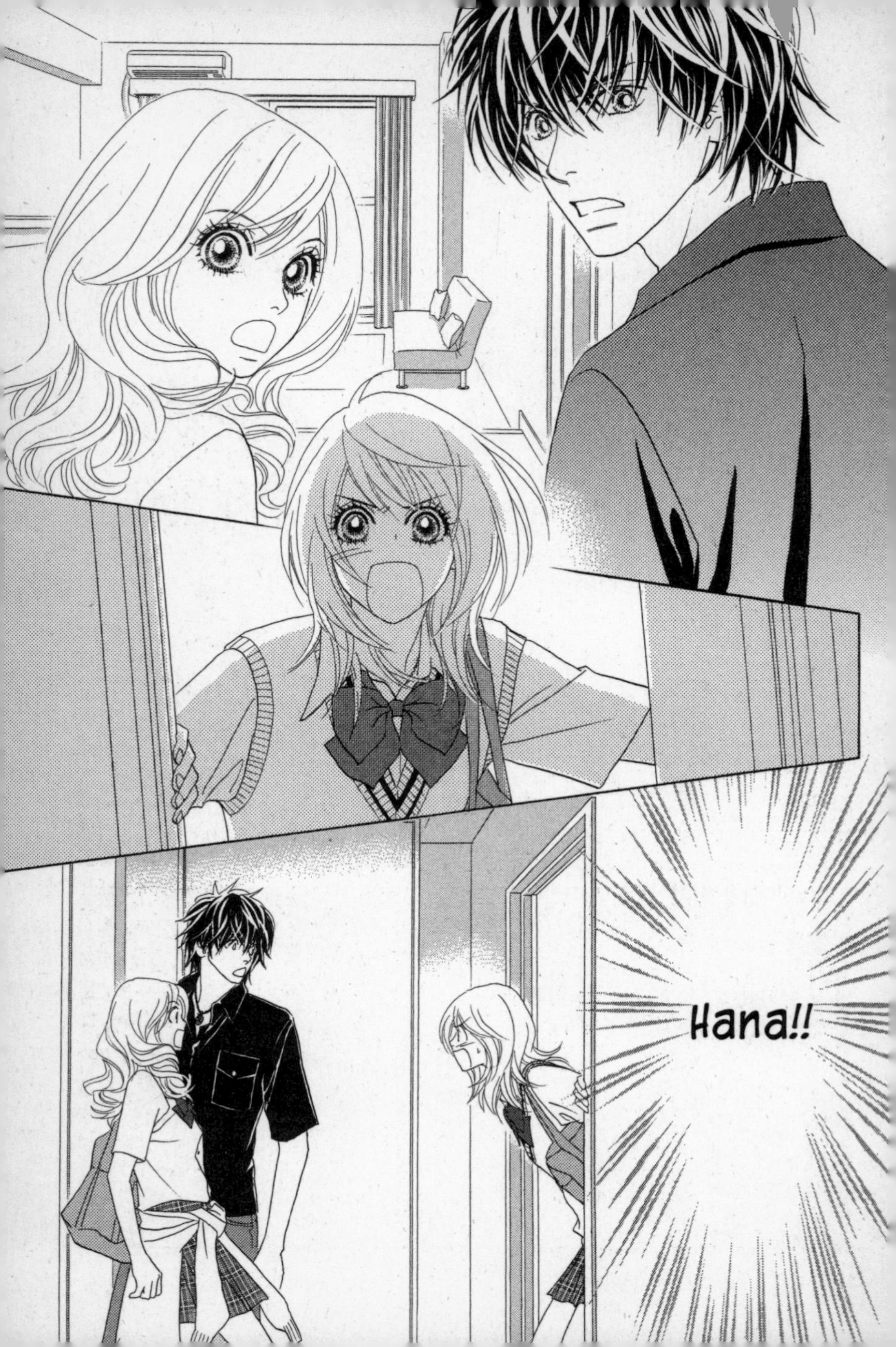
Hana!!

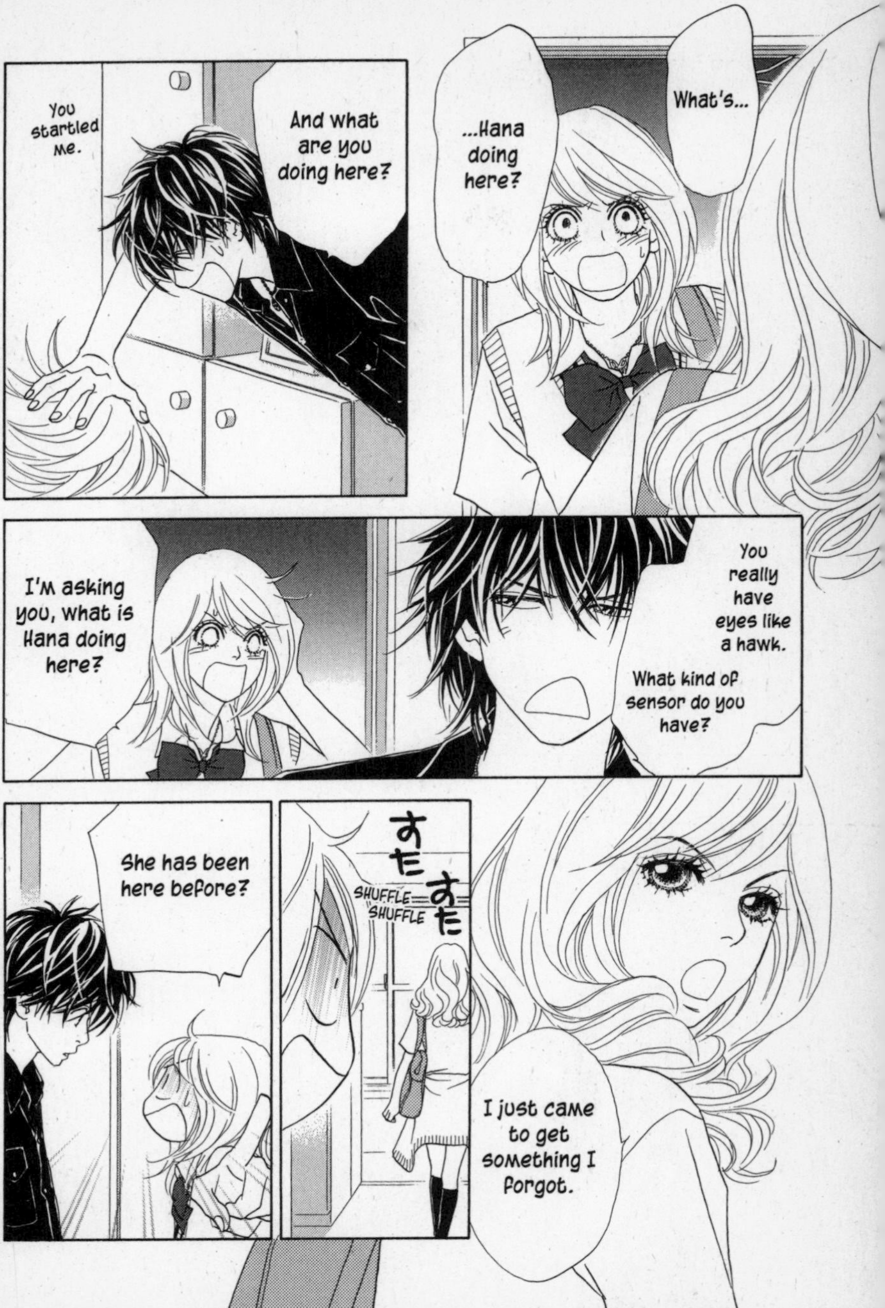
What's...
...Hana doing here?
You startled me.
And what are you doing here?
You really have eyes like a hawk.
What kind of sensor do you have?
I'm asking you, what is Hana doing here?
I just came to get something I forgot.
すたすた
SHUFFLE SHUFFLE
She has been here before?

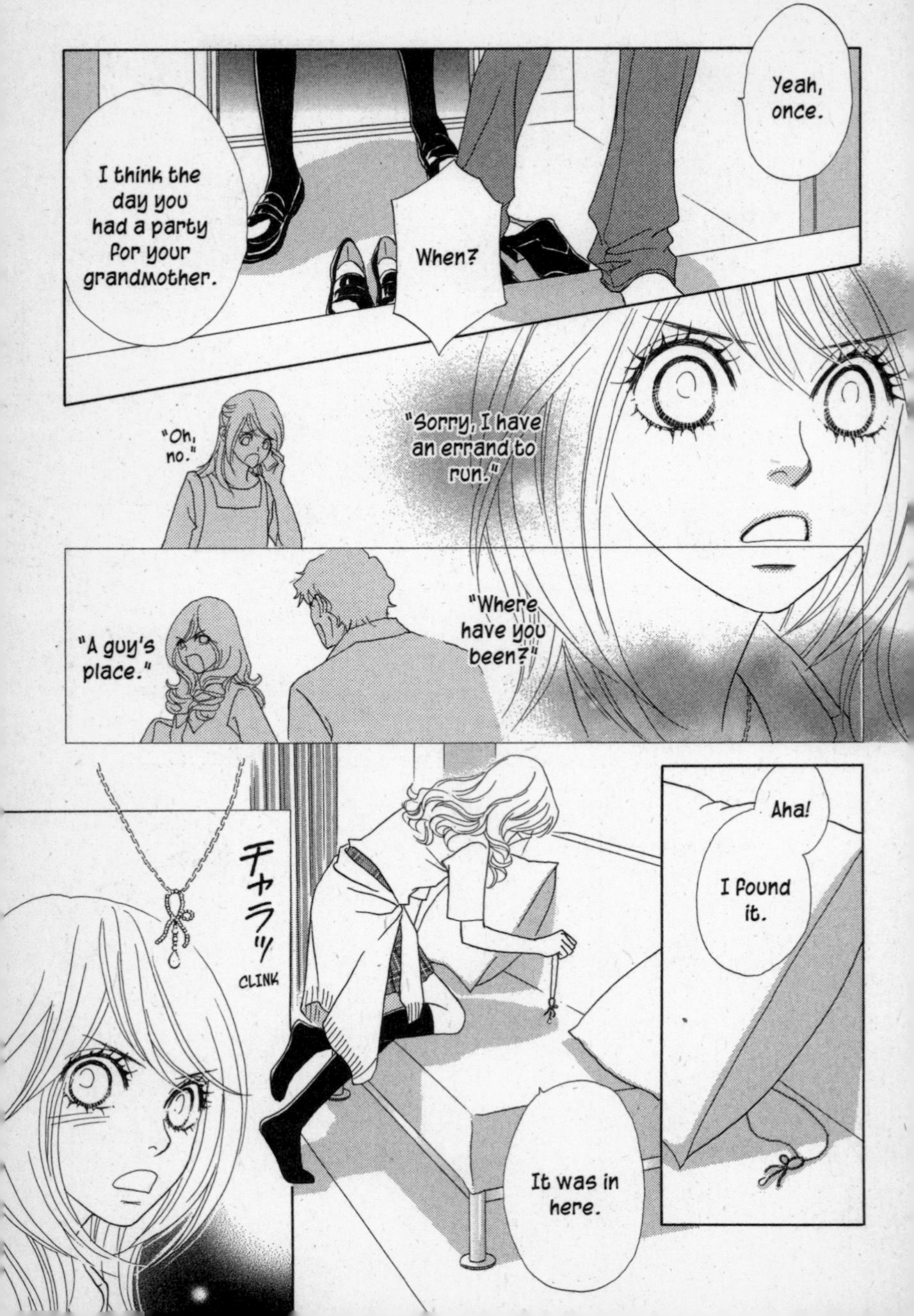
Yeah, once.
When?
I think the day you had a party for your grandmother.
"Sorry, I have an errand to run."
"Oh, no."
"Where have you been?"
"A guy's place."
Aha!
I found it.
It was in here.
チャラッ
CLINK

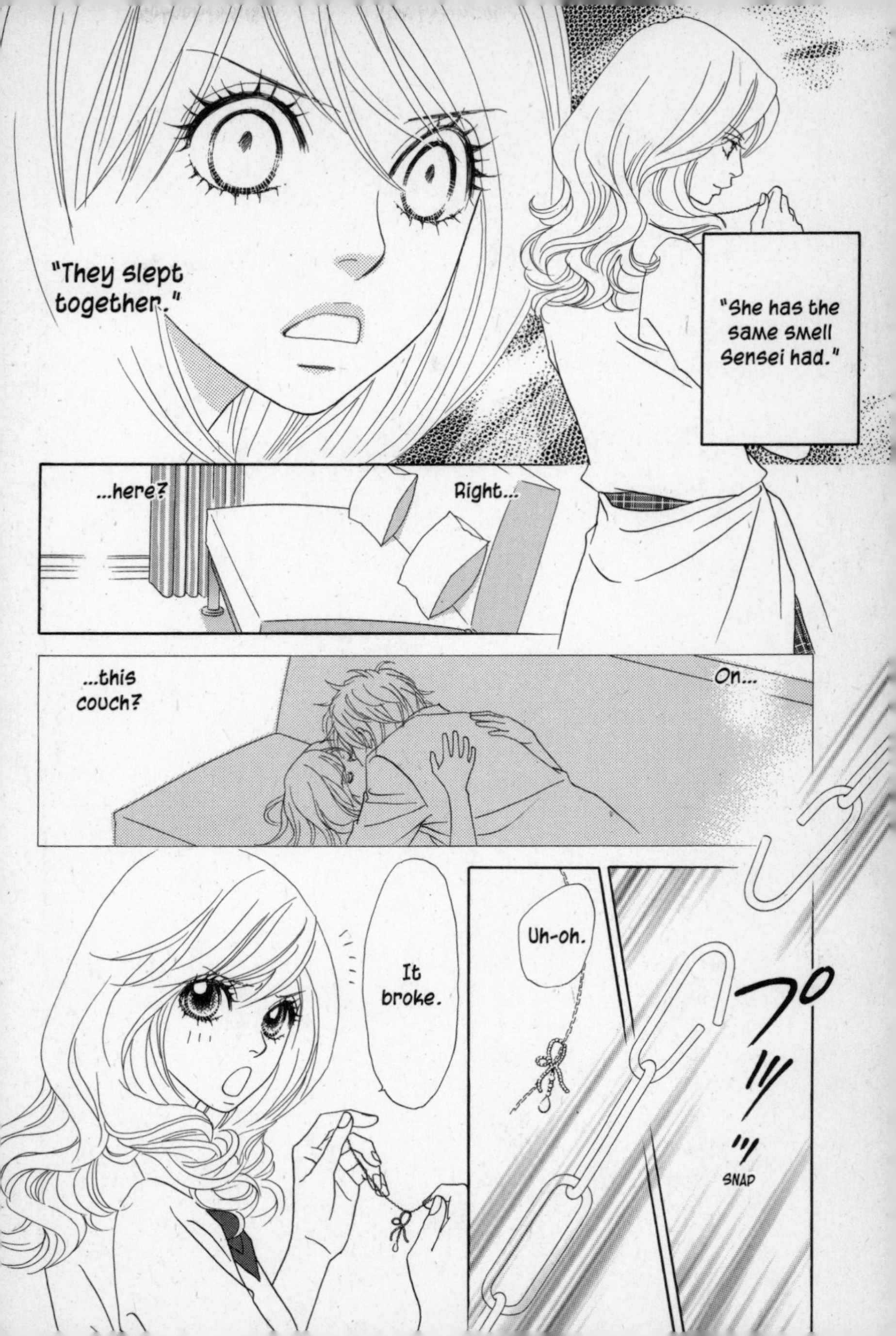
"She has the same smell Sensei had."
"They slept together."
Right...
...here?
On...
...this couch?
Uh-oh.
SNAP
It broke.

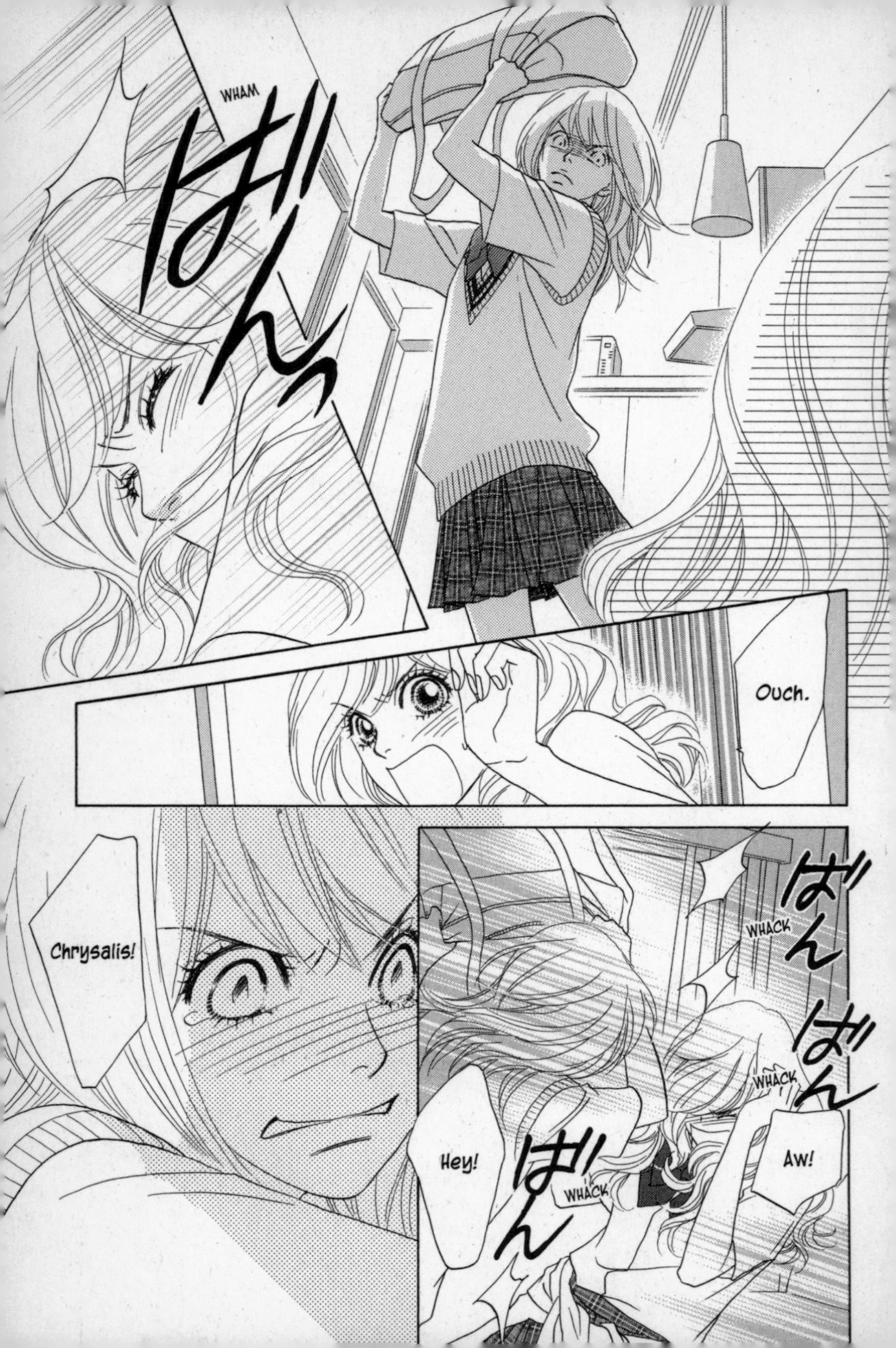

WHAM
ばんっ
Ouch.
ばん
WHACK
ばん
WHACK
Aw!
Hey!
ばん
WHACK
Chrysalis!

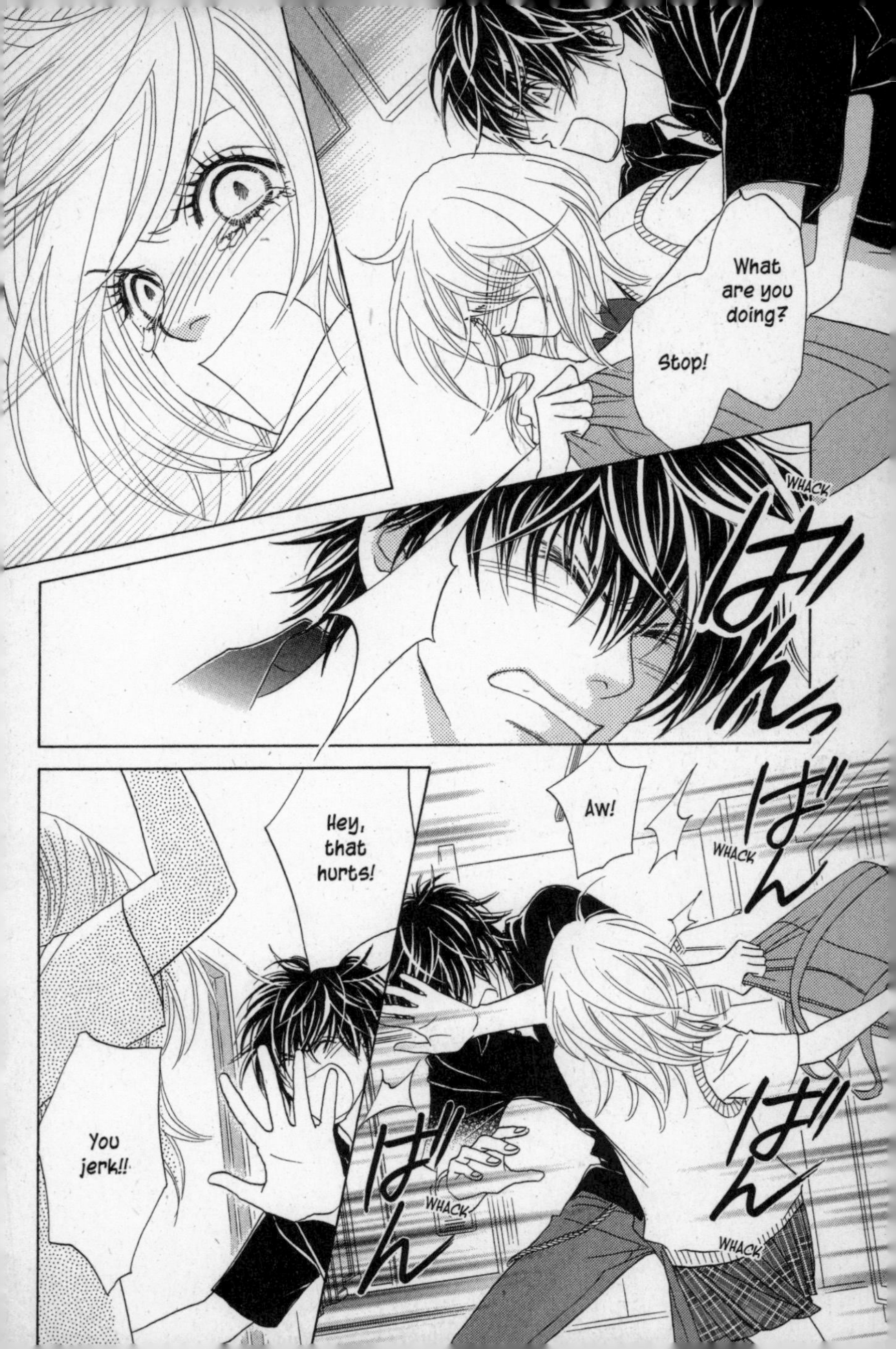
What are you doing?
Stop!
WHACK
ばんっ
Aw!
WHACK
ばん
WHACK
ばん
Hey, that hurts!
WHACK
ばん
You jerk!!

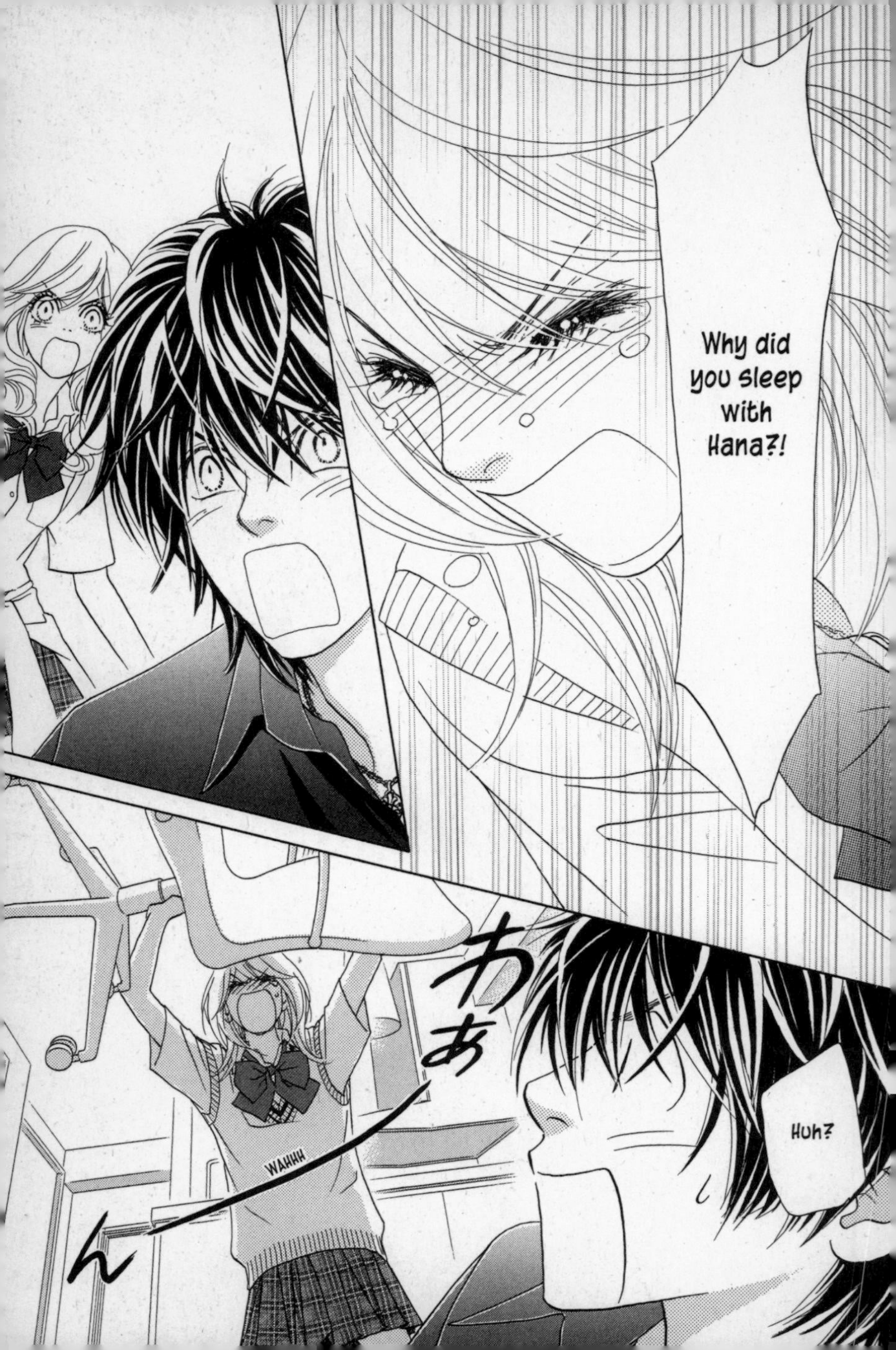
Why did you sleep with Hana?!
Huh?
わあーん
WAHHH

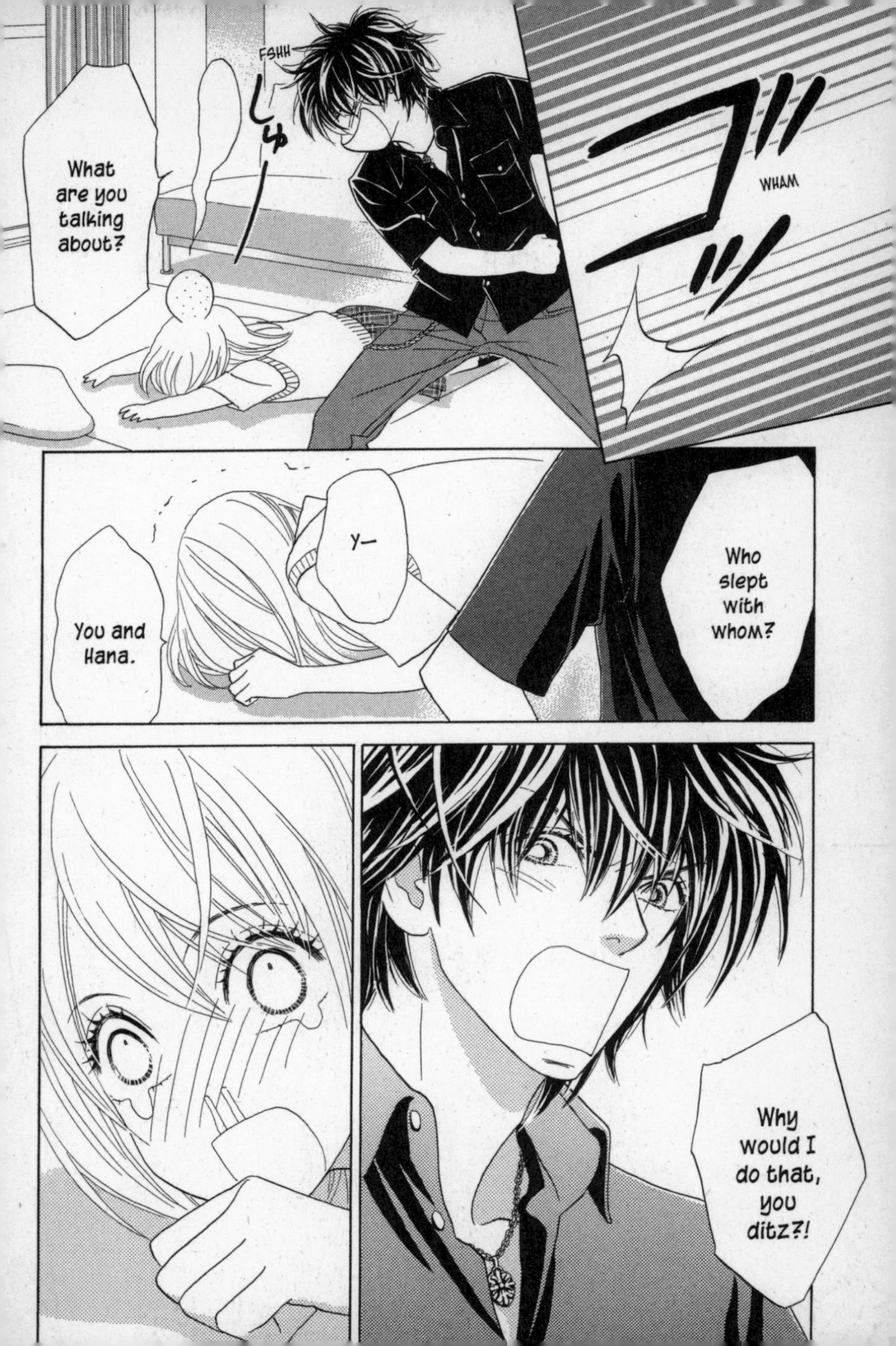
ゴッ
WHAM
FSHH
しゅー
What are you talking about?
Who slept with whom?
Y—
You and Hana.
Why would I do that, you ditz?!

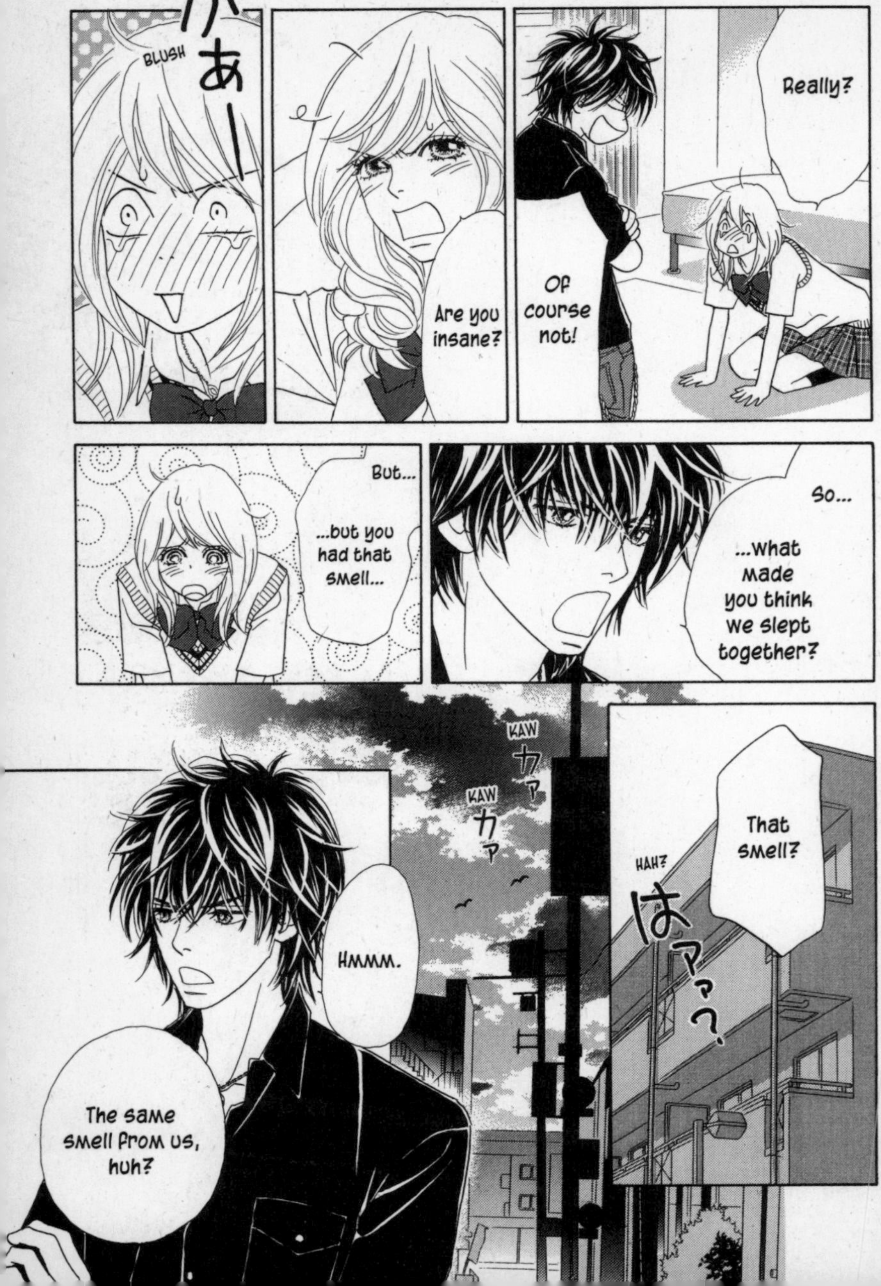
Really?
Of course not!
Are you insane?
かぁー
BLUSH
So...
...what made you think we slept together?
But...
...but you had that smell...
That smell?
HAH?
はァァ?
KAW
カァ
KAW
カァ
Hmmm.
The same smell from us, huh?

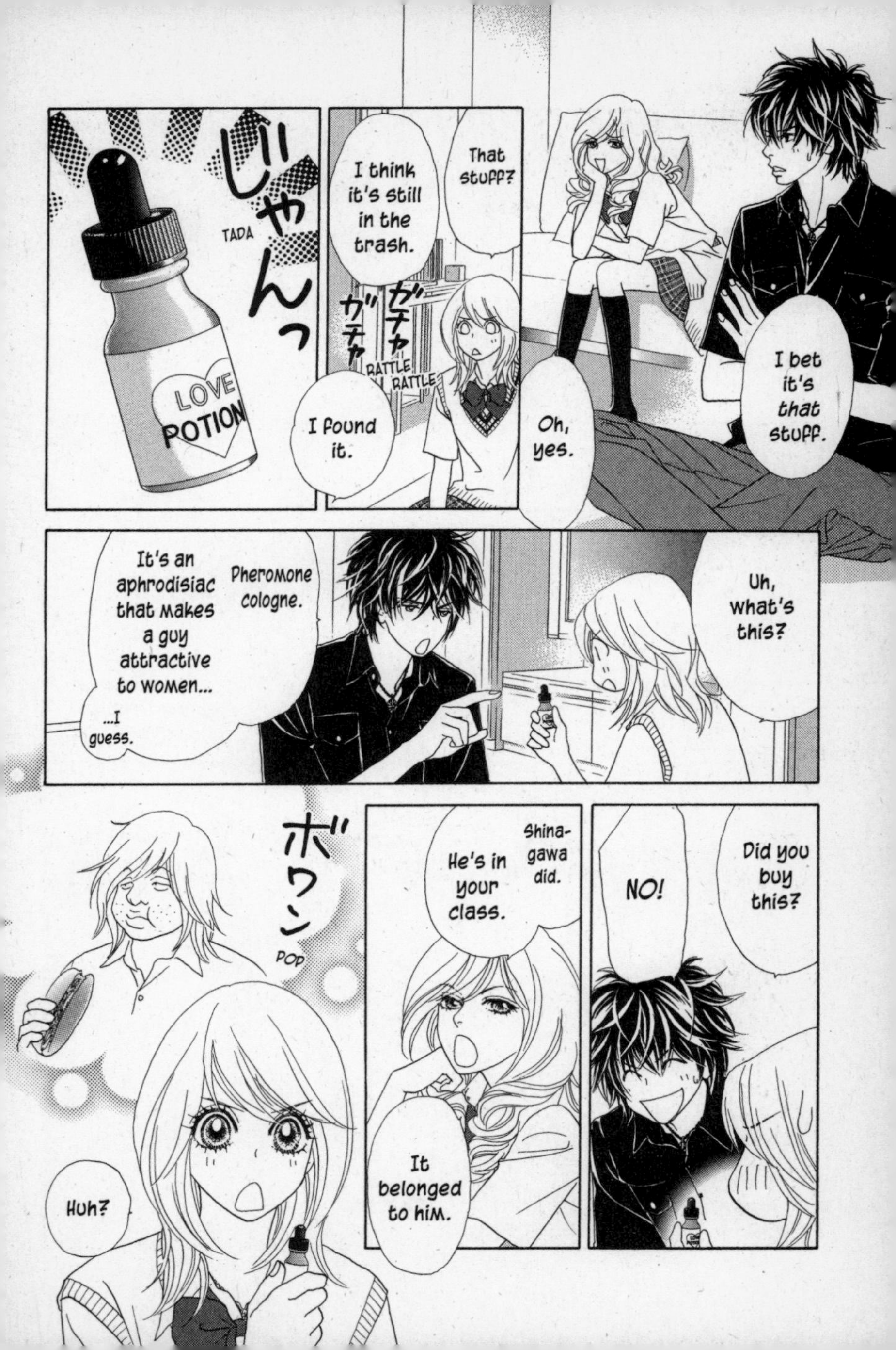
I bet it's that stuff.
Oh, yes.
That stuff?
I think it's still in the trash.
ガチャガチャ
RATTLE RATTLE
I found it.
じゃんっ
TADA
LOVE POTION
Uh, what's this?
Pheromone cologne.
It's an aphrodisiac that makes a guy attractive to women...
...I guess.
Did you buy this?
NO!
Shinagawa did.
He's in your class.
It belonged to him.
ボワン
POP
Huh?

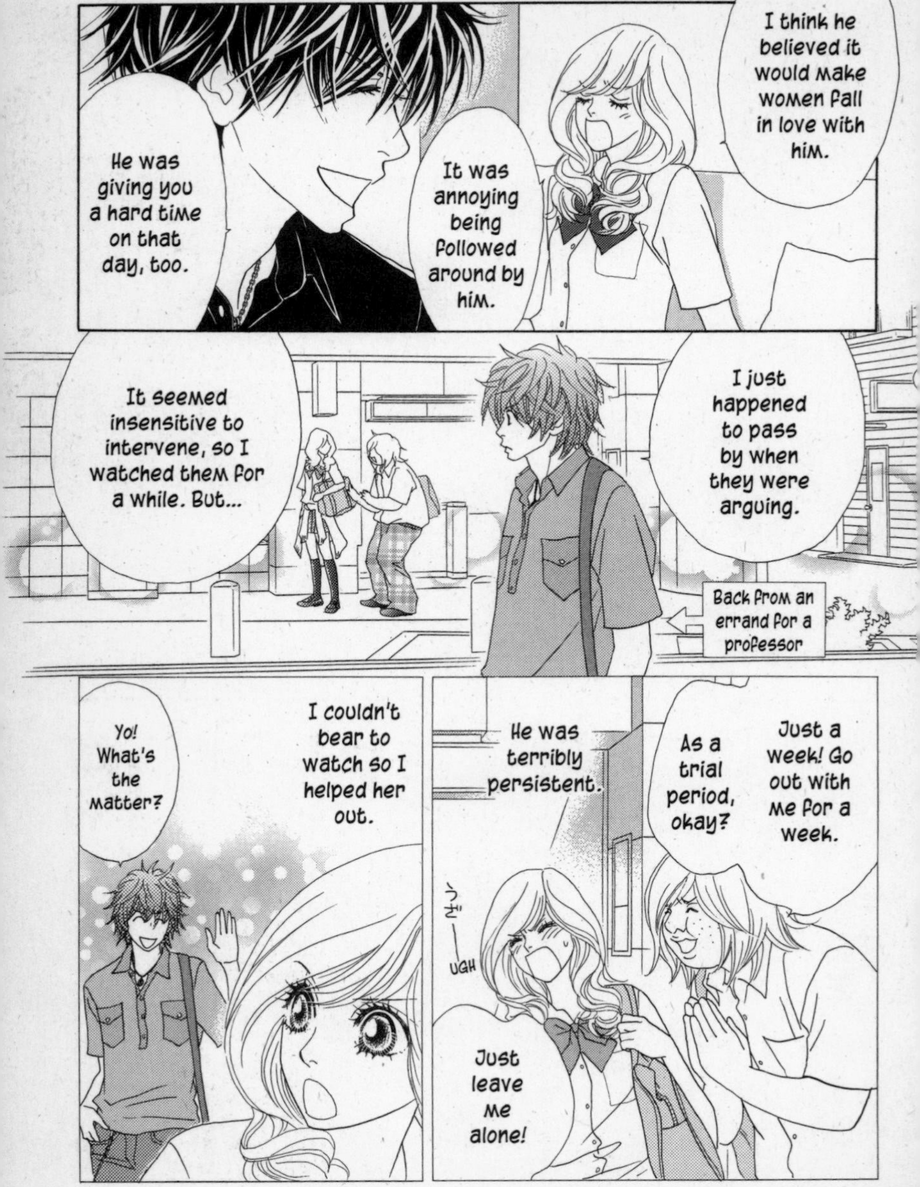
I think he believed it would make women fall in love with him.
It was annoying being followed around by him.
He was giving you a hard time on that day, too.
I just happened to pass by when they were arguing.
Back from an errand for a professor
It seemed insensitive to intervene, so I watched them for a while. But...
Just a week! Go out with me for a week.
As a trial period, okay?
He was terribly persistent.
うぜー
UGH
Just leave me alone!
I couldn't bear to watch so I helped her out.
Yo! What's the matter?

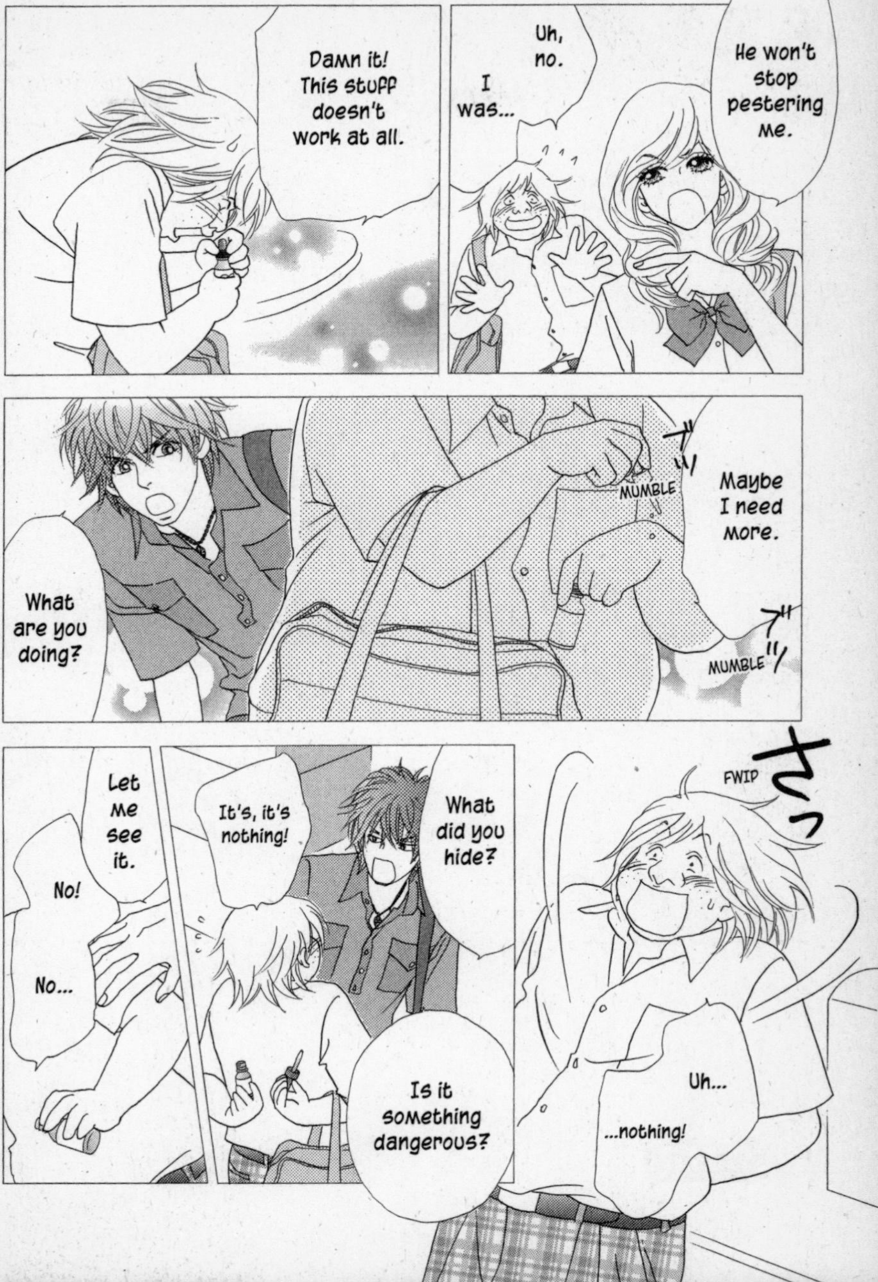
He won't stop pestering me.
Uh, no.
I was...
Damn it! This stuff doesn't work at all.
ブツ
MUMBLE
Maybe I need more.
ブツ
MUMBLE
What are you doing?
さっ
FWIP
Uh...
...nothing!
What did you hide?
It's, it's nothing!
Is it something dangerous?
Let me see it.
No!
No...

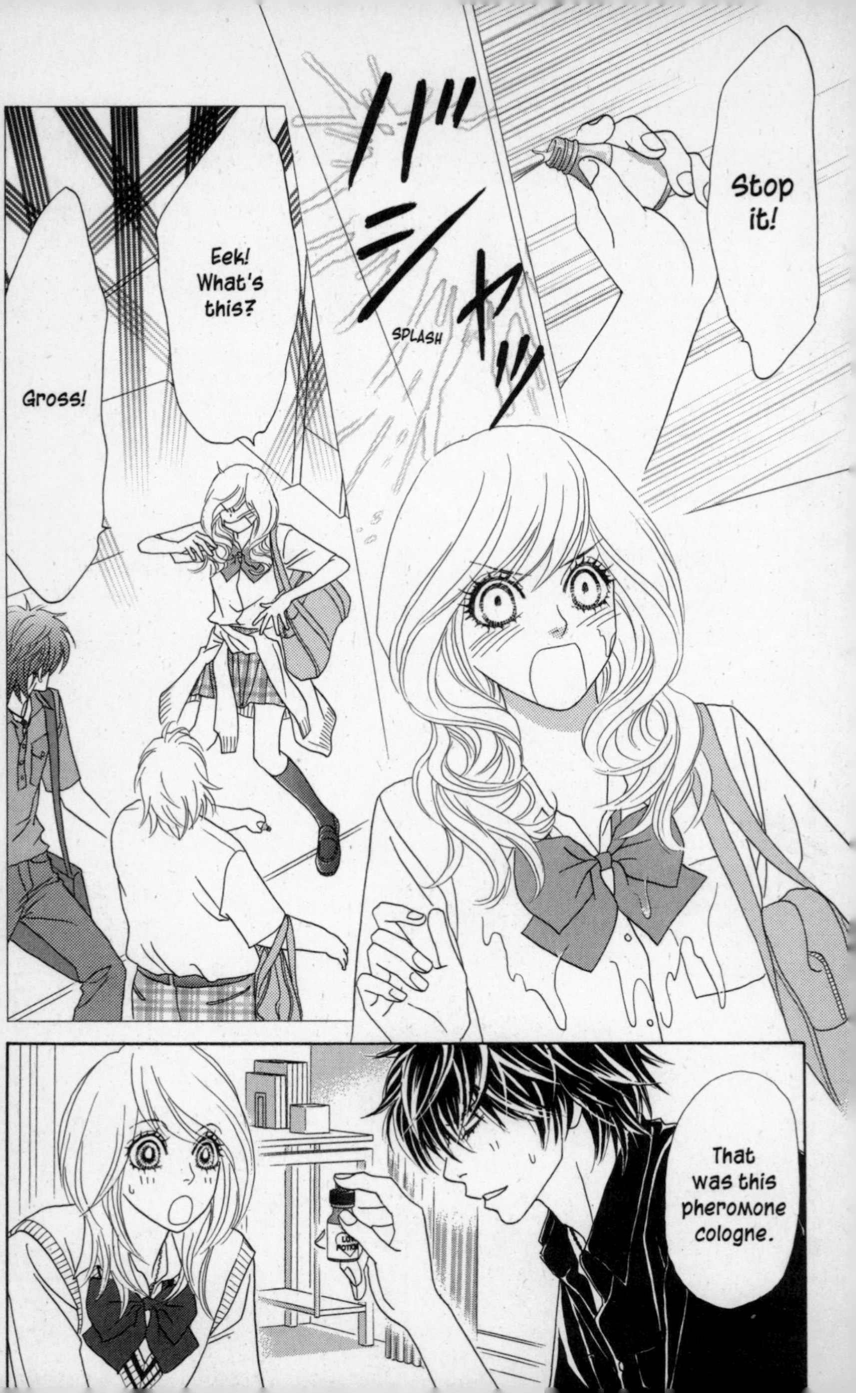
Stop it!
バシャッ
SPLASH
Eek! What's this?
Gross!
That was this pheromone cologne.

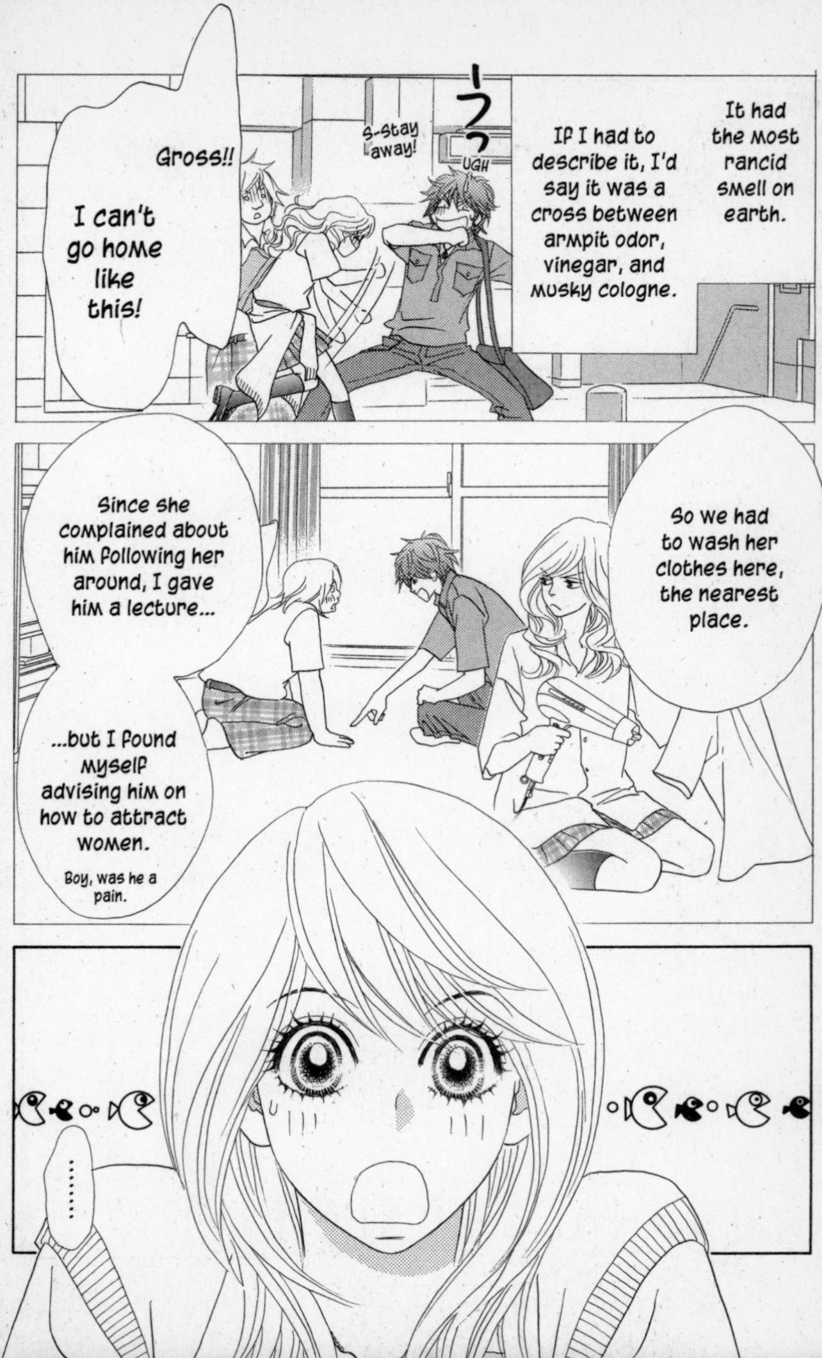
It had the most rancid smell on earth.
If I had to describe it, I'd say it was a cross between armpit odor, vinegar, and musky cologne.
UGH
S-Stay away!
Gross!!
I can't go home like this!
So we had to wash her clothes here, the nearest place.
Since she complained about him following her around, I gave him a lecture...
...but I found myself advising him on how to attract women.
Boy, was he a pain.
......

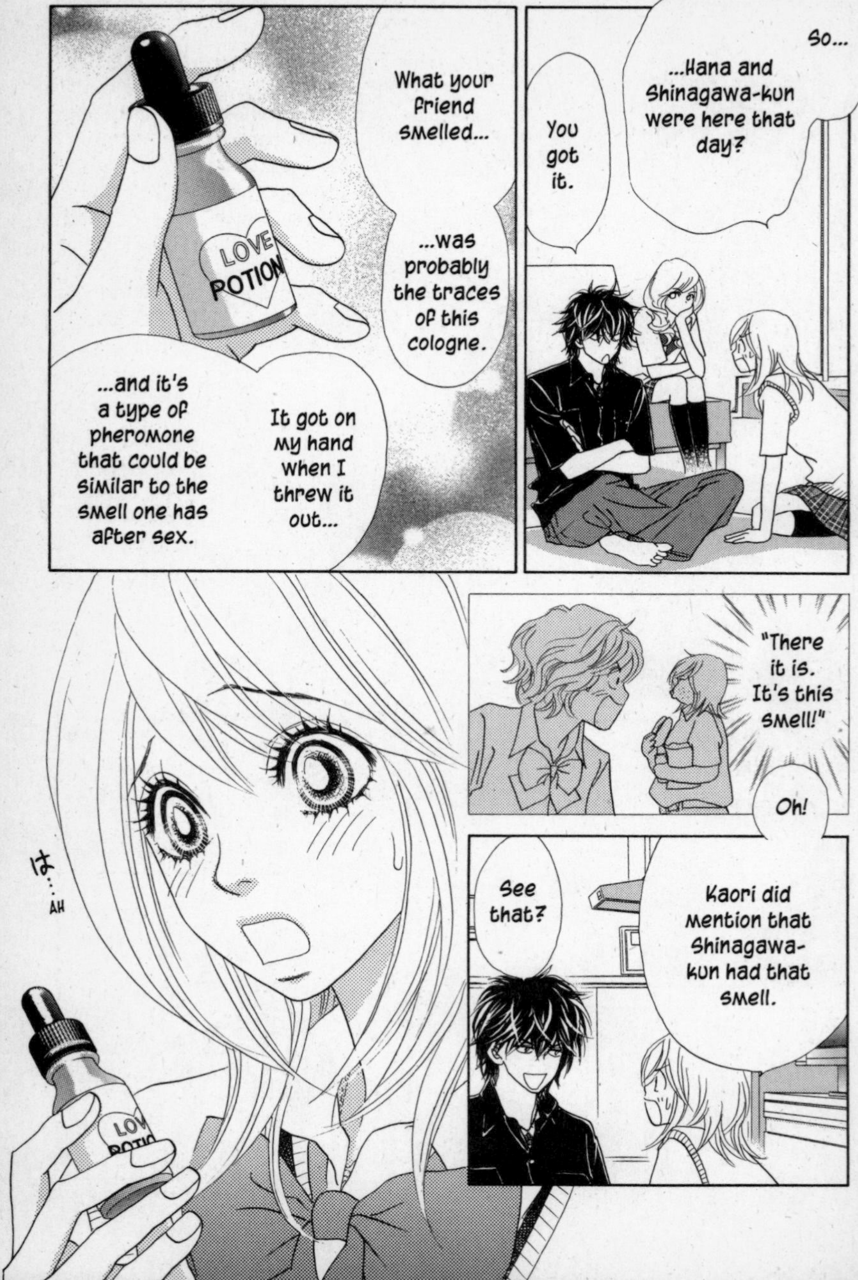
So...
...Hana and Shinagawa-kun were here that day?
You got it.
What your friend smelled...
...was probably the traces of this cologne.
LOVE POTION
It got on my hand when I threw it out...
...and it's a type of pheromone that could be similar to the smell one has after sex.
"There it is. It's this smell!"
Oh!
Kaori did mention that Shinagawa-kun had that smell.
See that?
は… AH

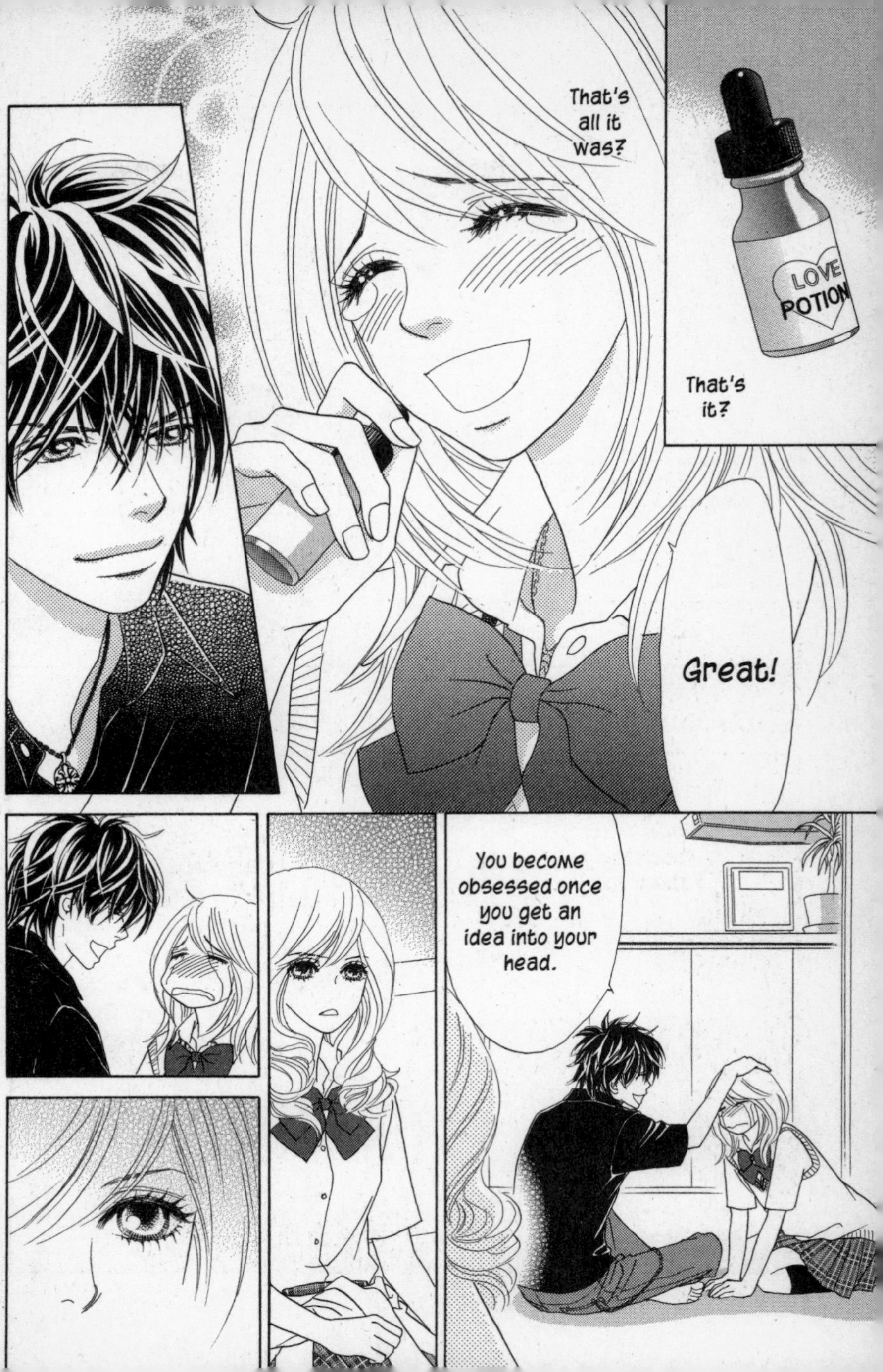
That's it?
That's all it was?
Great!
You become obsessed once you get an idea into your head.

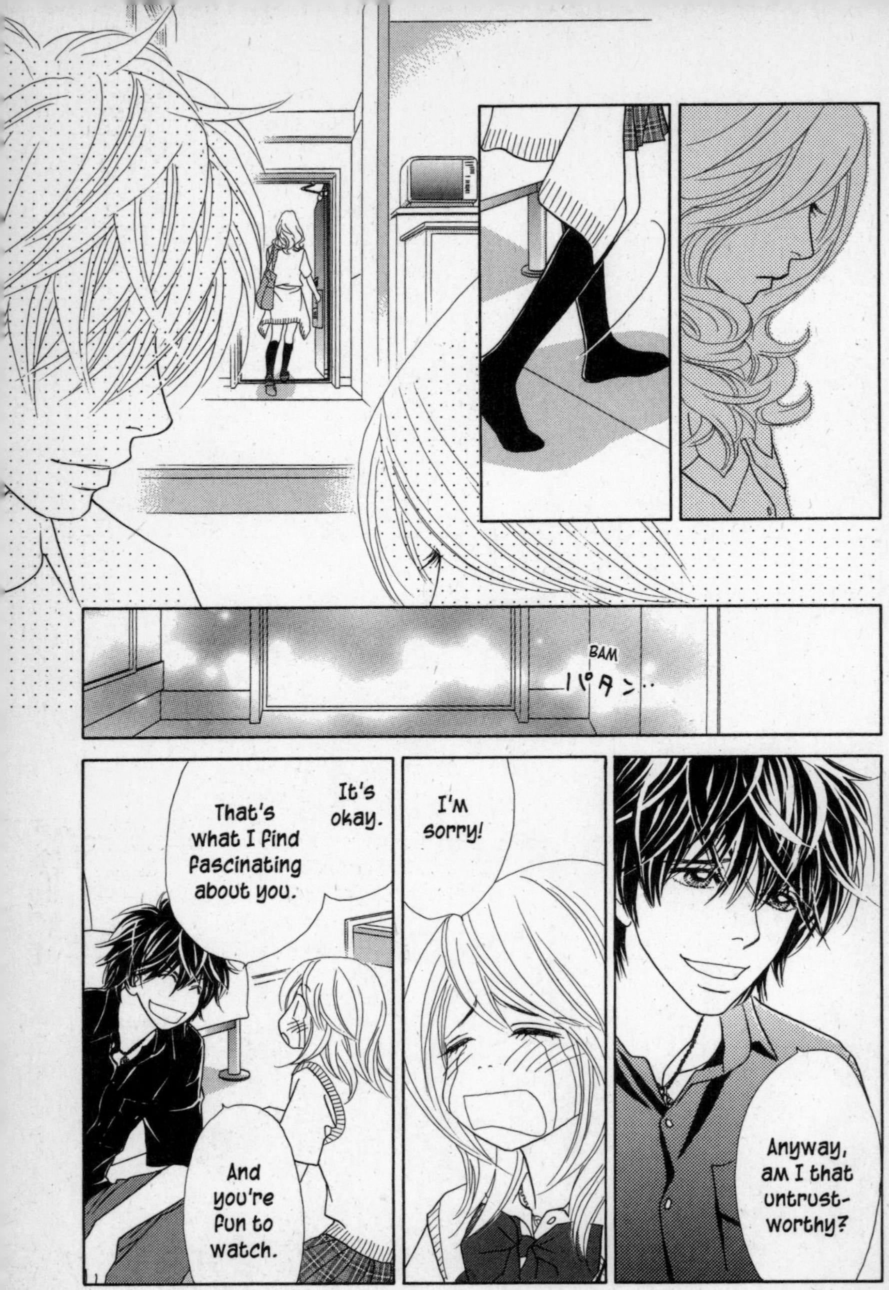
BAM
パタン‥
Anyway, am I that untrust-worthy?
I'm sorry!
It's okay.
That's what I find fascinating about you.
And you're fun to watch.

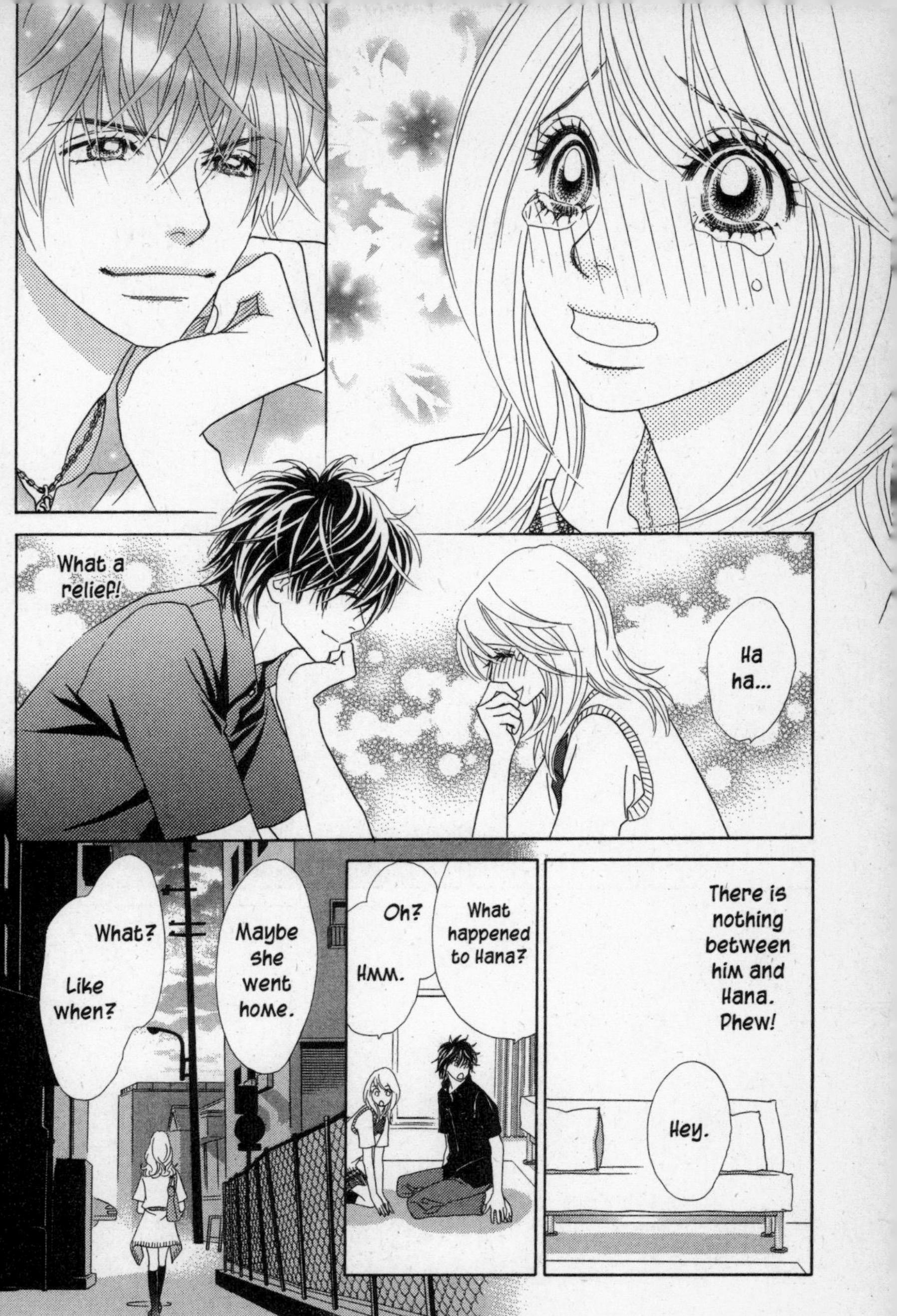
Ha ha...
What a relief!
There is nothing between him and Hana. Phew!
Hey.
What happened to Hana?
Oh?
Hmm.
Maybe she went home.
What?
Like when?

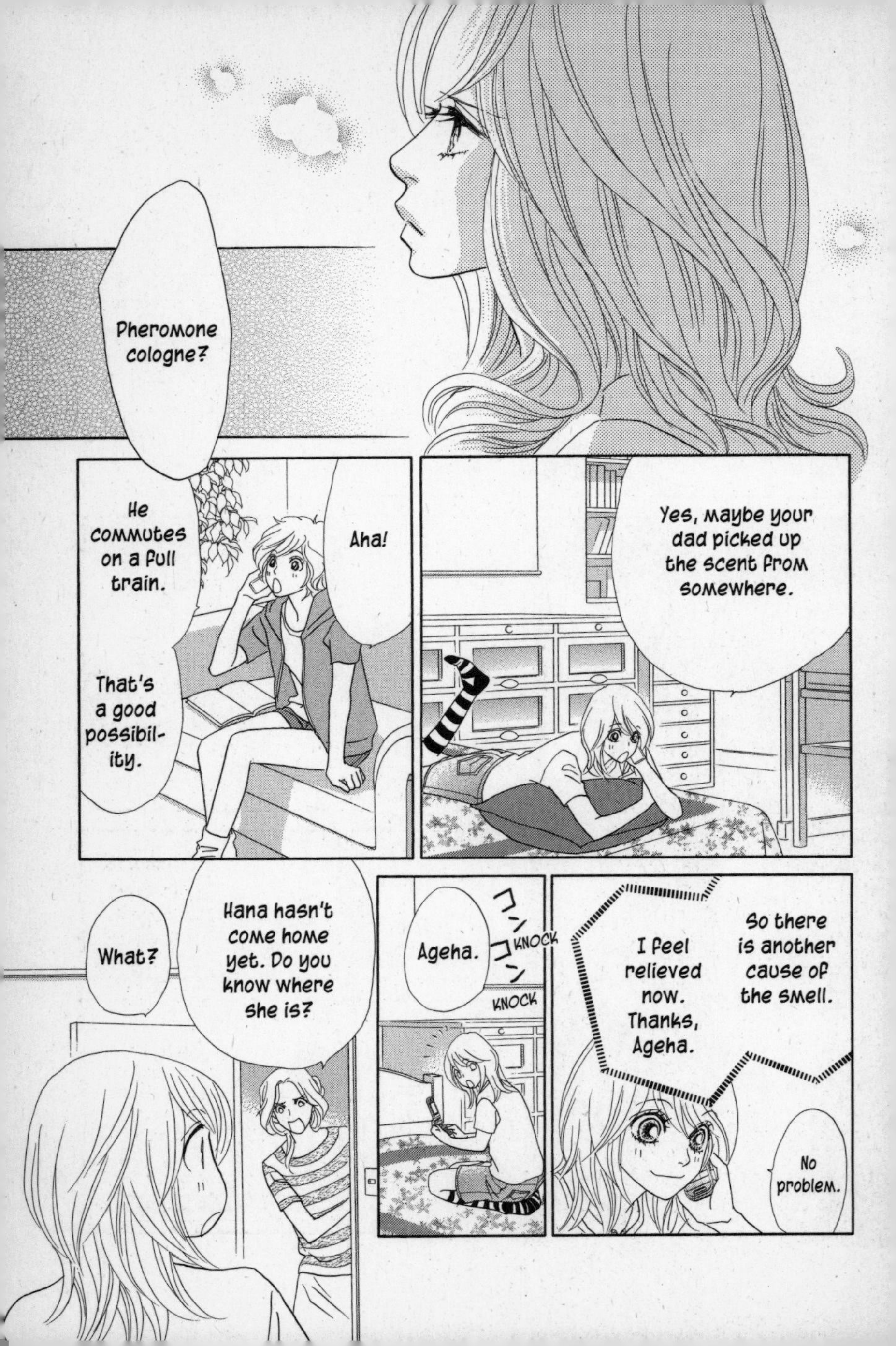

Pheromone cologne?
Yes, maybe your dad picked up the scent from somewhere.
Aha!
He commutes on a full train.
That's a good possibility.
So there is another cause of the smell.
I feel relieved now. Thanks, Ageha.
No problem.
コンコン
KNOCK
KNOCK
Ageha.
Hana hasn't come home yet. Do you know where she is?
What?

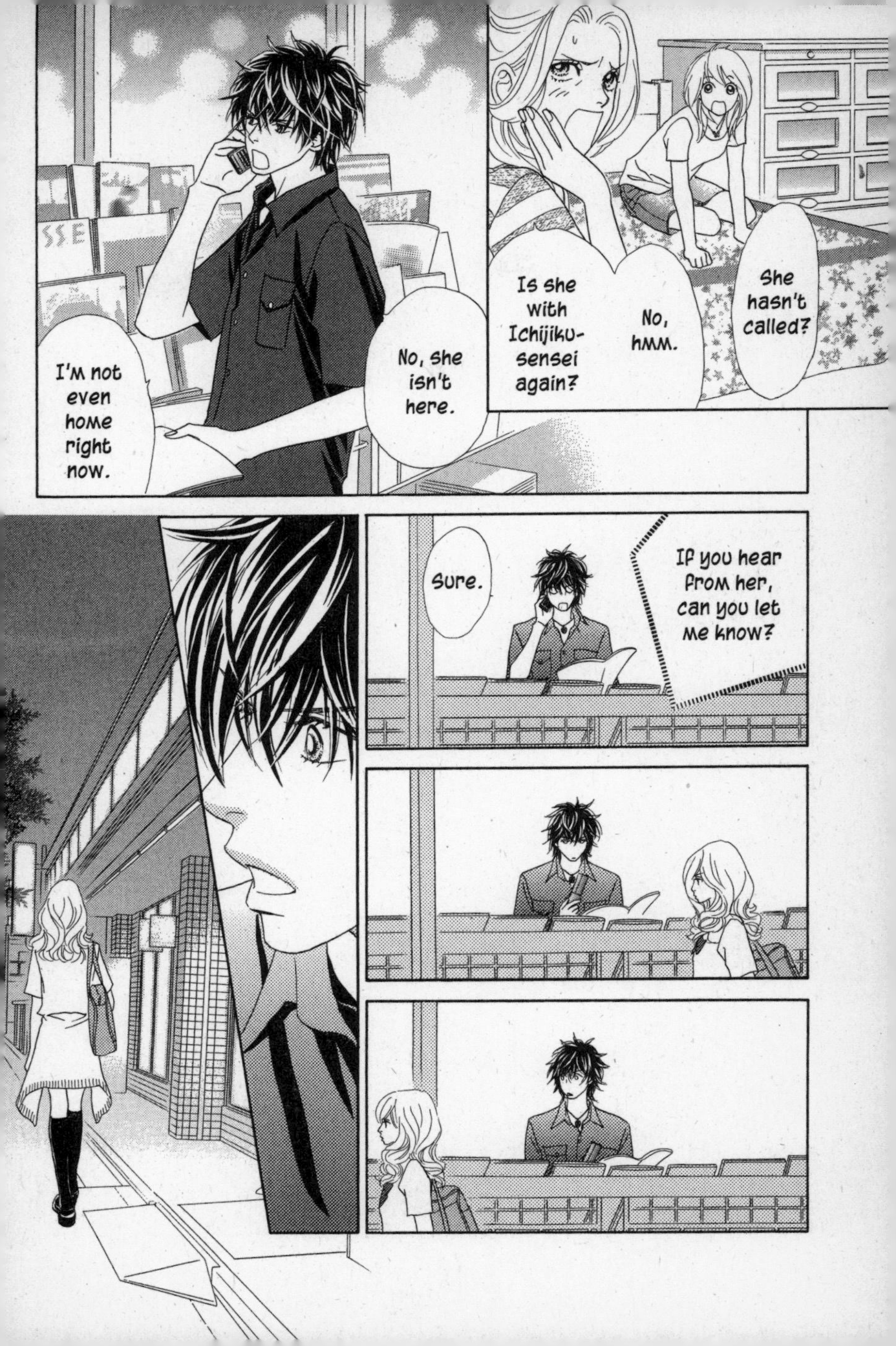
She hasn't called?
No, hmm.
Is she with Ichijiku-sensei again?
No, she isn't here.
I'm not even home right now.
If you hear from her, can you let me know?
Sure.

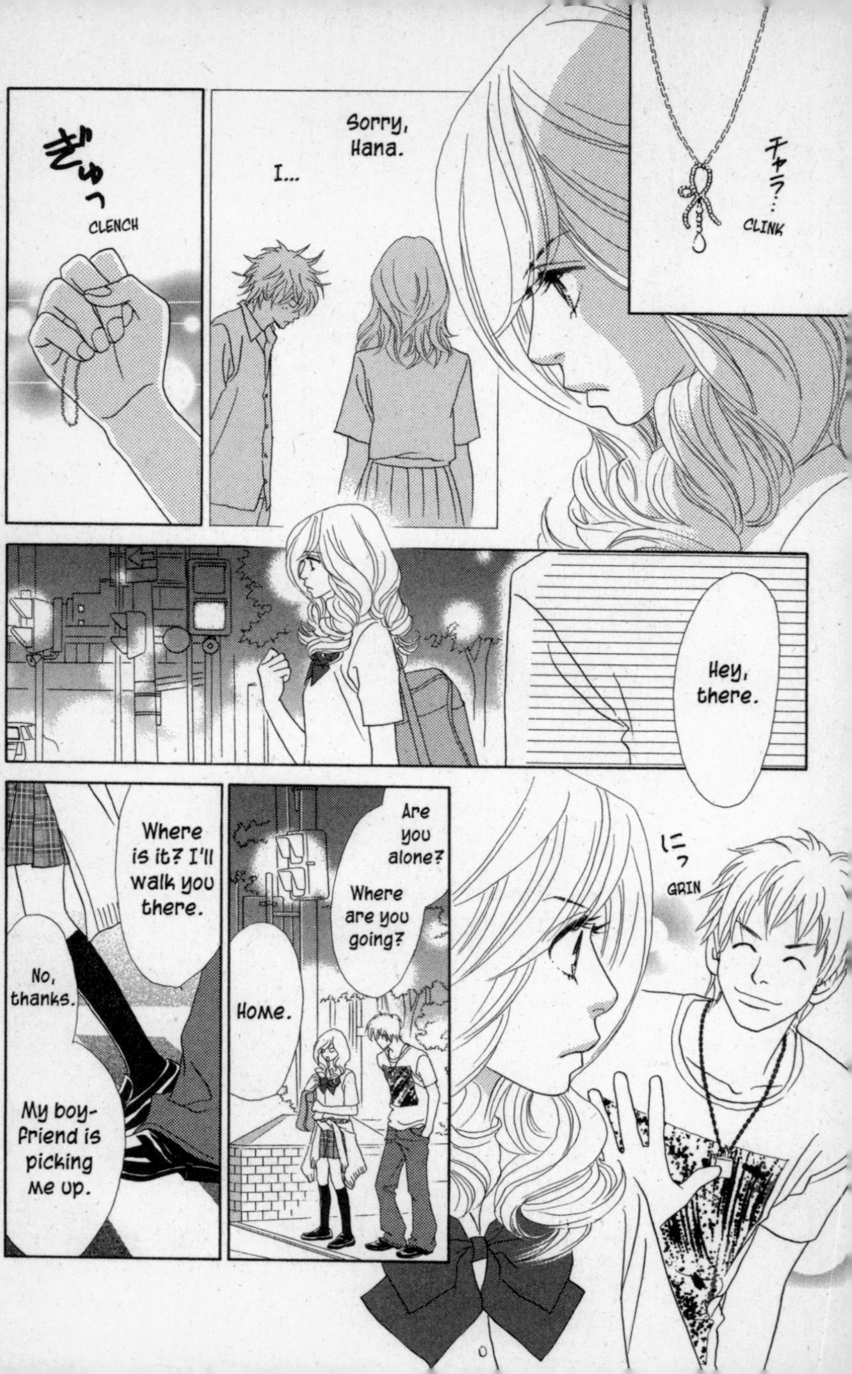
チャラ…
CLINK
Sorry, Hana.
I...
ぎゅっ
CLENCH
Hey, there.
にっ
GRIN
Are you alone?
Where are you going?
Home.
Where is it? I'll walk you there.
No, thanks.
My boy-friend is picking me up.

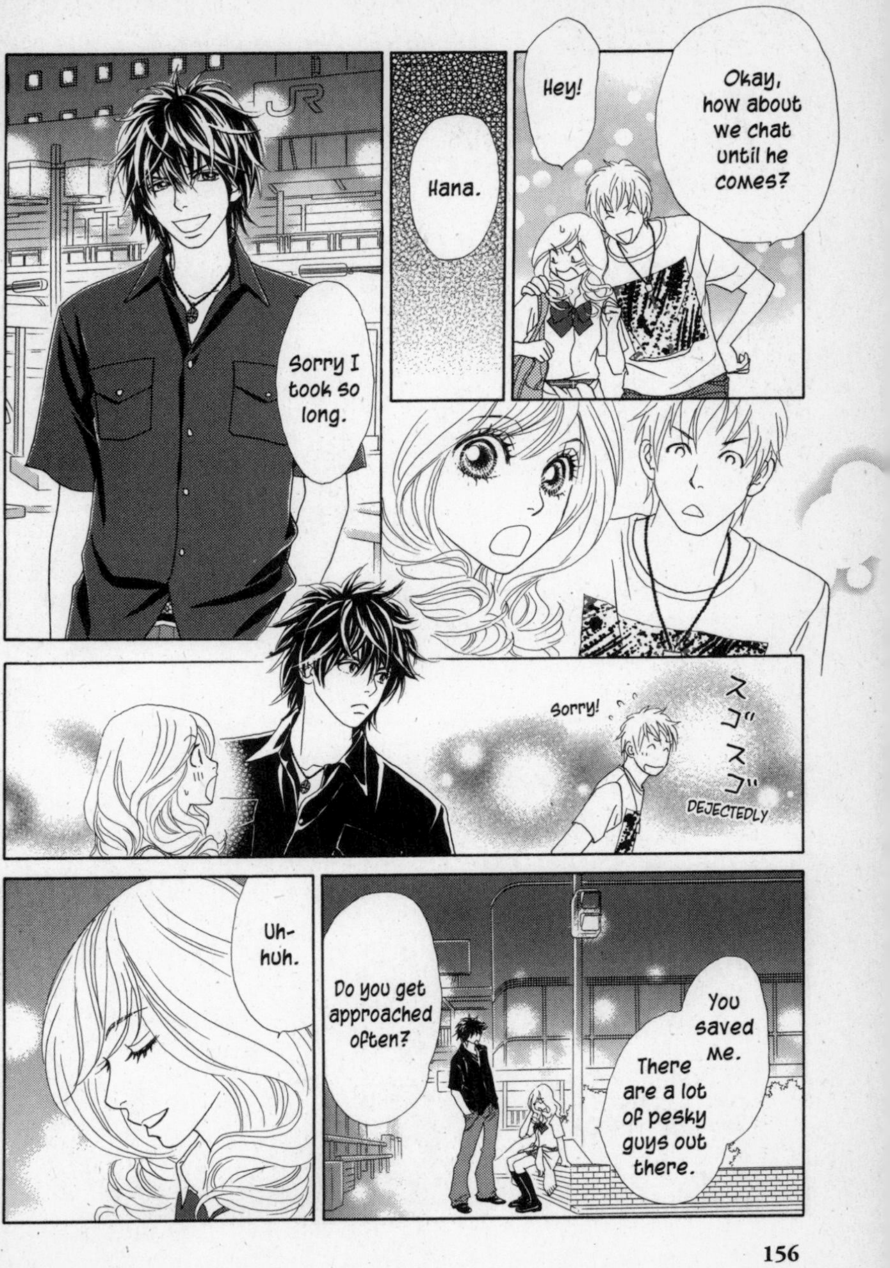
Okay, how about we chat until he comes?
Hey!
Hana.
Sorry I took so long.
スゴスゴ
DEJECTEDLY
Sorry!
You saved me.
There are a lot of pesky guys out there.
Do you get approached often?
Uh-huh.

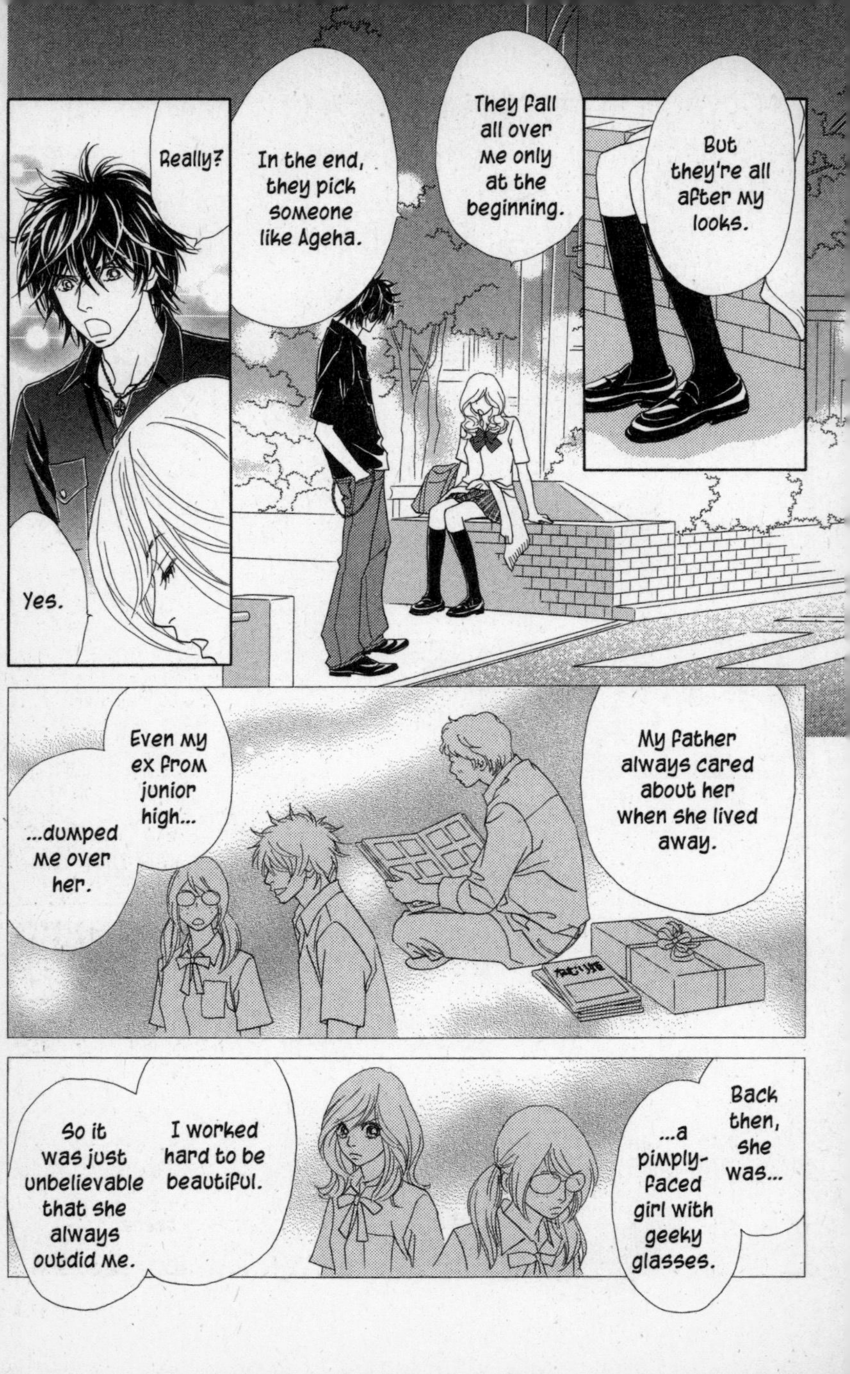
But they're all after my looks.
They fall all over me only at the beginning.
In the end, they pick someone like Ageha.
Really?
Yes.
My father always cared about her when she lived away.
Even my ex from junior high...
...dumped me over her.
Back then, she was...
...a pimply-faced girl with geeky glasses.
I worked hard to be beautiful.
So it was just unbelievable that she always outdid me.

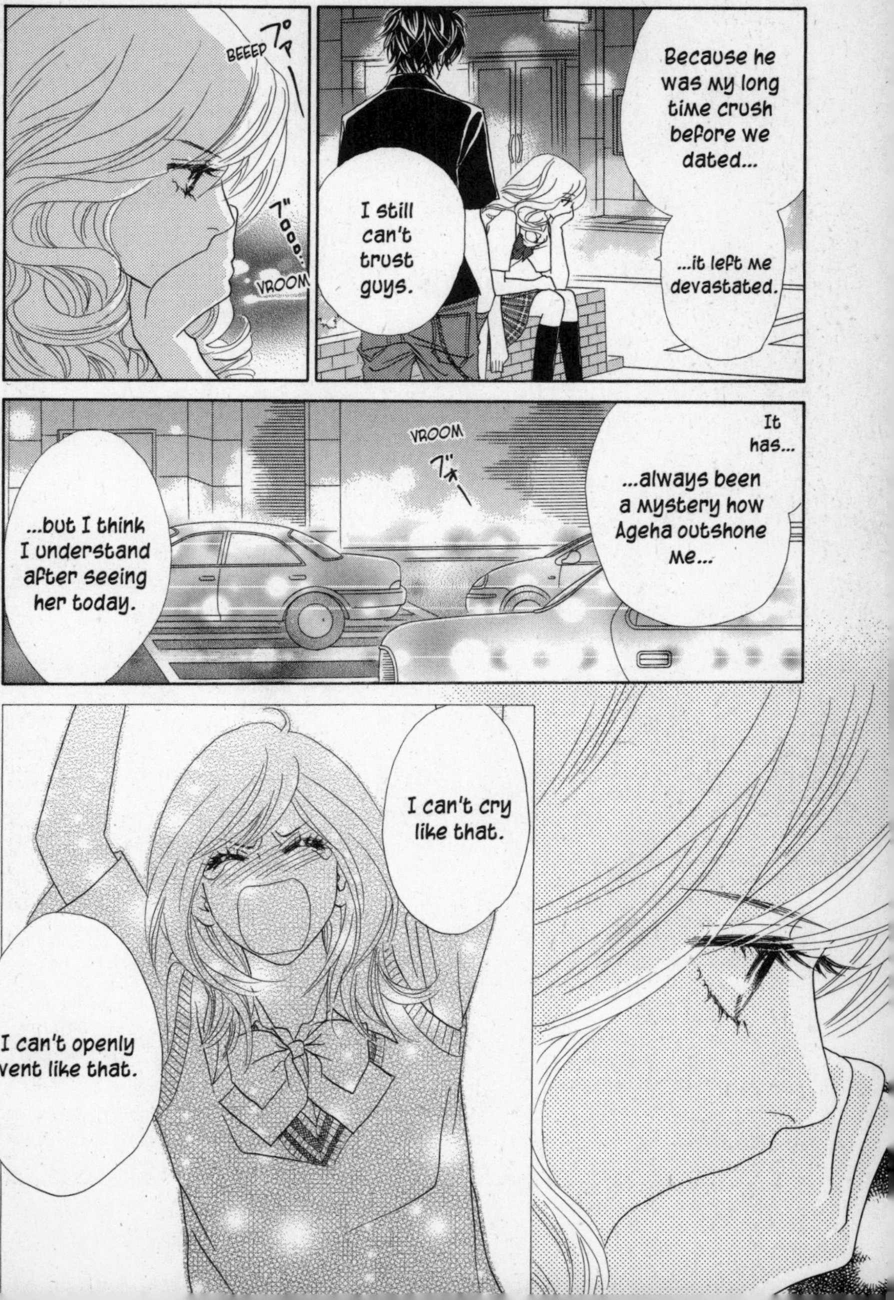
Because he was my long time crush before we dated...
...it left me devastated.
I still can't trust guys.
BEEEP
VROOM
It has...
...always been a mystery how Ageha outshone me...
VROOM
...but I think I understand after seeing her today.
I can't cry like that.
I can't openly vent like that.

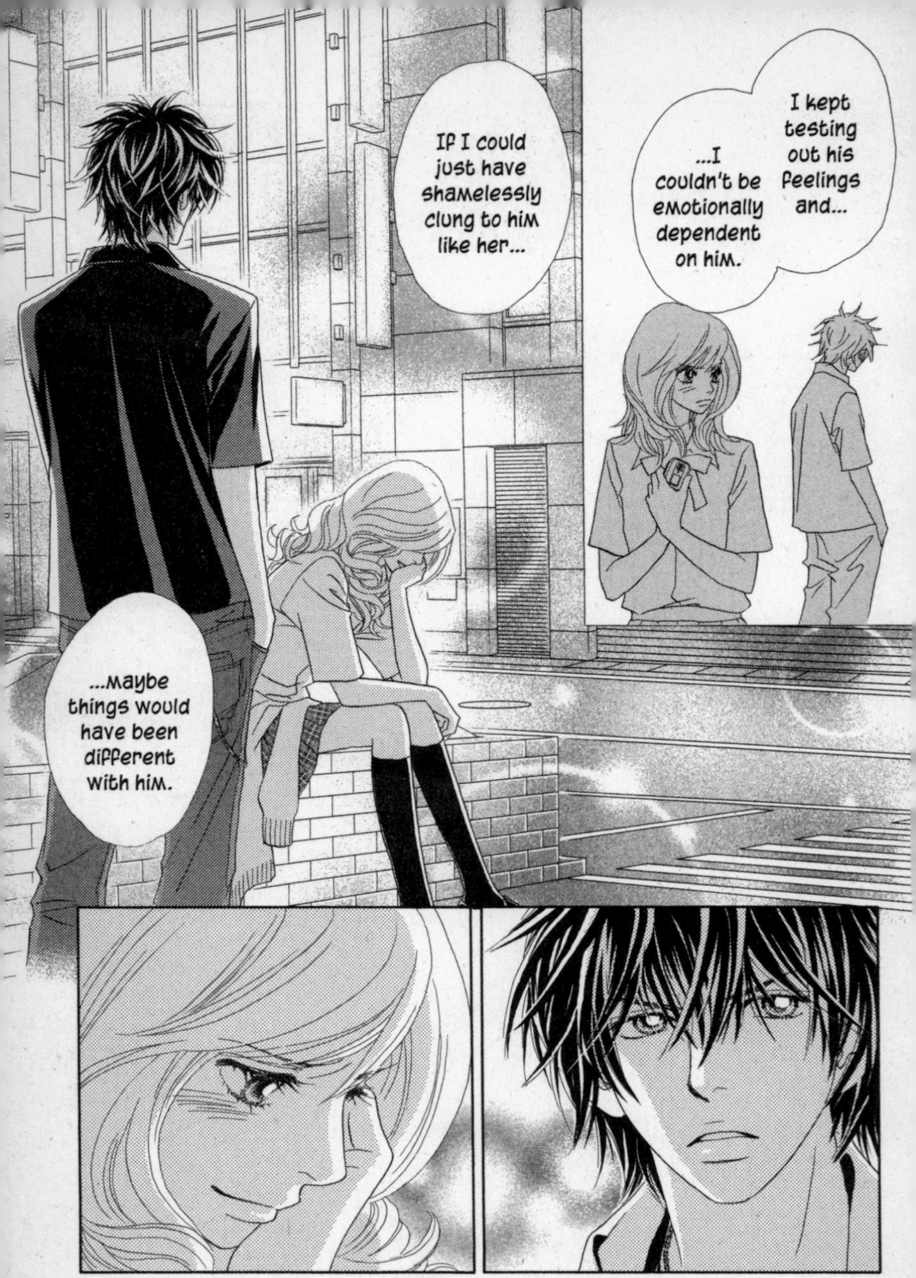
I kept testing out his feelings and...
...I couldn't be emotionally dependent on him.
If I could just have shamelessly clung to him like her...
...maybe things would have been different with him.

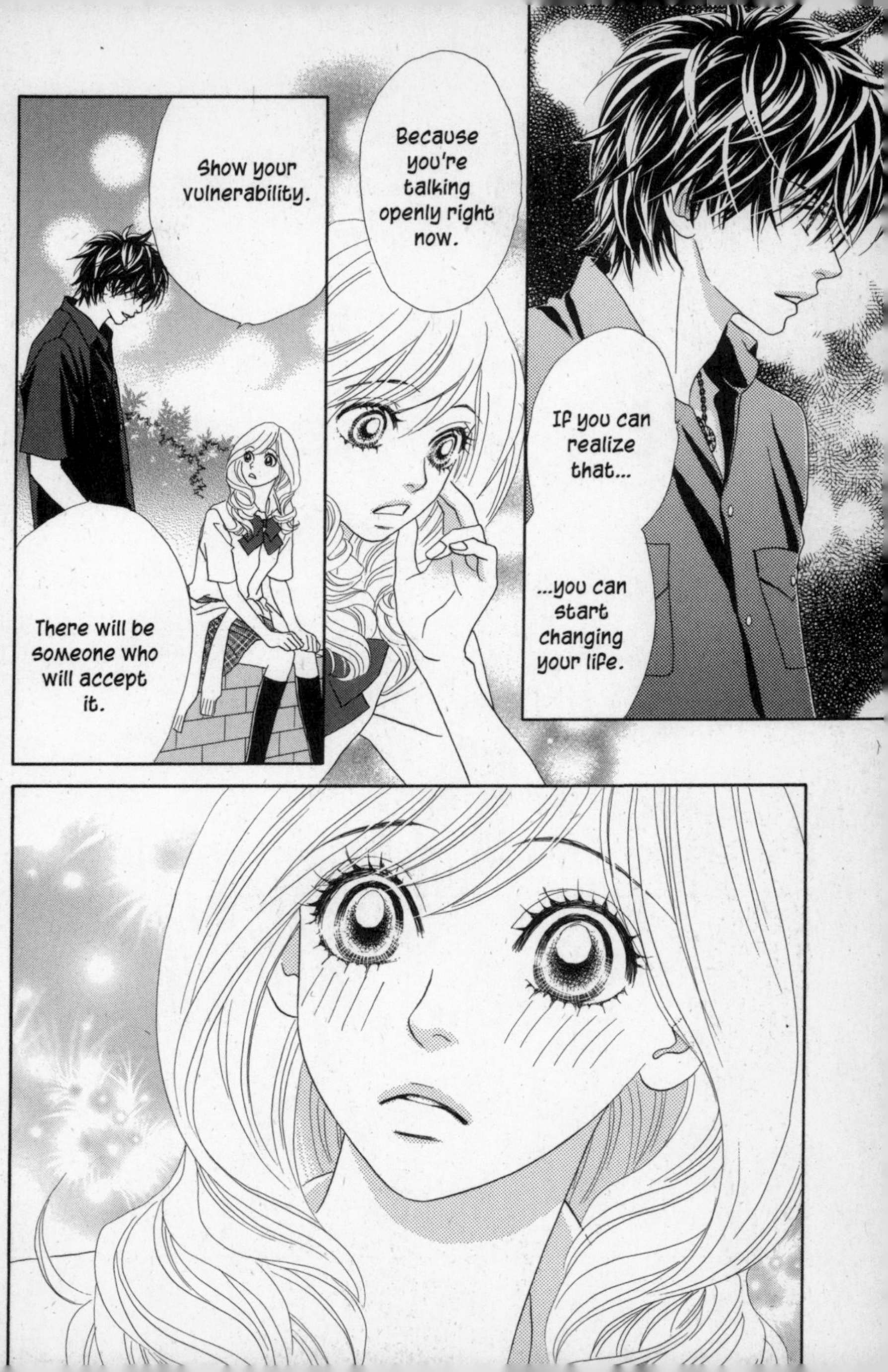
If you can realize that...
...you can start changing your life.
Because you're talking openly right now.
Show your vulnerability.
There will be someone who will accept it.

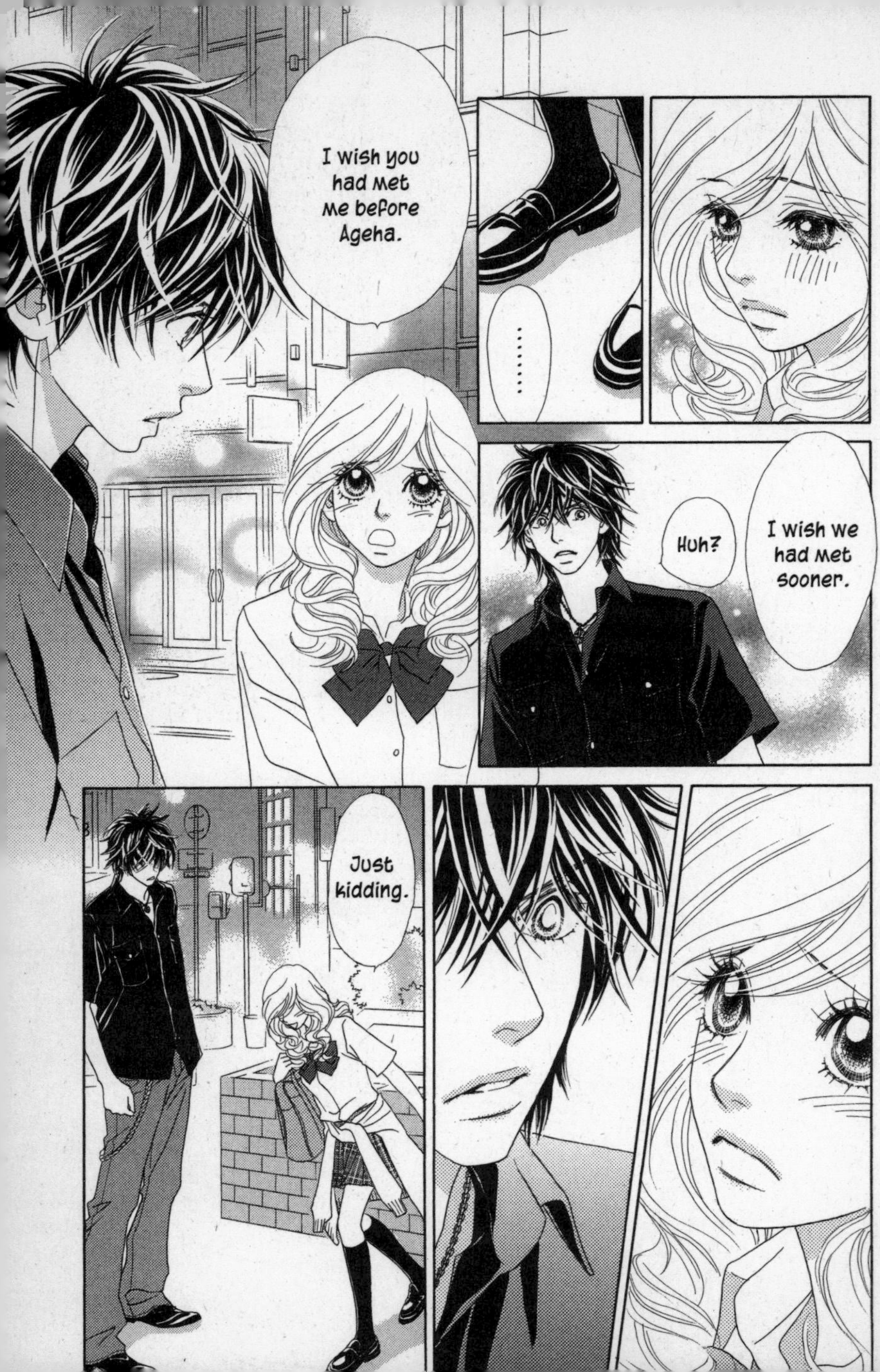

......
I wish we had met sooner.
Huh?
I wish you had met me before Ageha.
Just kidding.

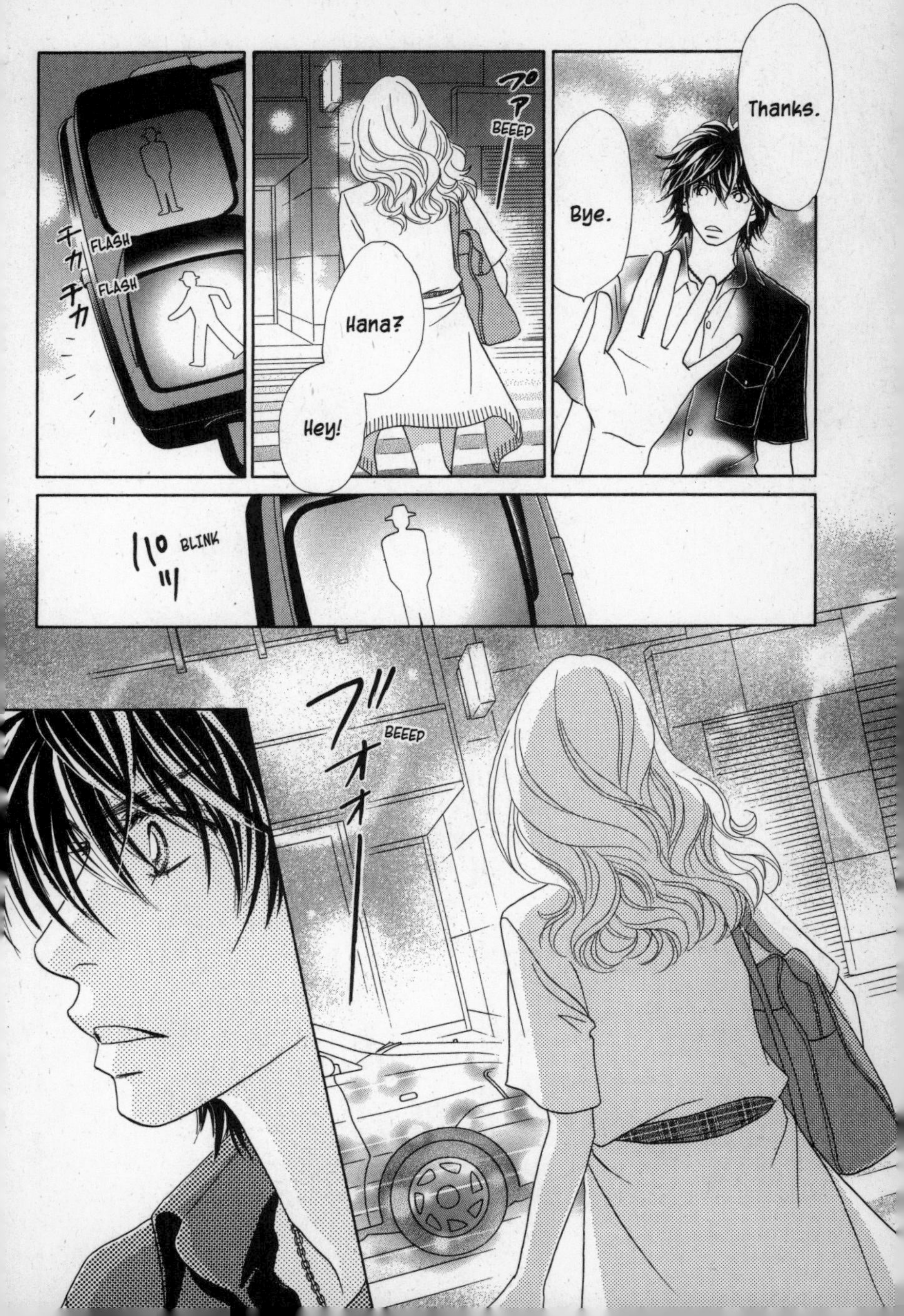

Thanks.
Bye.
プア BEEEP
Hana?
Hey!
チカ FLASH
チカ FLASH
ハッ BLINK
ブオー BEEEP

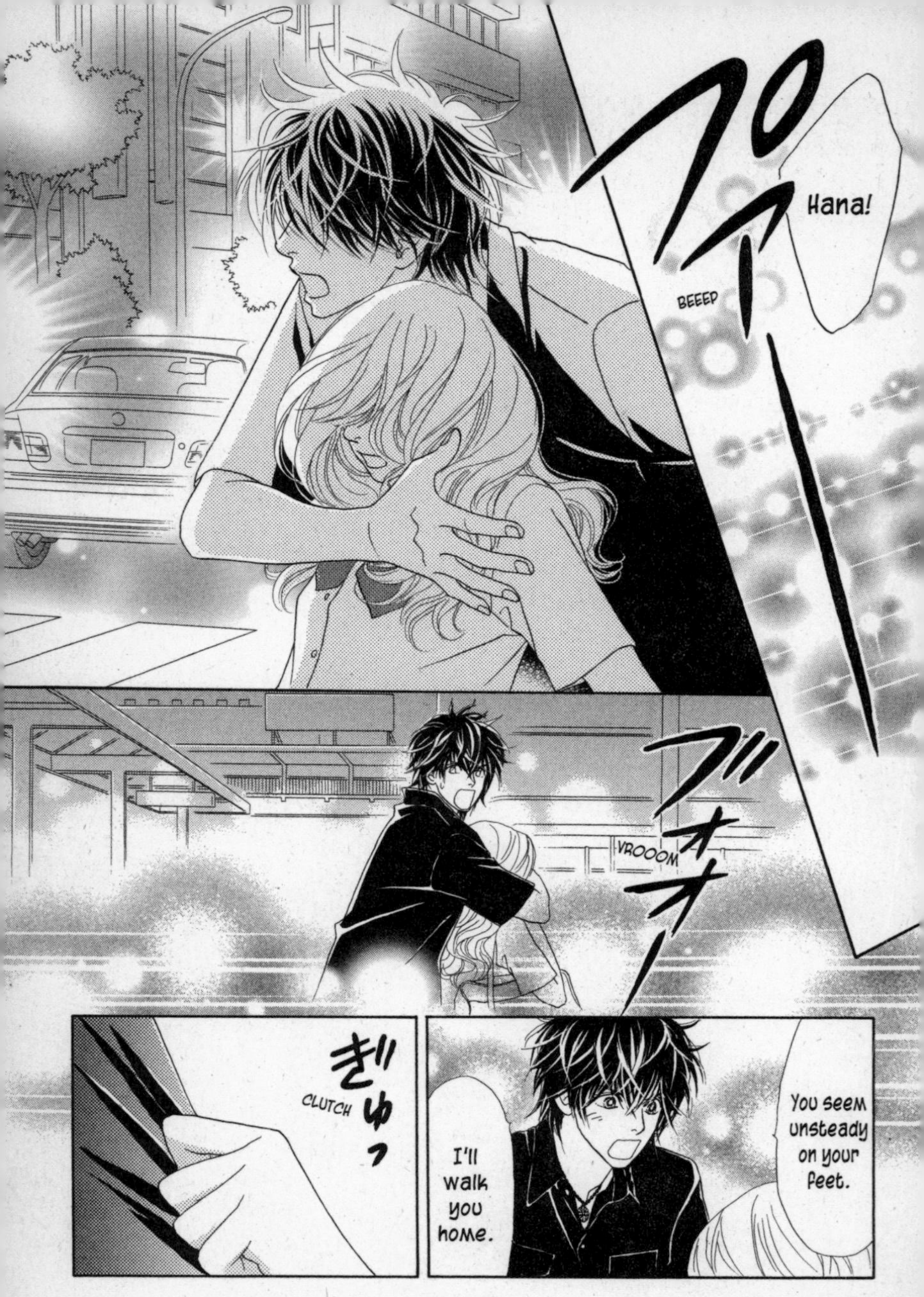

プァー
BEEEP
Hana!
ブォオー
VROOOM
You seem unsteady on your feet.
I'll walk you home.
ぎゅっ
CLUTCH

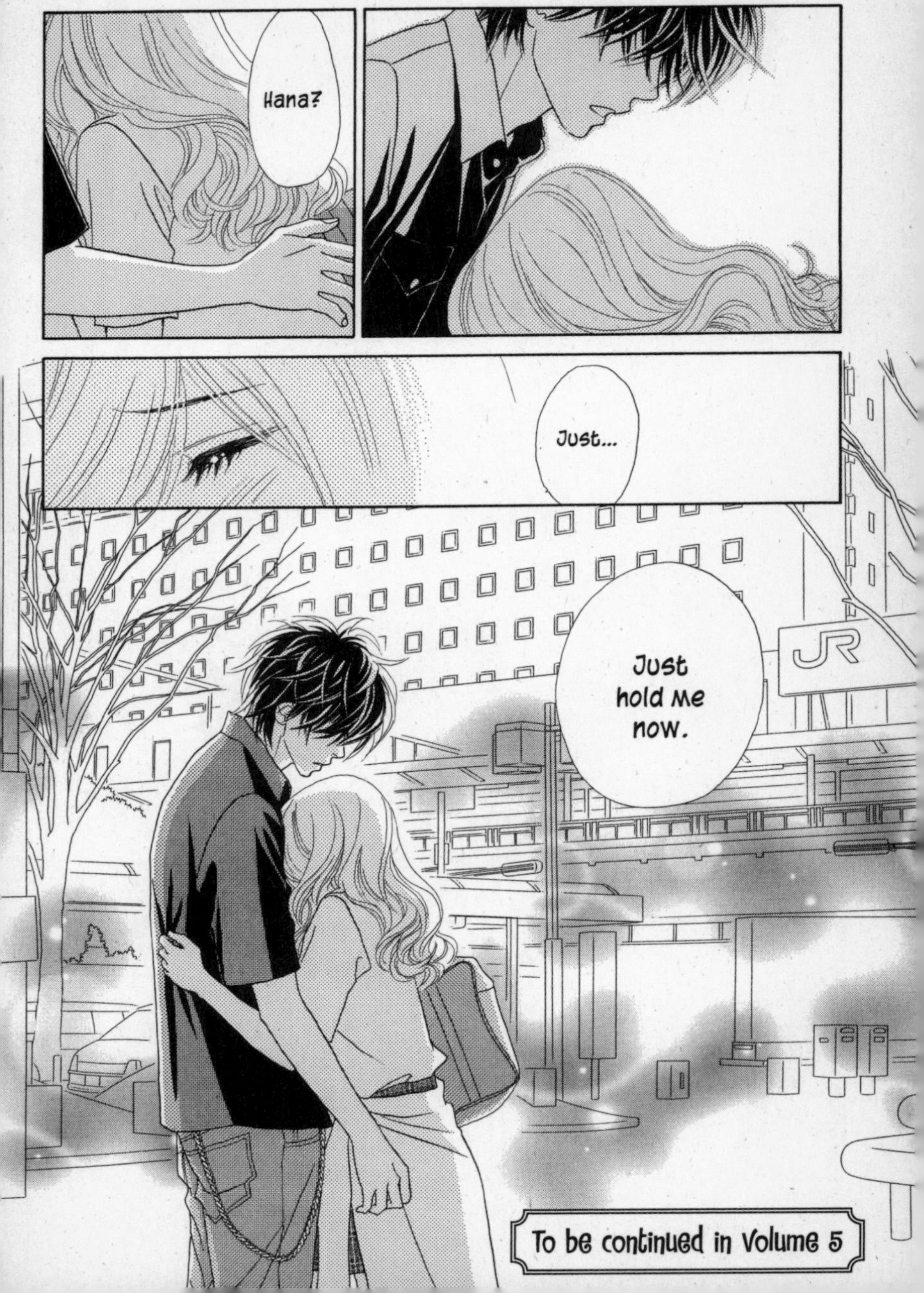
Hana?
Just...
Just hold me now.
To be continued in Volume 5

Staff

Aiko   Amemori
Tomomi   Kasue
Satsuki   Furukawa
Akiko   Kawashima
Ayumi   Yoshida
Hiromi   Inui

Editor
Toshiyuki   Tanaka

March 6, 2008

Miwa   Ueda

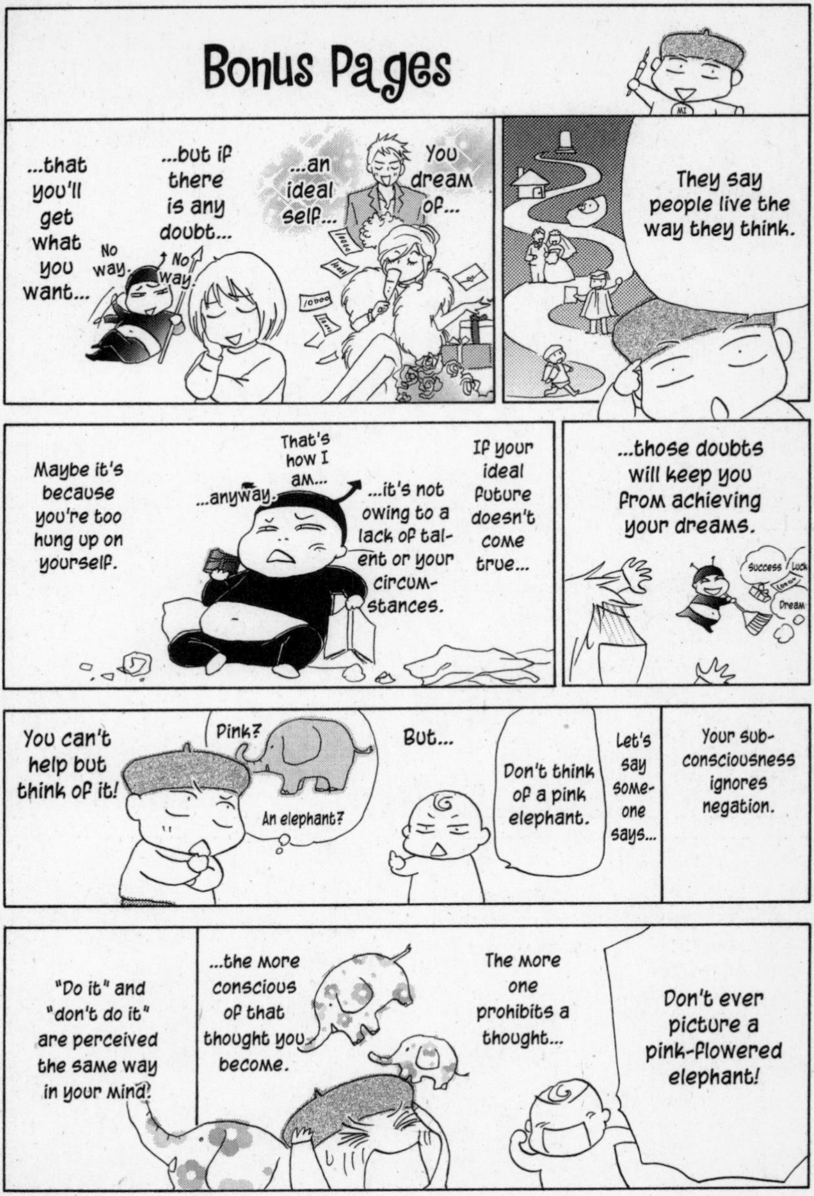
Bonus Pages
They say people live the way they think.
You dream of...
...an ideal self...
...but if there is any doubt...
No way.
No way.
...that you'll get what you want...
...those doubts will keep you from achieving your dreams.
Success
Luck
Dream
If your ideal future doesn't come true...
...it's not owing to a lack of tal-ent or your circum-stances.
That's how I am...
...anyway.
Maybe it's because you're too hung up on yourself.
Your sub-consciousness ignores negation.
Let's say some-one says...
Don't think of a pink elephant.
But...
Pink?
An elephant?
You can't help but think of it!
Don't ever picture a pink-flowered elephant!
The more one prohibits a thought...
...the more conscious of that thought you become.
"Do it" and "don't do it" are perceived the same way in your mind.

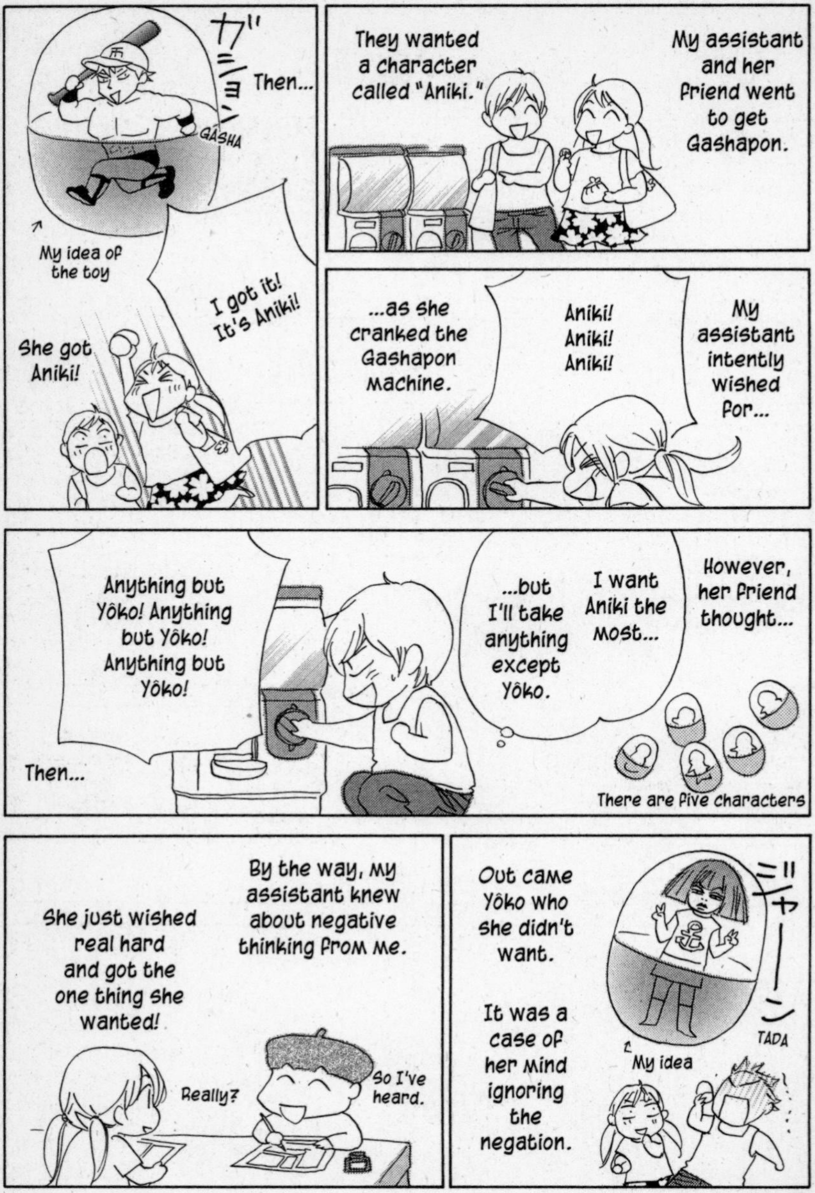
My assistant and her friend went to get Gashapon.
They wanted a character called "Aniki."
My assistant intently wished for...
Aniki! Aniki! Aniki!
...as she cranked the Gashapon machine.
Then...
ガシャン
GASHA
My idea of the toy
I got it! It's Aniki!
She got Aniki!
However, her friend thought...
I want Aniki the most...
...but I'll take anything except Yôko.
There are five characters
Anything but Yôko! Anything but Yôko! Anything but Yôko!
Then...
ジャーン
TADA
Out came Yôko who she didn't want.
My idea
It was a case of her mind ignoring the negation.
By the way, my assistant knew about negative thinking from me.
She just wished real hard and got the one thing she wanted!
So I've heard.
Really?

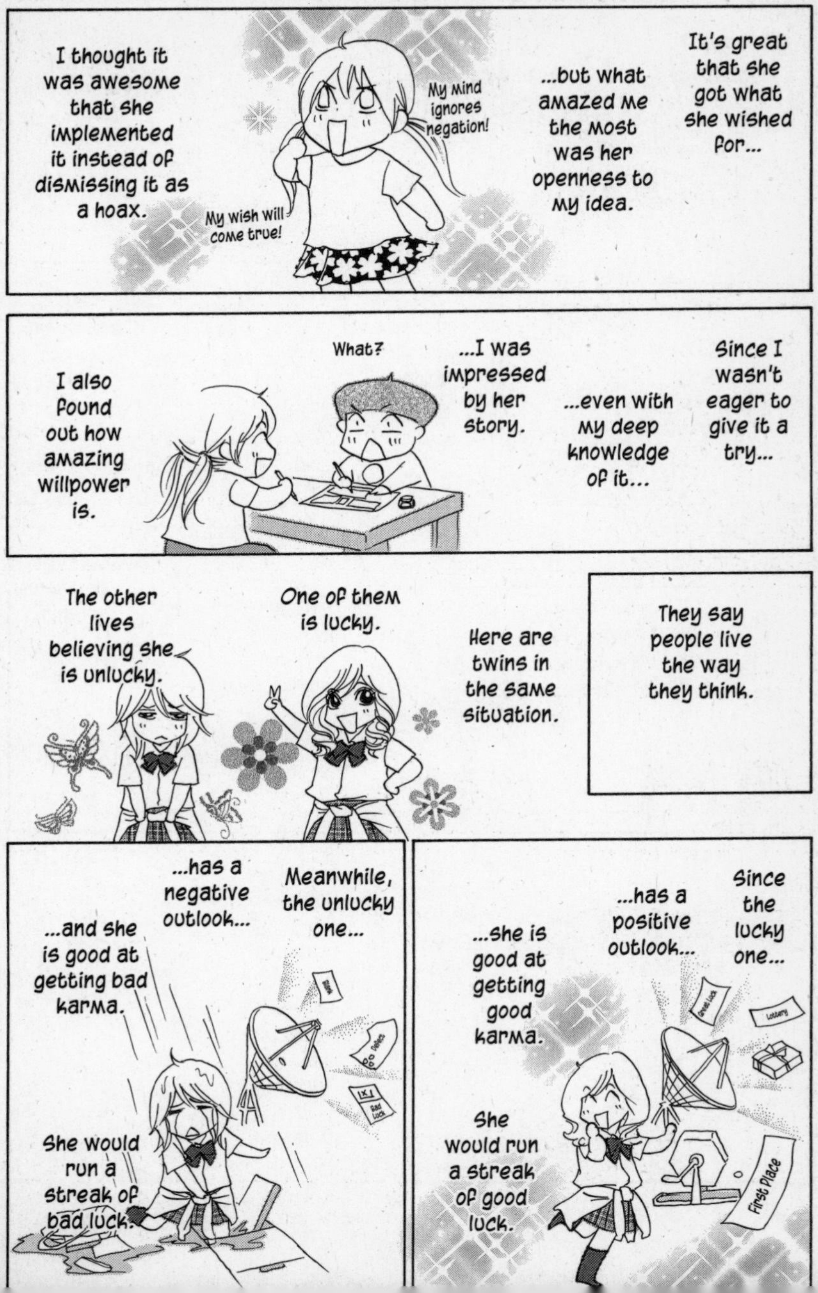
It's great that she got what she wished for...
...but what amazed me the most was her openness to my idea.
My mind ignores negation!
I thought it was awesome that she implemented it instead of dismissing it as a hoax.
My wish will come true!
Since I wasn't eager to give it a try...
...even with my deep knowledge of it...
...I was impressed by her story.
What?
I also found out how amazing willpower is.
They say people live the way they think.
Here are twins in the same situation.
One of them is lucky.
The other lives believing she is unlucky.
Since the lucky one...
...has a positive outlook...
...she is good at getting good karma.
Lottery
First Place
She would run a streak of good luck.
Meanwhile, the unlucky one...
...has a negative outlook...
...and she is good at getting bad karma.
Bad Luck
She would run a streak of bad luck.

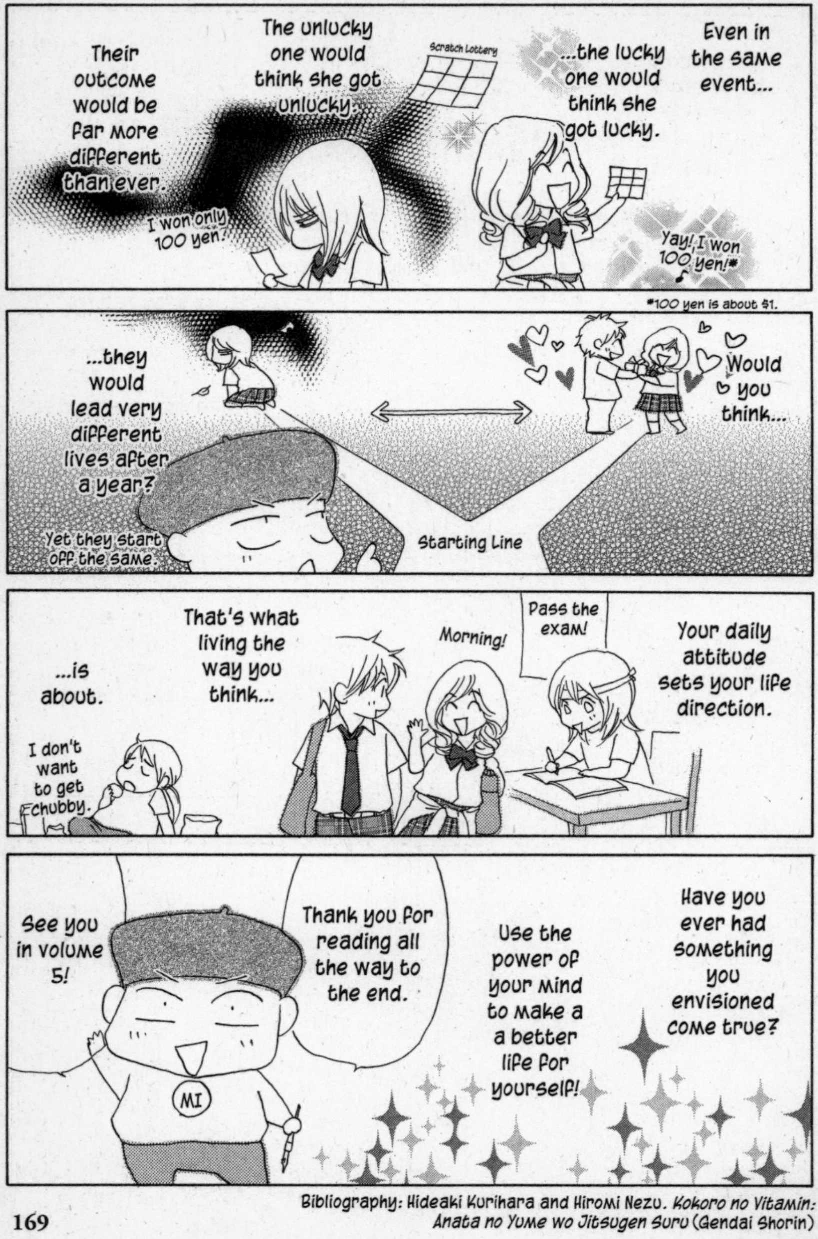
Even in the same event...
...the lucky one would think she got lucky.
Yay! I won 100 yen!*
Scratch Lottery
The unlucky one would think she got unlucky.
I won only 100 yen.
Their outcome would be far more different than ever.
*100 yen is about $1.
Would you think...
...they would lead very different lives after a year?
Starting Line
Yet they start off the same.
Your daily attitude sets your life direction.
Pass the exam!
Morning!
That's what living the way you think...
...is about.
I don't want to get chubby.
Have you ever had something you envisioned come true?
Use the power of your mind to make a a better life for yourself!
Thank you for reading all the way to the end.
See you in volume 5!
MI

Bibliography: Hideaki Kurihara and Hiromi Nezu. *Kokoro no Vitamin: Anata no Yume wo Jitsugen Suru* (Gendai Shorin)

About the Creator

MIWA UEDA was born on September 29, in Hyogo, Japan.
Her original series, *Peach Girl*, won the Kodansha Shojo Manga
of the Year Award in 1999. *Papillon* is her latest creation.

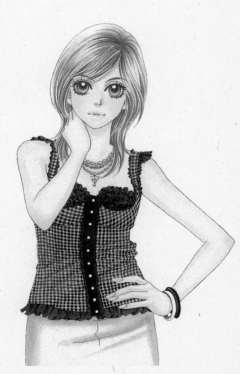

Translation Notes

Japanese is a tricky language for most Westerners, and translation is often more art than science. For your edification and reading pleasure, here are notes on some of the places where we could have gone in a different direction with our translation of the work, or where a Japanese cultural reference is used.

Butterfly and Flower

The full Japanese title of this series is *Papillon: Chô to Hana*. Ageha and Hana's names contain the Japanese characters *chô* and *hana*, which mean "butterfly" and "flower" respectively. The title, *Papillon*, is French for "butterfly"—a good title for a story about a girl undergoing an amazing transformation, like a caterpillar becoming a butterfly.

Kyû-chan

Ichijiku's nickname comes from a Japanese character in his last name, which can also be read as *kyû*.

Altoids, page 24

Ageha actually mentions Frisk, a Belgian brand of curiously strong breath mints that is popular in Japan. Since Frisk is so unfamiliar to Americans, we've replaced that reference with one to Altoids.

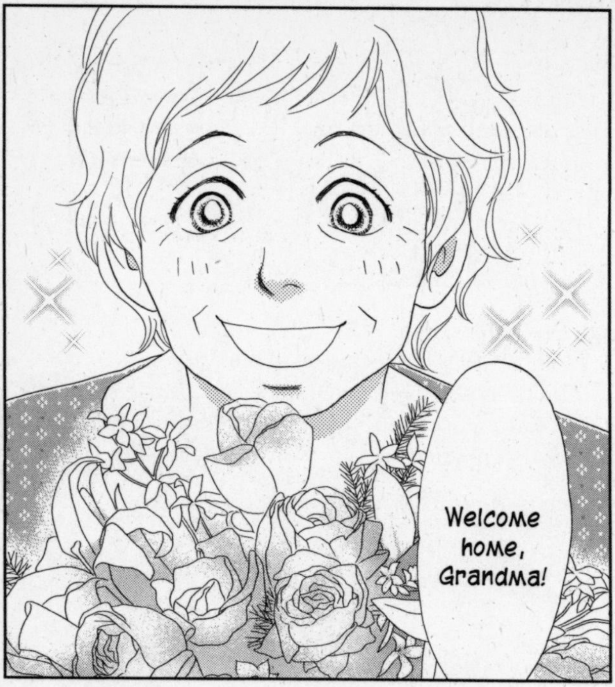
Welcome home, Grandma!

"Welcome home, Grandma!" page 86

Ageha is actually saying, literally translated, "Congratulations on getting out of the hospital, Grandma!" However, since it is more customary in English-speaking countries to welcome patients home rather than to congratulate them, we changed it accordingly.

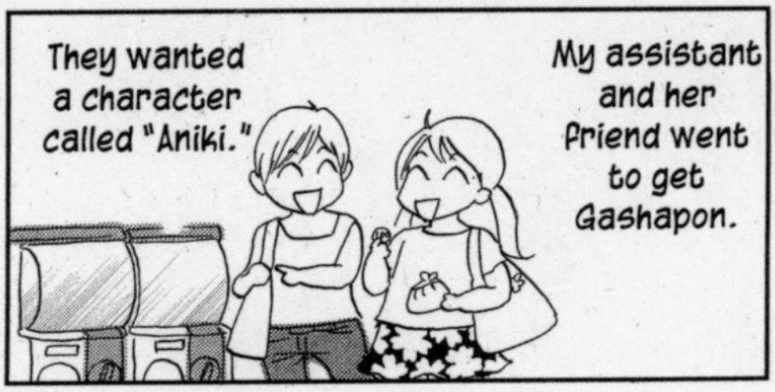
My assistant and her friend went to get Gashapon.
They wanted a character called "Aniki."

Gashapon, page 167

Gashopon is one of several ways Japanese refer to a capsule toy vending machine, but it is also a registered trademark owned by Bandai, the Japanese toy company. The name comes from the cranking sound, *gasha* or *gacha*, and the dropping sound, *pon*, such machines make.

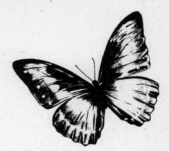

Preview of *Papillon*, Volume 5

We're pleased to present you a preview from volume 5. Please check our website (www.delreymanga.com) to see when this volume will be available in English. For now you'll have to make do with Japanese!

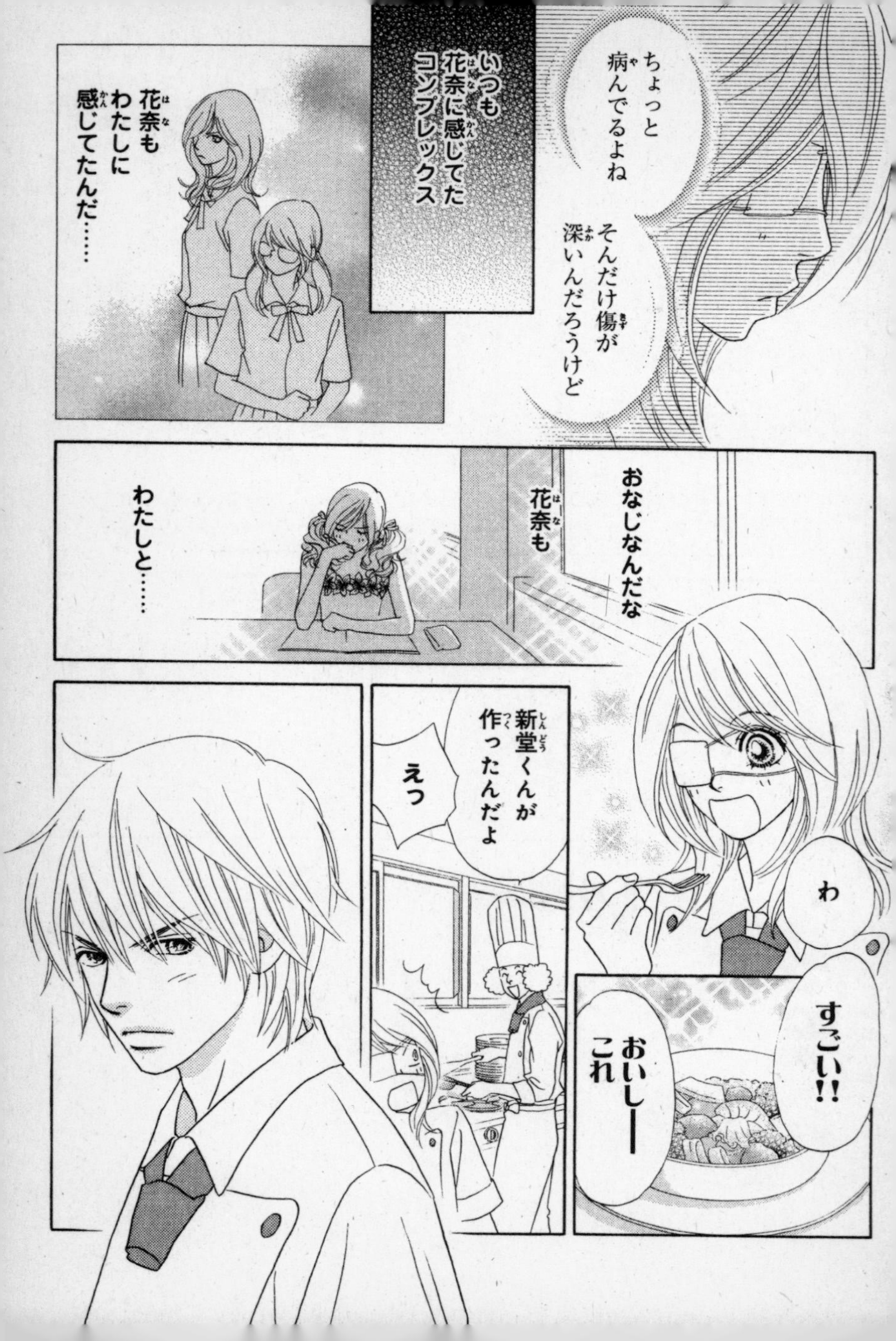
ちょっと病んでるよね
そんだけ傷が深いんだろうけど
いつも花奈に感じてたコンプレックス
花奈もわたしに感じてたんだ……
おなじなんだな
花奈も
わたしと……
わ
すごい!!
おいしーこれ
新堂くんが作ったんだよ
えっ

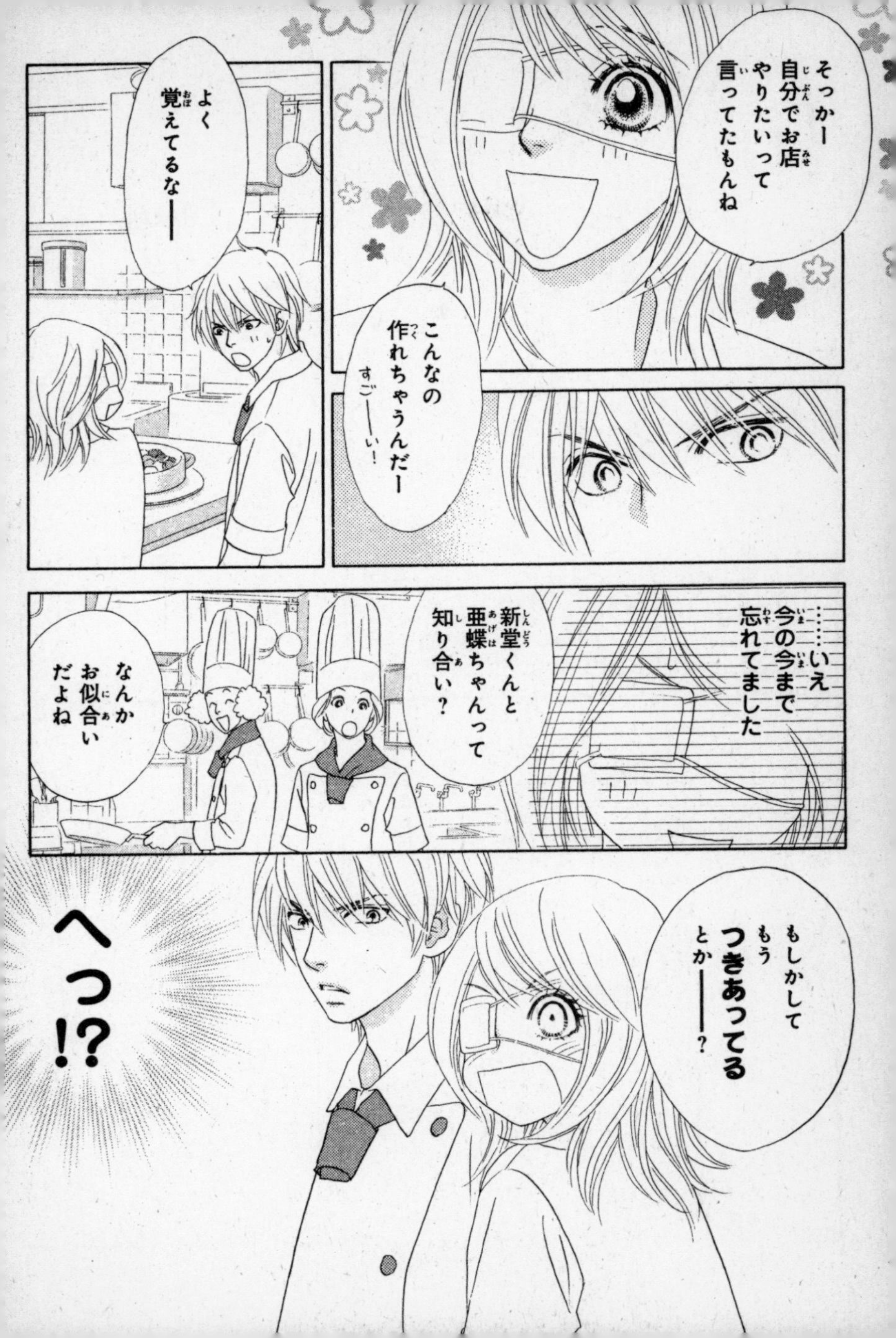
そっかー
自分でお店やりたいって言ってたもんね
こんなの作れちゃうんだー
すごーーい!
よく覚えてるな――
……いえ 今の今まで忘れてました
新堂くんと亜蝶ちゃんって知り合い?
なんかお似合いだよね
もしかしてもう つきあってるとか――?
へっ!?

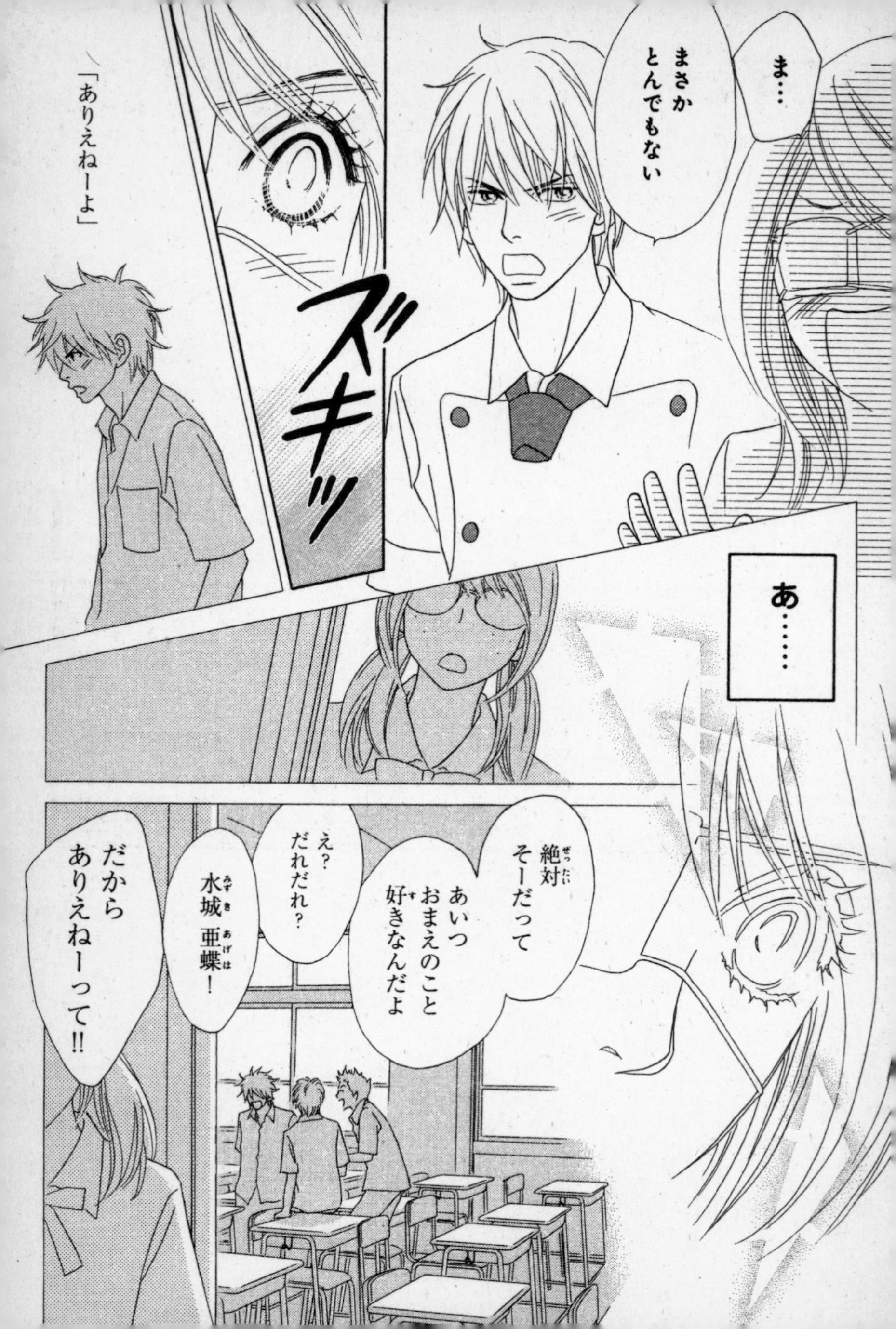
ま…
まさか
とんでもない
ズキッ
「ありえねーよ」
あ……
絶対
そーだって
あいつ
おまえのこと
好きなんだよ
え？
だれだれ？
水城亜蝶！
だから
ありえねーって!!

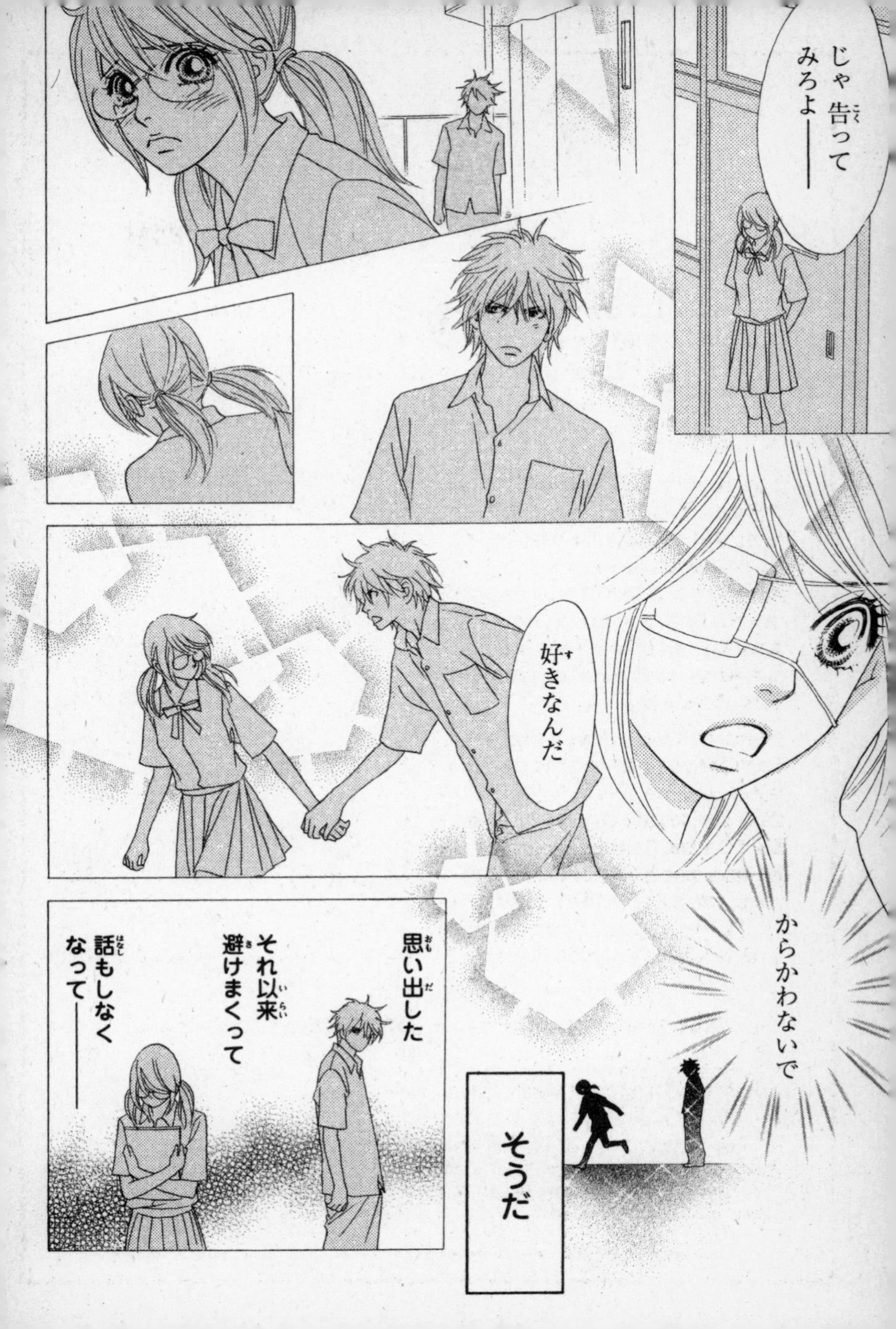
じゃ告ってみろよ――
好きなんだ
からかわないで
そうだ
思い出した それ以来避けまくって話もしなくなって――

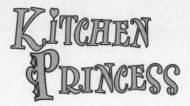

KITCHEN PRINCESS

STORY BY MIYUKI KOBAYASHI
MANGA BY NATSUMI ANDO
CREATOR OF ZODIAC P.I.

HUNGRY HEART

Najika is a great cook and likes to make meals for the people she loves. But something is missing from her life. When she was a child, she met a boy who touched her heart— and now Najika is determined to find him. The only clue she has is a silver spoon that leads her to the prestigious Seika Academy.

Attending Seika will be a challenge. Every kid at the school has a special talent, and the girls in Najika's class think she doesn't deserve to be there. But Sora and Daichi, two popular brothers who barely speak to each other, recognize Najika's cooking for what it is—magical. Could one of the boys be Najika's mysterious prince?

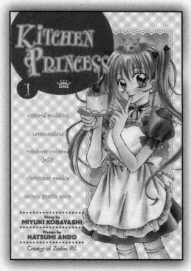

Special extras in each volume! Read them all!

VISIT WWW.DELREYMANGA.COM TO:
- Read sample pages
- View release date calendars for upcoming volumes
- Sign up for Del Rey's free manga e-newsletter
- Find out the latest about new Del Rey Manga series

RATING T AGES 13+

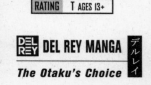

DEL REY MANGA
The Otaku's Choice

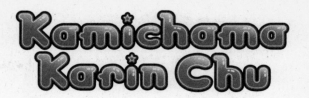

Kamichama Karin Chu

BY KOGE-DONBO

A GODDESS IN LOVE!

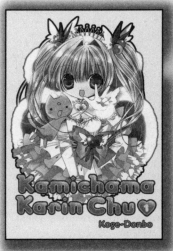

Karin is your lovable girl next door—if the girl next door also happens to be a goddess! Karin has a magic ring that gives her the power to do anything she'd like. Though what she'd like most is to live happily ever after with Kazune, the boy of her dreams. Magic brought Kazune to her, but it also has a way of complicating things. It's not easy to be a goddess and a girl in love!

• Sequel series to the fan-favorite *Kamichama Karin*

Special extras in each volume! Read them all!

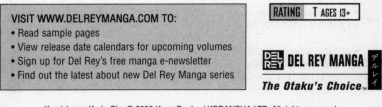

VISIT WWW.DELREYMANGA.COM TO:
• Read sample pages
• View release date calendars for upcoming volumes
• Sign up for Del Rey's free manga e-newsletter
• Find out the latest about new Del Rey Manga series

RATING T AGES 13+

DEL REY DEL REY MANGA デルレイ
The Otaku's Choice™

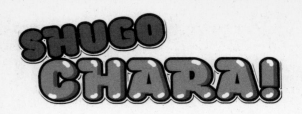

SHUGO CHARA!

PEACH-PIT

Creators of *Dears* and *Rozen Maiden*

Everybody at Seiyo Elementary thinks that stylish and super-cool Amu has it all. But nobody knows the *real* Amu, a shy girl who wishes she had the courage to truly be herself. Changing Amu's life is going to take more than wishes and dreams—it's going to take a little magic! One morning, Amu finds a surprise in her bed: three strange little eggs. Each egg contains a Guardian Character, an angel-like being who can give her the power to be someone new. With the help of her Guardian Characters, Amu is about to discover that her true self is even more amazing than she ever dreamed.

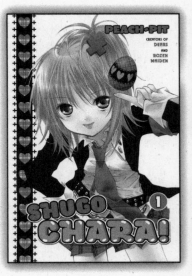

Special extras in each volume! Read them all!

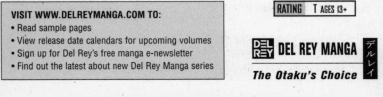

VISIT WWW.DELREYMANGA.COM TO:
- Read sample pages
- View release date calendars for upcoming volumes
- Sign up for Del Rey's free manga e-newsletter
- Find out the latest about new Del Rey Manga series

RATING T AGES 13+

DEL REY MANGA デルレイ

The Otaku's Choice

GAKUEN PRINCE

BY JUN YUZUKI

CRAZY FOR COEDUCATION!

Joshi High is an elite school that most girls in Japan only dream of attending. Then one day everything changes—the all-girl school goes coed. There's just one catch: The girls outnumber the boys. So begins a wild, no-holds-barred competition for the boys of the school. Which smart and independent-minded girl will rise above the fray?

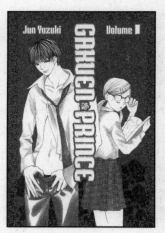

Available anywhere books or comics are sold!

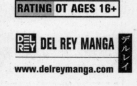

TOMARE!

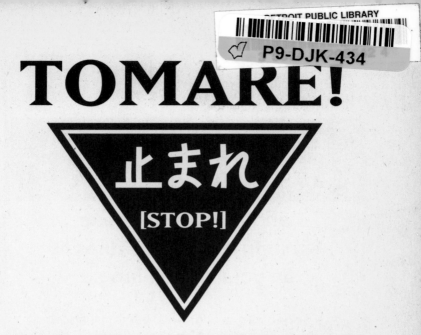

止まれ

[STOP!]

You're going the wrong way!

Manga is a completely different
type of reading experience.

To start at the *beginning*,
go to the *end*!

That's right! Authentic manga is read the traditional Japanese way—
from right to left, exactly the *opposite* of how American books are
read. It's easy to follow: Just go to the other end of the book, and read
each page—and each panel—from right side to left side, starting at
the top right. Now you're experiencing manga as it was meant to be!